The Muse Within

Jon-Roar Bjørkvold

The Muse Within

Creativity and Communication,
Song and Play from
Childhood through Maturity

Translated from the Norwegian by
William H. Halverson

Aaron Asher Books
HarperCollins*Publishers*

HarperCollins books may be purchased for educational, business, or sales promotional use. For information, please write: Special Markets Department, HarperCollins Publishers, Inc., 10 East 53rd Street, New York, NY 10022.

FIRST EDITION

Designed by Jessica Shatan

Library of Congress Cataloging-in-Publication Data

Bjørkvold, Jon-Roar.
    [Musiske menneske. English]
    The muse within : creativity and communication, song and play from childhood through maturity / Jon-Roar Bjørkvold; translated from the Norwegian by William H. Halverson. — 1st ed.
      p. cm.
    "Aaron Asher books."
    Translation of: Det musiske menneske.
    Includes bibliographical references and index.
    ISBN 0-06-019025-6
    1. Music in education. 2. Music—Instruction and study. 3. Creation (Literary, artistic, etc.) 4. Music—Psychological aspects. I. Title.
MT1.B6313   1992   92-52549
780'.7—dc20
MN

92 93 94 95 96 CC/HC 10 9 8 7 6 5 4 3 2 1

Zeus had brought the world into being, and the gods beheld in mute wonder the magnificence that lay before them. But, Zeus asked, is not something still wanting? And the gods replied that yes, one thing was wanting: the world lacked a voice whereby all this wonder could be expressed in words and in music. In order for such a voice to sound there was need for a new kind of divine beings—whereupon the Muses sprang into existence as the children of Zeus and Mnemosyne, goddess of memory.

—PINDAR

CONTENTS

Translations and Tears   ix

Preludium   xi

1. Before Birth   *1*

2. The Playing Child Learns to Live   *11*

3. The Culture of Children at Play   *21*

4. Three Worlds of Singing Children: Norway, Russia, and the United States   *57*

5. The Muse-ical Child Goes to School   *119*

6. Child Culture and Music Education   *171*

7. "If You Love Somebody, Set Them Free!"   *257*

8. The Muse Under Siege   *277*

9. Old Age   *335*

Postludium   *349*

Bibliography   *351*

Acknowledgments   *367*

Index   *369*

TRANSLATIONS AND TEARS

Dr. William H. Halverson of Columbus, Ohio, has created a truly unique translation of my book. As the proud father of five daughters he has added to its heartbeat. As the author of a widely used philosophy textbook he has added to its brainbeat. And as a true lover of poetry he has added to its wordbeat.

That this was to be no ordinary translation was evident to me in the opening lines of his letter accompanying the first pages of the manuscript:

> Herewith my loving translation of *The Muse Within*. I hope you like it! I expect, of course, that you will want to make small changes to further improve this version of your book, but I very much hope you will feel that I have caught the spirit, the inner music of your book. I feel that we are singing from the same score, but you must be the judge of that. If it doesn't occasionally bring a tear or two to your eyes I must start over again.

Yes, Bill, I like it! It has brought many tears of joy to my eyes during the year we worked together on the translation, sending hundreds of typescript pages to each other across the Atlantic. I know that it has also deeply touched my Norwegian friend and colleague Dr. Dag Schjelderup-Ebbe, who has been a most valuable partner in this work. We have all been "singing from the same score"—and loving it. If my readers should hear some of that same inner music as they read the book, it will surely be because they too have been gripped by the power of this translation.

JON-ROAR BJØRKVOLD

PRELUDIUM

Storm and foam and fury. Three terrified people — two children and their father — in a twenty-two-foot wooden boat on a roaring, swelling sea.

Good Lord, what had I done now? Another crazy thing. Taking the children out in this dreadful weather! I who couldn't dock a boat without slamming it against the pier even when the sea was smooth as a mirror.

The young boy, trembling with fear, cowered against the bottom of the boat. He knew perfectly well my limitations as a seaman. Tears mingled with rainwater on his frightened little face.

Chaos on the sea, chaos in my soul. I was on the verge of totally losing control. Everything was drenched. "Damn!" I said to myself. "What's the use of flares when the matches are soaked!"

Suddenly her voice struck me. It was the voice of the twelve-year-old girl, singing carefully and hesitantly at first, then more confidently and with firm intensity. Her song rose higher and higher, up above the engine housing and the blue canopy, against the wind and the pelting rain. Her voice never wavered, not even for a moment. And what did she sing, this young girl who knew her life to be in danger? Was it "Nearer, My God, to Thee"—that old hymn associated with the sinking of the *Titanic?* Not on your life! It was a verse by Alf Prøysen, the beloved Norwegian writer of children's songs, set to the cheery tune of "Jingle Bells"! Through the howling wind I heard her sing:

> My name is January, and I am quite a chap,
> And when I come, you'd better wear
> Your warmest coat and cap!
> But I have much to give
> If you would like to ski:
> The snow that lies upon the slopes
> Is all a gift from me!

January, snow and skiing—in this maelstrom of raging sea and storm in the middle of July! For one brief moment I felt laughter welling up in my throat before the icy hand of terror gripped me anew. Nausea overcame me. I threw up.

But the brave girl continued to sing. Verse after verse, over and over again. Singing had become a survival strategy, the lifeline we all needed: *"We shall overcome!"*

Slowly I began to realize how the song was taking hold of me. I was recovering in body and mind, as after a fever. Fear no longer raged through me. It was still there, to be sure, but now to a remarkable degree it was under control.

Through the driving, almost horizontal rain I caught a glimpse of the singing girl. Her face was ashen against the orange life jacket, and she trembled as much from the wind and water as from the danger she felt. And yet she was dauntlessly secure. By singing she had regained the control that I lacked. Her grip on her younger brother was as tight as her grip on the song—like two sides of the same coin. *Molto serioso.* The boy had stopped crying. He sat with his head leaning trustingly on his sister's shoulder. Nothing remained of the former terror but a few deep sobs that convulsed his little body from time to time. The angry waves could no longer reach him, though the sea continued to heave and roar around the boat with undiminished might. The song's strength had vanquished the storm in all of us. Isn't that what a poet once called "soul-fire against the elements"?

We reached land safely—but none of us will ever forget that boat trip. It is indelibly recorded in our minds and bodies as a salty, uncomfortable gnawing in the pits of our stomachs. More clearly than the whining wind and the raging sea, however, I remember the singing girl and the miracle she wrought that memorable day not so long ago.

The indomitable power of expression that imbued this young girl and her singing points to a priceless reality that is shared by all humankind. I shall speak of this reality as "the Muse Within." Her manifestations appear in all countries and in every culture. She is present in every stage of life, from its dawning in the unborn fetus to its waning in old age. She appears in the primal cry of the newborn infant, in the spontaneous singing of children in a sandbox, in Mahalia Jackson's gospel vibrato, in Louis Armstrong's trumpet playing, and in Shostakovich's symphonies. Mozart cultivated her from *The Magic Flute* to the *Requiem*. Bach called her forth in his mighty *Passions*. She sparkles in the Indian *raga* and is revered in the Nigerian *nkwa*. Stephen Foster embraced her in his immortal songs. Grieg could not have lived his life without her. She sings in the dancer's hips, in the poet's words, in the child's spontaneous play with color and form. Her song flows like a fundamental life force in our veins, with a potential for sounds and forms and variations still unknown. This song enables us to see more clearly and to feel more deeply. It helps us to achieve insights and perceptions that leap beyond our previous level of understanding—insights and perceptions that would otherwise be inaccessible to us.

We all need the Muse Within, for we are what I shall call *muse-ical beings*. To lose our *muse-icality* would be to lose a profoundly essential part of our humanity. I think it is important, therefore, that so far as possible we try to understand the Muse Within, to comprehend more fully the origin, the distinctive character, and the myriad manifestations of this creative force that is the common heritage of every member of the human family.

The scope of our inquiry is extremely broad and for that very reason generally taboo in a culture such as ours that prizes special-ization. Our investigation has to do not only with human develop-ment and play, children and child culture, creativity and music, but also with schools and pedagogy, social development and poli-tics. Thinking about the Muse Within requires us to think in ecological and holistic terms. If we do not try to see our subject in a larger context—one that transcends the established boundaries of disciplines and genres, cultures and age groups, even science and poetry—we shall lose sight of the Muse Within.

Our discussion begins where human life begins: with the prena-tal stage, when sounds, movements, and rhythms are imprinted within the fetus as fundamental patterns for life. We then go on to consider the differing manifestations of the Muse Within in the various stages of life: from the babbling of the newborn to the spontaneous singing of children; from the child's first encounter with school and formal instruction to the teenager's musical liber-ation; from Dmitri Shostakovich under Stalin to musical games and dance in old age.

The book's aspirations are as naïve as those of a child: with all the power you possess you stretch forward to embrace the life you have been given; you try to get a firm grasp on some elements of this life; and then you reinterpret what you have grasped to create fragments of meaning.

The Muse Within

Big sister, age five: "Am I going to get a brother or a sister?"

1
Before Birth

This is something every mother knows: the unborn child responds to *sound*. Let an eighth-month fetus hear the piercing sound of a trumpet or a piece of silverware striking a glass in close proximity to its mother's belly: the unborn child will respond with a hefty kick.

This, too, every mother knows: the unborn child responds to *movement*. When a woman in a late stage of pregnancy lies down to sleep, the fetus often becomes restless and protests with angry kicks: it wants the rocking and the *rhythm* created by the movement of its mother's body to continue.

The Basic Elements of Music Are Imprinted in the Unborn Child

Sound, movement, rhythm: these, the basic elements of music, are imprinted upon the child's sense apparatus long before birth.

Speculation about the musical dimension of life in the womb is as old as Western civilization (Sundberg 1979). In Plato's *Laws* we read that the unborn child must have physical exercise. Here movement is regarded as basic.

> ATHENIAN STRANGER: Am I not right in maintaining that a good education is that which tends most to the improvement of mind and body?
>
> CLEINIAS: Undoubtedly . . .
>
> ATHENIAN STRANGER: And do we not further observe that the first shoot of every living thing is by far the greatest and fullest? . . . And

the body should have the most exercise when it receives most nourishment? . . .

CLEINIAS: But, Stranger, are we to impose this great amount of exercise upon newly born infants?

ATHENIAN STRANGER: Nay, rather on the bodies of infants still unborn.

CLEINIAS: What do you mean, my good sir? In the process of gestation?

ATHENIAN STRANGER: Exactly. I am not at all surprised that you have never heard of this very peculiar sort of gymnastic applied to such little creatures. . . . (*Laws* 788c–d, 789a–b)

Plato's Athenian Stranger, who many think is Socrates, even discusses whether laws should be enacted requiring pregnant women and nurses to engage in certain bodily movements for the sake of the young—for example, a law "that the pregnant woman shall walk about and fashion the embryo within as we fashion wax before it hardens" (*Laws* 789d).

The Bible also speaks of the experience of the child before birth. St. Luke tells of Mary's meeting with Elizabeth, the wife of Zachariah.

And when Elizabeth heard the greeting of Mary, the babe leaped in her womb; and Elizabeth was filled with the Holy Spirit and she exclaimed with a loud cry, "Blessed are you among women, and blessed is the fruit of your womb! And why is this granted me, that the mother of my Lord should come to me? For behold, when the voice of your greeting came to my ears, the babe in my womb leaped for joy. (Luke 1:41–44, RSV)

It is clear, therefore, that modern research on the relation of the unborn child to sound, rhythm, and movement—the basic elements of music—is not being conducted in a vacuum; it can claim a rich background both in universal human experience and in historical documents of great cultural importance.

SOUND AND MEMORY
Research on the fetus's experience of sound is currently in a period of rapid development.

We know for certain that the fetus hears sounds long before the mother notices any specific response. From the sixth month the fetus responds to sound with an increased heart rate (Verny 1982, Eisenberg 1976). It is even possible today to detect minor hearing problems from the thirty-fifth week of gestation (Jensen 1985). Moreover, it is not just aurally that sound reaches the fetus; it is also transmitted in the form of vibrations from the mother's body via the water in the amniotic sac, thus affecting the fetus's entire body. In this way sound becomes a *total* bodily experience for the developing fetus.

Researchers have studied not only the fetus's passive experience of sound but its *listening*—i.e, its more conscious awareness of sound. Between the twenty-eighth and the thirty-second weeks of gestation the fetus's nervous system reaches a stage of development virtually identical to that of a newborn child, and the brain stem also matures rapidly. Neurologically, everything is in place for the fetus to store up impressions of sound in its long-term memory. The fetus's awareness of sound also increases at this time. It is believed that the fetus is able to *remember* sounds from at least the eighth month, and perhaps much earlier (Verny 1982, DeCasper 1980).

These facts lead to a very interesting question: Is there a *learning connection* in human beings between life before birth and life after birth, and can it be substantiated by the recollection of sound?

An American researcher, Anthony DeCasper, carried out several experiments which showed that "within the first three days of postnatal development, newborns prefer the human voice, discriminate between speakers, and demonstrate a preference for their mothers' voices with only limited maternal exposure" (DeCasper 1980). These findings led DeCasper to advance a bold hypothesis: that sound preferences after birth are influenced by what is heard prenatally. To test this hypothesis, sixteen pregnant women were selected to read to their respective fetuses from a well-known children's book by Dr. Seuss, *The Cat in the Hat.* Tightly rhymed and rhythmical throughout, it begins as follows.

The sun did not shine.
It was too wet to play.

So we sat in the house
All that cold, cold, wet day.

The women were instructed to read the whole poem aloud twice
a day during the last six and a half weeks of pregnancy. DeCasper
estimated that by the time of their birth each of these fetuses had
heard the book being read for about five hours.

When the children were born, DeCasper employed a sucking
test he had used in earlier research. The newborn babies were
linked to a tape recorder by means of headphones and a nipple
was placed in each baby's mouth. If the baby sucked in one
rhythm, it would hear a tape of its mother reading *The Cat in the
Hat;* if it sucked in another, it would hear its mother reading
Nancy and Eric Gurney's *The King, the Mice and the Cheese.*

Once upon a time,
In a faraway country,
There lived a king . . .

But the newborns didn't want the latter poem! Its rhythm was
altogether different, and there were no rhymes. They signaled
their preference for the poem from their "preinfancy" by sucking
in such a way as to get what they were used to: their mother's
voice reading their "good old favorite," *The Cat in the Hat* (De-
Casper and Spence 1982).

But what was it about the first poem that was attractive to these
infants? Was it really its familiarity, born of constant repetition
during the weeks preceding birth, or was it rather the hypnotic
regularity in rhyme and rhythm of the poem itself?

To answer this question, DeCasper and Spence altered the
phonetic character, rhymes, and rhythms of the poems, and were
able to confirm that newborns were also able to pick out more
irregular poems their mothers had read to them in the womb.
Indeed, they were able to do this *whether or not* the poem was read
by the mother: "the greater reinforcing value of the target story
was independent of who recited the story" (DeCasper and Spence
1986, p. 143). More recently DeCasper, in collaboration with a
group of French researchers, has produced direct evidence of the

fetus's ability to remember prior to birth. By measuring changes in pulse and blood pressure, DeCasper and his colleagues concluded that immediately before birth the fetus's behavior demonstrated that it recognized poems previously read aloud by its mother (DeCasper et al. 1986).

An effort is now under way to identify the longer-range effects of a systematic exposure to sound such as we have been discussing. Current research on this question is focused on the period from gestation to preschool age (Shelter 1987).

Another interesting question that has been studied (e.g., Verny 1982) is whether the fetus is in some sense able to "understand" differing emotional overtones in its mother's voice. Changes in the mother's psyche produce changes in her biochemistry and movements as well as in her tone of voice and language. The fetus, by virtue of being literally a part of its mother, is exposed to all of this. It is now widely believed that little by little the fetus learns to recognize its mother's moods fairly well. If, for example, endorphins ("well-being hormones") are released when the mother talks or sings, the unborn child will share in the total positive emotional experience. Indeed, some researchers claim that the fetus receives various types of biochemical imprints that can be triggered by a number of things including song (Thurman, Chase, and Langness 1987). The child, in other words, appears to acquire a symbiotically conditioned key to the mother's personality and unique temperament, with far-ranging consequences for later life.

Thus we may say that the child's language training starts long before the moment of birth. Moreover, it is in the most literal sense a *mother tongue* that the fetus begins to learn, for it is above all the mother's voice that reaches the unborn child. This is important despite the fact that this voice undoubtedly sounds different to the child than it will after birth because of the filtering that occurs before it reaches the womb.

The fetus hears its mother's voice without apparent difficulty. Other people practically have to shout—at about the seventy- or eighty-decibel level according to one researcher (Jensen and Flottorp 1985)—to penetrate the flesh and water surrounding the fetus and make themselves heard. The father's voice, therefore, stands in a qualitatively different relationship to the fetus than the mother's. Despite this difficulty, it is important that the father communicate with the unborn child, both for his sake and for that of the child. Even if the child does not directly hear the father's voice, his singing or talking in the company of his pregnant wife will have an effect on *her* emotional life. Thus the unborn child will at least have indirect contact with its father, albeit through biochemical processes mediated by the mother. The pathways to the child's heart are more complex than we in our prosaic, positivistic practicality had previously thought.

The central figure in all of this, however, is the mother. She—for better or for worse—is the principal source of the impulses that will reach her unborn child. But note: this *mother tongue* that the child begins to acquire in the womb is at root a musical mother tongue as well, for it is the *musical* qualities of the mother's voice—the tone, the rhythm, the tempo, the dynamics—that acquire meaning for the fetus, not the ordinary meanings of the words that she happens to be using.

As early as 1928 the Russian psychologist Lev Vygotsky, in clear opposition to the prevailing Piaget theory, maintained that the newborn child was a social being (Vygotsky 1975). DeCasper's findings carry Vygotsky's perspective even further: a human being is in a limited way a social individual *before it is born*. The fetus senses, remembers, and learns—not, of course, in the same rich ways that a five-year-old child does, but nonetheless in ways that give evidence of a little mind at work within the developing body. Many of us have burned into our memory the oft-published picture of the fetus in the classic head-down position, sucking its thumb. The picture conveys an important truth: the child is preparing in earnest for that imminent moment when the umbilical cord will be cut and it must suddenly learn to survive without the nourishment that has sustained it throughout the gestation period.

The sucking reflex is essential to the life of a newborn child. How many mothers—and fathers—have felt a kind of primal joy when their newborn takes milk for the first time? But the fetus is developing another capacity that is no less important for survival and development: *the capacity for social life*. It is the mother's voice that mediates this process, that builds a bridge from microcosm to macrocosm, that gives continuity, familiarity, and confidence in

the transition from fetus to newborn. Here the musical sounds—
of speech, song, and laughter—with which the fetus became
familiar during the months in the womb serve as words of dedication that usher the child into the human community as a communicating, social being. Just as the newborn child hungrily devours milk from its mother's breast, so with equal hunger—albeit
in a less obvious way—s/he devours the mother's familiar voice.
This is the first social and human anchoring place in a strange and
unknown world. Firmly rooted in the muse-ical experience of the
womb, the child begins a process so demanding that an enormous
reservoir of motivation, cleverness, and adaptability is required in
order to survive and thrive. *Homo sapiens* is born with a muse-ically
conditioned social competence of considerable scope.

MOVEMENT AND NEUROLOGY

During the gestation period, physical movement as well as sound
plays a decisive role in the development of the fetus. Researchers
have long known that bodily movement—both that of the fetus
and that of the mother—is essential for the formation and maturation of the child's brain.

The Russians were among the first to do research in this area.
In the late 1950s B. N. Klosovsky showed how movements of both
mother and fetus produce changes in the fetus's nervous system
that stimulate chemical processes that in turn directly affect the
brain's maturation and capacity to function. Like DeCasper, Klosovsky maintains that exterior influences play a role in the development of the child *before* birth. Thus modern neurology confirms
Plato's 2,500-year-old insight regarding the importance of physical exercise during the gestation period.

Sound, rhythm, and movement, then, do play important roles in
the physical as well as the psychological development of human
beings even during the fetal stage. Long before birth the foundation
is being laid for the emergence of the person as both a social and
muse-ical being. We are born as individuals whose muse-ical development has already begun. Thus it seems reasonable to propose
that a more deliberate human relationship with the unborn child—
preferably one involving a conscious attempt at communication—
would enhance the life of the child after birth. *Both* the child and

the relationship between parents and child would be strengthened.

This area of research is still in its infancy. Only the barest beginnings have been made thus far in the coupling of prenatal and postnatal psychology. Nonetheless, I think there are sufficient grounds for this practical advice to those—both mothers and fathers—who are expecting a child: *Talk to your unborn child! Dance with your unborn child! Play with your unborn child! Sing for your unborn child!* Give your child an elixir of love fashioned from muse-ical ingredients. Play music that will put the mother-to-be in good spirits. If the child does not hear this sound as music in the conventional sense, never mind: at the very least the child is assured an experience of good biochemical fellowship with its mother.

Everything possible must be done to enhance the woman's pregnancy and make it as harmonious, stable, and joyful as possible. It is during this time that the foundation is laid for the lifelong psychic health of the child.

An Addendum Regarding a Muse-ical Incubator for Premature Babies

I have often been asked: What can be done with *premature* babies, who sometimes must spend the first several months of life in an incubator? How can their muse-ical needs be addressed, deprived as they are of mother's voice, heartbeat, and movements? While no research has yet been done to measure directly and systematically the effect of this deprivation on premature babies, their desire for contact with an "other" is beyond doubt. Neonatologists have long been aware, for example, that incubator babies who are able to do so invariably move toward the humming sound of the motor that controls the temperature and humidity within their enclosed world. Some neonatologists have also expressed concern because these babies experience relatively little human touching, and because much of what they do experience is associated with pain (being pricked with a needle, for example). It should be emphasized, however, that premature babies without brain damage appear by and large to grow up reasonably well despite their deprivation during the incubator period.

Still, on the basis of what we now know about the ability of the fetus to respond to its first impressions of mother's voice, there is reason to advance the following hypothesis: conditions for the healthy development of premature babies could be improved by closer contact with the mother's voice. It is but a short step from this hypothesis to the recommendation that a new type of incubator be developed to help compensate for the muse-ical deprivation of premature babies.

There is good reason to believe that many premature babies, like their full-term counterparts, can learn to recognize their mothers' voices. A simple way to provide for this opportunity would be to play a tape in the baby's incubator. The tape should contain both ordinary talk and the sorts of songs that mothers normally sing to their babies, with frequent changes of "repertoire" during the incubator period. The mother's heartbeat should also be recorded on the tape, to function as the natural underlying rhythm of her voice, carefully fine-tuned to the semantic content and emotional overtones of her words. The father's voice, too, should be on the tape. Hearing the loving voices of both parents may compensate somewhat for the many other stimuli of which the child is necessarily deprived in an incubator.

It is quite possible that ongoing voice stimulation of the kind here envisioned would contribute to a further stimulation of the auditory capacity of the brain and of the ear as a functional organ of hearing. Again, it is the normal full-term pregnancy that provides the frame of reference.

Taking another clue from the normal pattern of pregnancy, I would further recommend the development of a new type of muse-ical incubator equipped with a special *rocking mechanism*—a computer-controlled device accurately simulating the pattern of the mother's bodily movements. We all know that children like to be rocked and sung to. Why not try to provide a similar muse-ical and human environment for babies who must spend the first several weeks of life in an incubator?

So far as I have been able to determine, no systematic effort has yet been made to allow premature babies to regularly hear their mothers' voices, nor do these children (except in cases of suspected or confirmed apnea) receive "motion stimulation" during this critical phase of life. I think a muse-ical incubator like the one described here should be developed and placed in use without delay.

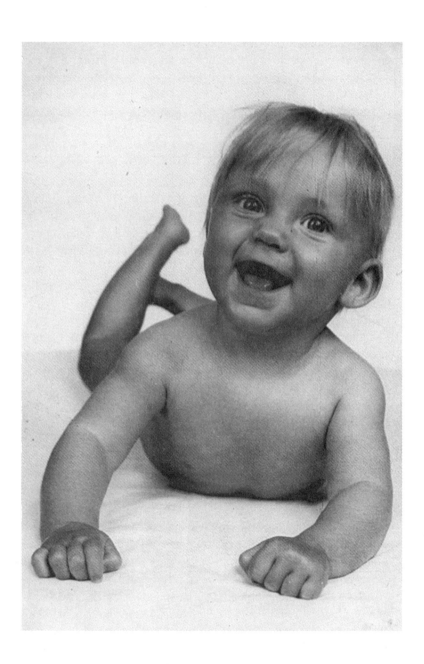

2

The Playing Child
Learns to Live

The primal cry with which a child enters the world contains a powerful existential impulse that is at the heart of every honestly felt muse-ical manifestation that will appear in later life. The newborn breaks the long silence of the gestation period and literally cries for its life. In this most critical stage of life, the child first hears its mother's voice as direct, living sound. Perhaps she, too, cries out in the pain that attends the birth of her child. But the child already "knows" this voice, whether the mother is crying or laughing, talking or singing. In this voice are rich possibilities for closeness and security, recognition and social contact. Throughout the gestation period the child has been preparing to meet its mother as a partner in conversation—a "virtual other," as Norwegian psychologist Stein Bråten puts it in an article describing the development of the "dialogic mind" (1988).

It is important, therefore, that the mother talk to the child as it lies upon her breast and they try to catch their breath after the strenuous activity in which they have just been engaged together. In this classic first meeting between mother and child, it is precisely the mother's voice that is uniquely able to provide a feeling of nearness and familiarity. The anchor of the umbilical cord has been taken away. Now there is a need for new, immediate anchoring points: breasts, milk, skin, bodily warmth, smell (which is also imprinted prenatally as "chemical learning"), the already familiar rhythm of mother's body and breathing—and *a voice*. All play a role in helping the child to organize his/her world—emotionally, cognitively, socially. The mother stimulates the child and the child the mother in such a way that the result is far more meaningful than either could have produced alone. That is the great blessing of all creative human interaction.

From Primal Cry to Protocommunication

In the last twenty years or so, the prevailing view of the newborn child has changed from a purely biological view (newborn as a physical organism with considerable potential for development) to a more humanistic psychological view (newborn as an independent and *social* individual). In many ways the work of Colwyn Trevarthen represents this change. His conclusions are based primarily on video recordings of mother-infant interactions that he has microanalyzed, not least with respect to voice and movement. He has also studied the ways in which mothers sing to their babies in different countries and cultures.

Trevarthen describes the newborn infant as an equal partner with the mother in the communication process from the very beginning of their life together after the child's birth (1978). Mother and child, he says, are "as tightly organized as well-matched . . . musicians in a duet" (1987). He carries this musical analogy even further in another article.

Rhythmic and melodic features of utterances in motherese suggest that the mother is offering a leading pulse to the infant, in much the same way as a conductor announces the beat with a particular routine figure of movements of his baton, sometimes after calling attention by rapping on the lectern. When mother and baby "get into the swing" of communication, they can be perfectly in agreement about a beat, for at least a few bars. This can lead to exquisite overlapping or turntaking that closely resembles the inculcated taking of parts by musicians. Protoconversations create musical forms of participation, the shared beat tending to a slow andante or adagio. (1988, p. 16)

What is going on here is a kind of sound game between two muse-ical people. To put it in the words of the well-known song by Irving Mill and Duke Ellington: "It don't mean a thing if it ain't got that swing!"

Without structure there is no communication. Without structure there is no ordered understanding of reality. Without structure there is no human consciousness. The evident *timing* that occurs in the dialogue between mother and child exhibits, therefore, a central feature of muse-ical communication—not only during the neonatal stage, but in all such communication. This timing creates altogether unique structural possibilities for the development of the individual's specific "dialogic mind." Mother and child "swing" together in a common rhythm, and in so doing strengthen each other's identity.

Trevarthen claims that the newborn can even take the lead in the earliest "conversations" between mother and child. He suggests the possibility of a completely internal common code, a *primary intersubjectivity*, whereby mother and child, in their own little communication world, exchange sounds and movements only they understand. Obviously, the infant's sounds have no semantic meaning. "But they are conversational in the sense of combining the interest of two persons in an exchange of signs," says Trevarthen (1987). These sounds are the first survival communication that in muse-ical terms concern something more important than most of the intellectual conversations we will engage in later in life: the confirmation of the will to live and the urge to social fellowship (1983). Helpless, yet powerful in its own way, the wrinkled little bundle of humanity finds its muse-ical anchor as a social being— a position from which no human being ever willingly departs.

Trevarthen argues that this interplay between mother and infant presupposes that the child possesses from the very beginning a communicational competence in relation to its mother—an "innate intersubjectivity," as he calls it. This claim is, of course,

consistent with DeCasper's findings regarding the ability of the
newborn to recognize its mother's voice. Indeed, Trevarthen takes
note of DeCasper's work in connection with his own research
(e.g., 1987).

The infant also learns incredibly fast to use its own voice in
various ways in "conversations" with its mother. By age two
months, according to Trevarthen, the infant is able to make remarkably mature and inflected sounds when "talking" with its
mother. Several researchers have shown that infants quickly develop a large repertoire of vocal sounds adapted to a range of
feelings.

In the intense contact with the squirming infant that occurs at
the changing table, on mother's lap or shoulder, or in the rocking
chair, the communication repertoire of mother and child is further
developed. The mother invents a unique language for her child—
baby talk, a very special form of "muse-ical mother tongue"—
with an ever closer bond between them as both her motivation
and her reward. Baby talk typically covers a wide range of vocal
inflections and contains many subtle nuances. It appears that
mothers normally can produce this special muse-ical language
only in the presence of their child: s/he is the instrument, the
holder of the key to this secret storehouse. In the child's absence
the mother reverts to normal speech: the muse-ical spell is broken
and can be restored only in a playful new dialogue between
mother and child (Fernald 1976). Research also shows that the
intonational and rhythmic patterns of baby talk are understood by
the infant, who responds systematically and confidently with
bodily movements, facial expressions, and voice (Snow 1977,
Papousek and Papousek 1981). Little by little the child masters the
whole repertoire of expressions, including the tiniest details.

The power of communication grows. The infant soon learns a
large number of meaningful sounds, long before any of them
become recognizable words. The meaning lies in the *music* of the
sounds—the nuances conveyed by changes in intonation,
rhythm, tempo, and dynamics. Every parent has observed, for
example, the many different kinds of crying of which their children are capable. One kind means "I'm hungry," another "I
hurt," yet another "I'm angry," and so on. And we must not

forget fake crying, which means "I don't really need anything, but I want your attention anyway!" Each kind of crying has its own unique sound: a certain pitch, intensity, duration, and rhythm (Wolfe 1969). New parents understand very well what their child wants as they drowsily stagger out of bed night after night to comfort the little despot who has suddenly taken over their lives (Sarfi, Smørvik, and Martinsen 1984). The child also adjusts its voice to match the changes in rhythm and tempo of its mother's voice. This behavior is especially clear in the child's reactions to its mother's singing. In its voice and movements, the infant-musician will often intuitively continue to mimic the music even after the mother has stopped singing. The rhythmic alterations between child and mother are, as Trevarthen puts it, "intersynchronized" (1987).

Trevarthen suggests that mother and child may be equipped with a common "inner clock" that governs patterns of movement, rhythm, tempo, and beat within a preestablished framework. It is possible, in accordance with DeCasper's findings, that such an inner clock is acquired prenatally, perhaps as one of the first ways by which the fetus internalizes the mother's unique pattern of movements. One can easily imagine that the clock governing the mother's personal movement pattern is imprinted within the fetus, suspended as it is in the fluid of the amniotic sac, sensing every detail of the mother's bodily movements.

Other researchers, too, have studied the "intersynchronization" of rhythmic patterns between mother and infant (e.g., Stern 1977). Condon and Sander (1983), using quite original micro-techniques, filmed the early muse-ical communication between very young infants and adults. They found that the infants' movements, usually thought to be helpless and random, were in fact precisely synchronized with the rhythm and tempo of the language of the adults. Condon and Sander's conclusion is most interesting.

This study reveals a complex interaction system in which the organization of the neonate's motor behavior is entrained by and synchronized with the organized speech behavior of adults in his environment. If the infant, from the beginning, moves in precise,

shared rhythm with the organization of the speech structure of his
culture, then he participates developmentally through complex,
sociobiological entrainment processes in millions of repetitions of
linguistic forms long before he later uses them in speaking and
communicating. By the time he begins to speak, he may have
already laid down within himself the form and structure of the
language system of his culture. (1983, p. 101)

The mother tongue, then, is imprinted within the infant's body
as a total muse-ical complex whose basic elements are sound,
rhythm, and movement. Condon and Sander, contrary to Noam
Chomsky and other linguists, hold that this first mimetic process
is not solely a matter of genetic-biological preprogramming. Like
Trevarthen, they emphasize instead the social competence of the
newborn infant. It is on the basis of the totality of its biological and
social birthright that the infant from the moment of birth further
develops its already established potential for communication. De-
Casper's studies of prenatal learning, which were undertaken after
Condon and Sander's findings, strongly confirm the claim that the
newborn infant is an inherently social being (as Vygotsky had
averred many years earlier). The work of Margaret Donaldson, a
student of Piaget, unambiguously supports the same conclusion
(1979). More and more the focus of researchers is on *the infant as
a social being*.

This little social being dramatically enlarges his or her world
during the first year of life. At every step of the way, bodily
movement, rhythm, and the intonation of language are of decisive
importance, not least in relation to the mother, the child's constant collaborator in the most important duet the child will ever
play.

SING WITH YOUR NEWBORN CHILD—
EVEN IF YOU "CAN'T SING"!
We have seen how important the mother's voice is for the first
stage in the development of the child's ability to communicate,
founded as it is on the muse-ical symbiosis of mother and child
during gestation. Mother's voice is the child's portal to social life.
The newborn's first hearing of its mother's tender words is a *déjà*

entendu of tremendous importance. It would be most unfortunate, therefore, if a mother never sang for her child because she was intimidated by a Western tradition of *bel canto* singing that says, "You don't sing nicely: do something else!" That is as silly as if one said to her, "Your breasts aren't pretty enough: don't nurse your baby!"

For the newborn there is no more important, no more beautiful voice in all the world than that of its mother. This voice contains the whole of mother's love in a concentrated form. What opera star would dare to compete with the incomparable wonder that transpires between mother and child? It is extremely important that the child gain access to the special emotion and communicative power inherent in its mother's and—to a lesser but nonetheless important degree—its father's voice. Therefore I say: sing to your newborn, even if you think you can't sing. It's good for all of you.

STAGES ON THE PATHWAY TOWARD CHILD CULTURE

Grace Wales Shugar is one of many researchers who have traced the development of communication skills from the child's first communication with its mother to a fully developed ability to communicate with its peers in a complex child culture. Shugar (1988) has identified various stages along this pathway.

At the beginning of the process it is strictly a matter of the personal relationship between the infant and its mother. The child is totally unaware of a world beyond the mother. At about three months one can clearly see how things outside the circle of mother-child communication begin to capture the child's attention. The mother (or mother and father) is no longer the whole of the child's world; the parents serve also as facilitators of the child's play with things within its reach. At this stage it is still difficult for the child to combine these two forms of attention. Either it "talks" with the parent or it plays with something: it can't do both at the same time (Trevarthen 1987). Toward the end of the first year, however, it masters the skill of "double attention." The child and the parent or other adult can now play together and communicate at the same time.

By now the child is an experienced communicator. As early as age seven months s/he will have developed the ability to enjoy a good joke. Increasingly s/he is able to initiate humorous exchanges—produce unusual sounds, make funny faces, etc.—and as a reward hear the infectious laughter of adults (Trevarthen 1987). Moreover, this all transpires theatrically and muse-ically: it is still the music of the language, the *how* and not the what, that gives the exchange its unique communicative power.

During the second year of life the child's interest turns increasingly toward other children, especially those of similar age. Shugar diagrams this stage as follows:

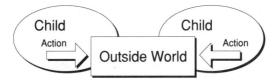

Here two children, one slightly older than the other, are playing with the same object in a kind of parallel game in which they do not communicate directly with each other. Each lives for the most part in his/her own ego-centered world, but the object with which they are playing happens to be in the worlds of both.

At the next stage the children continue to play with the same toy, but now a relationship has been established between them as well. They communicate with each other. The two worlds have become one.

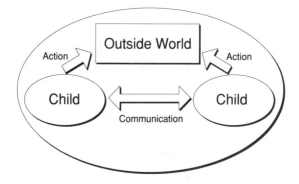

Soon the two children are able to play with two different toys within the context of one and the same game—as when two toddlers crawl around on the floor, each holding a toy car, regulating traffic by word and deed, *zo-o-om*ing and *br-r-r*ing and *honk*ing as they play and sing.

From this point on the child must learn to make its way in two arenas of life: the family and the world of other children. The child moves back and forth between what Urie Bronfenbrenner has called the *micro*-level and the *meso*-level of its life (1979). It is important at this stage that play serve as a bridge-builder between these two quite different milieus so that the child can integrate them in an ever larger but meaningful whole.

Two-year-olds still need an adult nearby for security and stimulation in order to play together smoothly (Trevarthen 1988). Thereafter, independence from adults and increased interest in play and companionship with other children develop with lightning rapidity. The child's language clearly reflects how contact with other children now begins to play an important role. If the family has moved to another part of the country, the children will often begin to mimic the regional accent and speech patterns rather than those of their parents. Mastery of the dialect of local child culture is a condition of entry into the group and full participation in its social life.

Once the process begins, it moves quickly. First there is one playmate, then a large group; first one game, then many. A magical new chapter opens for the child during the third year of life, one of companionship as well as loneliness in the company of other children at play. Time and life march on, and child culture rapidly assumes an important role as a matrix for the child's further development.

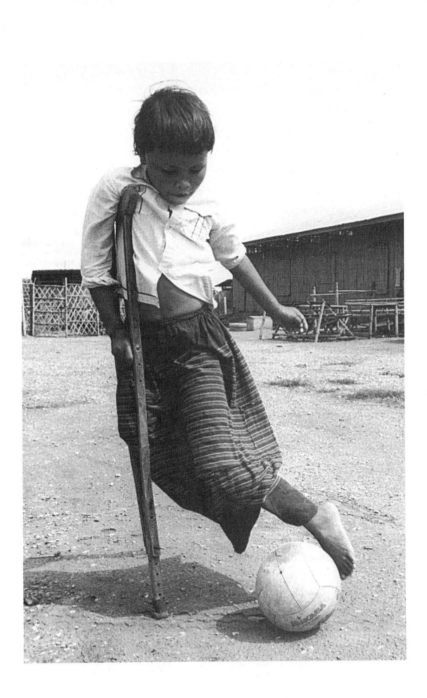

3

The Culture of Children at Play

THE TRIUMPH OF INCONVENIENCE

Summertime at the cottage on an island off the coast of Norway. A bright, clear day with the refreshing sea nearby and a blazing sun overhead. Eighty degrees in the shade! Rare in this part of the world—an absolute dream for a vacation. When did we last experience a day like this?

The parents have made their way down to the new sundeck, carefully situated in a south-facing cleft in the rock to catch the sun and avoid the wind. A cozy, charming place. Contented adult bodies stretch out lazily in the warm sunshine without a care in the world. The transistor radio is playing softly in the background, the suntan lotion has been applied, the first sip has been taken of a nice, cool beer. Ah, this is living!

Suddenly the idyll is interrupted:

"Where the devil are the kids? Have we forgotten them as we lay here sunning ourselves? They were here just a minute ago. Has something happened to them?"

The frightened parents look around in every direction. Then they hear it: a soft buzz of talking and singing—*under* the sundeck!

Surprised, the parents crawl quietly over to the edge of the deck and peer down. Sure enough, there they are—all three children—down in the shadows. Squeezed together between a pile of sharp stones and a mound of wet, soggy dirt, in the farthest corner of their private little cellar. It must be chilly and unpleasant, but there they sit, in almost total darkness, in a space so cramped that even they can move around only on hands and knees. There, in the shadowy darkness of their newfound cave, oblivious to the inherent discomfort of their surroundings, they are busily playing together. It is *the triumph of inconvenience*.

IN CHILD CULTURE
At about age three children enter seriously into the activity of playing with other children. They develop ever wider horizons regarding the possibilities for play in companionship with others and move quickly from solitary play to a more selfless interest in other children. They alertly and eagerly pick up the "rules of the game" from the older children, who are the undisputed leaders of the group activity by virtue of their mastery of those rules. The hunger for learning at this stage is insatiable, and the ability to learn is enormous because the process is absolutely essential to life. There are many skills to be mastered: body language, the subtleties of the spoken language, humor, songs. All are keys that will open the door to the fellowship of *child culture*, a muse-ical community of friendship and bickering, warmth and coldness, play and rivalry. No child can remain outside this culture without suffering harm. Like the primal cry, the entry into child culture has to do with the struggle to survive through participation.

The play of preschool children has a broad range. Naturally the *traditional games* are important elements in the daily life of these children. Hopscotch, for example, is played according to established rules in Scandinavia, Russia, and the United States—and no doubt in many other countries. The very point of the game is the mastery and interpretation of the rules in the mock-serious interplay between the uncertainty of the beginners and the sure mastery of the "veterans" whose good-natured cheating is part of the fun.

Equally important, however, are the *open games*. These, too, have rules and norms, but to a large extent they are created by the children themselves, who are free to change them at will in a process that resembles improvisation on an established theme. Role-play games are examples of open games: Mommy-Daddy-Baby, Cops and Robbers, and others. Here the meta-level, the deliberate fiction of the entire setting of the action, is a vital dimension, and children enter into it with complete dedication. "Let's pretend . . ." is the magic phrase that defines the rules of such games—and the success of the pretending is evident in the real fright experienced by a three-year-old robber unlucky enough to get captured by a four-year-old cop!

Lastly, there are *original games*, in which children, drawing on their natural propensity to play, exhibit great creativity, originality, and curiosity as they go about the exploration of reality in their own unique way. Even here, however, there is an underlying structure—a kind of cultural gravitational field—that sets certain limits to what can and cannot be done. Child culture, like any other, has its own repertoire of norms that govern the behavior of all members of the cultural group, and these norms clearly have a formative influence on any games the children may invent.

These three types of games give a measure of structure and continuity to the everyday life of children. The relationship between the individual child and child culture could almost be called one of symbiotic reciprocity, for the two belong together like wind and weather. On the one hand, child culture provides support and structure for the child's mental development and sense of identity. But on the other, each child is also an essential living element that constantly renews and preserves the culture in all its variety and uniqueness. The child's field of play widens—from playing alone to playing with others in the family to playing as a member of a group of children—and the reward to be won is the same as the one we observed in the case of the newborn child: more structure creates the possibility of more awareness, more communication and closeness, more socialization and learning.

The games of five- or six-year-olds tend to be more firmly structured than those of their younger counterparts. These games are as spontaneous and creative as ever, but to a much higher degree than previously they are imbued with the rules, norms, and values of the group. The younger children constantly observe and seek to emulate the older ones and are initiated into the secret labyrinths of the cultural game. Here is living folk culture being preserved in a genuine oral tradition. Here one finds friendship and enmity, demonstrations of toughness, forbidden words. Singing games and hopscotch. Playing tricks and playing ball. Bike riding and swinging. The imperceptible detail makes all the difference and defines the make-or-break issue of the day: if you don't master the code you are lost. Everything is governed by child culture's own unwritten rules regarding what, where, who, why, and how.

Where do we find this child culture in our modern industrial society? We find it wherever two or more children are gathered together and reveal their private code of rules in their play. In a rumpus room where one child visits another to play cars. In the sandbox, perhaps the one at the preschool or in the park. Or, as time goes by, in the schoolyard during recess or after school. Games and play are living realities everywhere.

Adult society, too, is built up—and civilized—through the forms and functions of play. Dutch cultural historian Johan Huizinga, in his classic *Homo Ludens*, shows that play is the original form of such important social activities as courtroom proceedings, war strategies, various peaceful social rituals, and art. The postmodernists of our day are approaching the same idea from another direction when they describe society's political life in its entirety as a kind of game.

The engine that drives all forms of play, be it rigorously rulebound or free, is a bold, creative, and insatiable curiosity. The wonder and desire to explore that are at the heart of play start with the familiar but seek the unfamiliar. This venturing from the known toward the unknown is something that the child can master only through a kind of creative duality. From one point of view, child culture is basically conservative. Well-established norms, values, and traditions form the basis and framework of this culture. New impressions are for the most part adapted to established processes and forms. At the same time, however, child culture has a need to *break* with the conventions, to modify norms and rules. *Cultural disobedience*—an element of protest against existing forms and standards—is therefore an essential feature of the "cutting edge" of child culture.

It is through changes in their own knowledge and skills that children change the world—for themselves and for others. The world can never be the same again once you learn to ride a bicycle without training wheels. Friedrich Schiller observed long ago that children have an inborn need for play. Life must be discovered and created by every single child, generation after generation, so long as there are children in the world. *As we create, we are created,* to borrow from the great Moravian educational reformer John Amos Comenius. A daunting task at times, but a necessary one.

At all times, children's playing is governed by the categorical imperative of all games: *Thou shalt play in earnest!* The slightest hint of condescension is enough to get one expelled from the group. Children abandon themselves to play like a flock of birds in flight, be it in giggling and laughter or in a gloomy hiding place. They are both vulnerable and invulnerable. Their lives are lived within the protective framework of play, which includes everything from the most ordinary objects and events of daily life to creations of their fertile imaginations. Play: the magic mixture of scabs and dreams that teaches us about life.

THE ECOLOGICAL CHILD

In *The Ecology of Imagination in Childhood* (1977), the American writer Edith Cobb has discussed the relationship between environment and play with particular attention to the ways in which play contributes to the development of children's imagination. With a deep awareness of the complex relationships among environment, play, and imagination—inspired in part by Gregory Bateson's *Steps to an Ecology of Mind* (1972)—Cobb sees children's play as part of a dynamic ecosystem that includes elements of both nature and man-made culture.

It is Cobb's thesis that the child comprehends reality and forms impressions of reality through the body's nervous system and

sense organs in a way that is directly and organically related to
nature's own energy forms. The body's pulse and nature's pulse
are two sides of the same coin, according to Cobb. In sense
experience, the child achieves extension into surrounding nature,
and nature, for its part, achieves organic absorption in the child.
Cobb therefore uses the term *biocultural* to describe the sensing and
creating forms of understanding that emerge in the child's play—
forms that are anchored in physical life but actualized in cultural
expressions and symbols. According to Cobb, this biocultural
balance between man and nature, and between thought and body,
is the source of imagination and the dynamic spring from which
further cultural development may flow. The child ventures forth
into the world "out there" within the context of a whole that it
does not yet know, but of which it nonetheless is an obvious and
immediate part.

> In the creative perceptions of poet and child we are close to the
> biology of thought itself—close, in fact, to the ecology of imagina-
> tion, in which the energies of the body and mind as a unit, an
> ecosystem, and the energies of nature combine in a mutual en-
> deavor to adapt to nature, to culture, and to the societies devised
> by man to embody culture. (p. 109)

In this balanced ecosystem children feel at home, because it is
here, as a part of the whole, that they and their playing belong.
Once again we are reminded of the children under the sundeck,
in a harmonious whole consisting of themselves, their play, and
their narrow cave of stone and gravel, acting creatively in a way
that literally is completely natural.

> The child's world, his surroundings, are not separated into nature
> and artifact. His environment consists of the information fed back
> to his own body by environmental stimuli. This responsiveness
> includes all levels of the child as a functioning organism. . . . Life
> is a matter of mutual, functional interaction or intercourse with the
> environment. This mutuality is equally nourishing and productive
> of life and form to the mind and to the body. . . .

The child's ecological sense of continuity with nature is not what is generally known as mystical. It is, I believe, basically aesthetic and infused with joy in the power to know and to be. These equal, for the child, a sense of the power to make. (pp. 29, 23)

The collapse of the tightly woven ecosystem consisting of nature and the creative cognition that is natural for children can produce crises of great significance not only for the child's mental health but also for its learning process in school and society. We shall return to this point in Chapter 5, "The Muse-ical Child Goes to School."

ANALOGICAL CORRESPONDENCES

There are almost as many pathways into child culture as there are children. Take swinging, for example. The big kids are tough. They swing so high that they almost go around in a complete circle, and they leap off into the air, seemingly without fear and with perfect timing, to see who can jump the farthest. As Italian musicologist Giuseppe Porzionato expressed it (1989), with particular reference to the child's neurology: *"Se mi muove . . . apprendo!"* ("I move . . . and learn!").

But a four-year-old knows how to handle a swing too. There she sits, securely planted on a tire suspended from a rope, swinging back and forth in lazy, undulating movements. Her best friend is beside her, and they are singing as they swing, their song rising and falling as the swing goes up and down, up and down. The movements of the swing, the movements of their bodies, their words, and their singing are warp and woof of the same fabric— a unified experience such as they have known many times before, going way back to the time when they were in their mothers' wombs. The song expresses in melody and rhythm what the swing conveys to the child's body in the form of purely physical oscillation; the two complexes are expressions of the same underlying reality. What we have here is one example of many *analogical correspondences* that unite the child's forms of understanding with forms of expression, and in so doing have an integrative effect on the child's personality as a whole. Thoughts, words, songs, feelings, and the whole repertoire of body movements are interwoven analogically as different aspects, or modalities, of the child's total experience. All of these elements are found in full flower in the spontaneous play of children. That is why play is so important in the process of bringing the child's inner and outer worlds into a harmonic relationship with each other. In play, the analogical balance between self and world becomes part of the ecology of the child's mind.

PLAY AS A WAY OF BEING—
HERE AND NOW AND BEYOND TIME AND SPACE

Many discussions of children's play do not go beyond the observation that play is a form of folklore. But play is more than that: it is a way of being, a *state of mind* in continuous motion. The impulse to play, as we have seen in the case of the newborn child, is built into the central psychic and sensorimotor processes that give the child a capacity for psychosocial development. Children do not just play: they live in and through their playing, with a capacity for total flexibility—both here and now and beyond time and space. Children *are* what they play. It is through play that they build new highways into the unknown—including, when necessary, regions that lie beyond the here and now.

I myself remember well that as a little boy I *was* Jesse Owens.

"SKINNY-ELF" AS JESSE OWENS

It was Grandpa Rudolf who said it. "Look at *those* legs! Sprinter's legs! It's as if I were looking at Jesse Owens!"

Me? Jesse Owens? Astonished, I looked down at my skinny legs. Me?

I had always known that I was skinny. I was sent to a Red Cross camp after World War II to put on a little weight. The camp was called Tomtebo, which means "home of the elves." I didn't like it, refused to eat, refused to sleep, refused everything, and managed to get sent home earlier than planned. I got out of camp, but I couldn't get rid of the name the other boys gave me: "Skinny-Elf."

"Your legs are like matchsticks, Skinny-Elf!" they said when I went out bare-legged in the summertime. "Don't break your leg when you kick, Skinny-Elf!" laughed the captain of our neighborhood soccer team if I ever got close to the ball—which didn't happen very often.

But here was Grandpa saying that my legs were like Jesse Owens's legs. I had never seen Jesse Owens, but I had certainly heard of him. My father often talked about him, and so did Grandpa. "Four gold medals in the Berlin Olympics in 1936: long jump, 100 meters, 200 meters, and relay. All world records; 10.2 in the hundred meters was his best performance. Hitler was livid and stalked out of the stadium before it was over. Absolutely unbeatable, quick as lightning. Yes, Jesse ran in competition with horses too—and won." Eyes glistening, I had devoured the legend with each retelling, over and over again.

Now I *was* Jesse Owens. At least my legs were. I examined them carefully when nobody else was home. There was a big mirror above a chest in the front hall of our house, and right opposite, not more than three or four feet away, was the doorway to the children's room. Just the place for Jesse Owens! I braced my feet firmly against the doorway, leaned forward, and grasped the edge of the chest with my hands in the classic posture of the champion sprinter streaking toward the ribbon. Jesse Owens in front of the crowd at the Olympic stadium in Berlin. For I *was* Jesse Owens as I posed there in front of the mirror, enjoying myself and the muscles I didn't have. I was as white as any native-born Norwegian, but in my mind's eye I was black like Jesse Owens. I could see it all in the mirror—the magnificent body, the gleaming black skin, the chest muscles. And in my heart I heard a wonderful song—a song about myself, the invincible Jesse Owens. At the same time, I could hear the jubilation from the packed stadium as 100,000 people cheered in collective ecstasy. They were shouting to *me*. This was no Skinny-Elf with legs like matchsticks. *Nosiree!* This is Berlin, 1936, and I can do a hundred meters in 10.2.

Or, come to think of it, wasn't it 10.1? I think I broke the world record several times there by the big mirror in the front hall, without moving my legs a single inch. Yes, I'm sure of it: Skinny-Elf *did* shave a tenth of a second off Jesse Owens's old record.

Nobody beat him, nobody equaled him. He was like a black panther racing through the sound barrier. The gold medal was mine, then and there, beyond time and space.

CHILD CULTURES MEET AND CHILDREN LEARN

As school age approaches, the expertise of children in the art of play reaches a preliminary climax. Let us see how a little Norwegian boy, thoroughly steeped in the child culture of his own country, experienced an encounter with American children.

THE STORY OF THE RED RUBBER BALL

He is seven years old and a newcomer in a foreign land. His name is Kjartan, but in America this is soon shortened to Tan. You need a name that fits the phonetics of the language, or you become invisible. Besides, Americans like nicknames.

Tan has scabs on both knees and is beginning to lose his teeth like millions of other seven-year-olds the world over. He is thin and ungainly, with thick blond hair that curls over his ears.

For Tan the United States is the promised land of big cars, cowboys and Indians, skyscrapers, and Disneyland. And here he is, unable to speak a word of English.

His parents go with him to school the first day. "All eyes on me!" says the teacher as she points toward her eyes to get the pupils' attention. Tan is confused. He jabs me in the ribs and whispers, "Why is she trying to poke her eyes out?" His mother and I feel a gnawing anxiety as we begin to realize how infinitely far our little boy has to go to find his way in this new and different world.

Time passes—days, weeks, months. Lonely and a bit wary, Tan leans against a tree and watches. The schoolyard is filled with children noisily playing all kinds of games that are totally incomprehensible to the little boy from Norway. Seven hundred American children are shouting, screaming, singing, laughing, hollering, running. Seven hundred models for him to follow. But there are so many new and unfamiliar games, so many strange sounds, so many faces he has never seen before. The patterns of the play, the rules and mores, are hidden from him as if by a fog.

It hurts, being on the outside like this. But the hurt doesn't just make him feel bad: it also drives him with tremendous force. He wants to break out of this loneliness. He wants to join the rest of the children, participate in their games, have fun with them, be one of the gang. So he doesn't give up, despite great pangs of insecurity. He hungrily takes in everything he sees and hears, tries putting it together this way and that. It's like a jigsaw puzzle with thousands of pieces, and every piece must be in just the right place before you can discern the whole picture. He must understand the combinations, grasp the complexity, penetrate the impenetrable. Each tiny detail is tested against a provisional concept of the whole and vice versa in a continuous and fruitful interchange through which, step by step, he closes in on his prey. From an adult perspective, the odds of a child succeeding in this process appear infinitesimal, but millions of children have managed it before, and now it is Tan's turn. It demands every ounce of courage and perseverance he can muster.

Determined, immovable, he leans against his tree and watches closely. He begins to feel the rhythm of the play. His body begins to move in a kind of inner dance as he senses the passion and the motion of the children around him. Everything is recorded both sensibly and muse-ically as he concentrates with an intensity fired by an unquenchable desire for social companionship. He will become one of them. He *must* become one of them. It is, quite literally, a struggle for life.

For more than three months Tan stood by that tree in the schoolyard, watching silently as the other children played. Not a word of English crossed his lips—and we, his parents, suffered. It's hard to see your own child so lonesome, so totally left out. We were about to go and talk to the principal, but Tan stopped us, insisting that everything was fine.

One day, shortly before Christmas, Tan came to me. Our conversation—in Norwegian, of course—went something like this.

"Dad, I want a red rubber ball!"

"Really? What for?"

"I'm going to play handball with the other kids."

Something important was about to happen: Tan was going to go out and *play*. With other American children. And he wanted his own ball! I practically ran to the local supermarket and soon returned with a big, soft, red rubber ball.

Tan took the ball and squeezed it, carefully and affectionately. Like a dog sniffing out a new acquaintance, like a violinist trying out a new bow. Quietly he began humming a song as his fingers explored the contours of his new possession. And then, suddenly, it was his—dedicated, as it were, ready to be used. As familiar to him as if he had owned it for years. With the ball under his arm, still humming, he went outside.

Then, watching through the living-room window, I saw it: Tan *walked* differently—like an American boy, with a little more spring in the hips, a different rhythm in his step. In no time at all he was playing with the others, unquestionably a member of the group. This was *American* handball. I saw them serving against the wall of the garage, throwing, ducking, hitting the ball up in the air, running. And the game had its own unique vocabulary: "Bounces!" "Slider!" "Watermelons!" "Redboard!" "Backstop!" "Pops!" "Waterfall!" "Black magic!" Tan ducked, ran, served, and hit the ball in the midst of all these American children— indeed, as *one of them*. He was no longer Norwegian in his play. To be sure, he still couldn't speak the language of his new playmates. But never mind: he *ran* in American, he *threw* in American, he *caught the ball* in American—yes, by God, he even stood and *waited for his turn* in American! With every ounce of his being the boy was *playing in American*. Fluently. Freed by a ball, in fine-tuned harmony with the other children in the neighborhood.

I trembled with joy. The entire code of this new child culture was being implanted in the boy's body as an integrated totality.

"Now he'll start to *speak* American too!" I suggested that evening. "It won't be long."

And I was right. Just a week later it began. With the naturalness of a child. This was something quite different from the fumbling, stilted school English of his parents. Nasal vowels, the characteristic American "r," singing sentence rhythms, and perfect American intonation. John Wayne! The words flowed with inborn timing and rhythm. It was no adult teacher who had produced this. The desire to play with the other children had been his motivation, the interaction with those children had been his schoolmaster, and a big red rubber ball had been the liberating medium. The ball released a new body identity. New body movements produced a new kind of play. The new play produced new language. And new language produced new human belongingness and cultural companionship—the very thing he had craved so deeply during the long months as an outsider.

We took the ball back to Norway with us. Tan insisted on it, though it practically filled his backpack. Now he is Kjartan once again. The ball, dusty and unused, lies under the bed of a thoroughly Norwegian boy. In Norway, nobody plays American handball. Neither does Kjartan. But the big red ball did not live its earlier ball life in vain, for once it was magic in Kjartan's life. It emboldened a seven-year-old boy from Norway to take that decisive leap in a foreign land: to play and talk American—without a safety net!

PLAY AND INNOVATION

In the all-consuming self-forgetfulness of play lies the key to self-transcendence. Thus play is the experimental laboratory for learning, where the conquest of reality—seen and unseen—is continually being anticipated. Standing alone there by his tree, Tan was at the same time "one of the gang," playing right along with the other children through the power of imagination. In his insatiable hunger for new friends, Tan became one of them—one of the boys—in a dynamic synthesis of dream and outer reality that we might call *cocreative learning*. Models of the surrounding world were taken in as inner representations and conceptions in a child's mind. There the impressions could ripen freely until they were ready to spring forth in manifest fullness: "I can!"

Every day children must cross the border into the unknown, for each day's experience contains new challenges that they must come to terms with in one way or another. Some things should be internalized and become part of their personalities, other things they must have the strength to reject. These daily challenges must be mastered if the child is to develop further—cognitively, emotionally, and with respect to sensorimotor skills. In these ever new demands for mastery lies a natural dynamic for human growth. In the ability to formulate or experience tomorrow what is still unknown today lies also an inner dynamic to change reality.

Piaget spoke of *accommodation, adaptation,* and *assimilation.* In creative concentration the little boy *is* O. J. Simpson, and in his imagination he outruns and outmaneuvers an entire opposing team, though in sober reality he is the only one around. All children have the capacity to live in an imaginary world without for a moment losing contact with their immediate surroundings. *Logos* and *mythos* become one. They themselves control the role change. As newborns they learned this art of meta-communication, and they retain the ability to shift perspective, in their playing and in their talking, throughout childhood (Bateson 1972).

The magical transformations of play are as old as they are important and are deeply ingrained in all folk culture. One encounters them frequently in folk tales. Asbjørnsen and Moe, for example, in their collection of Norwegian folk tales, tell the story of the boy who made himself into a lion, a falcon, and an ant. *Why* did the boy do this? Well, silly, how else could he manage to fly all over the world, escape from a bird's cage, slay the nine-headed dragon, crawl through a crack in the mountain into the home of the trolls, crawl through the keyhole into the lair of the six-headed monster, kill the monster, and win the hand of the king's daughter and half the kingdom as well? In the same way, the mild-mannered reporter Clark Kent can instantly change himself into Superman to defeat the terrible Lex Luthor and save his beloved Lois Lane. Superman can do all sorts of wonderful things: fly, leap tall buildings in a single bound, bend steel in his bare hands, and so on. Skinny-Elf was not Superman, but he could run faster than anyone else in the world—even faster than Jesse Owens.

Animals can play, but they can never leap out of their skins through imagination. Imaginative transformation is a specifically human skill. I am reminded of a Russian proverb: "Take away the fairy tale—and then try to explain to a man why he should go on living."

The Swedish children's writer Astrid Lindgren has written about the same theme in a beautiful and moving way. The opening of her novel *The Brothers Lionheart* deals precisely with the idea of crossing a boundary. Here we meet the scrawny, mortally ill Rusky.

"How can things be so terrible," I asked. "How can things be so terrible that some have to die, when they're not even ten years old?"

"You know, Rusky, I don't think it's that terrible," said Jonathan. "I think you'll have a marvellous time."

"Marvellous," I said. "Is it marvellous to lie under the ground and be dead?"

"Oh," said Jonathan, "It's only your shell that lies there, you know? You yourself fly away somewhere quite different."

"Where?" I asked, because I could hardly believe him.

"To Nangiyala," he said.

To Nangiyala—he just threw out the word as if it were something everyone in the world knew about. But at the time, I had never heard it mentioned before.

"Nangiyala?" I said. "Where's that?"

Then Jonathan said that he wasn't quite certain about that, but it was somewhere on the other side of the stars. And he began to tell me about Nangiyala, so that one almost felt like flying there at once. . . . (p. 8)

We grown-ups who have read Astrid Lindgren's book know that Rusky went to Nangiyala, for we have been there with him. A snow-white dove came and got him and carried him over the border to Nangiyala, "on the other side of the stars." We know that there he and Jonathan became the valiant brothers Lionheart who conquered both the monster Katla and the cruel Tengil and his men. Just like in the fairy tale. We have been eyewitnesses to the whole story, thanks to the remnants of our childlike capacity for fantasy.

The Greek word from which "fantasy" is derived means, literally, "making visible"; it has to do with the mind's ability to create inner images. "Imagination," which is a synonym for "fantasy," has the same connotations: it comes from the Latin *imago*, which means, among other things, "picture," "mental picture." The Russian language incorporates the same connection: the word for "imagination," *voobrazjenie*, is derived from *obraz*, which means "picture" or "image." It is not only with our eyes that we see. The brain has other avenues of vision, and they are accessible to both the sighted and the blind. Play stimulates our inner vision. So also do books and music. Astrid Lindgren once said in a radio interview (Bøhle 1988b) that it was music that had the power to transport her to the world of Nangiyala. Music, by virtue of its direct access to the human body and senses, has a unique ability to inspire the imagination. Deeply felt music can stimulate quantum leaps into other forms of experience and understanding. That is one of the reasons we cannot get along without it. We are by no means speaking here of a flight from reality, but of a strengthening and enlargement of our perception of reality such that the inherent *mystery* is perceived once again. The distinction between reason and imagination becomes totally inconsequential.

> Fantasy represents the seeking mind's effort to find meaning, connection, order—to reach understanding. Fantasy is not the opposite of reason but its prerequisite. To follow one's fantasy in a creative flight of imagination is for the child the natural way of achieving insight. (Berefelt 1981)

WHAT IS A ROCK GUITAR?

Arne is a six-year-old Norwegian boy who has mastered the art of play and has seen rock videos on television. He likes the English word "heavy" (as in "heavy metal"), though he doesn't know for sure what it means. But it's a neat word.

No piggy bank in the world could hold enough money to buy such a thing as a rock guitar. Not Arne's, in any case. But he solves his guitar problem in his own way. Intuitively anchored in the magic of spontaneous song, Arne goes into the kitchen one day and finds the finest rock guitars a little boy could ever want.

First the cheese plane. The shape is just right, with both a neck and a body. Triumphantly, Arne crouches down like the rock players he has seen on television. In an instant it is as if he were electrically charged: the electricity of play has taken control of him. The chubby little left hand holds the neck of the cheese plane. The right hand strums chords with a heavy, professional rock beat. It all comes straight out of his favorite video: "Come and take me, baby, come and take me now!" His foot beats time, his body jerks rhythmically. The song begins to intoxicate him. The cheese plane *is* a rock guitar. And Arne is the star, standing there in the middle of the pulsating sound from a band that only he can hear.

Encouraged by his initial success, Arne looks further. How about a *fork?* Wouldn't that do too? Sure enough! He opens the broom closet and finds an old badminton racket. An obvious choice. And a whisk broom. He plays on them briefly but quickly lays them aside: they look almost too much like a real guitar. The music has gone to his head. His boldness increases, *accelerando.* Arne is ready for something stronger. What shall it be?

The fresh mackerel—the one Mother bought at the fish market earlier in the day: a guitar! The floor lamp is dragged from the living room into the kitchen: a spotlight! A sweat sock is slipped over a big wooden spoon: a microphone! Everything is now swinging within the magic circle of Arne's make-believe as the mackerel drips fishy water on the floor for the sake of spontaneous rock. By now Arne's entire body is trembling to the rhythms of the vividly imagined rock music. Objects have become superfluous: a completely imaginary guitar has now taken their place, the same "pretend" guitar that most youngsters play at one time or another. The most submissive guitar in the world, the one that gives you absolute control. Arne starts a new tune, drawn from his parents' repertoire: "One, two, three o'clock, four o'clock rock! . . ." He plucks harder and harder, totally absorbed in rhythm and melody and movement, until every last ounce of energy is spent. Then, exhausted, he goes quietly to sleep on the kitchen floor.

PLAY, REASON, UNDERSTANDING, AND HUMOR

Play can break through the confines of what we may call *technical reason* and introduce new possibilities when reason is in danger of becoming too narrowly confined. All human mental activity is, of course, grounded in reason, but reasoning according to the canons of deductive logic is only one such activity. Valuing, willing, deciding—these, too, are grounded in reason. And so is imagination. Imagination is reason seeking to transcend itself, reason reaching for the beyond, reason with wings, and play is one of the important ways whereby reason acquires wings. It is through this capacity for play that literature, the visual arts, and music achieve much of their impact. The *play* of the various art forms with a given body of material creates rich new ways of reshaping the everyday Euclidian world and introducing the dose of suprarational asymmetry that alone can enable important elements of the human spirit to break free. Picasso's Cubist paintings of the human figure are a good example. An artist's creative play with his or her material can transcend time and space; indeed, at its very best it can overleap the ordinary boundaries of thought, sensation, and reason.

Play and song have a Dionysian dynamic that is not based on technical reason. Technical reason reduces the world to categories by means of ordered concepts. The playful imagination, by virtue of its relative freedom from such concepts, has the power to elevate us above the categorial knowledge already achieved. It carries us beyond our limiting preconceptions into the new country that lies "on the other side of the stars." The open, wondering quality of play becomes an emancipating power that liberates us from the absolute sway of technical reason.

The idea that childlike play is a qualitatively different mode of understanding is closely related to Schopenhauer's views on the special status and function of music for humankind. Music, for Schopenhauer, is the *vox humana*, the quintessential human voice; it is therefore the medium that most powerfully transcends reason's massive conceptual barrier of established knowledge and brings the human being into immediate contact with the inner essence of existence. More recently, Roland Barthes advanced similar ideas regarding the power of music to lift us out of the banal and overused clichés of everyday life and open up new modes of understanding (Barthes 1975, Bjørkvold 1988a).

Children find in play the same kind of liberation that Schopenhauer and Barthes, each in his own way, attribute to music. The Muse Within is the source of both music and play; they are examples of what we might call "muse-ical breakthroughs." Children are muse-ical beings at an early stage of development, and for them the breakthrough typically occurs in the form of play. Indeed, Barthes himself was so consciously playing when he experimented with conceptless forms of expression that he called his technique *ludish*, from the Latin *ludere*, "to play" (see also Engdahl 1983).

Sometimes a powerful muse-ical breakthrough can be achieved by simple means, not least through *humor*. I shall give one example that combines music, literature, and theater. In *The Cherry Orchard*, Chekhov wrote a scene in which the lovesick Epikhodov stands playing and singing to his beloved Dunyasha. The audience can clearly see that Epikhodov is playing a guitar, so we are startled when he says, "How nice it is to play the mandolin!"

"What in the world is going on?" we ask. "Surely that's a guitar he's playing. Did the actor get his lines wrong?" And Dunyasha, who is sitting on another man's lap and is not at all in love with Epikhodov, reinforces our altogether reasonable puzzlement as she says irritably, "It's a guitar, not a mandolin." But Chekhov and Epikhodov deftly take the last trick as the lovelorn man replies, "For one who is crazed by love, it is a mandolin." And suddenly it happens: technical reason's ordinary limits are transcended in a flash of muse-ical logic.

The masterful linking of apparently disparate elements breaks in upon us as a flash of new insight, which is then released in laughter—the puckish originality of wit as mental acrobatics, from "ha-ha" to "aha!" (Skoglund 1987). The idea that one can move from humor to discovery is a key principle in Arthur Koestler's analysis of the essence of humor (1965). This phenomenon is absolutely central in child culture; it is a productive element in

children's playful thinking and an essential aspect of their psychological health. It is also directly related to the childlike insight that
is part of the special talent and approach of many scholars and
scientists.

Because of the phenomenon of muse-ical breakthrough, it is
quite literally child's play for those who are inspired by the Muse
Within to square the circle. We all know, of course, that a circle
is forever round, a square is forever square, and "never the twain
shall meet." But it is precisely in the unexpected clash between the
narrowly rational and the muse-ical poles that humor occurs. And
the laughter that follows expresses the joy we spontaneously feel
when, without warning, we are caught up in humor's liberating
journey across the border of rationality.

Humor is an important part of child culture: riddles and jokes
flourish among children everywhere and are passed on from generation to generation. Riddles are perhaps the most common type
of children's joke. Here is a typical example.

> *Question:* What do you call a canary that flies into an electric fan?
> *Answer:* Shredded tweet.

Many children's jokes have to do with school.

> *Boy to his friend:* The teacher said we'd have a test today, rain or
>   shine.
> *Friend:* So why are you so happy?
> *Boy:* Because it's snowing!

Children often tell jokes involving games or sports. This one is
typical of the genre.

> *Basketball Coach:* Gosh, Tim, you've grown another foot this sum-
>   mer!
> *Tim:* No, coach. I've still just got two!

These examples illustrate typical features—plays on words,
ambiguities, absurdities—that children instinctively like. One

study undertaken in Norway found that over half the jokes told by five- to eight-year-olds are based on word play and other linguistic phenomena (Selmer-Olsen 1987). That is not surprising, for as soon as children begin to master the basic principles of the language and get their little world reasonably well ordered, they start to play and experiment. This, too, creates form, meaning, and a new type of control. Children want to be free, to be out of the cage, to formulate and feel something new. That, of course, is one of the functions of humor: the unexpected departure from convention, the bold and clever twist of meaning that yields flashes of new insight and unanticipated satisfaction. And the child who has the ability to be genuinely funny on the spur of the moment—not just by retelling old jokes, but by inventing new ones that make everybody laugh—is accorded a very special position in the group. When everything clicks, such a child can initiate a euphoria of muse-ical intoxication, a flight of ecstasy. That is why such children are especially admired, loved, respected—or feared for their talent—like the jesters in the Renaissance courts.

Later in this book we will see how an adult jester, Dmitri Shostakovich, used humor as a means of survival in the face of the existential anxiety he was forced to endure for much of his adult life.

THE MUSE-ICAL IMPERATIVE
It is by no means always easy to cross the border into new understanding and knowledge. It is costly, demanding. It can be life-threatening, both physically and psychologically. Nonetheless, children are constrained by a kind of inner necessity to make constant new attempts to achieve muse-ical breakthroughs. They muster everything they have in order to leap farther and farther out into waters a thousand fathoms deep. This is not a well-regulated enterprise with full insurance in case of accident. There is no advance guarantee of safety, of indemnity, of a happy ending. A new leap may emerge from conflict, pain, and aggression; wonderment, fantasy, and longing; humor, cunning, and impudence; courage, rashness, and fear. The lonely Rusky experienced many of these emotions as he lay in his bed waiting to die. He was

preparing himself for the leap over to Nangiyala. And it is not just a matter of *daring* to leap, with all the existential risk that implies; it is equally a matter of being *able* to leap with the total abandon that playful imagination requires if the intended goal is to be reached. The slightest dissonant hint of reservation, holding back, doubt—and the string snaps, the spell is broken.

The intense mixture of a wide range of competing emotions—everything from lightheartedness to desperation—can produce tremendous creative power. And this power is essential if we are to be equal to the challenge, to bridge the chasm between the known and the unknown. The point is not just to get where we are going; it is equally important to feel the creative energy coursing through our veins, to be keenly aware that we are moving toward answers to questions we scarcely know how to ask.

Moreover, all forms of expression must be available to children if they are to succeed in breaking new barriers. Body, speech, singing—all play a role in creating the fundamental concepts by which the child attempts to master the complexity of experience. And the child's need to express him/herself functions as a constant inner urge, an imperative that cannot be ignored.

Astrid Lindgren depicts this very point in another of her children's books, *Ronia, the Robber's Daughter*. Ronia is wandering around in the woods looking for Birk. It is spring in the evergreen forests of Scandinavia, and the greening of the earth is mirrored in the longing and budding infatuation between the two children.

> And here she was now, diving headfirst into spring. It was so magnificent everywhere around her, it filled her, big as she was, and she screeched like a bird, high and shrill.
>
> "I have to scream a spring scream or I'll burst," she explained to Birk. "Listen! You can hear spring, can't you?" (pp. 77–78)

Ronia cries out her joy "like a bird." The primitive power of her voice gives shape and expression to Ronia's sensations with the strength of the primal cry. Deafening and beautiful. Ronia's spring-cry is far removed from the carefully honed beauty of an operatic aria. She is not crying out for the sake of an aesthetic

ideal. Her spring-cry is an existential form of expression, a fundamental way of articulating her own experience of reality: "I have
to scream a spring scream or I'll burst!"

Descartes found in the ability to doubt a proof of the existence
of the rational being: *"Dubito, ergo cogito; cogito, ergo sum."* ("I doubt,
therefore I think; I think, therefore I am.") Children find in the
ability to sense a proof of the existence of the muse-ical being:
"Sentio, ergo canto; canto, ergo sum!" ("I sense, therefore I sing; I sing,
therefore I am!") This *muse-ical imperative* is creatively necessary for
both sensation and reason. It was expressed in literary form by
Henrik Ibsen, who experienced the same drive to expression as a
creative writer. The opening lines of his first play, *Catiline*, are
these: "I must! I must! Deep down within my soul a voice commands, and I will do its bidding."

Play as a Fixed Point Amidst the Chaos of Life

Anyone who has hovered over an infant and lovingly tried to
engage it in play has probably experienced intense joy in the
immediacy and contact as child and grown-up interact in a fine-
tuned duet. Odors good and bad, sparkling eyes, soft skin, happy
sounds. You hold your hands over your eyes, then take them
quickly away: "Peek-a-boo!" The baby laughs merrily, in delight
tinged with fear. Encouraged by the child's laughter, you do it
again—and again, and again. Rarely are two people closer than
this. *Play* springs into being—that creative life form that thrives
only in the intersection between fantasy and reality, originality
and ritual, wild humor and heartrending seriousness. Under suitable conditions, by the age of three or four months the baby has
developed into a marvelous little clown, humanity's eternal *homo
ludens.*

From the time the newborn begins to play with its fingers and
toes, play is a crucible in which personality is formed. Through a
playful approach to life the child tests the limits of language and
the capabilities of the body in immediate contact with the jumble
of impressions and challenges that are the stuff of daily life. It is
here that the foundation is laid for social understanding and

growth, for basic attitudes, and for each individual's unique pattern of abilities and coping skills.

Many researchers have studied the decisive importance of play in human life, among them the late D. W. Winnicott, a British psychoanalyst. Play, according to Winnicott, is the essential bridge-builder that connects the internal, subjective world of concepts and ideas with external, objective reality. Play is the transitional object that creates continuity and meaning between the dream and everyday reality.

It is essential for human beings to preserve an authentic contact between inner and outer reality in a delicate balance between subjective imagination and more objective rationality. The censoring resistance of rationality can be tempered through play in a process of creation rather than suppression, with the conscious and the subconscious learning to tolerate each other as they engage in a stimulating interplay that makes the mind more whole. Insofar as individuals succeed in keeping these channels open in both directions—and insofar as the channels are vital and strong—they can become creative, integrated people.

Opportunities for play, the wellspring of creativity and inventive imagination, must be protected and strengthened. Song, which is an auditory form of play, is an essential element in the muse-ical bridge that joins the individual's inner and outer worlds. Friedrich Nietzsche expressed this point beautifully in *Zarathustra:* "How delightful it is that there are words and songs. Are not words and songs rainbows and invisible bridges between that which otherwise is eternally separate?"

If the muse-ical seam that joins the inner and outer world is weakened, the wings of imagination are clipped and the capacity of sensation and understanding to create muse-ical breakthroughs is diminished. The result, according to Winnicott, is that the person so affected ends up in a posture of resignation and submission relative to his or her surroundings and their inherent demands. This, in Winnicott's view, can mean the difference between health and sickness, life and death.

Those who are bearers of the Muse Within dare to inseminate inner dreams with outer reality and to let outer reality be enriched by inner dreams, not in a fractured either/or, but in a life-giving both/and.

In an article entitled "Imagination as Creative Transcendence," Marit Akerø (1987) presents the thesis that the proper function of imagination is not just to shift the boundaries of ordinary reality *outward* in an endless quest for utopia as an extension of that reality, for imagination has the capacity to shift the boundaries *inward* as well. Herein lies tremendous potential for change, both of ourselves and of the reality around us.

Little Arne's flight of fancy with a mackerel shifted the boundaries of reality in both directions. Both inner and outer space were filled with song and thereby enlarged. This phenomenon embraces not only the trivialities of everyday life but also such weighty matters as human forms of cognition, self-understanding, and fitness for life. From this perspective, it is crucial to maintain the vitality of the human capacity for play from the very beginning to the very end of life.

The question as to *how* the vitality of the human capacity for play can be preserved leads inevitably to a closer consideration of the *pedagogical* concepts and principles that determine the shape of Western education today. What do we do with children during the transition from child culture to school culture and adult culture? What are our priorities? *Why* do we have these priorities? *On what basis* do we affirm them? Later in this book we will discuss these and related questions, with child culture itself as our frame of reference.

We know that play is a natural part of the life and culture of children. In the area where developmental psychology adjoins social anthropology, it is therefore the task of child-culture research not only to establish the existence of play but also to delineate its outward manifestations, patterns, and cultural meaning. On such a foundation we will be better equipped to undertake a much-needed discussion of the pedagogical dogmas of high-tech society in the context of humankind's muse-ical distinctiveness.

THE ETYMOLOGY OF "PLAY" AND "MUSIC"

The original meaning of the word "play" clearly appears to contain such muse-ical elements as sound and movement. The Norwegian word for play, *lek* or *leik,* is derived from the Gothic *laiks,* which means, among other things, rhythmic movement, dance (Grimm 1885). The Old Norse *leikr* connotes similar meanings: communal play, dance, sacrificial dance. In modern Icelandic a composer is called a *tonleikar,* i.e., a person who plays with sounds. We see, then, how a basic element in a human mode of expression—movement—finds verbal expression in the concept *lek,* with sound as the implied structural factor. The word *lek* comes to denote the entire range of cultural manifestations of the muse-ical being qua muse-ical being.

This same muse-ical nucleus is found in the corresponding words in many other languages: *play* (English), *Spiel* (German), *jeu* (French), *igra* (Russian), and so on. In all these languages the word has a double meaning: it can pertain either to a game or to making music.

It is not surprising that this is so. Play includes movement and sound as important elements of a larger whole: this is the human being's perceptual basis from the very beginning of life, as we have seen. This is the sense apparatus with which the child begins, and which develops further in that never-never land at the intersection of imagination and reality that is the home of play. It is this sense apparatus that reaches full creative maturity in preschool child culture. It is universally human, yet conditioned by national circumstances and traditions.

As we shall see later, the spontaneous muse-ical expressions that occur within child culture are much closer in both form and function to the concept of play than to the traditional adult concept of music. It is not easy for us as adults to be cognizant of the spontaneous singing of children, for more often than not it occurs in the form of fleeting outbursts in the course of their busy play. Our ordinary adult concept of music becomes unwieldy and is of no help to us.

Let us look at one simple example in which singing is important.

No child is admitted as a member of child culture until s/he can hop on one leg. Every two-year-old knows this, and to this end practices day in and day out—although the plain truth is that s/he runs a considerable risk of getting a bump on the head or a bloody nose in the process. But nothing could be worse than being excluded from the group, and so the practicing continues. Finally the child's muse-ical intuition discovers a solution: I must sing and hop *at the same time.* But isn't it difficult to do two things at once? Wouldn't it be easier to do just one thing at a time—hop first and then sing? Absolutely not! Singing and hopping complement each other perfectly. One day the two-year-old knows this with his whole being, and with a song in his heart as well as on his lips he hops elatedly over the floor in perfect, singing balance. To the child, it is all one thing, not two.

Hop-ping, hop-ping, hop-ping, hop-ping

Since antiquity, when music and play were constituent elements in a unified whole, the concept of music has developed steadily in the direction of aestheticization, specialization, and professionalization. That is why it is so easy for us to overlook authentically muse-ical manifestations as they occur within child culture. The concept of *music* in the narrower sense, which is clearly rooted in adult culture, limits our understanding of reality, and as a result something of fundamental importance in the experience of children largely escapes our attention.

Our Western concept of music includes an aesthetic dimension that controls our selective perception; it functions as a kind of subjective filtering mechanism. This aesthetic dimension, which among other things includes norms regarding pitch and tonality, is totally foreign to child culture. Nor does this concept of music, rooted as it is in the classical tradition, capture the sense of functional and expressive unity that is the warp and woof of the spontaneous singing of children. Culture stands against culture, the child's approach to life against the adult's—with children as the obviously weaker and more vulnerable party.

At a more basic level, this generational conflict concerns the relationship between written culture and oral culture, or what we might call the adult tradition of *literacy* and the child tradition of *orality*. The focus of the former on letters and words implicitly invites analytical distinctions and the drawing of clear boundaries. The written word is a symbolic abstraction; it stands apart from physical perception and sensation. The formulation of precise concepts tends inevitably toward systematic division and specialization. The tradition of orality, on the other hand, finds expression in sounds that penetrate directly—physically—into the body and the senses. The two modes of perception are totally different. Walter J. Ong, in *Orality and Literacy* (1982), elaborates on the contrast between written language and oral language.

> Sight isolates, sound incorporates. . . . Vision comes to a human being from one direction at a time: to look at a room or a landscape, I must move my eyes around from one part to another. When I hear, however, I gather sound simultaneously from every direction at once: I am at the center of my auditory world, which envelopes me, establishing me at a kind of core of sensation and existence. . . . You can immerse yourself in hearing, in sound. There is no way to immerse yourself similarly in sight. (p. 72)

Corresponding to these two traditions are two radically dissimilar forms of consciousness, the oral and the written. Ong's insightful discussion shows how written language structures our thinking qualitatively in ways that are totally different from what occurs in cultures that do not have a written language.

Let us see how African and Western cultural orientations differ in their ways of regarding "music." In traditional African societies we find an oral, muse-ical culture that is functionally interwoven into both everyday life and festive occasions, ordinary work and sacred rituals. In principle, therefore, it is similar to the oral culture of children.

The African perception of music-dance-humankind-world as an organic whole is reflected in concepts of sensation that are different from those held by most Westerners. Africans experience what we might call *unitary sensation,* and this important fact about their culture is reflected in their language. It appears, for example, that many African languages do not have a word for "hearing" or "listening," presumably because such a word would be too restricted in meaning to capture the "integrated sensing" that is for them the central reality, a single complex experience in which one simultaneously sees and hears and is moved to dance as one's body vibrates in response to the sound that is one element in the total experience. *Sikia* is the word used by the African Bantu to denote the experience of sensing with one's whole being. A Swahili-English dictionary lists the following meanings for the word *sikia:* "(1) hear; (2) pay attention to, notice, understand, perceive; (3) heed, obey. Mostly of the senses of hearing, but also of other senses except taste" (Johnson 1971, p. 429).

It is through such integrated sensation that "music" is experienced in the African manner — as something one hears and listens to, but also as something one sees, responds to physically (dance), understands through, respects, and even obeys. It is just so, I maintain, that *children* experience the world from infancy into early childhood. The child's concepts are formed in synchronous, muse-ical totalities. Sometimes the dominant impression may be visual, at other times aural, but the totality is always there as the background that gives meaning to each element. Our Western urge to specialization is such that we have divided sensation into a collection of isolated skills that can then be mapped and studied one by one. When children go to school, in the rite of passage from muse-ical being to pupil, they learn little by little to believe that their adult mentors are right. Sensing part of the whole replaces integrated sensation, with many profound consequences, not least for learning.

In an article published in 1987, ethno-philosopher K. Anyanwu of Lagos gives a description of the thinking, attitudes, and processes underlying African artistic manifestations that would also be highly accurate as a description of the pervasive muse-ical character of child culture. If we follow this thought to its logical conclusion, it is tempting to postulate a universal muse-ical fellowship among oral folk cultures all over the world, irrespective of geographical location and ethnic origin. These otherwise dissimilar cultures seem to be united by fundamental attitudes that are the fruit of the Muse Within that is shared by all.

Let us follow Anyanwu's discussion in greater detail as he draws a series of instructive contrasts between Africa and Europe.

> The logic of art or of aesthetics is the logic of integration or coordination whereby the individual and the universal are fused together, while intuition and imagination transform the sensuous and the intellectual experience into one aesthetic continuum. . . . African thought makes no clear-cut distinction between subject and object, mind and body, self and world. . . . Life-Force, Sound and Word are identical. In other words, Sound is the model of reality in African thought. It is the raw material out of which certain meaningful and significant structures are shaped, organized or created. But Sound is the model of music. We have to regard Sound as the principle of creativity, intelligibility and rationality in African thought; and an epistemological attitude based on this model is bound to differ radically from the Western modes of knowing. . . .
>
> "I think; therefore, I am," wrote Descartes. But the remark no longer seems to have validity. . . . The Negro-African could say: "I sense the Other; I dance the Other; I am." . . . Art is rooted in Life-Force. . . . It would lose its meaning, purpose and significance if divorced from the process of life.

Here, then, we see child culture's *canto, ergo sum* reformulated as an African *salto, ergo sum:* I dance — therefore I am. Indeed, these are two variations of a muse-ical proof of our existence that are equally foreign to the traditional Western way of thinking.

Song and dance are profoundly important for Africans of all ages as well as for children everywhere. Song and dance *internalize* their contact with the world that surrounds them, the totality that both intuitively feel and of which they know themselves to be a part. Muse-ical ecstasy gives the African contact with the divine in an animistic world where everything is perceived to be a bearer of divinity. Spontaneous singing gives children a feeling of belonging in relation to their environment, thereby bringing it nearer and making possible the further investigation of reality. Song and dance release the power and spontaneous energy that provide access to the wholeness within which humankind lives bioculturally and ecologically, to use Cobb's expression.

Adult Western musicians can also experience "integrated sensation" in happy moments of inspired music-making. The Danish musician Peter Bastian concludes his book on music and awareness on precisely this point: "The sounds are like fine threads that unite me with my surroundings; they are like long, thin feelers through which I can touch the world" (Bastian 1988, p. 182). Obviously, we are dealing here with universal muse-ical processes, phenomena that occur in Lagos and in Oslo, in Moscow and in Long Beach. Music anthropologist Kenneth Gourlay (1984) speaks to this very point in a stimulating article entitled "The Non-Universality of Music and the Universality of Non-Music."

> In so far as it is possible, genuine understanding of what other people do demands a new start. We must begin, not with the supposition that some form of "music," as we know it, is a universal, but that the greater probability is of the universality of some form of expression, for which as yet we have no name, other than that it is "non-music" . . . in a broader sense of a form of creative expression that subsumes what are commonly designated "musical sound," "dance," "drama" and "ritual," and which is not the prerogative of an elitist minority but belongs to the community. This form of expression is used on occasions of heightened feeling, when speech is inadequate, and it is necessary for communication to attain a new level of intensity.
>
> Such an approach will negate the validity of our specialist training and restore something of that "wholeness" and integration which is the hallmark of nonfragmented societies in which human beings are able to fulfill themselves through creative expression. Only then will the search for universals have any significance. (p. 36)

Since the African relationship to the world is so much closer to that of children than is the adult Western view, it is useful to look more closely at African concepts of "music." "In no African language about which we have information," observes Gourlay, "and in many used by other peoples who have oral rather than written traditions, is there a word corresponding to the English term 'music' " (1984, p. 28). We find one principal African concept relevant to music in the Swahili word *ngoma*. Danish ethnologist Steen Nielsen describes the relation between music and *ngoma* as follows.

> The word *muziki* is used to denote "music" in our sense, but the word was obviously borrowed from Europe so it really didn't help me very much.
>
> *Ngoma* is a Bantu word, but it appeared that its primary meaning is "drum," "dance" and "festivity"—all words having something to do with music, but according to our concepts other things as well. The inner coherence in the concept *ngoma* is so strong, however, that it really is impossible to isolate music from the other elements. (1985, p. 35; see also Ledang 1988)

It is *sikia*, the word for integrated sensation, that discloses the full meaning of *ngoma* with illuminating consistency.

Other African cultures exhibit the same type of integrated muse-ical thinking. In Cameroon the word *wún* means "sing, dance"; in Nigeria the word *nkwa* has the meaning "song, dance, play." And if we go halfway around the world to the Polynesian islands in the Pacific, we find the same fundamental insight common to all oral cultures. On Samoa the notion of *pese*, "song," is always combined with *siva*, "dance," because the two activities are indissolubly bound together. The essence of the matter, common to oral cultures everywhere, is that singing provokes bodily movements and so cannot be separated from them—which is exactly what very young children *in all cultures* experience.

It is also interesting to note how "music" is reflected in a picture language, where concepts are presented visually rather than abstractly as in our Western languages. In modern Chinese, the word for "music" is pronounced *yüeh* and its character is written like this (see DeWoskin 1982).

If we examine the etymology of this character, we find that it was constructed from the following components (see Hsüan 1968).

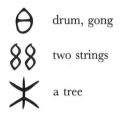

drum, gong

two strings

a tree

In the character for *yüeh*, these elements are combined into a single unified whole. The concept depicted by this character, like the African *ngoma*, connotes dance (drum), ritual (gong), sound (strings), and closeness to nature (a tree). Add to this the fact that *yüeh* signifies both music and joy, and it is clear that the Chinese concept of music also includes an element of emotional excitation. This is in fact a central characteristic of all manifestations of the Muse Within; indeed, it is the *sine qua non* for the experience of muse-ical authenticity, exhilaration, and ecstasy.

In the Nordic countries, the Sami (Lapp) *joik* exhibits a degree of spontaneous animation and ennobling identification between song and surroundings that is similar in many ways to the concept of *ngoma*.

Hereafter in this book I shall use the term *ngoma* to denote the form of muse-ical play characteristic of child culture. I do this for the sake of both simplicity and precision, and as a sign of muse-ical solidarity among oral folk cultures all over the world. I can find no better word, for we music experts—teachers and researchers alike—have never felt any urgent need to look for one. Why should we? The concept of music has always revolved around *us* as the center of the Western European music universe. And children's music—what is it but a primitive forerunner of what may develop into something of importance in the fullness of time? So we have thought for much too long, with our eyes directed only on our own narrow horizons.

Nor is it merely a matter of shifting the focus from ourselves to the child and formulating new concepts suitable to the muse-ical experience of children—as if that were not demanding enough. No, what is needed goes even deeper: we must try to change the very structure of the literate mind that permeates us through and through (see Ong 1982). We must try to grasp at least a few fragments of a more oral way of thinking. It is impossible for us book-learned adults to free ourselves from our accustomed ways of thinking. Our entire world, for good and for ill, is formed in the image of these concepts. But if we don't at least try to open up, we will unthinkingly continue to judge children's spontaneous singing according to aesthetic standards appropriate to the Vienna Boys' Choir, smugly pronouncing it ugly and unmusical. That is how Europeans judged the *ngoma* of the Bantus in comparison with Schubert's lieder and Tchaikovsky's *Nutcracker Suite*.

But the European experience of music, too, was once characterized by a sense of organic wholeness, as we learn from the ancient Greek myth about how the Muses came into being, recounted by Pindar in the ode that appears at the front of this book.

The Muses Are Born and the World Sings

The word "music" derived from this beautiful myth: Zeus gave the Muses *mousiké techne*, the ability to practice the musical arts in song and dance. The concept of "music" in our restricted sense of the word was altogether foreign to the thinking of the Greeks. The Muses, through their *mousiké techne*, were to express something universal: the splendor and *harmonia* of the whole universe, from the tiniest element of the individual soul to the incomprehensibly vast reaches of the firmament. This was also Plato's point of departure in his political philosophy, which stressed the significance of musical training in the formation of character *(ethos)* from earliest childhood on. Man and his music were a part of the universe and its music; each element was in balance with every other element as a part of the whole.

The Muses—the divine muse-ical beings—were created precisely to give the world the voice that had been lacking. They were a manifestation of life, just as the primal cry of the newborn infant is a manifestation of life. Seen in this light, all playing and singing children are the legitimate heirs of the Muses.

The Muses, then, according to the ancient myth, gave the universe an audible voice—a voice that could create new universes of pictures and concepts in the mind. This is what happens when children begin to express themselves. New worlds can be created through something as direct and simple as song. C. S. Lewis makes use of the same idea in his children's tale *The Magician's Nephew*, one of the stories in the Chronicles of Narnia. It seems natural to conclude this part of our book about the Muse Within in a truly childlike spirit, with a few magical lines about the founding of Narnia, from a story in which Song itself is the voice of creation.

> The Lion was pacing to and fro about that empty land and singing his new song. It was softer and more lilting than the song by which he had called up the stars and the sun; a gentle, rippling music. And as he walked and sang the valley grew green with grass. It spread out from the Lion like a pool. It ran up the sides of the little hills like a wave. In a few minutes it was creeping up the lower slopes of the distant mountains, making that young world every moment softer. . . . Far overhead from beyond the veil of blue sky which hid them the stars sang again: a pure, cold, difficult music. Then there came a swift flash like fire (but it burnt nobody) either from the sky or from the Lion itself, and every drop of blood tingled in the children's bodies, and the deepest, wildest voice they had ever heard was saying:
>
> "Narnia, Narnia, Narnia, awake. Love. Think. Speak. Be walking trees. Be talking beasts. Be divine waters."

Poet and juggler (Han Dynasty, c. 200 B.C.–200 A.D.)

4

Three Worlds of Singing Children: Norway, Russia, and the United States

From a global perspective, Norway is a very small country, a pleasant social democracy on the northern edge of Europe with a fairly even distribution of prosperity. It has never been a major player on the international political stage. Norwegian children are not indoctrinated with a sense of national pride that must be defended against dangerous foreign enemies. Companies that make toy guns and tanks and battleships do not find much of a market in Norway. Norwegians love their flag and proudly display it on appropriate occasions, but it is not a normal part of the furnishings of a Norwegian kindergarten. Nor are the walls decorated with portraits of the king, prime minister, or party leader. One is much more likely to encounter the king or the prime minister on a weekend ski trip—a fact that is indicative of the democratic solidarity between great and small that still characterizes Norway. Such a thing would be unthinkable in any of the superpower countries of the world.

Nor do Norwegian children have to carry upon their slender shoulders the heavy weight that must be borne by the children of the mighty: the need to be the world's best, smartest, strongest, and biggest. Norwegian children will not build or pilot the next generation's spaceships to Mars and Jupiter. School-like formal training still does not play a dominant role in Norwegian kindergartens. Gifted children are not singled out for special treatment at an early age. Norwegian children even start school at a later age than their counterparts in either Russia or America.

For Russian preschoolers, the situation is quite different. In 1985, when I conducted my study of Russian children, the Soviet Union was still a dictatorship and one-party state. Like their parents and grandparents before them, the children whom I studied had been taught at an early age to rally around national symbols and national leaders. Lenin's portrait adorned the wall of every kindergarten, for Lenin had served for generations as a collective father figure and powerful unifying force. The "great war for the Motherland"—the struggle against Hitler's armies during which the Soviet Union suffered more casualties than any other European country (over twenty-six million, according to recent official statements)—was kept alive in the memory of Russian children. For that reason, toy guns and tanks and such were very popular in the USSR and were not—as in Norway—regarded as negative influences; they were part of the process of developing a patriotic outlook. "Mother Russia" was to be the object of every child's deepest commitment and was acclaimed not least in music, literature, dance, and painting—all of which played important roles in preschool training.

Although Russian children were clearly treated with great love, respect, and warmth, they could not escape the academic pressure stemming from the high aspirations of their superpower homeland. As the next generation's leaders they had to be the best in as many fields as possible in order to protect their country's place as a major world power. As early as age seven, the most gifted pupils were identified and sent to schools where they could concentrate on developing their special competence in mathematics, dance, music, languages, sports, and so on. No other country in the world placed such a high priority on preschool and kindergarten research and training as the USSR. As early as 1963 Urie Bronfenbrenner pointed out that the Russians were spending more on their preschool program than on their space program. Although play activities were regarded as extremely important (Usova 1974, Leontiev 1976), the content and organization of the kindergarten program bore the unmistakable stamp of the rigid school system of which it was an integral component. Part of the price of superpower competition was the shortening of carefree, playful childhood.

The political system in the United States is of course vastly different from that of the former Soviet Union, but the superpower syndrome is equally evident. The United States plays a crucially important role in world affairs, both militarily and economically. The result for children is in many important ways very much the same as it was for Soviet children. Considerable emphasis is placed on national values; there is much talk about "the American spirit" and "patriotism." An important aspect of superpower patriotism is the willingness to fight and die for one's country. Billions of dollars' worth of GI Joe toys, model tanks, planes, battleships, and other military toys are offered for sale to millions upon millions of American children, subtly cultivating their tolerance for the real thing.

In American kindergartens, George Washington is a beloved national symbol; children learn at an early age to honor him as "the father of our country." The flag, too, plays an important role as a symbol of unity in the midst of enormous ethnic diversity. Each morning, in schools all over America, children stand and face the Stars and Stripes, right hand over heart, and recite the Pledge of Allegiance. To an outsider, this exercise has the appearance of what might be called "nationalistic morning devotions." It is one of the ways in which American children learn to worship at the shrine of democracy. Interestingly, the Pledge became an issue in the 1988 presidential campaign when then-candidate George Bush strongly defended its importance for American children and, indeed, for the entire nation.

Even as American children recite the Pledge, some of them are vaguely aware that "liberty and justice for all" is the ideal, not the reality. They may observe, for example, that minority children— blacks, Hispanics, Asians, Native Americans—are generally poorer and attend less adequate schools than most (though by no means all) white children; that English, especially American English, is considered superior to other languages; that the president does not always tell the truth—for example, regarding the Watergate break-in. A series of events in postwar American history— the assassination of President Kennedy, the forced resignation of President Nixon, the scandals associated with the Reagan administration—appear to have made a deep impression on the minds of children and young people. Indeed, one senses in conversations with American youth that the contrast between these facts and the ideals embodied in the Pledge of Allegiance (and other documents, notably the Constitution) creates a problem for them: from childhood onward they must live with a vague sense that there is a troubling contradiction between the dream and the reality.

American children also start school at an earlier age than their counterparts in most European countries, typically at age five. In America there are periodic demands for improvement in the so-called three R's: reading, writing, and arithmetic. In the 1950s, the launching of Sputnik unleashed a call for more rigorous training in science and engineering; today the challenge that primarily drives American educators is growing competition with that economic superpower in the Far East, Japan. Less and less time seems to be available for play in American kindergartens as academic pursuits take priority. Like the Russians, Americans have also developed special programs for gifted children, "the best source of leaders for our nation's future."

Clearly, then, Norway, Russia, and the United States differ in many ways. But let us ask: *To what extent is there a common child culture irrespective of these enormous cultural, social, and political differences?*

As we noted earlier, the unborn child senses a world of sound and movement. This fundamental *common experience* unites human beings all over the world, regardless of later differences in language, culture, and political systems. The inborn muse-ical understanding of the world is a common human potential that gives the infant the capacity to master *whatever* languages and cultures s/he may encounter. *A playful* ngoma *is a universal life necessity.*

Guided by these views, I began my research with the working

hypothesis that there is spontaneous singing of some sort among playful children in all cultures. Such singing would be evidence of a common *muse-ical mother tongue* that would undoubtedly take different forms in cultures and traditions that are in some respects radically different. It would point to a common reality beneath the cultural diversity.

THE OSLO STUDY

Oslo has about half a million inhabitants—a total population equivalent to that of a single district of St. Petersburg or Los Angeles. Yet, because of the vast forests that lie within the city limits, with respect to land area it is one of the largest cities in the world. It is a modern city, with all that implies: a hectic jumble of traffic jams, shops, movie theaters, restaurants, and people constantly on the go. Yet its streets are narrow, like those of a small town, and unspoiled nature is so close at hand that one can board a trolley and in twenty-five minutes be transported from the commotion of the city to the serene tranquillity of endless miles of forests and hills.

Oslo's history stretches back in time longer than that of St. Petersburg and Los Angeles together. Its university was founded long before California became a state. In Oslo, children still take it for granted that they can go out and play hide-and-seek without the chronic fear, so common in large cities elsewhere, that they will be kidnapped, raped, or murdered.

In Oslo the world's first children's ombudsman carries on his work at the national level. It is the capital city of a country that has the highest statistical rate of child traffic fatalities in all of Europe but also the lowest general infant mortality rate and very nearly the highest mean life expectancy in the world. Oslo has more children's brass bands than any other city in Europe, and nearly all of them contribute to making Constitution Day (May 17, Norway's equivalent of the Fourth of July) into a magnificent celebration by marching proudly through the city in the children's parade.

Though the cost of attending a preschool in Oslo is steadily increasing, the waiting lists for entry are getting longer and longer.

The public schools are equally accessible to rich and poor, but teachers are poorly paid relative to other groups in society. A metropolis that is not yet used to being multicultural, Oslo finds it altogether too easy to balance tight school budgets at the expense of the children of immigrants from Turkey and Pakistan and elsewhere who have recently learned to call this city their home.

Oslo boasts a beautiful fjord that is slowly getting cleaner as antipollution measures begin to produce results, and large tracts of hills and forests that are available for all to enjoy. The water in the nearby streams is still so pure that one can drink it without fear of disease.

These, in a nutshell, are some of the important features of the local milieu that children in Oslo learn to take for granted, but that make their experience quite different from that of children growing up in St. Petersburg or Los Angeles.

SPONTANEOUS SINGING

The Oslo study was based on systematic observation of children's spontaneous singing and playing in three public kindergartens during one entire school year. A principal objective of the study was to broaden the understanding of children's communication potential by viewing such spontaneous behavior as *linguistic* phenomena, i.e., as part of children's natural mode of communication. The methodology of the study was what anthropologists call "passive participant observation." I was with the children, but I did not organize or direct their activity in any way. I simply observed it and kept notes on what I observed.

The first results of this research were published in Norway in 1985 under the title *Den spontane barnesangen: vårt musikalske morsmål* ("Children's Spontaneous Singing: Our Muse-ical Mother Tongue"). What I found was that this underlying "muse-ical mother tongue," which is as natural to children as laughing and crying and moving their limbs, constitutes an intersubjective code of communication that is an essential feature of child culture. In what follows, I shall describe this code in greater detail and discuss its significance for human development.

Among the myriad activities that children engage in each day—everything from potty rituals and tying their shoelaces to malicious teasing and innocent playing in the sandbox—spontaneous singing enters in as a natural and essential element. It is at the center of child culture's muse-ical *ngoma* of physical movements, words, and song. It gives rhythm to their playing, form to their movements, and warmth to their words. It is critically important for children to master spontaneous singing, for it is part of the common code of child culture that gives them a special key to expression and human growth. This kind of singing, which springs forth without adult encouragement and is therefore spontaneous, is governed, like all other facets of play, by child culture's norms and rules in both use and form.

It is the concrete situation at a given moment that determines what will be sung. Obviously a child's angry outcry in the midst of a quarrel is totally different from contented humming while coloring a picture. Spontaneous singing, just like ordinary speech, is capable of being adapted to fit a given social situation. No such situation is norm-free. On the contrary, personal expression—in words, physical movement, or song—always occurs within the confines of the common codes set by the culture. Unfortunately, this contextual perspective on child culture and its song tradition has been largely overlooked.

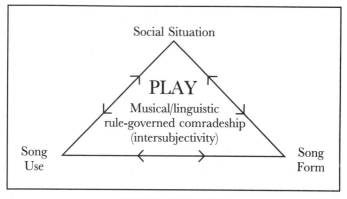

CHILD CULTURE

The concrete play situation, the musical practice, and the musical form mutually influence one another at all times, always within the context of a socio/muse-ical totality. The whole context is imbued with the common rules, values, and norms of child culture—transmitted by the children themselves from generation to generation—as the controlling frame of reference. This frame of reference is embodied in systems of symbols that are determined by cultural conventions, symbols that all children in a given culture understand and accept. Within this total context, real communication occurs among children as they translate (decode) the symbols within a common framework. (Interestingly, the word *communication* is derived from the Latin *communicare*, to *make common*.)

SONG FORM

When children begin to sing in response to some event in their daily lives, their song must necessarily have a *form*. But forms are not imposed haphazardly; form-giving is governed by a set of common norms that the children themselves apply in each concrete situation. They know perfectly well what they have to do to get their way. Something that sounds like noise and pandemonium to an adult ear sometimes turns out to be part of a sophisticated system of spontaneous song communication.

Early in life, children begin to use what I shall call *fluid/amorphous* songs. These evolve in a completely natural way from the infant's babbling as part of its first playful experiments with voice and sound. This type of spontaneous song, with its fanciful glissandi, micro-intervals, and free rhythms, is quite different from what we adults traditionally identify as song.

Children employ two types of songs in addition to the fluid/amorphous type: *song formulas* and *standard songs* (i.e., songs from the standard repertoire). The latter, in which children freely adapt existing songs to fit their current situation, are naturally far more complex musically than the former. One might think, therefore, that standard songs would be the latest type to appear in the child's development. This does not seem to be the case, however. Most children hear standard songs at a very young age; this is a precious part of their earliest playing as they sit on Mother's or Father's lap and bask in their affection. What mother has not sung favorite songs to her child while changing a diaper?

Song formulas, on the other hand, are primarily a means of communication between children; thus they play no significant role in the child's life until s/he is ready to start playing with other children, typically at age two or three. The "significant others" in the child's life (parents and other adults versus other children) appear to be more important in determining choice of song type than the degree of musical complexity. That appears to be why children normally begin using standard songs before the musically simpler schematic type.

Children often make recognizable attempts to "sing along" with their parents and/or older siblings before they are a year old—literally before they can walk. My eldest daughter, Tiril, had a large repertoire of standard songs by the time she was twenty months old. She enjoyed taking part in a simple form of antiphonal singing in which her mother and I would start the song, she would join in, and if we dropped out just before the end, she would usually finish alone. Many times it was also evident that she was hearing a song "in her head" even when she wasn't singing aloud. She would start a song, fall silent for a few seconds, then sing the last note aloud at approximately the "right" time, as if her singing was governed by an internal metronome. The astonishingly accurate *timing* made it clear that the interruption was for her something more than mere silence. The song was continuing as an inner monologue at about the same tempo until she finally sang the last note aloud. She sang the whole song from beginning to end, but in a form that combined the use of her inner (private) and outer (public) voices.

During the next five months, enormous further development occurred. Tiril was exuberant when she was with us, her parents, because she quickly became aware that singing created a special warmth and magic that we all experienced together. Singing was coziness and human contact. Just a month past her second birthday, this daughter of mine had an active repertoire of over thirty songs, several of which had many verses. One of her favorite Christmas songs had six verses, and she knew them all. Admittedly, Tiril grew up in an environment more conducive to singing than do most children. Nonetheless, her example shows how early

children can master a relatively large repertoire of standard songs
if they are exposed to them in the context of meaningful experiences with people they love.

Little by little, children naturally bring standard songs into their
playing with other children. During the preschool years these songs
constitute an invaluable fund of raw material that the children
transform in various imaginative ways. We have all surely heard
examples similar to the following, in which a little boy alters "Frère
Jacques" to chide his sweaty brother for not taking his bath.

Most such improvisation involves textual changes, but occasionally children will venture to change the music as well.

As children approach the age of three, *song formulas*—short,
fixed musical phrases with well-defined intervals and rhythms—
become much more prominent in their singing. Who has not
heard children sing out phrases such as the following?

Children typically are first exposed to this type of song during infancy when their parents or older siblings engage them in play. It
happens, for example, in the game of "peek-a-boo." In one version
of this game you cover your face with your hands and say, "Where's
Mommy?" The child stares at you, spellbound. Then you suddenly
take your hands away, and with a big smile you half say, half sing:

or: There's mommy!

And the little one laughs with joy. The descending major third
here is an example of what has been called mixed syntax, a typical
blend of song and speech that children also learn to use extensively
(Oksaar 1988).

Children do not develop a complete repertoire of song formulas until they begin to communicate with other playing children on an ongoing basis. Then, as they enter step by step into the inner sanctum of child culture, this aspect of their muse-ical mother tongue becomes an active and functional part of their communication system.

Song formulas are part of a child-culture tradition that has been passed down through many generations. In my study of four- to seven-year-old children in Oslo I found that the following were the most common.

Teasing and tattling

Imitative

Calling and announcing

Imitative

Calling and announcing

Imitative

Aggressive

Descriptive

Descriptive

Descriptive

Imitative

Alerting, calling attention

The development of a child's general conceptual framework and patterns of expression is not a one-dimensional, linear process. Children do not burn their bridges as they enter new territories in their ongoing conquest of the world. Their bold exploration of the new presupposes a secure footing in the old and familiar. The spontaneous singing of a six-year-old, therefore, includes all three song types. From the perspective of the child who has mastered all three, fluid songs and song formulas are by no means more "primitive" than standard songs. Only an expressive vocabulary that includes all three song types is adequate to the whole range of the child's emotional, communicational, and social needs.

Song Use

In their everyday activities children appear to use songs in three principal ways that I shall call analogical imitation, symbolic representation, and background coloration.

A. Analogical imitation: Song as a concrete part of play

The little girl bends intently over the paper on which she is drawing a "picture." The pencil goes around and around in an irregular but nonetheless rhythmical pattern, and as her hand moves over the paper she *sings* what her hand is doing.

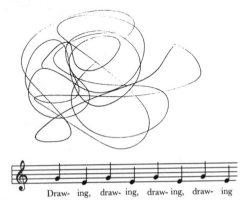

Draw- ing, draw- ing, draw- ing, draw- ing

This is movement-play in song, a typical example of play and song as a unified *ngoma,* irrespective of cultural setting. Melody, words, and action constitute an integrated whole in which the song is an aural reflection of the arm's movements as well as the marks that are appearing on the paper. Kinesthetic, visual, and auditory sensation are in perfect balance as contrasting *analogical correspondences* of the total sensation. The little girl's total experience is *sikia*, as in African Bantu culture. She is not singing *about* the fact that she is drawing: she is *singing the drawing*. One could almost say she is part of the drawing herself, if she is sufficiently absorbed in the experience. She has for the moment abandoned her subjective individuality and become part of a larger totality in which subject and object are one. It is by virtue of such processes that play can be said to occur both here and now and beyond time and space. Inner and outer reality are united as a consequence of the child's secure anchoring in his/her *ngoma*. It is through such total sensation that children accumulate the strength to advance steadily toward higher levels of understanding and to become more and more themselves.

In our specialized world, this drawing and singing child might very well be made an object of study—not, unfortunately, as a totality, but as a phenomenon various aspects of which are of interest to different observers. The art teacher will be primarily interested in the child's scribbling as a first halting effort to handle a drawing pencil, and will perhaps explain how she will advance from scribbling to closed circles and other meaningful shapes as motor control improves. The gym teacher might observe the movements of the child's arms and fingers and note the degree of coordination between gross and fine motor skills. The music teacher will perhaps be looking for the first promising sign that the child is beginning to develop an ear for intervals of the kind that can be written in ordinary musical notation and used in "real songs." Before you know it, *ngoma* has vanished—and the child as well.

Let us consider another typical example of spontaneous, analogical sound-play. This time the little girl is playing with a paper airplane, and her song—a long, continuous glissando—mimics the movement of her hand through the air as the plane crashes to the ground.

Here song and movement imitate each other, becoming complementary analogues in a self-evident, synchronous unity. In one
integrated move the girl succeeds in communicating thought,
feeling, and form. The spontaneous song is *objectified* in her playing
as the descent of her song's glissando becomes part of the descent
of the paper airplane. This is a child-culture version of techniques
familiar from the sound tracks of animated cartoons.

As long as the song is used as a direct imitation in sound of
specific outward movements, the analogical relationship among
song, play, and imagination is usually easy to see. Fluid song,
however, is widely used in connection with a variety of inner
feelings, often without any associated play activities. The abstract
and essentially subjective character of such feelings makes it difficult to demonstrate their intimate relationship with song, but
that such a relationship exists is certainly beyond doubt. Here, too,
we are dealing with a process of analogical concretization in which
the song realizes in sound the energy, the tension, and even the
changes of the child's inner feelings. The song becomes, we might
say, an integrated part of the child's mood. Little Steinar's inner
disquiet may express itself like this in song as he huddles by himself
in a quiet corner of the classroom.

This is a lonely monologue in song. Follow the line from left to right: it begins hesitantly, grows in strength and shrill intensity, and finally dies away in quiet contentment. Any parent who has listened to a small child bewailing its fate when unwillingly sent to bed will surely recognize this song.

B. Symbolic Representation: Use of "Song-words" to Tease, Report, Call, Command, Ask, Reply
Countless generations of children have heard or sung a cruel little song that, with adaptations as necessary, goes like this.

You are a dum-   my; dum-my, dum-my you!

Here the use of song is *symbolic* rather than objective. The song is no longer a concretization of play, an embodiment of outward action or inner feeling. Now it is functioning on a symbolic level, as a proxy for something else—in this case, teasing.

Unlike the glissando mimicking the descent of the paper airplane, there is no analogical relationship between this song and what it represents. It is just one particular spontaneous song-word that is different in certain respects from other spontaneous song-words. The syntax of this brief musical utterance as expressed in intervals and rhythm (and in our example, in the text) makes it a symbol of *teasing*. Every member of child culture understands this song-word in this way, even when there is *no* text. All one need do is hum the phrase to a playmate, and the meaning is clear enough. A song formula such as this triggers an *intersubjective reference* that is partly cognitive and partly emotional in origin. It is precisely this common reference that makes this song formula a linguistic symbol rather than a more indefinite signal of some kind.

Song communication of this type among children is by no means limited to teasing. Song formulas of various kinds, each clearly defined by its own particular pattern of intervals and rhythmic structure, can be used to relate information, call, command, question, and reply—all within a muse-ical context common to all children. As with ordinary speech, these songs can be subtly varied to reflect the individual characteristics of a child's voice and rhythmic preferences. They are a priceless fountain of expressive possibility wherein the voice becomes a mirror of the child's soul.

C. Song as Background Coloration

A third way children use spontaneous song is as a more or less casual accompaniment to play. For example, a little girl is building a sand castle, and as she plays she begins humming a few bars of Bruce Springsteen's "Born in the USA." What she is mainly doing—the activity that has her attention—is building the sand castle, not singing a song. Nonetheless, the song is an important part of her total experience, for it serves as *an emotional source of energy that stimulates spontaneity*. We are dealing here with a song accompaniment that occurs within the framework of play. The song, in this case, has a *signaling* function: unlike the symbolic "song-words" discussed earlier, it does not "refer" to anything. As a part of the total play experience, however, song as background coloration is as important for children as analogical imitation and symbolic representation.

THE INTERPLAY OF FORM AND USE

My earlier studies have shown that children, guided by the "rules of the game" peculiar to their culture, systematically unite a specific use with a specific form in their spontaneous singing (Bjørkvold 1985). I shall speak of this in what follows as the *complementarity* of form and use. It does not occur with absolute regularity, but it is sufficiently consistent to reveal a clear pattern of prevailing preferences.

Fluid song appears to be associated primarily with analogical imitation. This type of spontaneous song is used in both solitary and group play; indeed, one could easily imagine the paper-airplane example in a play situation involving several children. On rare occasions fluid song is also used as a type of expressive communication through which a child acts out his or her inner feelings.

The most typical use of fluid song, however, is as a vehicle for introspection. We saw this in the example of the inner song mono-

logue, where little Steinar sat by himself in a corner of the classroom and became absorbed in a kind of musical reverie. In such
a moment, fluid song becomes a powerful means of revealing
deeper layers of feelings and dreams. In the subjective inner world
the child then enters, song can become the confidential bearer of
forbidden thoughts—and nobody else can interfere. Fluid song is
well suited for this purpose, for its form is so flexible and subjective
that you can make it your own in any way you choose. There is
no need for anyone else to understand what you are "singing."
The song code in this case is completely *intrasubjective;* it applies
only to the individual "singer" at this particular time and place.
It is *unique* in the literal sense of that word.

All of us have need from time to time of an imaginary friend
who always understands and agrees with us, a faithful companion
who is always there, ready to give comfort and protection—and
to take the blame when something goes wrong. Song—invisible,
and often scarcely audible—can be such a friend for children,
perhaps for many more children than we realize, much like
"Binker" in A. A. Milne's famous children's poem.

> Binker—what I call him—is a secret of my own,
> And Binker is the reason why I never feel alone.
> Playing in the nursery, sitting on the stair,
> Whatever I am busy at, Binker will be there. . . .

Song formulas, by virtue of their terse, standardized form, are
especially well suited for communication and are thus employed
primarily in what we have called *symbolic representation*. They are
used in quarreling as well as in friendly role-playing, always in
such a way that other children immediately understand the intended meaning. Here shared comprehensibility is fundamental.

As I have shown (Bjørkvold 1985), the statistical correlation
between song formulas and their use for symbolic representation
is very high. In principle, song formulas function just like spoken
words in a child's communication system, for both are simply
sounds with semantic content.

The semantic content of song formulas can never be stated with the same precision as that of the words of a spoken language. The *meaning-scope* of such songs is less well defined, and they typically carry a strong emotional charge as well. This does not mean, however, that song formulas are less useful to children for communication than spoken words. As a matter of fact, it is often in precisely those situations where spoken words are not adequate that these formulas are employed. In such cases, the broader meaning-scope and greater emotional charge of the songs give the communication a strength and solidity that spoken words alone could not achieve.

Earlier analyses (Bjørkvold 1985) show that one and the same song formula can have more than one meaning. Song formulas, like words, can be homonyms: they can sound the same but have different meanings. The prototypical song-formula motive of child culture (G-A-G-E), for example, can be used for narration and description as well as for provocation. In practice, however, the most frequent use of this motive among children is for teasing.

Two other song formulas—a descending minor third and a descending major third—are widely used by children, and both exhibit homonymy. Both are used for calling: their primary meaning is "Come here!" This meaning is especially associated with the descending major third. Descending thirds, major or minor, are also used for narration and description, the setting within child culture constantly clarifying the actual meaning for a given group of children. The children always understand, for usage is governed by rules of meaning prescribed by the child culture of which they are a part.

Children's song formulas exhibit another interesting feature related to the complementarity of form and use. There is clear evidence that *usage of the different song formulas is governed by the social development of the particular group*. In a group where few of the children know each other, they are hesitant, waiting to see what will happen. Their social activity is in an embryonic phase, and the need for a "song vocabulary" with which to communicate is correspondingly limited. At this stage, children primarily communicate, play, and sing with and for themselves. This, too, is important, for in the privacy of solitude the child is always right, always wins, and always has control. After the children have been together in school for a full year, however, the situation is totally different. By that time they have spent hundreds of hours together playing, fighting, laughing, crying, and their use of song mirrors the dramatic change in their development as a social group. Increasingly, the song formulas are used in play as natural and essential modes of expression in a situation that more and more requires them to enter into complex social relationships with their fellows—for better or worse. The converse is also true. Because the need as well as the opportunity to be alone in the group decreases, their use of introspective song declines over time. Children's spontaneous singing always mirrors their lives, individually and collectively (Bjørkvold 1985).

Finally, standard songs are used more or less equally in all three of the ways identified above. Here the text appears to be the main determinant of how a given song will be used. If any one use predominates, perhaps it is as what we have called background coloration. Here, as in the sand castle example, the original text of the song is often retained unchanged. But standard songs are also used for emotional introspection, just like fluid songs, sometimes in the form of wordless humming, sometimes with a few fragments of the familiar texts.

PER'S BUTTERFLY

Per had always had trouble with spoken language, but song seemed to call forth words and feelings in a way that nothing else could. Even at the age of five it was difficult for him to say his name clearly enough for anyone to understand. But Per loved to sing, and he sang constantly—and with good reason. Song enabled him to communicate, both with himself and with others.

One day Per heard a song he found absolutely entrancing, one that was strangely different from anything else he had heard in preschool. It was a Henrik Wergeland poem set by Eivind Groven. It went like this.

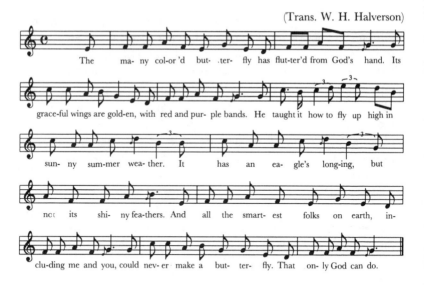

(Trans. W. H. Halverson)

The ma-ny col-or'd but-ter-fly has flut-ter'd from God's hand. Its grace-ful wings are gold-en, with red and pur-ple bands. He taught it how to fly up high in sun-ny sum-mer wea-ther. It has an ea-gle's long-ing, but not its shi-ny fea-thers. And all the smart-est folks on earth, in-clu-ding me and you, could nev-er make a but-ter-fly. That on-ly God can do.

The preschool teachers repeated this song for the children over and over again for a period of several weeks. It is a difficult melody, rhythmically, melodically, and with respect to tonality. It is not a "typical" children's song by any means. Nonetheless, or perhaps for that very reason, it slowly took root in Per. He embraced this "impossible melody" as a kind of muse-ical example of the triumph of inconvenience. The melody seemed to become a part of him, to fill his entire being. He went about constantly singing or humming this demanding song, in his own little version.

Yes I am a but-ter-fly, but-ter-fly, but-ter-fly!

I had seen muse-ical miracles before, and now I saw another. As Per ran this way and that, flapping his arms and beaming and singing about his precious butterfly, he *became* that butterfly. I was reminded of the original meaning, in Greek, of the word *enthusiasm:* having a god within. No longer was Per a tongue-tied little boy who couldn't even pronounce his own name: he was a butterfly, newly created by a muse-ical god within, a five-year-old butterfly in a green sweater and soiled blue jeans. In magical moments such as this, one understands clearly the truth of Dostoevsky's statement that *when the mathematical unit is the human being, two times two no longer equals four.* In such play the child's capacity for wonder is muse-ically exposed. This is what Edith Cobb calls "the genius of childhood—a cosmopoetic exploration of mind and world. . . . The highest poetic endeavor has its inception in the child's need to be what he wants to understand, and to express that knowledge in some outward form" (1977, p. 50).

Per sang with and for himself, but children also use standard songs for purposes of communication. Textual improvisations are typical in such cases: in response to the needs of the moment, children will often give a quick twist to the text, thereby transforming it into something more suitable for their purpose. Little Paul, for example—like many four-year-olds—has a crush on his Sunday-school teacher, whose name is Heather. When she teaches the children the hymn, "Fair Are the Meadows," Paul can't resist creating his own version in her honor.

As an eyewitness to this episode I can vouch for the fact that Heather blushed, notwithstanding a reassuring age difference of at least twenty-five years between her and her admirer!

In contrast to song formulas, in which the specific pattern of musical intervals is of primary importance, the use of standard songs for communication is determined mainly by their texts. The primary reference, therefore, is *denotative,* with the tune functioning more as an emotional context or *connotative* reinforcement. Who knows what associations Paul and Heather may have had with this song? Perhaps Paul's mother sang it to him when he was a babe in arms, and perhaps Heather had often sung it and heard it sung by others at Christmastime. If so, the happy memories associated with the song surely enriched the meaning of the altered text for both Paul and Heather. It is in precisely this way that standard songs are able to serve so effectively as bearers of the feelings as well as the thoughts of children. To be sure, they lack the finished form of an art song, but what enormous expressive power they have nonetheless!

Children sometimes employ great wit and humor as they adapt standard songs to situations that adults would never think of *singing* about. Consider this transformation of "London Bridge."

(Vivian Zahl Olsen)

Or take this well-known table prayer sung by children on both sides of the Atlantic—

O you who feed the lit-tle birds, now bless our food, O God. A - men.

—and its irreverent revision.

O you who ate the lit- tle bird, be nice and spit it out a -gain.

A few specific findings are worthy of note. Most important, it appears that children's interest is by no means limited to songs that grown-ups traditionally regard as "children's songs." With a voracious appetite for life, they refuse to be bound by what we adults think they can handle, gladly embracing songs that are sometimes quite complex, both textually and musically. They need such songs, too, as a point of departure for the investigation of their own reality—as part, we might say, of their musical vocabulary. That reality is not nearly so shallow and simple as many teachers of young children assume when they condescendingly try to limit them to "clap-and-point" songs. It has been shown that children often intentionally disregard this type of song when they want to comment muse-ically on their situation at a given moment (Bjørkvold 1985). The vacuous has no standing in the realm of the meaningful. Remember Per and the song of the butterfly!

Many of the standard songs that play a role in the daily life of children are derived from old traditions, musical games, and jingles that have been a part of child culture for many generations. Most, however, are borrowed from the surrounding adult environment. Interestingly, the mass media—notwithstanding the steady stream of music blaring forth day and night from radio, television, videos, and cassettes—do not appear to influence preschool children's repertoire of standard songs as much as is generally believed. The reason appears to be that mechanically produced sound makes much less of an impression on children than the nearness and affection of another human being. A simple song sung unprofessionally but *lovingly* to a child sitting on a parent's lap reaches more deeply into the child's consciousness than the near-perfect voice of a singer on a CD. Both my own research in Norway (Bjørkvold 1985) and a later Danish study (Alkersig and Riemer 1989) show that only about twenty percent of children's repertoire of standard songs come directly from the media. The rest are derived from a living song tradition extending from our own time back through many, many generations.

OUR MUSE-ICAL MOTHER TONGUE AND ITS FUNCTION

Music anthropologist Alan P. Merriam distinguishes the concepts *use* and *function* as follows: " 'Use' . . . refers to the situation in which music is employed in human action; 'function' concerns the reasons for its employment and particularly the broader purpose which it serves" (1964, p. 210). Accepting this distinction, we turn now to a discussion of the functions of spontaneous children's singing, i.e., the underlying significance such singing has in their lives, both individually and as a social/cultural group.

Spontaneous singing, as we have seen, is children's *muse-ical mother tongue,* even in a narrower linguistic sense. It is part of their many-faceted communication system. In recent years this view appears to have gained acceptance internationally among scholars concerned with children and language (Söderbergh 1988, with Bjørkvold 1988b). Spontaneous singing has some of the same functions in children's lives as spoken language, and some functions that are different.

Modern language research has identified the following as the main functions of human speech generally: creating contact, communicating information, and marking identity. These three functional areas are closely related, and all are clearly evident in the spontaneous singing of children.

The *contact-creating function* has its origin in the earliest muse-ical dialogue between mother and infant. That is the experience in which the child discovers the enormous contact-creating potential in the melodious modulations of the human voice. It is there, in the mother's arms, that the first contact with another human being is established and the process of socialization begins. This process continues during the preschool years. Spontaneous singing becomes a double mirror that can be made to reflect either the inner or the outer world with equal effectiveness. This capacity of spontaneous singing also accounts for its most important *emotional* function, which is to create contact with deeper layers of feeling in our own hearts and to express emotion in a way that touches others. Through spontaneous singing, children master in a remarkable way the very thing that Winnicott identified as the essential role of play as a psychodynamic process: to be a vital mediator between inner and outer reality. When this mediation occurs, two objectionable alternatives are avoided: one in which the child withdraws into him/herself for protection against surroundings perceived to be threatening, the other in which the child becomes totally lost in an "outward" life that lacks adequate inner and emotional moorings. The healthy child is able to take the considerable risk of establishing vigorous *contact* with the world, to engage it creatively, critically, questioningly. That is how it must be if new challenges are to be met and the world's myriad secrets unraveled—which is the task set for preschool children by the "booming, buzzing confusion" of the world around them.

Spontaneous singing also serves a *therapeutic* function. It is an added safety valve that strengthens communication, both for children with normal speech and for a child like Per, who coped with his speech problem by singing instead.

Spontaneous singing can of course play a role in communicating knowledge and information, thus contributing to learning and cognition just as ordinary speech does. We have already discussed several examples in which song, by virtue of its stronger emotional charge, also has a clear *imagination-freeing* function and an accompanying *breakthrough* function in the process by which children move toward ever higher levels of awareness. Most five-year-olds know that $1 + 1 = 2$, but they can also sing themselves into a magical world in which $1 + 1 \approx x$—and suddenly new and important insights are open to them. Thus we may say that spontaneous singing also has an important *awareness-broadening* function. A song fragment can be the key that gives form, life, and sound to a new experience, making it emotionally and cognitively accessible to the child.

In spontaneous songs incorporating humor, the irrational flaunting of the norm is often the dynamic element that makes the result humorous. The very point of such songs is to challenge established boundaries and norms, to turn them upside down by viewing them through the oblique prism of impish humor. Bold and original, often possessing a unique ability to spontaneously "seize the moment," witty children are constantly searching for increasingly authentic life experience.

All these song functions are naturally incorporated into the play of children, which is inconceivable without spontaneous singing. At one moment song is the bubbling center and principal activity of the group, at another it is a shining silver thread thoroughly interwoven with other threads in the complex fabric of play. But song is not merely an important part of the *ngoma* of play; song also has a clear *structuring* function for play, giving it outer and inner form, rhythm, dynamic drive, pulse, and emotional energy.

These functions of spontaneous singing enter in turn into the process called *socialization*, whereby children are prepared for life in culture and society. Spontaneous singing as a badge of identity is part of this process.

Within the complex fabric of interpersonal relationships that make a collection of individuals into a group, each child has a unique role to play. In the social life of a group in which there are winners and losers, puppy lovers and bosom buddies, the bold and the timid, each child contributes on the basis of his or her presuppositions and individuality. All children know the rules of the game of child culture as well as football players know the rules of football. In the spontaneous singing of kindergarten children there will always be a leader, a number of good followers, and some who reluctantly tag along. Some see to it that the song gets started and make sure that it goes well; others, less confident, are nonetheless indispensable. Each child has his/her own idiomatic way of infusing song into play, a personal repertoire and a personal form within the context of the total group. All children who are members of a group participate in such activity, some more frequently and vigorously than others. I can truthfully say, however, that in such groups I have never encountered a child who did not sing at all.

As the dynamics of the group play themselves out, spontaneous singing naturally does its part to mold each child's sense of uniqueness and *individual identity*. The particular way you express yourself in spontaneous song—just like the way you talk, handle yourself in a dispute with another child, etc.—says something both to yourself and to others about who you are and where you stand within the group. Indeed, it appears that a child's singing can spell the difference between respect and indifference, between friendship and isolation.

Child culture, as we have seen, defines itself by rules, norms, and values that give it uniqueness and cohesion. These marks of the group's identity do not constitute a static system; they are products of the continuous working of creative forces that are constantly testing boundaries even as they attempt to preserve them. Here children develop as part of a sister/brotherhood. Because each child's way of singing is unique, this form of expression contributes significantly to establishing each child's sense of *cultural identity*. Spontaneous singing, deeply anchored as it is in mind and body, helps to assure a kind of structural continuity in child culture. This is a matter of considerable importance, for structural continuity—a pattern of fixed processes and forms that remain substantially unchanged from day to day—is vitally necessary if children are to cope with and organize their own lives, language, norms, moral code, national traditions, customs, and habits.

Music anthropologist John Blacking, in *How Musical Is Man?* (1973)—a study of the music culture of the Venda people of South Africa—draws the following conclusion.

Musical behavior reflects varying degrees of consciousness of social forces, and the structures and functions of music are related to basic human drives and to the biological need to maintain a balance among them. . . . Thus forces in culture and society would be expressed in humanly organized sound, because the chief function

of music in society and culture is to promote soundly organized
humanity by enhancing human consciousness. (pp. 100, 101)

This generalization is equally true for child culture and the development of the child's consciousness. Through spontaneous singing, children clear a pathway in their own lives and in so doing
secure for themselves the vitality and cohesion of child culture. At
the same time, the sense of belonging, confidence in a cultural
identity, and the beginnings of socialization are all present in
children's creative *repudiation* of the norms and their playful investigation of the unknown.

QUALITY AND MUSICALITY

The quality of children's spontaneous singing consists primarily in
the extent to which it expresses existential presence, genuineness,
and sincerity. The similarity to African culture is striking. Again
we quote Anyanwu: "If proportionality or symmetry is a criterion
of beauty, then most African art works are not 'beautiful.' In fact,
the basic function of African art is to create *meaning,* and this
suggests that what is *meaningful* is *beautiful*" (1987, p. 256). Ideally,
this statement should apply to all music, including Western art
music. I will return to this idea later.

It is not easy for one schooled in the standards of art music to
adopt other criteria for judging singing. Consider the following
detailed description of African song, which in many respects parallels the singing of children.

Even more than the drum, the human voice is at the heart of
African music. . . . The voice is never "trained" in the Western
sense to produce sounds remote from those of speech; the vocal
music of Africa bears a very intimate relationship to speech. . . .
They use a dazzling variety of types of singing, depending on the
dramatic situation required: head tones, chest tones, grunts, whispers, whistles, amazingly realistic imitations of bird, animal and
other natural sounds, undulations and yodels; all are part of their
repertory of sounds. Unlike Western singers, Africans deliberately
cultivate strong differences between the various registers of the

voice, even emphasizing the breaks between them, from a growl to a falsetto, even almost a scream, as well as using with virtuosity the various harmonic and non-harmonic sounds of which the human voice is capable. (Small 1977, pp. 50, 51)

Out of respect for children, we must train ourselves to appreciate such singing. Consider Per's butterfly song. Neither the beat nor the pitch was exactly "right" in the manner of boy sopranos who are able to move adult audiences to tears. What kind of voice did Per have anyway? Was it alto or soprano? It doesn't matter, for in child culture the distinction is irrelevant. The alto/soprano distinction is a historically conditioned way of categorizing voices within the Western *bel canto* tradition. In reality, a human voice is like a human face: each one is absolutely unique and can never be duplicated. Each voice expresses its owner's unique inner life and experience. For that reason, every child's voice is beautiful and important, each in its own way.

Naturally there are many music teachers who understand these truths and, as the fine musicians and teachers they are, do their work accordingly. I believe, however, that there are also many for whom this is *not* the case, and the consequences for children's musical and human upbringing, play, and learning are very serious indeed.

At the very heart of child culture's playful *ngoma* lies the child's natural muse-icality as a unified psychosocial phenomenon within a larger ecological whole. Song and movement are part and parcel of an existential process whereby the child's whole body functions as an expressive instrument that sends powerful signals both inward—helping the child define and understand him/herself—and outward toward the world. We must look, listen, and learn from the children themselves if we want to understand at least in some measure how the Muse Within manifests herself in the earliest stages of life.

THE ST. PETERSBURG STUDY

Let me first sketch a vignette of St. Petersburg (still called Leningrad at the time of my study) as I saw it through Norwegian eyes after visiting the city several times and living there for half a year. The contrast with Oslo was enormous.

St. Petersburg is one of the largest cities in a country that until recently prided itself on being a great superpower. The cruiser *Aurora* anchored in the Neva River is a constant reminder that this proud city was the cradle of the Revolution. It is also the site of the imposing Winter Palace, former home of the czars, which was stormed by the Bolsheviks at the beginning of the Revolution, and of the adjoining Hermitage, one of the largest art museums in the world. During World War II it acquired the name "City of Heroes" as over a million people lost their lives in the course of the German blockade that lasted for almost three years. Even today, children are constantly reminded of this tragic chapter in the city's history through eyewitness accounts from parents and grandparents of the suffering, destruction, and death that they observed.

St. Petersburg was founded nearly three hundred years ago as Russia's "window to the West." It is unusually beautiful and architecturally pure, boasting a large nucleus of buildings in eighteenth-century classical style, designed by the leading Italian architects of the day. Majestic Nevsky Prospekt, a broad thoroughfare, bisects the city like a gigantic arrow culminating in an enormous arrowhead: the gilded spire of the Admiralty building. It is a proud cultural center with an abiding love for circus, theater, ballet, music, and the visual arts and an astonishing degree of artistic sophistication among learned and lay people, young and old—at the theater, in the concert hall, and in the endless lines in front of every ticket window. In a city with a centuries-old tradition of political censorship, one Friday afternoon I observed Plato's *Dialogues* and Grieg's *Lyric Pieces* offered for sale in the newsstand at the main subway station—and in a few minutes both quickly sold out.

It was in St. Petersburg, a century and a half ago, that Glinka laid the foundation for the rich Russian tradition in art music. It was here that "the mighty five"—Balakirev, Borodin, Cui, Moussorgsky, and Rimsky-Korsakov—helped define Russian distinctiveness and national awareness as, with great artistic power, they introduced unmistakably national music to an international audience. In the course of just twenty years, St. Petersburg—home of the Kirov Ballet, the St. Petersburg Philharmonic, and one of the world's oldest and finest music conservatories—gave the world three of this century's greatest composers: Stravinsky, Prokofiev, and Shostakovich. The city maintained an elite school for "music prodigies"—a seeming paradox in a society supposedly built on the principle of total equality, where the *prima ballerina* is one of the best-paid citizens, and a boy with a violin case under his arm was regarded as highly by his peers as the captain of the hockey team.

Because St. Petersburg lacked the West's material abundance, its children were not as well clothed or as well equipped as their counterparts in Norway or the United States. But the warmth they evoked could be observed even on a bitterly cold winter day, when a stiffly aloof policeman suddenly flashed a big smile as he helped a little girl across Nevsky Prospekt.

All this is part of the experience of children in St. Petersburg, so different from both Oslo and Los Angeles.

RUSSIAN RESEARCH

What does child culture look like in St. Petersburg? How does it fare in a city with such impressive music traditions and such ambitious and systematic programs for the education of gifted children, not least the musically gifted? And to what extent is an understanding of children's muse-ical culture reflected in Russian research and pedagogy?

The most characteristic feature of Russian research in this area is its preoccupation with "elite" education rather than with the natural development of children's own spontaneous singing. However, some Russian scholars have begun to focus on what they call "preschool children's independent artistic activity" as a subject of research in its own right, apart from the traditional musical training of children. This in itself is an important qualitative step in a country with a strong tradition of singling out musically gifted children for intensive specialized training at an early age.

In a research report dealing with the "independent artistic activities" of preschool children in several republics of the former

Soviet Union, N. A. Vetlugina (1980), a student of Lev Vygotsky's, emphasized that preschool children's artistic activity is existentially motivated, a manifestation of their continuous life experience. She described children's imaginative creativity as "realistic," thus acknowledging that individual creativity is part of a total understanding of reality. Vetlugina stands within a strong Russian tradition that includes such scholars as Vygotsky, Luria, Leontiev, and Usova. That she identifies play as the activity most suitable for children's artistic expression leads one to expect a more detailed discussion of child culture and its manifestations. Surprisingly, Vetlugina's *Independent Artistic Activities of Preschool Children* does not include such a discussion. It is obvious that her thinking was strongly influenced by the result-oriented, elitist arts education so thoroughly entrenched in the Russian tradition. She freely acknowledged as much in a private conversation with me in 1985, in which she also emphasized the importance of future research on the spontaneous singing of Russian children as a manifestation of authentic child culture.

My research on the spontaneous singing of Russian children was, then, the first of its kind. My data are not extensive, but they represent a beginning. Having worked for many years in the field of Russian music, I received permission to do a field study of Russian preschool children for several weeks in the autumn of 1985. My research was conducted primarily in St. Petersburg, with supplementary material gathered in Moscow. My object was to determine the extent to which spontaneous singing appeared as a muse-ical manifestation in the play of children who lived in a country dramatically different from Norway and who had never been exposed to the seething media culture or the chaotic capitalism of the West. Restricted in scope as it was, the study was only intended to serve as a cross-cultural basis for comparison with the principal findings of my far more comprehensive study of Norwegian children. I was specifically seeking answers to two questions. Can one speak at all about *universals* in child culture, common features irrespective of national boundaries, documented through children's use of song? And to what extent does the spontaneous singing of St. Petersburg children manifest a national distinctiveness and identity with ethnocentric roots?

I found that preschool children in St. Petersburg had the same need to express themselves through spontaneous singing as Norwegian children. The process was the same, pointing to an obviously universal human need for play, expression, and communication. Five- and six-year-old Russian children weave singing into the fabric of their play just as Norwegian children do. They sit in a swing, glide rhythmically back and forth—and sing. Or they race around on tricycles—and sing. Their playground equipment was neither as shiny nor as modern as that in a well-equipped Norwegian preschool, but the fervor and the pace were the same. And we must not forget the sandbox, as important in St. Petersburg as in Oslo, a favorite place for spontaneous singing (to the words "varoom-varoom" and "toot-toot") as toy cars are maneuvered along narrow sandbox roads by expert sandbox dwellers. It goes without saying that in Russia, as elsewhere, ball and song live a symbiotic life together. Children love ball games, whether their society is organized according to the principles of capitalism, socialism, or social democracy. Ball-children of the world, unite!

SONG FORM

It can be stated unequivocally that all the *forms* of spontaneous singing used by Norwegian preschoolers—fluid-amorphous songs, song formulas, and standard songs—were also used by Russian preschoolers. But I did detect some differences between the two groups, principally the much less frequent use of the latter two forms. Among the St. Petersburg children, fluid/amorphous singing was far and away the dominant form of spontaneous singing. My Moscow findings confirmed this characteristic of Russian child culture, at least as found in preschools in two large cities.

My research also left the distinct impression that spontaneous singing in general occurs less frequently among Russian preschoolers than among their Norwegian counterparts. This impression is interesting in light of my findings from an Oslo study carried out during the 1970s. I discovered that preschool children who were steadily and systematically exposed to adult singing experienced what could be called an accelerated socialization into the world of adult music. The adult influence with respect to repertoire, manner of singing, and even situations in which singing appeared to be appropriate was so strong that the children in this preschool, to a greater degree than elsewhere, began to sing like grown-ups instead of like children. They were less inclined to improvise, more adept at singing the "right" text and melody exactly as they had been taught. Richer manifestations of the spontaneous singing typical of child culture were more evident where the adult influence was somewhat less prominent.

It is possible that systematic adult influence had an even more decisive socialization effect on the singing of Russian children. It should be remembered that a Russian preschool is much more like an ordinary school than is the case in Norway. For the older children there are fixed periods of instruction between the periods of free play, with desks arranged in tidy rows in one corner of the room. Special music teachers come regularly, typically two hours a week. Their goal is not only to increase the children's enjoyment of beauty and to cultivate their aesthetic awareness; there is also an ideological dimension meant to develop national pride and heighten a sense of Russianness. Consistent with the importance accorded music in Russian society, preschools are also equipped with an impressive array of musical instruments for both children and adults. Many schools even have their own music room.

It is clear that such conditions benefit children who are identified by standardized proficiency tests as musically gifted in the traditional sense. Systematic instruction stimulates these children to express themselves musically in accordance with the premises of their teachers. Thus they enter into an essentially adult singing tradition at an early age and learn to prefer it to improvised spontaneous singing in the context of free play with other children. One could speak here of a development from divergent to convergent musical expression, learning to conform rather than to create. The children judged less proficient on the basis of music tests preferred to remain in child culture, playing and singing in their own way with other children like themselves. In other words, they chose *ngoma* instead of music.

The song forms used by Russian and Norwegian children were quite similar. Most of those I observed in Norway appeared again in the spontaneous singing of Russian children—and with the same meanings, understandable by all. The implication is that there seem to be some *universal song forms* in child culture.

The calling pattern, for example—the descending major third—was the same as in Norway.

Sa-sha!   Tya-ta!
(Aunty!)

I found it interesting that when the pattern had to be altered to accommodate a three-syllable word, the alteration was always the same: an ascending major third followed by a descending one. Its roots, of course, lie in the intonation of the spoken language.

Ri-bya-ta!   Na-ta-sha!
(Guys!)

The intimate connection between the intonation of spoken Russian and the pattern of song played a significant role in Modest Moussorgsky's song cycle *The Nursery*, composed between 1867 and 1875. Moussorgsky was known for his ability to relate to children. The texts of these songs consist of conversations between a nurse *(njanja)* and a child about various scary events recounted in fairy tales. In the opening phrase of the song "With Nursey" ("Come and tell me, Nursey dear, that old tale you know so well, of the wolf, that wicked dreadful wolf!"), the child speaks to the *njanja* using the same intonational pattern of rise-fall Russian children use when calling each other with a word or name having three or more syllables. Moussorgsky had listened carefully to the music of the spoken language—the abrupt shifts in intonation as the mood changes from joy to terror, for example. With this music

1. With Nursey

Посвящается великому учителю музыкальной правды
Александру Сергеевичу Даргомыжскому

Слова М. МУСОРГСКОГО

in his ears, he composed melodies that are radically different with respect to rhythm, tempo, dynamics, and intervals from those one would expect to find in a traditional nineteenth-century art song. The Russian language, especially the language of Russian *children*, gave him a creative key to an entirely new form of melodic conception. "The goal," he once said, "is not beauty, but truth."

In the service of truth, fidelity to the music inherent in the language of children, he was able to write melody lines of extraordinary expressiveness, notwithstanding—or perhaps precisely owing to—the "choppiness" resulting from constant changes in meter.

Both ascending and descending thirds, then, were commonly used by Russian children. Nonetheless, not once did I hear a Russian child use the teasing formula so common in child culture elsewhere. How can the absence of this song formula from the repertoire of Russian children be explained? Is the form less universal among children than has often been supposed? Granted, my observations of Russian children were limited, and my sample was hardly large enough to support any far-reaching conclusions. What can be said, however, is that the teasing formula is certainly used less frequently by Russian children than by their Norwegian counterparts, for whom it is the commonest of song forms.

There is clear evidence that the teasing formula occurs with great frequency throughout the world—in Scandinavia, England, many countries of Central Europe, the United States, Australia, Singapore, and elsewhere. We do not know why Russian children appear to differ from other children in this particular way, but the apparent absence of this formula from their musical vocabulary casts doubt on the supposed universality of the teasing song formula. However, it is also true that discipline in Russian preschools is much stricter than in such schools in Norway, making it harder for a child to get away with teasing a playmate—in song or otherwise!

As might be expected, the standard songs sung by Russian children reflected the repertoire to which they had been exposed, and were distinctively Russian. Norwegian children, on the other hand, sang not only Norwegian songs but occasionally international hits, the musical wares offered by the mass media. In 1985 Russian society was still quite insulated from the influence of the pop-music industry. At the same time, however, indigenous Russian music—folk music as well as the compositions of the great Russian masters, from Glinka and Tchaikovsky to Prokofiev and Kabalevsky—had been cultivated to an extent unparalleled in any Western country. The constant playing of this distinctively Russian music was an integral part of cultural politics in the former USSR, a method of engendering in people at all levels of society a feeling of national pride and belongingness.

Russian children improvise on fragments of these songs and adapt them to the needs of the moment in exactly the same ways as Norwegian children (and, as we shall see, American children). The *form* is the same; what is different is the *content*. The following role-playing is universally appealing to children. A little girl, Katya, walks around singing her doll to sleep to the tune of an old Russian lullaby. The old song and the situation of the moment are united in the little girl's experience as she lovingly weaves the doll's name, Lydya, into the text. Here is the original song.

And here is Katya's version.

Song Use

The similarity in the *use* of song by Russian and Norwegian children was striking. The examples that follow, all recorded during my observations of Russian children at play, could just as well have been gathered in Scandinavia or the United States.

A. Analogical Imitation: Song as a Concrete Part of Play

Natasha, a little girl with typical Russian pigtails and a white hair ribbon, was pushing a chair across the floor. The motion of the chair was echoed in a long humming tone that continued without interruption until the chair crashed against the wall on the other side of the room. Another example: two boys were fighting with play swords, and as the mock duel progressed they became increasingly enchanted by the rhythm of their clashing swords and began to sing in unison.

> De,   de,   de,   de,   de,   de,   de,   de.

And yet another: a chubby little boy stood alone by the fence surrounding the schoolyard, rocking up and down, bending his knees, and singing.

> Dzjoo!   Dzjoo!   Dzjoo!

Not to mention all the little boys who crawled around playing with toy cars, with spontaneous singing as the audible fuel. Boys, not children, for the observed differences in play patterns between the sexes was much greater in Russia than in most Western countries: boys played with tanks, guns, and swords, girls with dolls and toy household goods. The concept of unisex toys did not appear to have taken hold in the USSR of 1985.

B. Symbolic Representation:
Use of "Song-words" to Tease, Report, Call, Command, Ask, Reply

It was evident from the use of common communication symbols in the course of their play that Russian children, like their Norwegian counterparts, also use spontaneous singing as a method of communication. Children sometimes use forms of spontaneous singing other than song formulas to tease, report, call, etc. Standard songs and fluid/amorphous songs are sometimes employed. I observed fewer instances of creative elaboration of standard songs among Russian than among Norwegian children, however. I am inclined to think that the heavy dose of formal instruction in traditional music is responsible for this difference.

C. Song as Background Coloration

Russian children made frequent use of song as a casual accompaniment to play. Tanya, for example, is pretending that she is out
in the forest picking *gribtsjiki*—small, tasty mushrooms—and as
she does so she hums a well-known Russian folk song, "Katjusja."

Grib- tsji-   ki   i - - - - i!   Grib- tsji- ki   i - - - - i!

Here "Katjusja," the text of which has nothing to do with mushrooms (it is a poem of love and longing), is clearly being used as
background or accompaniment in Tanya's play. Gathering mushrooms is what her private little game is all about. The song adds
sound and rhythm, emotional energy and warmth, important
elements in Tanya's total experience. Indeed, it is the song that
makes her game seem authentic, for it unites her inner pictures of
the game (the mushrooms growing all around her in her imagination) with the "real" world in which she is playing. Perhaps the
song so enlivens the inner pictures that she literally *sees* the mushrooms and the trees in the forest as she walks around the preschool
room playing her solitary little game. The song helps to break
through the confines of technical reason and show her the way to
all those delicious mushrooms that lie beyond the boundary.

FUNCTION AND MUSICALITY

There is no doubt that for Russian preschoolers, too, singing is
part of a broader muse-ical manifestation that includes physical
motion and talking as well as song in what might be called a
Russian variant of child-cultural *ngoma*. Their play occurs within
the "global and multifunctional" framework so typical of infants'
first attempts to relate to their surroundings (Vygotsky 1975),
which preschool children retain despite the division of these attempts into disparate functions as they grow and mature. It is this
broadly inclusive capacity to reach out to the world in what to an
observer appear to be many ways at once (though the child apparently experiences it as a single unified thrust) that constitutes the

basis for life experience, learning, socialization, the development of individual identity, and maturation. For Russian children, as for Norwegian children, play is the most important cultural arena, the familiar beachhead from which bridges can be built to other selves, to the perceived world, and even to the still unknown.

"SOVIETSKAYA MUZYKA" LOOKS TO THE FUTURE

The March 1988 issue of *Sovietskaya Muzyka,* the large and prestigious journal of the professional association of Russian composers, launched a critical debate concerning the music education of children and young people in the country—a topic that could not have been seriously addressed prior to Gorbachev's policy of *glasnost.* The debate was editorially entitled "On the Threshold of the Twenty-first Century," which is indicative of how important this matter is perceived to be for the further development of Russian society as a whole. Its relevance for our study is that it provides a glimpse of how Russians understand the place of music in the lives of children and young people.

A representative panel of experts was asked to respond to the following questions.

1. Is there a need in our country, with its exceptionally rich treasure of national traditions, for a common system for the musical-aesthetic training of children and young people?
2. The music education system that exists in our country was developed many years ago. Is it adequate for the needs of the present?
3. Most children who attend music schools do not become professional musicians after they graduate. Not only that: they don't make music as amateur musicians either, and only rarely do they attend symphony concerts or the opera. Why? And what do you think needs to be done to change this situation?
4. Are you satisfied with the role that music plays in the lives of your own children?
5. Do you think there is a connection between young people's music preferences and their general cultural life-style?
6. What is it, in your view, that the professional composers are not

giving the youth? Why do the young people so often prefer
music that they themselves have created?

7. Why, in your opinion, has the training of public school music
teachers continued for so many years without improvement?

8. Immediately following the Revolution the Russian authorities
thought that they had only to open the door to artistic treasures
and the people would naturally be drawn to them. As everybody
knows, that is what happened at the time. Today, seventy years
later, one can no longer state without qualification that this is so.
What, in your opinion, is the reason for this? (*Sovietskaya Muzyka*,
March 1988, pp. 2–3)

It is not difficult to discern in these questions a deep underlying
critique of a system that no longer functions satisfactorily. In the
debate engendered by these questions, music psychologist Arnold
Gotsdiner made the following interesting points.

A program of aesthetic training, if it is to be viable, must take
account of national conditions and traditions in each republic. . . .

Unfortunately, the psychological and maturational principles
governing the development of children and youth are overlooked,
especially their overwhelming need for social contact and self-
affirmation. . . .

There is no instruction in such vitally necessary practical
skills . . . as transposition, improvisation, and the playing of jazz
instruments. . . .

I repeat: the young seek independence and must, therefore, be
given opportunities for group activity and independent forms of
expression that are authentically theirs. (*Ibid.*, pp. 7–8)

The debate does not employ such concepts as "muse-ical child
culture" or "children's muse-ical mother tongue," nor does it
attempt to refine such concepts as "music" *(muzyka)* or "musicality" *(muzykalnost)* in relation to children's global and existential
mooring in the values and norms peculiar to child culture. It does
appear, however, that the premises for such a debate are now

firmly in place in this country where both children and music are regarded as very important.

The contrast between St. Petersburg and Los Angeles is at least as great as that between Oslo and St. Petersburg. After living for a year in the vicinity of this sprawling metropolis, I formed several dominant impressions.

Los Angeles is one of the largest cities in a country that prides itself on being a great superpower and has a population some sixty times greater than Norway's. It is a city where a bewildering array of TV channels broadcast programs around the clock, seven days a week, with frequent interruptions for commercials. In 1986, 784 murders were reported, and it is not safe for children to play outdoors after dusk—but a four-year-old child with the requisite charm and acting skill can earn a fortune as a superstar in TV commercials promoting popcorn and breakfast cereal.

Los Angeles is a city of multimillionaires living in luxurious villas and drug-addicted Vietnam War veterans sleeping in abandoned cars—contrasting products of the American dream. It teems with people of all races and shades of color, like the rest of this immense land whose diversity is so great as to defy generalizations.

In Los Angeles, "the entertainment capital of the world," children grow up with Hollywood, Beverly Hills, Sunset Boulevard, and Disneyland as part of their everyday environment. Here, throughout much of the twentieth century, movies, the most significant cultural invention of this century, were cultivated more assiduously than anywhere else, setting norms for hundreds of millions of people across the barriers of language and culture. Los Angeles is the only city in the world that has an airport named after a film star: John Wayne Airport.

The outward appearance of Los Angeles is also the object of good-natured American humor. People ask: Where are the skyscrapers? Where is downtown? For Los Angeles, unlike most large cities, is *horizontal*, consisting of a vast collection of smaller communities. Angelinos themselves sometimes speak of this place with self-deprecating irony as "forty suburbs in search of a city" or "the nowhere city of California."

In Los Angeles, gangs of young hoodlums engage in bloody street wars, and drug problems and the associated violence are of a magnitude totally unknown in Oslo or St. Petersburg. The right to buy and carry weapons, a legacy of frontier life, is taken for granted, and the milk carton on the breakfast table contains not only information about fat content and calories, but pictures of missing children above the poignant question, "Have you seen me?"

California's bright sun shines down on the private homes, the affluence, the marvelous beaches, and the myriads of open, friendly, tanned, and unusually helpful people who live in this remarkable place on the edge of the Pacific. California and Los Angeles boast some of the finest research and most advanced technology in the world. The *Los Angeles Times* is one of the glories of America's vaunted free press, so outstanding that the best products of journalism in Oslo and St. Petersburg pale by comparison.

How does child culture fare in this part of the world, different in so many ways from both Oslo and St. Petersburg?

NEIL POSTMAN AND THE "DISAPPEARANCE OF CHILDHOOD" IN AMERICA

The United States was an obvious choice as a site for my study of musical child culture from a transcultural and transpolitical perspective. It is the acknowledged leader of the Western world, and it seemed important to gather material that could be compared with my findings in Russia. Moreover, in 1982 Neil Postman published a book advancing the thesis that child culture in America was in danger of being destroyed by television. *The Disappearance of Childhood* created alarm in Europe as well as the United States, for Europeans are altogether too familiar with the phenomenon of America's terrifying problems today becoming Europe's tomorrow. Was this yet another example?

A reading of Postman's book makes it evident that its title is more dramatic than its content. It was as a student of the *media,* not of child culture, that Postman had entered the debate. He had no scientific, systematic data regarding child culture in America to back up his claims. His argument was based on nothing more substantial than anecdotal accounts and subjective impressions. Nonetheless, the myth of the disappearance of childhood in America took hold in Norway and elsewhere.

According to Postman, it was only with the invention of the printing press that a clear distinction was established between adults and children as more and more adults acquired a skill that children could not share with them: the ability to read and write. Literacy, Postman maintained, separated children from adults in a way that was qualitatively unknown in the Middle Ages, when a common oral culture was shared by all. Later, when children were sent to school to learn to read and write, and little by little to become adults, they began to identify themselves as a separate group—developmentally, socially, and in terms of their level of knowledge. Children, says Postman, became more clearly identified as children, adults as adults.

Against this background, Postman advances his principal thesis: television's audiovisual mass culture, which, like pre-Gutenberg oral culture, is shared by adults and children, is bringing about the disappearance of childhood as a specific category. You do not need to know how to read and write in order to understand what is presented on television, he says. Thus a fundamental difference between children and adults with respect to knowledge and the ability to acquire knowledge is removed.

Postman's analysis contains, of course, some interesting points, but it has *nothing to do* with child culture as a playful fellowship of young human beings. Children play, whether or not they have access to books. Childhood as playing culture is something quite different from childhood as reading culture. Children at play constitute an oral folk culture, physically and muse-ically, one in which the children themselves determine the values and norms. Childhood learning to read comprises a disciplined literate culture, abstract and intellectual, based on values, ideals, and norms set by adults. This point will be discussed further in the next chapter. For the present it is enough to say that Postman, in my view, is quite wrong in maintaining that school and the literate culture it represents are the principal guarantors of playful childhood.

That is not to deny that television may indeed play a role in weakening the interest of some children in books and enlarging the sphere of knowledge shared by adults and children. But so what? Insofar as television represents a threat to children's play, it is not because its method of communication is oral rather than written. On the contrary, *oral* forms of communication are entirely congruent with child culture. If television is a threat to children's play it is because it robs them of their time, not because it uses the wrong form of communication.

My working hypothesis as I began what was to be a full year of research was that the United States, notwithstanding its plethora of television channels constantly spewing forth an endless variety of programs, *must* have a playful child culture. On the basis of my findings in Oslo and St. Petersburg I had also developed a theory about universal play processes among children, and I hoped that my observations of American children would either confirm or disconfirm this theory.

CHILDREN'S SPONTANEOUS SINGING:
OUR MUSE-ICAL MOTHER TONGUE WORLDWIDE

Let it be said immediately that my observations in Southern California left no doubt that children's play is by no means "a dying art" in the United States. I observed countless instances of children at play both in Los Angeles proper and in nearby Dana Point, where I lived in 1986–87. This will come as no surprise to my American readers, most of whom observe the same phenomenon daily. The urge to play among children is universal.

In the schoolyards one quickly recognizes games and other playful activities common to children everywhere, irrespective of national boundaries and differing political systems: ball games, jump rope, tag, singing games, clapping games, and hopscotch. When American children jump rope to "Teddybear, Teddybear," the rhythm and the rules—yes, the inherent *magic* of the game— are absolutely identical to the Norwegian equivalent that I remember from my childhood and that my children and their friends still play today. I did note one interesting difference, however. American children, unlike their Norwegian counterparts, often initiated the game with a musical "introduction" that is a variant of one of child culture's most familiar song formulas.

Blue bells! Jing- le bells! E- vee, I- vee, o- ver!

I also observed many more ball games of various kinds among American schoolchildren during recess periods than I did in Norway. The availability of a large number of television channels did not seem to make them any less inclined to play ball than Norwegian or Russian children. Indeed, the very opposite may be true: watching professional sports teams on television may create dreams of becoming the next Michael Jordan, the next Orel Hershiser pitching the Dodgers to victory in the World Series. I understand such dreams, for I once *was* Jesse Owens.

Nor is playfulness by any means limited to youngsters in the lower grades, for there is also a thriving play culture among teenagers. In California, skateboards are enormously popular. One sees children and young people playing with them everywhere: sidewalks, streets (dangerous!), gas stations, parking lots, schoolyards. The range of skill reminded me of skiers: everything from beginners who can barely move without falling down to experts who perform incredible acrobatic feats of balance and agility. And surfboards: the hot sun and sandy beaches of Southern California attract an endless throng of young people who swim out into the surf, boards in hand, to prove their skill atop the biggest waves the mighty Pacific has to offer. These young people are contemptuously turning their backs on television's soap operas, talk shows, dating games, and all the rest in favor of "fun in the sun" in their Western paradise.

The subjects of my research in the United States, however, were not the sun-tanned devotees of surfboard culture but, as in Oslo and St. Petersburg, preschool and kindergarten children. I employed the same methodology as in the previous two studies so that the results might be comparable.

Many of the people who live in Los Angeles are recent immigrants, especially from Mexico, whose northern border lies only a couple of hours' driving time from the city. Indeed, it is now predicted that by the end of the century over half of the inhabitants of California will be Mexican-Americans. The existence of this large and identifiable subgroup made it possible for me to conduct separate studies among children of European and of Mexican descent. Moreover, it was not difficult to find kindergartens and preschools containing homogeneous groups of each. Many of the Hispanic children were from families who had entered the country illegally, and not a few lacked even a minimum mastery of English. They preferred to speak Spanish, both among themselves and with their teachers, many of whom knew a little Spanish.

Kindergarten is an integral part of the K-12 system of education in the United States, and this is reflected in the curriculum. The emphasis is on academics: the children are led through a fixed program of instruction in reading, arithmetic, science, and social studies, with "breaks" for play, rest, and other activities. During art class, it was far more common for children to be instructed to "draw a picture like the one in the book," or to color or cut out a predrawn picture, than for them to create pictures or cutouts of their own choosing. The children quickly learned to signal their desire to say something by raising their hand. In striking contrast to similar schools in Norway and Russia, singing and music activities were almost totally absent. According to my conversations with kindergarten teachers, development in the direction of a fixed curriculum for these predominantly five-year-old children has accelerated during the past twenty years. One suspects that the "superbaby syndrome" has had something to do with the transformation of the American kindergarten from a play-based to a book-based enterprise.

A kindergarten experience of this kind undoubtedly tends to suppress the development of children's natural playfulness. Only in the preschools, where increasing numbers of American children spend their weekdays while both parents are at work, does one find more typical manifestations of child culture—and even here the effects of the superbaby syndrome are discernible. One finds more free play and spontaneous singing than in a typical American kindergarten, but elements of the school curriculum are filtering down into the preschools as well. Many three- and four-year-olds are being encouraged to learn their letters and their numbers—and even to read—so that they will be "ready for school." The inherent absurdity of imposing such premature literacy on toddlers was effectively, albeit unwittingly, expressed in a ceremony at one such school in which the oldest children were dressed up in little caps and gowns and "graduated" into kindergarten! One wonders whether their parents laughed at the comedy of the spectacle, wept for their offsprings' vanishing childhood, or merely clapped in appreciation of what they assumed was a good thing.

In order to get a representative sample of the spontaneous singing activities of young American children, then, I found it necessary to make observations in both preschools and kindergartens. To facilitate comparison with similar observations in Oslo and St. Petersburg, I will present my findings under the same rubrics.

SONG FORM

All three of the song forms initially identified in my study of preschool children in Oslo were present in the spontaneous singing of American children as well.

Here are several examples of fluid/amorphous song. Brian, Chris, and Fred are playing together in a corner of the room, building a jet fighter and rockets out of Legos. At a certain point in their play they themselves *become* jet fighters: with a rocket in each hand they run around, arms outstretched, pretending to "bomb" each other, singing rhythmically as they play. Cesar, a little Mexican boy, drones absentmindedly as he plays with a jigsaw puzzle. Juliana goes around straightening up the activity stations, humming contentedly as she works. No words, no "tune" in the usual sense, just happy noise. If I had closed my eyes I could have imagined that I was in Oslo or St. Petersburg.

I observed many examples of the use of song formulas. The

calling formula observed in my earlier studies appeared again and again.

Each part of the world has its own ways of noting the passing of the seasons. In Southern California, the migration of the gray whales close to the shore is an annually recurring sign that spring will soon be here. Great herds of these forty-ton giants of the sea pass near Dana Point en route from the Barents Sea to the warm waters of the Gulf of California, where they will bear their young. The spectacle naturally makes a deep impression on children as well as adults. Young Ted expresses himself in song as he draws a whale.

Both the major and the minor descending third are used for calling by children in the United States.

The "teasing" formula occurs frequently in the spontaneous singing of American children, sometimes with texts that threaten as well as tease.

In the next example, Judy is hanging by her knees from the top of the jungle gym. She sings to let her playmates know how brave she is.

I am quite sure that even without understanding the words, Scandinavian children, upon hearing Judy's song, would comprehend its inherent meaning, for the song in conjunction with an act perceived as daring has a fairly universal significance. The same transcultural relationship is plain to see as Thomas crawls around on the floor, recklessly driving his toy car through the blocks.

I'm gon- na hit you! Out of my way, out of my way!

Finally, he parks his car in the block-garage. With a long, lingering tone he coaxes it into place, mimicking the sound of an idling engine. Even more complex formulas—musical aphorisms hovering between song formulas and jingles—are shared by the children of Los Angeles and Oslo.

Thanks for the dough- nut, splish, splash!

As- ke på du- ken, spell spar!

I observed relatively few instances of spontaneous use of *standard* songs among American children. The principal reason for this was not far to seek, for my research on the spontaneous singing of Norwegian children had shown me that the songs children adapted to their own purposes were by and large those they learned from their preschool teachers. The relative infrequency of such song use by American children, then, was a direct and predictable consequence of the virtual absence of adult-led singing in the kindergartens I observed. Extensive television-watching, which appears to be the rule rather than the exception in most American homes, also does little to promote singing among American children.

Nonetheless, I did observe a few examples of the adaptation of standard songs. One of the kindergarten classes in Dana Point, for example, had a "music hour" once a week for a period of several weeks. The songs the children learned during these few hours quickly became part of their repertoire and found their way into their daily experience. This was one of their favorites.

One day when one of the children wanted to chide a classmate who seemed a bit conceited about his reading ability, he sang this.

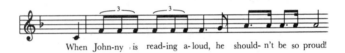

An old 45-rpm record of a song entitled "My Wonderful Bodymachine" was played occasionally. Its purpose was to teach the children to appreciate and take proper care of their bodies. Jennifer, however, found another use for the refrain, which she thought perfectly described her copy of a picture of a house.

Two songs are so deeply rooted in American folk culture that they might almost be called badges of cultural identity: "Happy Birthday" and "Jingle Bells." A birthday isn't a real birthday without the former, nor is Christmas complete without the latter. But both are used, *mutatis mutandis,* for many purposes other than the original ones. I once observed some boys who had watched the daring aerobatics of the Blue Angels on television, and who were now running around with arms outstretched pretending to be the intrepid pilots of those graceful flying machines. As they flew, they sang.

I'm fly-ing a plane. I'm fly-ing a plane!

One hears countless parodies of "Happy Birthday," of which the following is both representative and, I am told, widely known in American child culture.

> Happy birthday to you,
> You live in the zoo.
> You smell like a monkey,
> And you look like one, too!

I once heard a quite astonishing adaptation of "Jingle Bells" in a preschool that provided an environment where children were encouraged to express themselves with considerable freedom. It started with four-year-old Brian, who was playing on the floor with his plastic dinosaurs. He imagined that they were eating spring flowers, and as he played he began to sing. Then the children around him picked up his song, and soon the dinosaur version of "Jingle Bells" resounded so loudly that it could be heard throughout the building.

Di-no-saurs, di-no-saurs, eat-ing all day long! Di-no-saurs, oh di-no-saurs, eat-ing all day long!

Song Use

The patterns of use previously observed in Oslo and St. Petersburg appeared again among American children. In several situations the concrete examples were so similar as to be interchangeable, further supporting the supposition that child culture has a universal character and identity as a muse-ical life form.

A. Analogical Imitation: Song as a Concrete Part of Play

The American boys dropped their Lego rockets to the accompaniment of a spontaneous song that was identical to that of the Norwegian boy whose song mimicked his paper airplane as it crashed to the ground. The descending glissando that traced the path of the airplane and the path of the rockets was the same in both cases. And when Thomas carefully parked his play car in the garage with the help of a long, sustained note, he was singing from the same score as Natasha, who "hummed" her chair across the floor in that kindergarten in far-off St. Petersburg. It appears, then, that we are justified in positing a propensity to analogical imitation as an inherent feature of child culture, one shared by all children regardless of the national or political setting in which they happen to live. All children learn, play, and think in wholes, in ecological totalities whose elements are closely interrelated.

B. Symbolic Representation:
Use of "Song-words" to Tease, Report, Call, Command, Ask, Reply

I also found that American children are like Norwegian and Russian children in their use of song formulas as a method of communication. Moreover, the content of these songs does not appear to depend on the American context, for they serve the same purposes in the other countries. The three principal examples of song formulas I observed in the spontaneous singing of children in Norway—the descending major and minor thirds and the teasing song—are also the principal ones used by American children. It appears that a pair of five-year-olds from the United States and Norway, though they might not understand a word of each other's spoken language, would understand each other very well if one of them were to taunt the other with the teasing formula that is more or less common to their musical vocabulary.

I also note as a matter of interest that in California this formula was nearly always used with a descending third preceding the top tone, like this.

Only once during my year in California—while several young-sters in a swimming pool were energetically splashing water on each other—did I hear it used without this feature. My impres-sion is that American children typically use the formula as shown above, and this impression is confirmed by my conversations with American friends whose observations span many years.

The American version of the teasing formula, then, differs slightly from the Norwegian, which more often than not omits the descending third preceding the top tone. Thus my American data, too, fail to confirm the theory that the teasing formula is as universal in use and form as had previously been supposed. At a minimum it must be allowed that there are regional differences.

C. Song as Background Coloration

It is not easy for spontaneous singing to find its natural place in a kindergarten system where such traditional school values as disci-pline, quiet, and order prevail. Any unsolicited singing that might "disturb" other children is quickly silenced by conscientious teachers who undoubtedly mean well, but who know little about the importance of spontaneous singing in the natural development of children. Nonetheless, an occasional instance of cautious hum-ming did manage to get past the censor from time to time in the classes I observed. Indeed, humming—in short snatches in con-junction with reading, working a jigsaw puzzle, or some other activity—appears to be the principal form of spontaneous singing among American preschool children—always in an obedient *pia-nissimo*. This was especially true of the Mexican children, who found here an emotional refuge in an alien culture in which their inability to understand or speak standard English often left them bewildered and afraid. It was good to hum, perhaps in concert with some familiar and comforting Spanish words running through their heads.

To a European, the curriculum of an American kindergarten is something of an anomaly. Clearly, *white masculine* America has decided that the emphasis will be on intellectual pursuits in a quiet atmosphere, and that little or no time will be devoted to muse-ical activities. But how can this be in kindergartens that lie virtually in the shadow of a world-renowned center of movie music and dance? How can this be in the United States, home of a vital music culture that is admired throughout the world, one that draws its inherent strength and hypnotic power directly from Africa's own *ngoma?* Why do not American kindergartens also reflect that *other* America, the America of blues, soul, and spirituals, the heritage preserved through the singing of such great black artists as Billie Holiday and Mahalia Jackson? The whole world remembers how, not so many years ago, this music energized the civil rights movement as hundreds of thousands of Americans—old and young, black and white—joined their voices in the mighty freedom songs that would eventually shake the foundations of institutionalized bigotry. We Europeans watched in amazement as Martin Luther King and his followers harnessed the power of song to defeat the forces of hate and oppression: "Oh, freedom . . ." "We shall overcome . . ."

American educators explain that there isn't time for everything and that the curriculum must therefore be limited to those things judged most important for children's growth and learning. I would only point out as a fact that might suggest a reconsideration of these priorities that the dropout rate in American schools is steadily climbing and currently exceeds twenty percent at the high school level.

SONG FUNCTION

On the whole the data from my American study confirm that song is an integral part of children's spontaneous play. For these children, too, play and song were observed to be fundamental components of their experience of life and their natural mode of expression. In this they are at one with Norwegian and Russian children, and doubtless with children throughout the world. In the children of California, as in those I had observed previously, physical movements and muse-ical sounds were typically united in a manner clearly identifiable as an expression of the *ngoma* of child culture. The examples given above show how the songs of American children, too, sometimes take on a linguistic character, thereby fulfilling important functions in the children's lives, both individually and collectively.

It is not necessary to repeat what has already been said in considerable detail about the functions of song and play in the life and experience of children. Suffice it to say that for American children, as for the others I have observed, spontaneous singing is related to the internalization of life experience and learning as part of an ongoing process of maturation and socialization. It is also closely related to the development of individual and cultural identity.

IS THE SPONTANEOUS SINGING OF CHILDREN
A MUSE-ICAL MOTHER TONGUE OF UNIVERSAL SIGNIFICANCE?
The dream of finding the key to universals in music is old, and in a way almost dangerously alluring. The idea of music as "the common language of the heart" among human beings everywhere is an innate, intuitive notion among both the learned and the unlearned. We cannot resist at least posing the question: *Do* children everywhere share a common muse-ical mother tongue?

Many more scholars must study children's singing in many more countries before we can claim to have established a definitive answer. For now I can only offer a few provisional considerations regarding this fascinating question.

First, it seems clear to me that insofar as play and communication are universal human phenomena, children's singing is also a universal human phenomenon. Second, spontaneous singing as a cultural process, as discussed earlier in this chapter, is a universal *sine qua non* of child culture. Third, I am inclined to think that the spontaneous singing of children exhibits some universal features in both *use* and *function.* The significance of such singing for socialization, identity, cognitive development, communicative ability, and general human growth undoubtedly holds not only for children throughout the world, but for all oral and muse-ical folk cultures. Thus we are dealing here with universals that are not only transnational but *transgenerational,* for oral folk cultures include people of all ages. The astonishing parallels between K. Anyanwu's discussion of African folk culture and my findings concerning children's singing certainly suggest the likelihood that some true generalizations common to both groups may yet be established.

With respect to the question of common musical *forms*, the evidence suggests that we must be very cautious. I think it is likely that the *categories* of song forms that I observed in three different countries—fluid/amorphous, formulas, and standard—could be found in the spontaneous singing of children elsewhere as well. These categories are in fact so broad that they can be construed to include many elements of children's behavior in addition to spontaneous singing. Children's play in general, for example, could be studied and classified on the basis of a similarly dynamic understanding of its forms as they become manifest in us. Indeed, it is one of the central theses of this book that song and play are two sides of the same underlying reality.

My studies have also shown that certain characteristics recur in the song forms used by children in different countries. These regularities are most striking in the song formulas: descending thirds appeared, for example, in the "calling" formula used by Norwegian, Russian, and American children. The descending third has long been an object of special study by music ethnologists. Curt Sachs (1977) maintained, for example, that this simple motive is related to the physiology of the human voice, i.e., the natural tension-and-release mechanism whereby a short vocal outcry is produced. The teasing formula, the universality of which has often been asserted in the past, does not seem to be so widely used after all. My research, in any case, found it frequently used by Norwegian, somewhat less frequently by American, and never by Russian children.

My central conviction regarding this matter is that all cultural expressions are formed on the basis of a concrete human reality but are firmly anchored in the surrounding culture. No song form as such is universally given to us from above. Thus the wide dissemination of the teasing formula, for example, is probably to be understood as an ethnocentric product that has gradually made its way into the musical vocabulary of much of the earth's population. I suspect, in any case, that further research will show that many of the children of the world manage to tease each other in song *without* making use of this vaunted "original" teasing formula.

The ethnocentric origin of spontaneous singing can be seen most clearly in the use of standard songs. Despite the influence of the mass media, which spread a common body of music throughout the world with astonishing rapidity and enormous power, the music culture of each country retains a certain individuality by virtue of the national cultural milieu that places its inimitable mark on everything it receives. This national trove is the natural point of departure for children's use of standard songs. I have never visited Tibet, but I have no doubt that the songs of Tibetan children reflect Tibetan culture just as surely as those of Norwegian, Russian, and American children reflect the cultures of their countries.

This type of song material is for the most part communicated to children during the earliest and most impressionable period of their life—as mother, father, grandparents, and other loving adults sing to them. The phenomenon of adults singing to children is, perhaps, universal, but the content of what is sung varies from one culture to another. These songs take root in the children's consciousness long before the mass media launch their assault by means of cassettes, CDs, radio, and television. Thus human beings have an advantage over the mass media, as a result of which child culture always exhibits national characteristics even as it embodies universal processes of play, song, and general development. This understanding of the process whereby the elements of a national culture are transmitted from one generation to the next underscores once again how important it is for parents to *sing* to their children.

But the mass media also have an influence on spontaneous singing, providing a "second layer" of standard song material that is common to children in many countries. Thus it is not surprising that children who live oceans apart sometimes use such songs for their own purposes. Thanks to the mass media, "Happy Birthday" is known and loved by children in many lands. Moreover, because birthday parties are such important events in the lives of children, this song often has a special place in their hearts. We have already looked at its use by some would-be Blue Angels in a kindergarten in Los Angeles. In Norway I observed a little girl sitting in a sandbox making loaves of bread out of coarse, wet sand, and as she worked she sang.

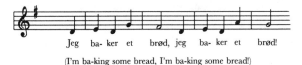

(I'm ba-king some bread, I'm ba-king some bread!)

It takes children to make the important point that a good recipe for bread should include song as one of the ingredients.

I knew, of course, that Norwegian children were familiar with "Happy Birthday," but I was flabbergasted one day as I observed a group of Russian preschool children playing hide-and-seek and heard one of them singing.

(I know where you are, I know where you are!)

What this example primarily shows, however, is that it is the occurrence of song as a playful sociocultural process among children that is universal. That children in three countries happened to use the same tune as the vehicle for their singing is accidental and of little importance. It is the predisposition to adapt for their own purposes the songs with which they are familiar that is universal, not the specific songs that have become their common property through the influence of the mass media.

The ongoing discussion about universals in music usually presupposes the Western European understanding of the concept of music. Earlier I tried to show that this concept is not adequate when one is discussing the unified muse-ical forms of expression and cognition characteristic of children. For this purpose one needs such concepts as *sikia* and *ngoma*. What we should be discussing is not music but *musikia,* a coinage that denotes the point where Western music and the *sikia*-world of children meet. In this context, studies of the spontaneous singing of children as a universal muse-ical mother tongue open the way to exciting new insights.

"I'm so happy. Only six months till I start school!"

5

The Muse-ical Child
Goes to School

> Be merciful, Lord.
> Show special compassion
> to those of thy creatures who are so logical,
> practical,
> realistic,
> that they are offended
> by somebody who can believe
> that there really is a little blue horse . . .
> —HELDER CAMARA

SILENT NIGHT

It was the first-graders' last day of school before Christmas vacation. Here we were: twenty-eight first-graders, thirty-three brothers and sisters, forty-two parents, and nine grandparents, all crowded into a classroom designed for thirty small children. But Christmas must be Christmas, even in school, and a special program to conclude the preholiday semester is a hallowed ritual in the life of every family with a first-grade child. It marks that special moment when your child, so recently a babe in arms, will make a public debut as a member of the class and performer of an assigned role in the Christmas program. The unruly horde as gentle flock, thanks to the teacher's magic wand.

The children were going to present a Christmas pageant, the roles having been assigned with due attention to their respective talents and sizes. The sheep had the easiest parts: completely covered with white acrylic costumes, all they had to do was crawl around on all fours and bleat occasionally. Many little sheep cavorted about the room, secure in the knowledge that they had no lines to remember. With a striking touch of pedagogical imagination, the teacher had given one of the most unruly boys in the class the part of Jesus. He was somehow squeezed into a manger that occupied a prominent place in front of the chalkboard. Overwhelmed by the importance of his role, he played a blissfully unperturbed Jesus, staring at the ceiling as his legs dangled clumsily over the sides of his little crib. Never before had he been so still for so long in a schoolroom.

There were also the three Wise Men, and Joseph and Mary—all slightly smaller than the babe in the manger. A couple of shepherds were there too, with colorful headbands and robes, each holding a ski pole in his right hand—the old type, made of bamboo. And of course the white-robed throng: the rest of the class, the heavenly host that according to St. Luke came down to the meadow near Bethlehem on that night long ago and sang praises to God. Draped in bedsheets, hair glittering with artificial jewels, a host of identical little angels.

Miss Hansen, the teacher, had worked hard with the angels, for it was their responsibility to bring the pageant to a suitable conclusion with a reverent performance of "Silent Night." She knew that this beloved carol would elevate the presentation above the ordinary, touching the hearts of the audience despite the hectic busyness of the season. She had even held extra rehearsals outside the regular school hours, teaching the children how to stand (feet twelve inches apart), how to breathe (with diaphragm support!), how to project their voices, how to deport themselves like a choir. She herself was a member of a choir and was confident of her expertise in this area. Drawing on her experience, she had even managed to teach some of the children the alto part. She eagerly awaited the moment when, in the third stanza of the carol, her little choir of angels would astonish the audience by singing in two-part harmony.

Some of the children were not allowed to sing in the angel choir, however. In a friendly but firm way, Miss Hansen had made it clear that four of the boys were better suited for other roles, especially Kjell, the naughtiest little rascal in the class. He seemed like a symbol of darkness in the midst of a celebration of light. Darkness was in his countenance, his voice, his soul. He clearly would have been out of place as a white-clad angel. No doubt Miss Hansen had thought carefully about how the droning monotones of Kjell and his three cohorts would spoil both the sound of the choir and the tender mood of the pageant. Naturally, every boy and girl in the class would participate in the program in some way, all in accordance with their talents. What, then, should Kjell and the others who couldn't sing be allowed to do? Miss Hansen had found an imaginative solution: they would be Christmas elves, right out of Santa's workshop! As soon as the concluding carol had been safely sung, they would come in with gifts for everyone. Miss Hansen had thought it through with attention to every detail.

For the most part, the pageant proceeded as planned. Oh, yes, one little sheep suddenly began bleating uncontrollably just as Melchior was about to present his costly gift to the baby Jesus, but that was merely amusing and detracted in no way from the performance. And then came the grand finale: the chorus of white-robed first-graders singing "Silent Night." There they stood among the sheep and the shepherds on the hillside near Bethlehem, feet placed just so, little diaphragms pumping assiduously, voices projecting just as they had been taught. These little angels left no doubt that they could carry a tune as they sang the familiar words.

Silent night, holy night . . .
Holy infant, so tender and mild,
Sleep in heavenly peace . . .

Even the alto part in the third stanza came through with great clarity—with the generous help of Miss Hansen's fine voice.

The moment was intended to be moving, and it was. The teacher quietly savored her triumph as expressions of childlike tenderness slowly transformed the weary adult faces in the audience. The hurrying and scurrying of the season were momentarily forgotten as the mood of peace and goodwill enveloped one and all. I too felt a tear trickle down my sweaty cheek as I sat in the back of that crowded room and listened to the program. And *my* daughter—wasn't she a sweet, darling little angel?

What happened next might be described as a swift journey from Bethlehem to bedlam. As if to provide comic relief, Miss Hansen slyly opened the door and admitted four wild little elves dressed in green and red—Kjell's little band of ruffians—who wasted no time in changing the mood from tenderness to pandemonium. Ignoring instructions, they tossed their gifts hither and yon in a wild display of pent-up energy and playfulness. Chaos, laughter, a babble of voices. The show was over.

Before leaving, we parents lined up to thank Miss Hansen for her work with our children and to wish her a merry Christmas. I was the last one to reach her, and it was just as well because she had a question for me. "As a specialist on children and music," she asked smilingly, "what did you think of our singing?"

What was I to say? She had conscientiously prepared the children for this program in accordance with her understanding of what ought to be done, and had even taken time for extra rehearsals with the angels. Which was more important for me in that situation, I wondered: to be polite and superficial, or to share my concern for those little monotones whose innate muse-icality I believed in?

Then I remembered little Per, and his song about the butterfly slowly began to echo in my head. And as Per's song grew louder within me, I remembered the face of a little boy who didn't talk much but often sang—off key. I kept this picture clearly in mind as I answered.

"Oh, yes, the singing, that was nice. Splendid, with that second part in the last stanza!"

Miss Hansen beamed with satisfaction.

"However," I said somewhat tentatively—and I saw her smile fade, but resolved to make my point anyway, hoping she would understand. "However, I think you should have included those four Christmas elves in your choir. For if God's son really was born in a stall in Bethlehem almost two thousand years ago, and if a heavenly host really did come down to earth to sing praises to God—well, I'm sure that in that multitude of the heavenly host there must have been many monotones just like them. Otherwise the song would never have been muse-ical enough to reach all the way to heaven."

Our Labyrinths

The newborn child encounters the world with innumerable possibilities. The child wonders and the adult responds to its wondering. The child asks and the adult answers. This is part of the inner dynamics of upbringing. The child's world grows constantly clearer and larger, but at the price of an equally constant diminution of the realm of the possible. Each answer excludes other possible answers, each insight other possible insights. If *this* is the way the world is, then it cannot be any of those other ways that to a child's mind might appear equally possible. Each question is a fork in the road, and with each answer a choice is made. Inescapably, necessarily, the child's world is steadily made to conform to that of the adult, however imperfect it may be. The child asks, "What is the world like?"—and we answer as if we knew! We give them *our picture* of the world, for that is all we have to offer. This is one of the unavoidable burdens of parenthood, one that sometimes makes us wish we could exchange roles with our child—or at least be a child once more.

> If I could go through it all again,
> the slender iron rungs of growing up,
> I would be as young as any,
> a child lost
> in unreality and loud music.
> —ROBERT LOWELL, "Realities"

The relationship between a child and its parents, however, is an integral part of a natural and spontaneous process of nurture. That parents make many important decisions for their children, and in so doing impose upon them their own convictions and values, is undeniable. At its best, however, this all occurs within a context in which each child feels that s/he is an integral part of a larger and meaningful whole. School, however, is a different matter, a setting in which the context and procedures of learning are determined not by nature but by human beings. What happens to a child's muse-ical potential when s/he goes to school? For schools, too, make choices for children. They, too, communicate ideas, values, convictions. How adequately do they protect and preserve children's inherent muse-icality?

We know that for altogether too many children, school turns out to be a cruel disappointment. They enter at age six, cheeks scrubbed, hair combed, eyes shining with anticipation. At eighteen, if they manage to see it through to the end, they sullenly accept their diploma and slink away in unconcealed disillusionment. What has gone wrong? Why—in Norway, Russia, the United States, and many other countries as well—do we have so many burnouts in our schools? All the debate about how to improve public education will yield nothing unless we unremittingly press the search for a better answer than we have found thus far to this critical question.

The Squelching of Childhood

I shall argue that the crux of the problem is a destructive collision between muse-ical child culture and a profoundly *un*muse-ical school culture. Schools are institutions engaged in the systematic repression of childhood. As a polemical point of departure, consider the following contrasts between the two cultures (hereafter referred to as the cultures-in-conflict list).

Child Culture	*School Culture*
Ecological integration	Pedagogical isolation
General life development	Progress in each subject
Existential	Formal

Child Culture	*School Culture*
Authentic	Secondhand
Continuity of time	Fragmentation of time
Wholeness *(ngoma)*	Specialization by subject
Canto, ergo sum	*Cogito, ergo sum*
Play	Study
Homo ludens	*Homo scribens*
Oral	Written
Being in	Reading about
Physical proximity	Physical distance
Testing one's own limits	Respecting boundaries set by others
Self-understanding	Teacher's evaluation
I can do it already	You still can't do it
Feeling of invincibility	Feeling of inadequacy
Muse-ical	Logical
Qualitative	Quantitative
Spontaneity	Following a schedule
Childlikeness	Forced maturity
Carpe diem! (Seize the day!)	Wait until you are older!
Exhilaration, ecstasy	Practicality
Intimacy	Distance
Courage	Uncertainty
Boldness	Caution
Empathy	Neutrality
Why	What
Creativity	Reproduction
Imagination	Technical reason
$1 + 1 \approx x$	$1 + 1 = 2$
Small blue horses	Harnessed horses
Emotional	Rational
Originality	Conformity
Improvised	Standard
The unexpected	The expected
Humor	Seriousness
Noisy	Quiet
Sensory	Intellectual
Physical movement	Physical inactivity

Child Culture	*School Culture*
I move—and I learn!	Sit still!
Unfolding of physical joy	Calisthenics
Egalitarian	Hierarchical
Self-control	Control by others
Freedom	Coercion
Commotion	Order
Uncompromising	Negotiable
Dionysian	Apollonian
Expanding limits	Confirming limits

When life forces encounter school thinking, continuity is interrupted. The child's urge to muse-icality, imprinted prenatally and reinforced in the relationship with parents and siblings and in play with other children, is suddenly confronted with powerful controlling forces that seem to oppose it at every turn. Many children fly high and far during their early childhood and assume numerous personae, from grimy-faced rowdy to soaring eagle. After a few years in school most of them no longer fly. They have become "muse-ically handicapped."

The transition from one chapter in the child's life to another, from one culture to another, is marked by an important rite of passage: the first day of school. The child trudges off, carrying within as a legacy of playful child culture the imperative that stands at the beginning of Ibsen's *Catiline:* "I must! I must! Deep down within my soul a voice commands, and I will do its bidding." In school the child suddenly confronts a new imperative and is told to heed it above all others: "You must! You must! High up, from the mouth of the teacher, a voice commands—and you will do its bidding!"

The primary locus of direction and control is suddenly shifting from self to other. The result? The autonomy of the process of cognition is shattered. Identity is threatened, tensions arise, and learning suffers. A disposition to learn must be rooted in a sense of freedom lying deep within oneself, or learning cannot occur. For what is learning? It is a *modification of the self,* a progressive alteration and extension of the self in relation to the world. If the self in all its human and muse-ical complexity is disdained, ignored, or even simply forgotten, the child will learn little. All children—indeed, all human beings—need this personal mooring in order to learn, whether in or out of school. The learner's sense of worth and respect for his/her own integrity are also critical: if our integrity is threatened, our ability to cope with life's challenges is also threatened.

Admittedly, the contrast between child culture and school culture is not absolute. *Of course* there are many schools in which spontaneity and creativity play important roles. One need not look far to find successful and happy pupils who spend their days in cheery classrooms with a warm, accepting teacher whom they will remember with affection for the rest of their lives. And *of course* one also finds in child culture such things as carrying out a plan, experiences of inadequacy, syllogistic reasoning, and moments of stillness. Indeed, the authentic kind of stillness in which a child is totally absorbed in an impression can be a vibrant manifestation of childlike spontaneity. In short, the world is not as neatly organized as the cultures-in-conflict list might seem to suggest.

Moreover, the degree to which schools acknowledge the legitimacy of the fundamental elements of child culture varies from one country to another. Norway, for example—perhaps because it does not carry the burden of being a superpower—has a much less authoritarian and less demanding program of instruction at the elementary level than either Russia or the United States. As of this writing, one still finds many schools in the United States where corporal punishment is permitted. In Russia, students in many schools are still expected to stand at attention beside their desks when answering a question.

Notwithstanding these qualifications, the list is useful as a way of setting in bold relief the astonishing differences between child culture and school culture. It demonstrates the important fact that we are dealing here with two *fundamentally different* cultures that are thrown into inescapable conflict when children go to school. The conflict occurs whether the children live in Norway, Russia, the United States, or—we surely are safe in concluding—any other country in the world.

I think an important clue to the progressive disillusionment of so many children during their school years is to be found in the numerous frontal collisions that inevitably occur when child culture and school culture meet. Children are notoriously at a disadvantage in relation to teachers, who are presented as authority figures who know what is best for them. Children can lose heart if the burden becomes too heavy to bear.

FROM AN ECOLOGY OF LEARNING TO THE STIFLING OF LEARNING

A *stifling of learning* occurs in the transition from child culture to school culture. The child is progressively detached from his/her muse-ical *ngoma* as s/he is subjected to alien forms of learning. Thus the child loses contact with something that lies very close to the center of his/her being, the vital crucible in which impressions and facts and values are molded into an authentic self. Indeed, for many children this process of detachment begins long before school, through the socialization process carried out by well-meaning parents and older siblings. For all children, however, the encounter with school represents something new: a massive and unremitting campaign to compel them to compartmentalize their learning. The intimate relationship between mind and body (Cobb), imagination and reason, inner world and external reality (Winnicott), is broken, and the authentic basis for learning is thereby weakened. Spontaneity is inhibited. Play and informality are banished to short recesses between class periods. The rationale for recess typically is that the children "should get some fresh air" before returning to the classroom for more learning. In fact, however, it is precisely during recess—the last bastion of child culture in the schools—that spontaneous play continues to yield authentic social, verbal, and sensorimotoric learning. In the school environment, the learning processes so common in the preschool years become rare (cf. Ziehe and Stubenrauch 1982). Even physical education is subjected to the dismal principles of a pedagogy in which quantitative thinking reigns supreme. For a child, it is a big jump from spontaneous activity in response to music to rigorous physical training, sit-ups and push-ups, stopwatches and records showing progress in meticulous detail. Even the enjoyment of physical activity is subordinated to the tyranny of numbers and the supremacy of technical reason as innocent schoolchildren are treated as if they were being prepared for Olympic competition.

Earlier we discussed in considerable detail the spontaneous processes through which children play, learn, and create. Impressions and expressions take multidimensional forms in which immediate and synchronous reciprocity among thought, action, and feeling give cognitive processes depth and a continuing grounding in the center of consciousness. Spontaneity is profoundly important for intimacy and warmth, involving, as we have seen, a pulsating network of analogical correspondences that unite the self with the world, thereby making reality intelligible. Bodily movement becomes the physical extension of thought, thought the psychological manifestation of the body. Respiration provides the coordinating rhythm that underlies thought, feeling, and bodily movement (Johnsen 1981). A stanza of a song makes an imagined scene or event vividly real and colorful. Such synchronization of the senses is called *synesthesia*. Children experience *sikia:* everything together in *one* unified whole, without division, where thought is physical perception and body is simultaneously mind. That is how they learn, from the very beginning of life, driven by a desire to conquer ever larger spheres of the physical and human world. Complex learning processes are in delicate ecological balance. It is through such processes, if all goes well, that children develop integrated personalities. They have spontaneous and immediate access to their own nearness and to the distance of others, with play as learning and learning as play. New phases in their cognitive-emotional development are merely expansions of this basic repertoire of complementary strategies of adaptation.

A child's ecological faculty of sensation functions as a tight network in which part and whole always work together and presuppose one another. If this fundamental muse-ical reality breaks down, the child's ability to learn is severely damaged. The squelching of childhood results in a *stifling of learning* as complex processes are divided into many unrelated fragments. Learning is no longer unified, authentic, and animated, as it must be if it is to take permanent root. Often the connections in the vital network are cut in pure ignorance by people who have good pedagogical intentions. Nonetheless, the consequences are tragic: the pathways binding feeling, thought, and body are closed; experience loses its depth, and learning its height. The cultures-in-conflict list may provide some clues as to how this comes about.

We are learning more all the time about what happens when nature's ecological balance is disturbed. When we deforest large areas of the earth, for example, we increase the probability of flooding. When we pollute a pristine Alaskan sound with petroleum, we introduce toxins into the food chain that endanger the lives of animals as well as humans. Growing concern for the environment is one of the major trends of our time. But how much do we really know about the ecology of the mind? Do we have any idea of the disastrous consequences we may be inviting when we "defoliate" the minds of children, depriving them of the unified way of dealing with the world that lies at the very heart of their being? Clearly, we need to broaden our thinking about ecology to include the *whole* of nature, in which human beings and their forms of living and learning constitute an important and integrated part. As Marcus Aurelius wrote long ago, in a passage addressed to himself, "This you must always bear in mind, what is the nature of the whole, and what is my nature, and how the one is related to the other, and what kind of a part it is of what kind of a whole" (*Meditations* II, 9).

No doubt the institutionalized stifling of learning is to some extent unavoidable, for children must lose some of their feeling of invincibility and naïve confidence in the adequacy of their present store of knowledge in the encounter with a formalized school system. They must, after all, be prepared for life in adult society. Schools are, among other things, the adult community's way of confirming and passing on the values regarded as essential to the continuity and stability of society.

Nonetheless, child culture also has a claim to respect and confirmation—indeed, it deserves to be recognized internationally as a basic human right. There is nothing in the social mandate of the schools that requires them to base their pedagogy primarily on adult values, as they do in country after country throughout the world. Impulses derived from children's own culture should be of central significance for the development of better schools and better societies. The basic idea is both simple and profound: "Learn from children—and children will learn from you!"

LITERACY AND ORALITY

To a large extent, the collision between child culture and school culture reflects the relationship between literate culture and oral culture in the Western world. Literate culture views itself as the superior form of culture. It claims a monopoly on values, prestige, and respectability, and its pretensions are rarely challenged. The written message is the means and the goal throughout the various stages of the educational process. Other cultures are characterized pejoratively as illiterate or primitive, often with overtones suggesting the general superiority of the white race. Walter J. Ong (1982) has proposed that these terms be replaced by the concept of *oral culture* in the hope that we might thereby escape some of our prejudices and reach a clearer understanding of the uniqueness, vitality, and values of such cultures. Ong is not interested in oral culture merely for its own sake, however. It is his thesis that a deeper understanding of oral cultures—their forms of communication and learning, their psychodynamic distinctiveness—will significantly enrich our understanding of what is unique about literate culture as well.

Children typically enter school as representatives of an oral culture. They are quickly immersed in a written culture that they are given to understand is vastly superior to their own. They are doubly unprepared, in the eyes of adults, for life in adult society: they do not yet know how to read or write, and tiny as they are, they are not yet complete human beings either physically or mentally. To be sure, such ideas are not explicit in the official pedagogy, but they are palpably present as an undercurrent. In the last analysis, schools are part of the adult world, places where the agents of literate culture attempt to mold children in their own image.

The situation today is paradoxical in many ways. While the

schools administer their writing-based programs, where all too often children are found wanting, a *secondary orality*—a new culture based on the printed word but communicated orally from child to child—is developing with lightning speed. Here, in the world of video players and computers, children often become instant experts. Armed with a competence for play derived from their own culture, they quickly surpass the hesitant fumbling with bewildering buttons and mysterious commands so typical of their parents' generation. What is called for here is curiosity and a playful attitude in interaction with a medium that provides auditory, visual, and tactile-motor sensations. Crowding around the computer screen, children can exchange experiences and show each other tricks in accordance with principles of oral communication common to child culture for generations. The danger is that this development will further widen the distance between children and the schools.

The prevailing view is that children go through a series of phases, and that schooling enables them to attain progressively higher levels of mental maturity and understanding. The highest level is what Piaget calls the symbolic-abstract phase: by the age of twelve, we are told, the child has finally acquired a rudimentary capacity to understand the world in the way that adults do. Neurologists confirm that by this time the brain's lateralization (distribution of functions to the left and right hemispheres) appears to have been completed in a long process of maturation, with logical-linear left dominance as the typical outcome.

But it seems fair to ask, Which came first, the chicken or the egg? Is the development of the twelve-year-old's capacity for abstract-symbolic thinking really a consequence of innate biochemical, neurological, and general psychological processes, common to all human beings regardless of their experience? Might it not rather be the case that this capacity results in considerable measure from the massive influence of literate culture as mediated by the schools? To what extent did Piaget, looking through Western European eyes, merely see himself in the mirror? Neurologists report that the brain continues to be formed up to the onset of puberty, thus leaving ample opportunity for the influence of environment. Is it not possible, then, that changes in patterns of function between the brain's two hemispheres can in some measure be traced back to the influence of the schools? It seems highly plausible that the dominance of literate culture in the early stages of the learning process leads in time to a corresponding dominance of abstract-symbolic thinking in thought processes.

It must be emphasized again and again that a child's "intelligence" includes much more than the purely logical-intellectual, for reason is a many-splendored thing. Howard Gardner, in *Frames of Mind* (1983), strongly opposes the one-sided cultivation of logical intellectualism in Western culture and emphasizes the importance of developing aesthetic-musical competence as an integral part of the learning and maturation process. He identifies seven forms of intelligence, all of which are in his view profoundly important for the development of the individual: linguistic, logical-mathematical, bodily-kinesthetic, spatial, musical, the ability to understand oneself, and the ability to understand others.

Gardner's work is a pioneering effort to create a much broader and more differentiated conception of the human capacity for understanding. Gardner stresses, among other things, the importance of musical intelligence for the understanding of reality. Unfortunately, he is often interpreted in such a way that he appears to fall into the typical Western trap of splitting up the human psyche into discrete skills. From my perspective, Gardner's various "intelligences" are best thought of as *modalities* of one underlying reality, *humankind's muse-ical intelligence.*

THE PEDAGOGY OF THE OPPRESSED

In 1970 the Brazilian educator Paulo Freire published an extraordinary book entitled *Pedagogy of the Oppressed,* in which he called attention to the frightening cleavage between the schools and the people of Latin America. The schools, as representatives of literate culture, were writing off as worthless the skills, needs, and ways of thinking of a whole continent, the daily life of many generations of victims of poverty and suffering. At best the schools were teaching their lessons to deaf ears; at worst they were contributing to the further oppression of their pupils. In many areas, according to Freire, schools "kill our curiosity, our inquiring mind and our creativity." Where the Brazilian schools saw a society filled with uncivilized ignorance and crying out for instruction, Freire saw a society filled with creative originality and cultural vitality. In the culture of the oppressed masses he found a key to the renewal of an ossified school system. He called it *the pedagogy of the oppressed:* a liberating school standing *with* the people in place of an oppressive school standing *against* them. Such a school, Freire argued, would have profound consequences not only for each individual but for the distribution of power and the political structure of the society. In 1985, Freire traced some of these implications further in *The Politics of Education: Culture, Power and Liberation.*

In the universal muse-ical life form as understood and described in this book lies an enormous potential for the development of a different kind of school, one in which the six-year-old is received with respect for what s/he already knows rather than with conde-scending sympathy because of the knowledge and skills s/he lacks. The condescension implicit in the traditional school is enshrined in the common American name for such institutions: *elementary* schools. Let us instead call this new type of school a *children's* school, not only because its pupils will be children but because its pedagogy will be governed by children's own characteristic forms of learning. Taking our clue from Freire, we might call this *the pedagogy of the Muse-bearers.*

It seems natural to ask: What should the central focus of the curriculum be in such a school? English? Mathematics? Foreign languages? Music? *The question misses the mark.* The central focus should not be on any subject, but on the child. Thinking in terms of an organized curriculum is itself a manifestation of a fragmenta-tion that militates against the muse-ical child's approach, in which the whole always determines the parts. In an ecological under-standing of learning and teaching, *everything that is taught—English, mathematics, music, whatever—should be muse-ical in form and content,* like so many streams flowing from the same mighty, inexhaustible fountain. How could the basis for a proper education for muse-ical beings be anything other than muse-ical? A firm commitment to such an approach in the classroom would enable children to preserve and use their innate and well-developed system of ecological learning processes, the underlying source of the physical, mental, verbal, playful, and musical analogical correspondences that enable knowledge to take root as true learning. Remember how seven-year-old Tan learned English in the course of several difficult and lonely months in Southern California—with a red rubber ball in his hand and a muse-ical imperative in his soul. Surely it must also be possible to keep this innate capacity for learning alive in the classroom to a much greater degree than is usually the case.

The idea of a school based on the child is of course not new. It has roots at least as far back as Rousseau's *Émile: "Réspectez l'enfance!"* ("Respect childhood!") Rousseau's thundering battle cry is as relevant today as it was in the eighteenth century. To respect childhood means, surely, to acknowledge the legitimacy of its inherent values, to grant it a voice in decisions affecting its welfare. But who consults children when decisions are made about the length of the school day, the nature of the pedagogy, or the content of the curriculum?

There is some evidence of a growing desire among teachers for a form of instruction more attuned to the needs of children, but we lack an adequate anthropological theory based on systematic studies of child culture to serve as a basis for such ventures. The teachers who are struggling to create real children's schools need the scientific support that might be provided by further research regarding the muse-ical interrelationship between play and learning. The weight of scientific evidence might then give further strength to Rousseau's demand to show respect for childhood.

"What about developmental psychology?" someone may ask. "Doesn't Piaget's description of the stages in the development of the preschool child constitute exactly this kind of scientific support?" The main features of this theory are indeed familiar: the sensorimotor stage from zero to two years, the preoperational stage from two to six, and the concrete-operational stage, which just happens to coincide—perhaps because we made it do so—with the earliest phase of formal schooling. Piaget's theories make a clear distinction between the preschool child and the schoolchild, and they also dictate that the characteristic features of preschool child culture cannot and should not be extended into the school setting.

In my opinion, this purely linear interpretation of stage theory represents a serious oversimplification of the relevant facts. Of course human beings constantly attain new levels in their journey from the cradle to the grave, but this in no way implies that the earlier achievements simply disappear. "The child is father of the man," as Wordsworth said. Each stage coexists with those that preceded it, thus providing an ever wider and deeper capacity for sensation and understanding. Six-year-olds are by no means just six-year-olds; they are the sum of everything they have been in the preceding years as well. The two-year-old and the four-year-old and the six-year-old live simultaneously in the same body and the same mind of the same first-grader. The different skills developed at various times are like the many registers of a pipe organ, and children are virtuosos who know their instrument well. They know how to alternate among the sensorimotoric, the preoperational, and the concrete-operational registers—and if the situation calls for it, to play *tutti* as well. Indeed, their virtuosity increases daily, for they are practicing all the time. This is a legacy of child culture shared by all children who are, as we say, "ready for school"— a vital resource that they bring along as they enter the classroom for the first time.

Throughout the six years preceding the first day of school, first-graders have demonstrated a determination to learn, an irrepressible will to persist. With unflinching courage, they have constantly met new challenges, scaled new heights, as single-mindedly as when they took those first uncertain steps toward Mother's or Father's outstretched arms. Such determination is based on something more fundamental than mere self-confidence. Children must be imbued with an innate feeling of invincibility and immortality in order to make their way in the world, to beat a pathway where they can run and sing and laugh and play—and therefore learn—with confidence. This is also the source of the triumph of inconvenience.

The first-grader's encounter with school obliterates this basic feeling of invincibility. The magic spell is broken—for upon entering school children are given to understand that *no* new pupil can do everything the school can do. This disillusioning recognition of their own inferiority relative to the school is part of the self-concept of all children, no matter how bright they may be. In the ledger of knowledge, all of them—the bright as well as the slow—are entered on the debit side. Thinking in terms of children's "deficits" is a traditional principle of organization in the school's hierarchical structure of knowledge control. This type of thinking is firmly entrenched and supports its case by pointing to a numbingly long inventory of knowledge and skills that the child must master enroute to membership in adult society. "Children must earn adulthood by becoming both literate and well-mannered" (Postman 1982, p. 88).

Pippi Longstocking, the Bobbsey twins, the Boxcar children: in the worlds of Astrid Lindgren, Laura Lee Hope, Gertrude Chandler Warner, and others, children are always perceived as heroes and heroines. Paradoxically, the word "childish" is often used as a term of derision, coloring and reflecting our Western attitude toward children. These negative connotations reveal something about adult society's view of children as immature, primitive, and incomplete candidates for adulthood. A more adequate understanding of the uniqueness and value of child culture should lead, however, to a redefinition of "childishness" in which the unequivocally positive content enshrined in the immortal stories and poems of childhood is restored once and for all. Much is at stake, for authentic childishness is the mother lode of all human creativity, originality, and candor. As the child matures during the long march from the first day of school to the last, the preservation of childishness as a resource profoundly important for life and learning should be an explicit objective. In this way, perhaps, *homo scribens* can become truly literate by remaining *homo ludens* at the same time.

In Praise of the Illiterate

Child culture is a form of oral culture that spans the globe. Numbering over 750 million strong, children under seven years of age constitute a majority of the world's illiterates.

In our enlightened Western world the very concept of "illiteracy" is a negative one. It is easy for us to regard someone who cannot read or write as primitive, ignorant, and unintelligent. We who are full of book learning tend to think that it is only their lack of literacy that prevents them from leading more rewarding lives. The reality is more complex, however. Those who are illiterate, as Paulo Freire has observed, constitute a highly diverse group of people. Freire has some words of warning regarding the ill-considered attempts of zealots to spread the gospel of literacy.

> In certain circumstances the illiterate man is the man who does not need to read. In other circumstances, he is the one to whom the right to read was denied. In either case, there is no choice.
>
> In the first case the person lives in a culture whose communication and history are, if not always, at least mostly oral. Writing does not bear any meaning here. In a reality like this, to succeed in introducing the written word and with it literacy, one needs to change the situation qualitatively. Many cases of regressive literacy can be explained by the introduction of such changes, the consequence of a Messianic literacy naïvely conceived for areas whose tradition is preponderantly or totally oral. (1985, p. 13)

Freire's statement regarding illiterates generally can be applied to the school's relationship to the oral culture of children. From a muse-ical point of view, the school's heavy emphasis on literate culture represents a drastic and by no means uniformly successful assault on another culture that is inherently oral. I trust it goes without saying that I am not challenging either the necessity or the importance of the ability to read and write. These are vital skills for people in our society, and the schools would be remiss in their responsibility if they did not teach them. The point is to soften the one-sided and unqualified stress on the unlimited superiority of literacy—even for children at the tender age of six or seven. This stress blinds us to the inherent value of child culture as a resource for learning and to the defects of prevailing methods of teaching reading and writing. We know perfectly well that our schools do not produce large numbers of passionate readers or enthusiastic writers. The ability to recite the alphabet and a few spelling rules by heart does not add up to an ability to read and write—and it most emphatically does not constitute a true love of reading or of literature.

The German author Hans Magnus Enzensberger addressed this very point in a speech given in 1985.

> One third of the population on our planet gets along without being able to read and write. Some 850 million people are in this situation, and the number will certainly grow larger.
>
> ... It is only we—i.e., the small minority of people who read and write—who could ever get it into our heads to regard those who do not have these skills as a small minority. Such an idea reveals an ignorance that I cannot accept.
>
> On the contrary: when I look at him more closely, the illiterate person appears to me to be in many ways an admirable figure. I envy him his memory, his ability to concentrate, his cunning, his inventiveness, his perseverance, and his keen hearing. . . .
>
> You may ask why a writer, of all people, argues the case for those who cannot read. . . . But the reason is obvious: it was the illiterates who invented literature! Their elementary forms—from the myth to the nursery rhyme, from the fairy tale to the ballad, from the prayer to the riddle—are all older than the art of writing. Without oral transmission there would be no poetry, without illiterates there would be no books. (1986, pp. 70, 71)

The vast majority of the languages of the world are spoken by people who are illiterate. Of some three thousand known languages, only eighty or so are associated with a developed written culture (Ong 1982).

Enzensberger contrasts the illiterates of oral cultures with the "secondary illiterates" of a society dominated by modern mass media—people who can indeed recite the alphabet by heart, but who can neither read nor write in a deeper human sense. Supported by the superficial consumerism of television and the tabloids, and without needed support from the school system, this mechanical and shallow human being has become a dominant figure in Western society according to Enzensberger.

[The secondary illiterate] is content, for the loss of memory from which he suffers causes him no pain. That he is not in charge is a comfort to him. That he is incapable of concentrating is something he regards positively. He considers it a good thing that he neither knows nor understands what is happening to him. He is mobile. He is adaptable. He wields a considerable amount of power. There is no need, then, for us to feel sorry for him. Also contributing to the well-being of the secondary illiterate is the fact that he has not the slightest inkling that he is a secondary illiterate. He considers himself well-informed, is able to decipher simple written instructions, pictograms, and checks, and he lives his life in a world that is hermetically sealed off from any temptation to self-awareness. . . .

The secondary illiterate is a product of a new phase in industrialism. [We now have] an economy in which the problem is no longer production, but the sale of goods . . . which requires qualified consumers. . . . Even as this problem has emerged, however, our technology has developed the adequate solution: the ideal medium for the secondary illiterate is television. (1986, pp. 73, 74)

SECONDARY ILLITERACY IN THE UNITED STATES

Is Enzensberger right? Where is the evidence? To what extent are we dealing here with anything more than a sharply worded and thought-provoking polemic from a Central European writer and intellectual?

Not long after Enzensberger's speech, evidence in support of his frightening thesis appeared in an official publication of the U.S. government. In 1987, some shocking official statistics were published in *The Nation's Report Card: Learning to Be Literate in America.* The alarm was sounded in the Preface.

Our high schools graduate 700,000 functionally illiterate young people every year—and another 700,000 drop out. According to Secretary of Labor William E. Brock, it is an "insane national tragedy" that 700,000 high school graduates get diplomas each year and cannot read them.

In 16 states, dropout rates range from 26 percent to 42 percent, and most big cities are at the high end of that. What's worse, most of those who do stay in school don't learn enough to meet even minimum academic standards.

Today, nine out of 10 colleges offer noncredit remedial courses in English and math to their incoming freshmen. The U.S. Department of Education says that as many as three out of five high school graduates who enter college require remedial work.

If current demographic and economic trends continue, American business will have to hire a million new workers a year who can't read, write or count. Teaching them how, and absorbing the lost productivity while they're learning, will cost industry $25 billion a year for as long as it takes—and nobody seems to know how long that will be. . . .

Clearly, we have to rethink our education system from the ground up. Reform and reorganization are desperately needed. (Applebee, Langer, and Mullis 1987, pp. 3–4)

According to this study, fully twenty-four percent of American eighteen-year-olds are functionally illiterate. Later in the report they are described as having a reading ability such as to enable them "to derive a surface understanding from relatively simple material." The report asserts further that only twenty-one percent of the students are capable of an independent summary and critical evaluation of more complex written material, which the report identifies as genuine literacy. The functionally literate, in other words, constitute a distinct minority among these students.

All parties to the debate concerning the condition of education in America acknowledge the validity of the statistics in reports such as this, but all do not agree on the necessity of drastic reform. Professor of literature Robert Pattison, for example, views what he calls "America's bankrupt literacy" as a built-in means of stabilizing the existing society. In any discussion of the justification and importance of creativity, a critical perspective such as Professor Pattison's should also be kept in mind.

When we in America give a man the tools of reading and writing, we expect him to become more efficient, not more intelligent. Mechanical skill with the technologies of reading and writing is essential for America, but not because it inculcates democratic habits or creates a judicious population. Reading and writing skills by themselves, it is thought, promote social cohesion and efficiency. They are necessary for productivity. . . .

Intentionally or not, the result of mass literacy in industrial America as elsewhere has been to train the citizen body only for social efficiency and obedience. . . .

Consider the alternative: a world in which the young are uniformly trained not merely in the mechanics of reading and writing, but in some critical attitude toward language necessary as a first step in the formation of literacy. This kind of educational endeavor . . . would produce not merely the functional skills requisite to the successful exploitation of a modern economy but the critical insight necessary for popular opposition to stifling institutions and oppressive ideologies. . . .

Stating the alternative makes it clear why this kind of literacy does not exist, why it is not likely soon to exist. None of our institutions desires it; very few citizens are eager for it. . . . Viewed in this light, the current state of literacy in America, far from being the unwanted disaster it is often advertised to be, is the state of events desired by the prevailing institutions. (1982, pp. 174, 175, 177, 178)

Many in the United States now acknowledge the necessity of a pedagogical renewal of the American school—if not for the sake of the children, at least for the country's sake. George Bush declared his intention to be "the education president." Japan, in the meantime, is steadily emerging as the new political-economic world power, with the United States tagging along as a weakened debtor nation. Reacting to this unsatisfactory state of affairs, many Americans are now demanding more "effective" schools, if not more creative pedagogy.

THE SITUATION IN NORWAY
It may be of interest to American readers to know how students in their country compare with students in a small and relatively homogeneous country like Norway. Unfortunately, no research

comparable to that discussed in *The Nation's Report Card* has yet been undertaken in Norway, so it is not possible to make a direct comparison of the extent of illiteracy and functional illiteracy in the two countries. Some relevant information is available, however.

A 1975 study regarding the children of Stovner, a suburb of Oslo, drew the following alarming conclusions: "It appears that large groups of children in Stovner are en route to becoming something very close to illiterate. Many of them appear to have lost the ability to learn to read, write, and calculate. Their problems appear to be intractable, incapable of solution by established methods" (Duve 1975, p. 13). On April 14, 1988, *Arbeiderbladet,* one of Oslo's largest newspapers, reported that the average final-exam failure rate among high school students in the general education program in the Oslo area was thirty percent. A spokesman for the schools said, "There is no reason to think that students in this area do worse than students elsewhere in the country." Countrywide results on high school final exams in Norway in recent years have also been disheartening. Of the students who passed the exam in 1991, for example, twenty percent received a grade of D. The comparable figure for 1992 was twenty-one percent. Four percent of the students taking the exam failed it altogether.

So there is reason for concern in Norway as well. A direct comparison with the situation in the United States is difficult, however, since high school there normally occupies students to age eighteen whereas in Norway the obligatory phase of education ends at age sixteen. But the proportion of Norwegian students who elect not to attend high school is probably counterbalanced by the rather large number of American students who drop out before graduating. Insofar as one can compare Norwegian students with their American counterparts, the Norwegian schools seem on the whole to be doing a somewhat better job.

It should also be noted that the high school curriculum in Norway has been broadened in recent years, which has clearly increased the general level of knowledge among Norwegian young people compared with their counterparts of some years ago. There is evidence, for example, that the conceptual and verbal vocabulary of Norwegian nineteen-year-olds is greater today than ever before. According to a study published in 1982, the verbal ability of military recruits as measured by standardized tests has been rising steadily since the tests were first administered in 1954 (Gerhardt and Hansen).

Nonetheless, it must be admitted that Norwegian schools succeed far too seldom in creating authentic readers and writers. Achievement levels among Norwegian high school students, too, are discouraging and frightening. For too many, learning to read and write is a negative rather than a positive experience. They suffer and the country suffers.

Enzensberger's and Freire's discussions of the vitality and creativity of the culture of the illiterate suggest the possibility of a more fruitful relationship between folk culture and advanced civilization in which the muse-ical resources of the former enrich the latter through the medium of a more muse-ical school. No doubt such a school cannot totally eliminate functional illiteracy, but perhaps it can at least help many more students to experience reading and writing as something just as natural and as important as talking to their playmates in a sandbox. That would be no small accomplishment.

Should Children Start School at an Earlier Age?

The Nation's Report Card says nothing about the possibility of harnessing the spontaneity and distinctive learning competency of child culture as a pedagogical resource in the schools. On the contrary, this report insists on the necessity of more "academic learning" and "an early start" if results are to be improved. Strangely enough, the extensive American research on the consequences of starting school at too early an age is not considered in the report's recommendations. One must look elsewhere to learn the findings of this research.

David Elkind was one of the initiators of the debate in the United States about the undesirable consequences of starting school too soon. His book *The Hurried Child: Growing Up Too Fast Too Soon* (1981) helped to define the issues surrounding the so-called superbaby syndrome, including the burnout and dropout problems, that were vigorously discussed throughout the 1980s. Elkind's opinion carries considerable weight, for he is an acknowledged leader in his field. He recently served as president of the National Association for the Education of Young Children, and his stand was also endorsed by Samuel Sava, leader of the National Association of Elementary School Principals (see Elkind and Sava 1986). It is clear that there is growing sentiment in the United States in favor of delaying the start of formal schooling.

Several research reports (e.g., Campbell 1984, Uphoff et al. 1985, 1986, Elkind 1988) strongly support Elkind and Sava's position. Among the findings of the research on high school students are the following:

- The number of burnouts is growing.
- The number of dropouts is growing.
- Achievement by the intellectually gifted is declining.
- The incidence of suicide, not least among females, is increasing.
- Social intelligence is decreasing.
- Children who start school at a later age appear to be much less likely to experience these problems.

Obviously one cannot attribute every case of dropout, burnout, or functional illiteracy to the practice of starting children in school too early. Many other factors, both social and familial, contribute. The research does show, however, that a too-early start and constant pressure to achieve have a significant negative impact on the development and potential of many children. Elkind underscored his concern about this problem in the title of his 1987 book, *Miseducation: Preschoolers at Risk.*

These findings and conclusions reveal some of the damage done by the "Sputnik shock" of the late 1950s, which created a demand for more rigorous education from the early grades onward. That Rudolf Flesch had just published his alarming account of the declining reading ability of American children (*Why Johnny Can't Read,* 1956) only added fuel to the fire. In the wild rush to "catch up in space" it apparently escaped everyone's notice that the

Russians had succeeded in launching Sputnik in spite of—or perhaps to some extent because of—a *later* start of formal schooling (at age seven) than that of American children.

The results of this "curriculum shove-down" in American schools have been quite disappointing. That should come as no surprise, for you cannot create a shortcut to learning readiness by tinkering with the time factor. Children need time, life needs time, and learning requires maturation. Nature itself teaches us this: tomatoes grown slowly in the fresh air and sunshine taste infinitely better than hothouse tomatoes. They are worth waiting for—and so are children.

It *is* possible to teach children a great deal at an astonishingly early age, for the capacity for learning is greater during the preschool years than at any other time in life. It is undoubtedly important, therefore, that children be introduced to literature, music, and the visual arts during this highly impressionable period of life. Failure to appreciate children's hunger for aesthetic quality as a force stimulating their creative imagination is itself a form of suppression. But the learning must occur muse-ically. The child's experience of beauty and his/her intellectual stimulation must be continuously and organically interwoven, with a keen spontaneity and inventive calm—and with an emotional nearness to adults—that most schools today are not able to provide. This cannot happen in eight weeks or even eight months of drilling on the ABC's. I am absolutely convinced that the experience of being read to frequently by a loving parent or an older brother or sister is in the long run a much better introduction to books for a six-year-old than classroom instruction. Formal teaching of the ABC's can wait; in the meantime many children, out of a sheer urge to discovery, will start reading on their own, often with the help of a parent or sibling. Indeed, systematic instruction is likely to be much more effective if children have first learned to love letters and words and books through informal exposure to them in an everyday setting.

RESPECT CHILDHOOD!

It was April, the first real spring day. Beneath the melting snow one could glimpse signs of new life striving to be born. There was a new warmth in the air, and delicious smells—harbingers of summer. What an exciting day in the life of a little girl! At last she could get rid of the clumsy padded coat and heavy boots that she had been obliged to wear all winter. It gave her such a marvelous sense of freedom to go outside with bare legs and light shoes: it was as if a heavy burden had suddenly been lifted from her slender little body. She was experiencing the wonderful lightness of being in that magical moment when winter is yielding to the insistent arrival of spring.

She was three years old. With that total concentration of which only children are capable, she was busily at work drawing her very first hopscotch diagram on a patch of asphalt where the warm sun had melted the snow from the driveway. It was the tiniest and most lopsided hopscotch imaginable: a man's footprint would have covered it completely. But it wasn't intended for *playing* hopscotch: the drawing was an end in itself. The girl was reveling in the joy of creation as she crouched there on bare knees and drew her hopscotch pattern, crooked, but strikingly beautiful. A child's signature in white chalk, testifying to the fact of growth through play.

The spot the little girl had chosen for her drawing was directly in front of the garage door. To put a car into the garage one would have to drive right over it. What were her poor parents to do with their brand new Ford LTD Crown Victoria?

It was no contest: *Respect childhood!* What is a car in comparison with the pride and joy of a three-year-old child? The Ford was parked in the street for an entire week, and the mini-hopscotch diagram lay there in the driveway, baking in the spring sunshine, nurturing the secret triumph in the heart of a little girl. A scant square foot of the earth's surface was for one brief moment under her control, conquered by play.

Then one day it rained, as it always does in April, and the hopscotch was washed away. But that's another story.

A MUSE-ICAL SCHOOL REVOLUTION IN RUSSIA

In 1989, the Western world celebrated the bicentennial of the French Revolution, that great cataclysmic event in human history that added the cry "Liberty! Equality! Fraternity!" to the world's vocabulary. The celebration took a form, however, that no one could have imagined as another revolutionary wave—one even mightier, perhaps, than that of the eighteenth century—swept over Europe, altering forever the political order that had prevailed for nearly half a century.

It is now becoming clear that *glasnost* and *perestroika,* the twin pillars of the 1989 revolution, will have profound consequences for Russian schools. Here, too, a revolution is under way, one that will radically change both the organization and the content of education in Russia. What is especially interesting about these developments is that the new ideology guiding the changes is *fundamentally muse-ical.*

A delegation from Russia visited Norway in 1990 to inform Scandinavian colleagues about their new school program. The main features of the new approach were summarized in the Norwegian press as follows.

1. Democratization: giving individual schools and communities a high degree of control over their own operations. The bureaucracy knows primarily about *control,* but what is now expected is *creativity.*
2. Cultural identity: A vigorous effort is now under way to give all registered minorities equal rights, with an education based on their own language and culture.
3. Humanization: The point of departure is no longer the nation or the group, but the *individual.* The dogmatizing of education is to be eliminated. There is today a high degree of interest in individualization, starting with the child's needs, taking account of "the whole person" and treating each pupil with dignity. The movement toward a society based on fundamentally humanistic ideals is very strong.
4. From technocracy to wholeness: New teaching plans are being

developed that reduce the technical-scientific dominance and give greater weight to the humanistic disciplines. The need for an *integrated* education that gives greater opportunity for the exercise of all talents is clear from kindergarten to the university level.

5. Differentiation: The new plans give significantly more options from which to choose and better support for realizing the choices made.

6. Active learning: Russian schools have been very traditional. The teacher has dominated the instructional process. Plans are now being made for pupils to play an active role.

7. Openness to new ideas is a central principle. Ideology is no longer to be allowed to squelch creativity. (Dalin 1990)

Even before Gorbachev came to power, a move was under way to change the time at which children start school from age seven to age six. This acceleration of formal education is now being combined with an inherently muse-ical approach in which instruction will be focused on the child, play, creativity, and integration. This is occurring in a society that traditionally has had a close relationship to the Muses of antiquity, for music, dance, the visual arts, and literature have always played important roles in the nation's life. Thus it will be most interesting to watch this program carefully in the years that lie ahead, for what happens in Russia inevitably has consequences reaching far beyond its own borders. If the creative power of a vital and deeply rooted Russian cultural life is now incorporated into a pedagogy that allows children's muse-ical learning potential to grow and flourish, the result could be quite a challenge for countries where the Muse Within is forced to languish because of a blind and one-sided belief in specialization and traditional academics as the only route to knowledge. A few other countries whose approach to education has traditionally been quite conservative—Japan and France, for example—have also begun to move in the same direction, though not so decisively as Russia. Whether they will rise to the challenge of creating a new vision wherein schools adapted to the needs of inherently muse-ical children play a central role remains to be seen.

FROM AN ECOLOGY OF LEARNING TO AN ECOLOGY OF TEACHING

Children learn ecologically; thus teaching must also be done ecologically. To be sure, it is neither possible nor desirable for the
school to become a copy of children's culture, but something must
be done to create greater continuity in the transition from preschool child culture to school culture. There is need for a new type
of thinking that starts with the premise that children are muse-ical
beings who are members of child culture. Only in this way can the
stifling of learning be decreased or eliminated. That would be
good for everyone concerned—the children, the school, and society as a whole.

The development of such an approach will require a great deal
of systematic work by many creative people in many different
schools. We need concrete examples of what does and does not
work to get the debate under way. What follows, then, is merely
an introduction, a preliminary sketch of some of the pedagogical
and organizational options that might be worth trying in a more
muse-ical school of the kind envisaged here.

THE MUSE-ICAL TEACHER

No school can become muse-ical without muse-ical teachers.
Thus it is not enough that teacher-training institutions help their
students to understand and respect children's essential muse-
icality. It is equally important that the professional preparation of
prospective teachers include systematic training to help them
maximize their own muse-ical potential. The fundamental characteristics of child culture must, so far as possible, become living,
breathing reality in the life of the teacher.

> Know you what it is to be a child? It is . . . to be so little that the
> elves can reach to whisper in your ear; it is to turn pumpkins into
> coaches, and mice into horses, lowness into loftiness, and nothing
> into everything, for each child has its fairy godmother in its soul.
> (Francis Thompson in the *Dublin Review,* July 1908)

Spontaneity, inventiveness, muse-ical energy, the gift of improvisation, playfulness, wittiness and warmth, professionalism and

naïve wonder, confidence and the ability to induce confidence: these are some of the qualities that must be developed in greater measure in teachers if the muse-ical intelligence of the school is to be significantly strengthened. It goes without saying that some of these characteristics are deeply ingrained in the personalities of many prospective teachers as a heritage from childhood. Unfortunately, the schools in which they will soon be working are likely to stifle these traits in young teachers as the vicious circle of traditional pedagogy runs its devastating course.

Much can be done, however, to stimulate further muse-ical growth on the part of individual teachers. One suggestion is that education students take a comprehensive course in creative play, improvisation, and dance as a means of revitalizing their inherent muse-ical capability. Practical concentration on their own development as creative people could bring prospective teachers into closer contact with their original vital powers, childhood's muse-ical legacy. Teacher and pupil could then meet in the classroom as vibrant, authentic human beings: the adult teacher who has gained new access to his/her own creative processes of learning, and the child who, in response to the inner muse-ical imperative, must constantly create in order to continue to develop as a person. Two kindred spirits who, despite their age difference, trust each other, sense the mutual kinship, and thus share the experience of learning as an existential necessity. Two for whom, at least now and then, magical moments occur even in the classroom.

ORGANIZING FOR TEACHING AND LEARNING

Reorganize the system whereby year of birth determines class placement! Draw upon the best experiences of the modern preschools as well as the old one-room schools and try something new! There is no other place in society where human beings are thrown together solely on the basis of having been born in the same year. During the preschool years, children find it altogether natural to associate with other children of various ages. When they finish high school they will enter a setting—a university, for example, or the world of work—where various age groups are once again mixed. That is the normal pattern. That is how we live, how we learn, how we work, both before we start school and after we finish. It is the source of some of the basic dynamism of human togetherness. Only in school are children subjected to an age-determined ghetto system in which there is alleged to be a great difference between a first-grader and a second-grader—truly a "class society" in the worst sense of that hackneyed phrase. No doubt it makes life much simpler for school administrators, but it is in many ways a misfortune for both pupils and teachers.

The system is absurd even if we look only at differences in physical development: in gym class the smallest child is constantly thrown into futile competition with classmates who are a head taller and weigh almost twice as much. The absurdity is compounded if we go on to consider mental development, for here the differences are even greater. Indeed, in this area there are two kinds of difference: an individual child may be highly advanced in one area of learning and lag in another, and there are enormous differences in overall mental development from child to child in the very same class.

These differences are documented by standardized tests in the United States, and the results I have seen are quite shocking. My son was a second-grader in 1986–87, and near the end of the year his class was given the widely used Comprehensive Test of Basic Skills. According to this test, there was a range of ten years in the achievement level of this group of eight-year-olds in mathematics alone. The weakest students were judged to be three years below the norm for that age group, while the best mathematician in the class scored at a level that would have been satisfactory for a fifteen-year-old. Consider the poor teacher, who must try to accommodate these enormous differences among children placed in the same class for no reason except that they happen to have been born in the same year. What teacher can hope to do justice to all the pupils under such circumstances?

Admittedly, one class is a small sample. Perhaps this class was not typical. Suppose, then, that the typical range of difference is only half as great, or even one-fourth as great, as in this particular class. Even so, the conclusion stands: the teacher is confronted with a degree of heterogeneity that makes effective teaching extremely difficult, and as a result the students suffer.

Children mature at different rates—socially, physically, intellectually, and emotionally. Some experience spurts of development that seem to change them almost overnight. Others develop slowly and steadily over a longer period of time, with variations from individual to individual. One can also make some generalizations. It is common knowledge, for example, that in many respects boys tend to develop more slowly than girls. Nonetheless, many children—the weak and the strong, the bright and the less bright, the mature and the immature—are hurt by the kind of segregation that results from the age-determined class system.

Abolish this system of pedagogical apartheid! Remove this painful display of dissimilarity based on a façade of similarity! Rather cultivate the differences by putting them in a context in which they are neither unusual nor stigmatizing but ordinary and completely natural.

The age-determined class system should be replaced by one in which differences in both physical and mental age are taken seriously and, indeed, used as a learning resource. One possibility: let the present grades one to three be treated as one large group, grades four to six as another. Then let flexible divisions be made within these large groups on the basis of differing levels of development in various areas, and let the child choose to some extent what to share and with whom. Such an arrangement, combined with a team of teachers trained to deal with diversity, might reasonably be expected to achieve better results than the present system.

What we are proposing is not just a mechanical redistribution of similarities and dissimilarities. More important, we are suggesting the channeling of a vital learning resource in such a way as to produce desirable results. Children are accustomed to learning with age differences, maturity differences, and differing talents as primary motivating forces. Surely this same learning resource could and should be tapped in the school setting, with teachers as partners and organizers of the process. The dynamics of difference are part of child culture and for that reason would immediately be perceived by the children as real, authentic, and functionally meaningful. It is much easier for a child to identify with an older playmate than with a teacher. Children who are older and more advanced in a given area help teach the others what they have learned, and in so doing strengthen their own self-esteem, while the less advanced strive to be more like them, perhaps thinking, "I want to do that too, so I have to learn it!" In this way children can progress even as they show consideration for their less advanced classmates. It is merely an extension of a pattern children are thoroughly familiar with from the world of play: one child shows another something that facilitates the mastery of Rubik's Cube, the yo-yo, the Frisbee, the skateboard. Peer instruction is without question infinitely closer to the pattern of child culture than instruction by the teacher under the best of circumstances. It brings the muse-ical world of childhood into the classroom in a thoroughly constructive way, not as pedagogical theory but as an experienced reality that enriches the learning experience.

A research project by a group of American scholars has uncovered striking proof of the value of peer instruction. Levin, Glass, and Meister (1984) undertook a broad national study to determine which factors were most important for learning in the schools. Norwegian educator Per Dalin (1988) has summarized their findings.

> Stanford University, the University of Arizona, and an organization called Research for Better Schools have collaborated on a project in which the following four strategies to improve schools were compared:
> a.   increased instruction time . . .
> b.   smaller class size . . .
> c.   systematic use of computer-assisted instruction . . .
> d.   using pupils as helper-teachers for other pupils.
> The results were quite astonishing. If we compare using pupils as a resource with the other three strategies, we find that it is nine times as effective as increasing instruction time and four times as effective as reducing class size or using computers in the instructional process.

Clearly, it is child culture's dynamic learning forms that lie behind and to a large extent explain the effects observed by Levin,

Glass, and Meister. Indeed, in view of what we know about the extent to which preschool children learn from each other, it is hardly surprising that peer instruction—pupils learning from other pupils—emerged as the overwhelmingly superior strategy for improving learning in the classroom.

Is it utopian to think that classes covering an age span of several years might become common in the 1990s? Certainly not. In Scandinavia, a trend in this direction is already emerging. In Norway, a number of schools have implemented a simple plan combining children in grades one to three in all subjects—a plan, incidentally, that costs no more than the traditional system. Friskolen 70 (The Free School 70) in Copenhagen, Denmark, has employed peer teaching for many years (see Dam 1989, Falbel 1989). Efforts have also been made in the United States to modify the age-determined grading system, often for the sake of specialized instruction in certain fields rather than in the name of child culture (Kantrowitz and Wingert 1989). I have the impression that multigrade classrooms, with students moving freely from one group to another depending on their progress in various areas, are becoming quite common in the United States. Perhaps the day is not far off when they will be the rule rather than the exception.

It is also desirable that the traditional forty-five-minute class period be replaced by a flexible schedule more suited to the attention span of young children. Children do not think, work, or play in forty-five-minute segments. Sometimes they need more time, sometimes less. If such flexibility could be achieved, I think it would be possible to harness children's natural modes of learning in new and exciting ways. Some schools have already had good experience with flexible scheduling in combination with mixed-age classrooms.

Changes such as those proposed here should not be avoided simply because they might be difficult to administer. As always in dealing with the schools, decisions should be made on the basis of what is best for the children, not what is most convenient for teachers and administrators.

MUSIC AND IMPROVED LEARNING

The idea that music is of fundamental importance for the development of character and reasoning ability is as old as Western culture. Plato, for example, argues in the *Republic* that because of its influence on the human mind, systematic exposure to music is essential to the health of the state. In modern times, both Pestalozzi (1746–1827) and Goethe (1749–1832) spoke eloquently in support of music as an important influence in the upbringing of children. Both stressed the importance of singing and other forms of music for the improvement of character and for the enhancement of learning in other areas. Music, according to Goethe, is useful as well as pleasant to the ear. In *Wilhelm Meisters Wanderjahre* (1821) he comes very close to advocating what we would call a muse-ical or *ngoma* pedagogy.

> When we teach children to transfer the sounds they sing to the signs they draw on paper, and to reproduce these signs in their throats . . . well, then they are simultaneously training their hand, their ear, and their eye. . . .
>
> Therefore, among all of the conceivable alternatives we have chosen music as a common element in the upbringing of children, for from music go valid connections in every direction.

More recently, Carl Orff (Germany) and Zoltán Kodály (Hungary) have had considerable influence by virtue of their eminence as composers, music teachers, and shapers of public policy with respect to music. Not surprisingly, therefore, many Central European countries have instituted ambitious programs of music instruction as fundamental elements of the total curriculum. Considerable research in this area has also been done in the United States (Hanshumaker 1980).

This interesting area of study does not lend itself to a quick survey, in part because much of the research has lacked a systematic theoretical basis and has been more or less ad hoc. Researchers have indeed been able to document in some cases that music has had a positive effect on children's achievement in other areas, but they have had difficulty identifying and analyzing the reasons. They have not viewed their findings against the background of the ecological learning system, not least because they have not made a systematic study of child culture and its spontaneous learning forms.

Much more research remains to be done before we can say with certainty that there is a positive correlation between music training and a general improvement in learning. In Hungary, especially, as a result of the influence of Kodály's ideas (discussed further in the next chapter), music training has been given an unusually prominent place in the school curriculum for many decades. The overall effect on the learning environment in the Hungarian schools is reported to be clearly positive. James Hanshumaker reports similar results from a test of the Kodály method in American schools.

Why should the Kodály method have a positive influence on learning and intellectual growth? Perhaps the answer lies in the fact that it builds on the relationship between *singing* and *speech* (the mother tongue). This relationship, in my opinion, is more important than the specific pedagogy of the system. The children's singing clearly helps to strengthen the indispensable conditions of ecological learning by encouraging flexibility and fostering a sense of complex interconnectedness. Interestingly, Hanshumaker cites other studies in which intensive instruction in instrumental music only was found to have *no* positive influence on children's learning in other areas. Perhaps learning to play an instrument, at least in accordance with traditional methods of instruction, quickly becomes so technically demanding and at certain stages so mechanical that the effect can be inhibiting rather than liberating. Singing, on the other hand, requires *no* corresponding technical mastery. The child can do it naturally, spontaneously, and the positive consequences for learning in general are demonstrable.

Ernst Weber (1981) has undertaken a critical review of some of the Central European experiments with increased music instruction in the schools. The methodology used in some of these experiments is rather questionable, however, so it is not always possible to draw solid conclusions based on hard data. Nonetheless, Weber notes certain general tendencies.

- heightened creativity (Salzburg, Munich, Berlin)
- greater ability to concentrate (all)
- enhanced reasoning ability (Hungary)
- increased motivation to learn (all)
- improved scholastic achievement (Hungary, Salzburg)
- improved sense of community with other children
  (Hungary, Salzburg)
- general maturing of personality (Munich, Berlin)
- greater emotional stability (Salzburg, Munich, Berlin)
- richer emotional life (Hungary)

It is important to note, however, that these desirable results cannot be achieved by just any type of music instruction. Only when the instruction is adapted to children's own spontaneous and playful learning style will it vivify and energize their learning generally. This is clear also from Hanshumaker's survey of some 768 studies of music and learning in the United States. The findings of his comprehensive review of the relevant literature agree on many points with those of Weber. Hanshumaker reports, for example:

- clear stimulation of vocabulary among first-graders
  (Wootton 1968)
- strengthening of oral language skills (Norton 1973, Shaw 1974)
- increased motivation for mathematics as a result of listening to
  music (Madsen and Forsythe 1973)
- general increase of motivation for learning through dance and
  drama (Norton 1973)
- general heightening of creativity (Simpson 1969)
- strengthening of social intelligence, sense of community, and
  self-confidence through dance (Montague 1961, Puretz 1973)
- improved motivation and decreased absences as a result of
  daily music instruction (Hood 1973)

Hanshumaker presents a balanced overview of the many research reports included in his survey, some of which describe experiments in which music instruction of various types did *not* correlate with improvements in learning in other areas. One possible explanation is that music, like anything else, can be—and sometimes is—taught in an unmuse-ical way. We shall look more closely at this phenomenon later.

Some interesting projects are also under way in Sweden to implement a more muse-ical type of instruction in the schools. In Uppsala, for example, a psychologist and a music teacher have jointly initiated a program in which dance and improvised musical games are included as a regular part of the curriculum for a group of primary-school pupils. This program, which has been in place since the 1981–82 school year, is based on Howard Gardner's theory of multiple intelligences. The development of the children who have received this special instruction has been carefully studied, and the effects of the dance-music experience appear to have been clearly positive (Ericson, Lagerlöf, and Gabrielsson 1988). These children, for example, generally scored higher than their control-group peers in concentration, sociability, motivation, and development of motor skills.

A somewhat similar program has been in operation for several years in Mjölby, a town near Stockholm. It is based on the premise that the relative paucity of physical movement in the traditional school is an obstacle to learning. The initiators of the program theorized that by giving pupils an opportunity for movement in muse-ical forms they could enhance brain lateralization and thereby improve the children's performance in such areas as reading, writing, and arithmetic. "Where is the central nervous system trained?" they asked. Their answer: "In the gym." This program has not been researched as thoroughly as the one in Uppsala, but two teachers who have worked with it for many years report that there is a connection between children's motor development and their learning ability, and that it is possible to develop children's agility and thereby improve their capacity for learning (Gustafsson and Hugoh 1987, p. 4). Through singing and physical expression the children further activate the same types of analogical correspondences that they naturally employ in their own culture. The muse-ical *ngoma* is harnessed as an engine of learning. If the ecological learning system of the child can be kept in balance, the result is likely to be positive for all forms of learning and thus, in principle, for all areas of study.

No doubt mathematics can be learned best in good mathematics classes, but must not such classes be muse-ically exciting exercises in human creativity—with pupils whose ecological learning equipment is fully intact—in order to be truly successful? The Danish educator Sten Clod Poulsen supports this view and argues that a deeper understanding of mathematics presupposes an adaptable, unified personality.

> The human psyche is a unified entity, learning is conditioned by its unity, the various psychological elements in consciousness are functionally interrelated. . . . Every instance of learning—of mathematics, for example—is permeated with emotional and social elements, and if these levels of personality are not harmonically integrated in the learning process they will set limits to the acquisition of learning—limits that *are not due to intellectual inadequacy*, but are an internal paralysis of thinking ability resulting from tensions between basic elements of consciousness. (1980, p. 84)

Integrated learning requires integrated—whole, complete—learners.

School and society are constantly articulating the need for more knowledge—and rightly so, in view of the degree to which the present one-sided approach to education has failed to achieve its goals. But there is only one way that knowledge can truly come alive, and that is through truly living human beings. Do today's schools provide the conditions for the growth of complete human beings? Are children allowed—nay, encouraged—to *live,* in the full sense of the word? May these questions continue to concern all of us as long as there are schools in which children spend a substantial part of each day during some of the most formative years of their lives.

The place and importance of music in the school curriculum

has long been a matter of serious disagreement in many communities. Regarded by many as a "frill"—a fine thing to have if you can afford it, but not really necessary—the music program is often the first area to be cut when a school levy fails and the budget has to be trimmed. The growing emphasis on career training in recent years has made music even more vulnerable to the budget-cutter's axe.

It now appears, however, that music can defend itself even on utilitarian grounds: music, when presented muse-ically, enhances learning in fields that have traditionally been viewed as unrelated to music. Nonetheless, the primary justification for including music in the curriculum remains what it always has been: it is one of humankind's deepest wells of *joy*—the soul-enriching experience that makes for a richer, fuller, and more creative life. What more glorious use could there be for music than that?

THE CAPACITY FOR WONDER AS A SCHOOL RESOURCE

The capacity for wonder is the child's key to learning. The muse-ical intelligence, the dwelling place of wonder, aspires to that which lies beyond. The child who is the bearer of this intelligence feels an inner urge to test deeper waters, to venture out toward forms, colors, perceptions, insights, understandings as yet but vaguely glimpsed or totally undreamed of. Once when you were a child you were transformed by wonder into a beautiful bird, and because of that you will always know for all time to come what it is like to fly—if only you can retain your childlikeness. Another time you were transported by wonder to Alice's Wonderland, and you remember the White Rabbit and the Mad Hatter as clearly as if they had been your closest childhood friends. It was wonder that enabled you to connect unknown sounds to words, and words to sentences, and sentences to meaning, and meaning to reality. The visionary thought, the leap beyond convention, presupposes imagination—one of the basic elements of wonder—by whose power the vision is perceived. Edith Cobb (1977) quotes Socrates in support of the view that the ability to behold the world with wonder is the highest level of intellectual activity, "for wonder is

the feeling of a philosopher, and philosophy begins in wonder"
(Plato, *Theaetetus* 155).

Reason is learning's secure frame of certainty, wonder is its
inquiring restlessness. In the dialectical friction between reason
and wonder, convention and vision, lie the inherent and indispensable dynamics of the learning process. Here the child finds
both the Batmobile and the Chevrolet that Mom drives to the
grocery store. The child must know without any doubt that $2 +
2 = 4$, and with equal certainty must be able to fancy that $2 +
2 \approx x$. Only then is s/he able to dive deeply into the whole of
reality with a true hunger to perceive it as it is. If the process stops
with the multiplication table, wonder's plasticity begins to fade.
And if wonder is petrified, so also is learning.

Moreover, it is not only the individual child who needs wonder's challenge to reason. The whole of society is dependent for its
continued development on wonder's creative potential, its capacity to achieve ever new insights. It is wonder that gives the present
a key to the mastery of the future. The capacity for bold wonder
is vitally necessary if the children of today are to create the society
of tomorrow, whose features are as yet unknown—one, therefore,
that even the most learned teacher cannot describe to them.
Perhaps this is what George Bernard Shaw had in mind when he
wrote, "You see things, and you say, 'Why?' But I dream things
that never were, and I say, 'Why not?' " (*Back to Methuselah*, Part
I, Act I). The school can cultivate wonder, show respect for wonder, be humble in the presence of wonder. It is the child's right,
the school's duty, and society's urgent need that wonder be preserved.

Mark Twain was perhaps guilty of a slight exaggeration when
he said that there are three kinds of untruths—lies, damn lies, and
statistics—but it can scarcely be denied that our society is in
danger of being tyrannized by numbers. The so-called scientific
method is held in such high regard that it is sometimes employed
in contexts where it is totally out of place, without the daring and
imagination that have characterized the research of the greatest
scientists. Without White Rabbits and Mad Hatters, all learn-

ing—including scientific inquiry—would eventually wither in a stupefying chain of trivial deductions.

More is at stake here than merely keeping open the borders of knowledge, important as that is. The nurturing of wonder is essential to the preservation of society's sensitivity and humanity, which open the way to a kind of understanding and appreciation of life that cannot be derived from statistics. The Norwegian poet Rolf Jacobsen has written of this in "Ask Again."

> The series of numbers laughs at us
> and claims that it can explain everything.
> It has jaws of iron
> and gnashing teeth.
> We ask and we ask
> and the numbers answer
> but they say nothing about the violins
> or about the joy between two arms.
> Then the computer sputters:
> "Question ambiguous.
> Ask again."
> (Trans. W. H. Halverson)

Learning needs play, sensitivity, passion, as well as wonder. Learning must find its way into the child's processes of imagination as a felt need, for within the magic circle of play everything is permitted. In a game in which anything can be connected with anything else, new knowledge can emerge as a creative modification of what was previously known. As Jacob Bronowski has written in *The Origins of Knowledge and Imagination* (1978):

> We must accept the fact that all the imaginative inventions are to some extent errors with respect to the norm. . . .
>
> If we ask "Why do we know more now than we knew ten thousand years ago, or even ten years ago?" the answer is that it is by this constant adventure of taking the closed system and pushing its frontiers imaginatively into the open spaces where we shall make mistakes. . . .

The creative personality is always one that looks on the world as fit for change and on himself as an instrument for change. Otherwise, what are you creating for? (pp. 101–102, 113, 123)

In child culture, learning is a process essential to life. New knowledge must be continually created. In school, the knowledge is presumed already to exist. The dice have already been cast, the winner of the prize is already known. The school's relation to learning, therefore, is totally different from the child's. Most schools have no inclination to create new knowledge. They simply transmit preexisting knowledge to those who do not possess it, i.e., the pupils. The sense of excitement in the learning process—the exhilaration of discovery, of doubt about the outcome—is missing as teachers recite what they already know to pupils who are being given answers to questions they have never learned to ask. Wonder is superfluous in such a classroom. Its place is taken by one of the worst enemies of learning: boredom.

Wonder can find expression not only in the so-called aesthetic areas—art, music, theater, dance—but also in such fields as English, social science, mathematics, and physical science. Any subject can evoke wonder if only the teacher is sufficiently museical to call it forth.

Matthew Lipman of the Institute for the Advancement of Philosophy for Children in New Jersey has started an interesting program that attempts to employ children's capacity for wonder to strengthen their reasoning and their ability to analyze and solve problems. Designed for children from age seven upward, it consists of courses on such topics as Reasoning About Nature, Reasoning About Language, Basic Reasoning Skills, and Reasoning in Ethics. Program materials have been translated into several foreign languages and have been used in Brazil, Australia, England, France, Austria, Iceland, and Denmark as well as the United States. The validity of such an approach depends primarily on whether it is truly adapted to the natural learning idiom of children or is just a way of initiating children into adult ways of thinking at a very early age. One Norwegian educator who has carefully studied the program concludes that it is on the whole well conceived and eminently worthy of use, provided that it is implemented in a way that "starts from the children's own world of ideas, with topics and problems that they find inherently interesting" (Opdal 1987, p. 359). As always, the muse-icality of the teacher is essential to the success of the program.

Music? Music!

Advocates for music often express the opinion that its importance in the school curriculum must be defended on the basis of its intrinsic value, not utility for other more "central" fields. Such a view accepts as given the division of knowledge into various specialized disciplines, which is totally foreign to children's natural way of viewing the world. Children are muse-ical beings who have learned to live, think, feel, and act in integrated totalities. To think muse-ically in relation to all fields does not detract in any way from music's unique dignity and value. No music teacher should feel that it is degrading to work with music in, say, a history class or an English class. Such an assignment should be looked upon as an opportunity to create continuity in life and learning between child culture and school culture. N. F. S. Grundtvig (1783–1872), the great Danish churchman and creator of the concept of the folk high school, once said, "First a human being, then a Christian!" Music teachers might well take as their motto "First a human being, then a musician!" It is for the sake of the child as a bearer of the Muse Within that we urge the incorporation of muse-ical elements as the basis of all instruction at the elementary level.

Naturally, we can also consider instruction in music as a subject in and for itself. In so doing, however, we must look critically at the manner in which music has traditionally been taught — once again for the sake of the children. Music can be many things: liberation or enslavement, ecstasy or despair. For music to be a positive influence in the lives of children requires much more than that it be given adequate space in the curriculum. What matters is the *content* and the *method of presentation*. These important issues will be discussed in detail in the next chapter. What do we find in the traditional music lesson: Music? Or music!

RUSSIA, CREATIVITY, AND POLITICS

The launching of Sputnik in 1957 showed the world—to the embarrassment of Americans and the surprise of almost everyone else—that the Russians were more advanced in space research than anyone had imagined. As we noted, the shock waves soon rippled through the American political and educational establishment. "Catch up with the Russians!" was the cry of many.

It may be that behind the economic ruin and deep human suffering that we observe today, a new shock is in the making in the former USSR. To be sure, many people in this once vast empire are today on the verge of starvation. For them, life is little more than a daily struggle for survival. Cultural institutions, too, are feeling the pinch as the general economic breakdown takes its toll on every aspect of society. But that is not the whole story. Russians today have greater freedom of action, greater freedom of expression in art, culture, and public debate than ever before. Might not all of this lead in time to a situation in which the United States once again finds itself trying to "catch up with the Russians"—not in space, but in the arts?

Former president Gorbachev explicitly stated that in his view the unleashing of the creative potential of Russian artists is the key to the renewal of their society. Leaders in the muse-ical arts— film, dance, theater, literature, music, painting—have been at the forefront of reform. That *Novy Mir (New World)*, the world's largest literary journal, has a circulation of nearly 1.2 million gives some idea of the importance of the arts in this enormous country. The great creative artists of the past—authors, composers, painters, sculptors—are revered as national heroes whose continued presence among the people is almost palpable. Most Russians have nurtured a love for these heroes since childhood, and their pride knows no bounds. Now: turn this deeply rooted cultural consciousness loose for a decade or two in a society that is committed to a policy of openness. Let Russian children spend their formative years in the midst of this ferment, and it may be that we will all suddenly get a new shock as this sleeping giant stirs to life with a mighty outpouring of creative power that finds expression in dramatic achievements in a wide variety of areas. Could the United States hold its own in such a *revolution of creativity?* It lacks a long cultural tradition upon which to build, and its children's heroes tend to be people who score touchdowns and hit home runs rather than those who write symphonies and paint pictures that will last forever.

It may be answered that during much of the present century Russia systematically purged many of its most creative spirits, whereas the United States was the beneficiary of a large influx of authors, composers, and performing artists who fled the terror of Hitler's Germany. It must be remembered, however, that the situation of artists improved with the death of Stalin in 1953, and the ranks of both artists and intellectuals have been replenished with men and women born since World War II. The refugees from Hitler's Europe have for the most part finished their careers, and it is unlikely that another such influx of artists and intellectuals will ever again occur. If there is indeed to be a new race for supremacy between East and West—not in science and space and armaments, but in the arts and in learning generally—the United States must depend for the most part on homegrown talent. It is conceivable that the entire balance of power between East and West could be upset by a revolution of creativity in which one of the protagonists is ill-equipped to compete because its cultural foundation, for complex historical reasons, has become too weak.

In the meantime it is well to remember that not everyone wants to see a dramatic increase of muse-icality and creativity. Gorbachev's courageous policies obviously made him vulnerable to a backlash from the political right within his own country. He implemented his policy of *glasnost* in the hope of generating enthusiasm, new thinking, and improved productivity—but at the price of undermining his country's traditional authoritarian stability and his own political security. How much in the way of unrest, free speech, uncensored journalism and literature, rock music, and radical plays and films can the Russian Federation tolerate before it breaks down altogether? Tensions are inevitable between creativity and control, imagination and dogma, freedom and order. Will the resurgence of ethnic pride and self-consciousness lead to chaos or to a mighty outpouring of muse-ical creativity?

A specialist in child culture has no special competence to answer such questions. What he can say is that Muse-bearers deserve to flourish not only for their own sakes but for the sake of society and its continuing need for learning, for productive work, for play, for beauty, for a high quality of life. All these are interrelated in the souls of muse-ical beings, for whom the ultimate unity of all things remains a vividly sensed reality, an ecological fact of life. The typical outlook of our time is quite different. We tend to think about and to sense the world in fragments, for the idea of culture and nature in ecological balance has been lost. A fragmented mind perceives a fragmented world. If our children can preserve into adulthood a greater measure of their muse-ical identity, their creativity, their sense of the wholeness of reality, perhaps the human race will have a better chance of surviving for at least a few more generations.

We adults, in the process of growing older, have lost altogether too much of our ability to sense the world as a unified whole and to live in that wholeness. We are products of a civilization that values specialization above all else, and in the process of educating us it has succeeded in fragmenting us to fit its countless specialties. Matthew Arnold was describing us when he wrote in *Empedocles on Etna:*

Hither and thither spins
The windborne, mirroring soul;
A thousand glimpses wins,
And never sees a whole.

Children, however, can still "see a whole." They sense via *sikia,* with both reason and imagination. For them, ordinary observation and naïve wonder, the mundane and the magical, are one. Bearers of the Muse Within, they can sing and dance and play their way into the wide and wonderful world of which they are a part, regardless of the particular culture or political system into which they happen to have been born.

Most adults want to retain their physical youth as long as

possible. That is why jogging, health foods, weight-loss programs, and face lifts are perennially popular, and why the cosmetics industry has flourished among us since ancient times. Might it also be possible to retain some features of our *mental* youth? In the process of development, shouldn't we try to preserve the pliant creativity of childlike imagination? *Must* the human spirit grow old and gray even as the body ages?

It is not enough to teach children to read better, or to write better, or to do better in arithmetic. If we stifle the Muse Within, we stifle their humanity. "Save childlikeness—and thereby save humanity!" was one of the central ideas in *Il mondo salvato dai ragazzini (The World Saved by the Children),* a collection of poems by Italian writer Elsa Morante. With the muse-ical outlook of a child, Morante wrote, the poet must "give reality back to the others— reality understood as the perpetually living value that is hidden in things" (Klem 1985). Children understand "the perpetually living value that is hidden in things." This is precisely what they are trying to master, precisely what they want to express in word, song, and play. This is their life. This is what makes their everyday world essentially and profoundly human.

Homo ludens: *Two muse-ical clowns!*

6

Child Culture and Music Education

MUSE-ICAL LEARNING AND LEARNING MUSIC

In the preceding chapter we discussed the stifling of learning that often occurs in the transition from child culture to school culture. I am reminded of an insightful passage in an account of his own childhood by the great Danish composer Carl Nielsen.

> It has often surprised me that people are in general so unaware of the fact that in the moment in which a child receives a strong impression—one that is strong enough to create a lasting recollection—in that moment the child is in reality a poet, with a poet's special ability to receive the impression, to express it, or merely to preserve it. The essential genius of the poet is the ability to observe and to comprehend in a unique way. Thus there have been times when all of us, each in our own way, have been poets, artists. The abrupt manner in which life and *adult authority* call the child from its lovely world of poetry and beauty into the world of hard, matter-of-fact reality must certainly bear the blame for the fact that most of us squander these abilities. The result is that imagination's divine gift, which is the birthright of every newborn child, is reduced to a mere fantasy or is totally lost.

The great poets, thinkers, scientists, and artists are only the
exceptions that prove the rule. (1927, p. 7)

Interconnectedness and balance, human nature and ecology, a
sense of the whole and total involvement therein: these are some
of the characteristics of childlike, creative competence. On such a
foundation it should be possible to develop a systematic music
pedagogy that takes proper account of the unique features of child
culture—a kind of muse-ical version of Paulo Freire's *Pedagogy of
the Oppressed*. I am convinced that this approach would strengthen
children's relation to music—not least as they make the critical
transition from singing child to playing instrumentalist—and
would be beneficial for both children and music, both dream and
reality.

FROM THE RED RUBBER BALL TO THE TRUMPET: GLIMPSES OF A BEGINNER'S FIRST YEAR WITH HIS FIRST INSTRUMENT

We found the trumpet at a flea market in the heart of New
Orleans, just before closing time. A faded label on the case told us
that it had once belonged to "Ronnie King." One of the clasps on
the case was broken. Inside was a well-worn Conn trumpet with
a big dent right by the mouthpiece. Gilded brass against deep blue
felt. Beautiful. Around us was a bewildering jumble of catfish,
oysters, garlic, pecans, and sugarcane. This was the French Quarter. Hearts pounding, we bought the trumpet without delay.
Thirty-five dollars.

We put the trumpet in the back seat of the car, where Tan's red
rubber ball was already waiting.

"Hi!"

Lying there side by side, the trumpet and the ball began to talk
about children, life, and play. The ball told about a brilliant shot
Tan had once made against a garage door, and the trumpet
described an equally brilliant blues performance by Ronnie King.
The trumpet bragged that Ronnie had known a couple of fellows
who once played with the great Louis Armstrong, and the ball
crowed just as loudly about Tan, who had played handball in

Southern California and learned to speak fluent American English in no time at all.

"Just because he was playing with me!" said the ball proudly.

"Play with me, too!" said the trumpet enviously as he tried to nudge the boy sitting in the back seat. "Get going, man! There's some great music inside me. I wanna be your pal!"

And that's exactly what happened. We started in September of 1987. There was no doubt about the method: no printed music! The music had to find its way directly into Tan's mind and body, without making a detour through literate culture's instruction-from-a-distance. That's how Tan had learned to talk like his American friends—confidently, as children do. Now, I theorized, he could learn to play the trumpet in the same way, as another expression of his muse-ical mother tongue. Our hope was that ball and trumpet would prove to be two sides of the same reality.

The first sound Tan was able to produce on his new trumpet was a true primal cry—a hoarse grating full of life and will. I was suddenly reminded of my own first attempt on a wind instrument many years earlier. I was sitting in my father's delivery truck with a big tenor horn on my lap. It was old and dented, badly in need of repair, but to me—starry-eyed at the thought of marching in the school band—it was brand spanking new.

"Give me a sound!" Father said encouragingly.

Who could resist such encouragement? I took the deepest breath I had ever taken and let loose with a mighty roar of a sound, cheeks puffed out as if I had a whole grapefruit in my mouth.

"Good grief, I thought for sure it was a horse that was about to be slaughtered!" said Father with a chuckle. But I knew it was no horse. It was a horn, and it was *mine.*

And now Tan was going through a similar experience with a trumpet. In my mind, the remembered sound of the tenor horn and the sound of Tan's trumpet were as one. I understood.

Tan was approaching his ninth birthday, so this was by no means a case of a four-year-old prodigy ready to perform "The Carnival of Venice" on television. He had all he could handle as he struggled to produce something resembling "Frère Jacques" in

C major, with short, labored blasts of air followed by an abrupt pause and a deep breath after each note. And why not? How else could he get any sound out of the horn? By the time he had wheezed his way through two verses his thin lips were swollen and exhausted.

Role models play an important part in the learning of children. The pattern of practicing alone all week long and then spending half an hour with a teacher, common though it is, is completely foreign to children's natural learning process. Trying to learn music this way deprives the child of much of the initiative, motivation, and human meaning associated with the identification with others that is so central to the child's experience of life and learning. Children must remain connected to their power source in order to mobilize their resources to keep on learning.

Tan's role models were two older sisters, Tiril and Tuva, both of whom played instruments. "Conquer new territory! Enter into yet another small corner of your promised land of secrets, skills, privileges, and adult recognition. *Play* your way in, with the trumpet as your instrument of conquest—like the people of ancient Israel who reportedly marched around Jericho blowing their trumpets till 'the walls came a-tumblin' down.' "

Surely Tan had an intuitive sense of the pattern of means and ends that was part of the experience of playing in association with others. Had he not perhaps mastered the whole process when he taught himself to speak English? Then, the companionship of other children in a schoolyard had provided the requisite context for learning. Now, his father's piano accompaniment would provide an authentic framework of rhythm and sound within which the budding trumpeter could teach himself to play.

It is a story that recurs again and again, from early childhood onward: if there is no vital learning context, the result is a learning vacuum. No child has ever learned the subtleties of his/her mother tongue except by living in the midst of a language milieu while acquiring the language. I think it is equally true that no child learns the subtleties of instrumental music except by living with the instrument in the midst of music's own swinging reality from the very moment s/he struggles to produce those first primitive sounds. Even "Frère Jacques" requires a beating musical heart if it is to live in the trumpet of a beginner.

Within a week, "Frère Jacques" had grown in significance as the duo became a trio. I played the piano as usual, and Tan's eleven-year-old sister Tuva played the French horn, so we had a round. With a child's intuitive sense of rhythm, Tan did his best to play along—generally in a slow tempo, and not infrequently with a few unintended notes, but always with a pulsating beat. If you lose that, you lose the whole feeling of music. I didn't have to explain that to Tan; he knew it instinctively. He felt it in his whole body—especially his feet, which from the beginning tapped out the beat as if someone had showed him how to do it. Tan made the wonderful discovery that two plus one equals much more than three when three instruments play together, even when one of the players is a beginner and the music is very, very simple. The Muse Within was already singing! Two months later I made the following notation in my diary.

> Tan has suddenly made a leap forward on the trumpet. Plays the Beatles tune "Let It Be" in F major. I accompany on the piano, give the tune a proper swing that Tan can enjoy. He aptly catches the rhythm and the C's and D's of the second octave, giving a real jazz twist to the sound.

Why "Let It Be" instead of some other song? Because Tuva was going on a school camping trip in the autumn, and her class had been learning "Let It Be" as their class song. Tuva was a sixth-grader, three years older than Tan, so that made "Let It Be" a big kids' song. Moreover, Tuva had been going around singing it so often that he couldn't get it out of his head. *Let it be, let it be . . . !* Tan had heard and hummed and sung and danced this song so many times that it had become a part of him. It was in his arms, his legs, his ears, his head. *Let it be!* He was going to share Tuva's camp experience—in his own way.

So the pedagogical link was simple enough: why not also *play* "Let It Be" with Tan, without further ado making the leap from a cautious repertoire of children's songs to the Beatles, with no pedagogical detours in between? I mentioned the idea to him, and he immediately jumped at this opportunity for social advancement. The motivation to play was fueled by his desire to be like his sister. In a very short time he had mastered the song—thereby advancing one step closer to the fascinating world of his sister and her friends.

How did he learn the fingering? It was simple enough: I had played in the school band for several years as a boy and was able to show him. Using my own mouthpiece, I had for some time been showing him how to play each new piece he tackled, letting him see and feel the fingering as well as hear the sound of the melody. In the process, he also learned quite a bit of music terminology: *chromaticism, F-sharp, third, octave.* This was part of the game, just like the specialized handball terminology he had learned in Southern California. Children pick up this kind of thing effortlessly, if only it is presented to them in a meaningful context. But still no printed music! Music was to have an opportunity to enter directly into mind and body, as a total sense experience. The *spontaneous process* method. *Ngoma. Sikia. Musikia.*

Did Tan practice hard at this stage? Not at all. He played for a few minutes every—well, *almost* every day. That was all. And that was enough, for nine-year-olds have other things to do, other games to play, other worlds to conquer. Three hundred play cars naturally had first priority, not to mention a couple of thousand Lego blocks and various other treasures. And to top it all off, it was just at this time that Tan, like many children his age, fell in love with reading. Earlier that autumn I had written in my diary:

One evening recently, long after normal bedtime, a thin, naked little boy came tiptoeing into the family room. We knew that he was in the middle of his second Hardy Boys book: *The House on the Cliff.* Now he looked concerned:

"Something sad has happened!"

"Oh?" we said, surprised. "What's that?"

"Fenton is gone!"

Forty more Hardy books are waiting for Tan—and much, much more.

Tan's experience illustrates an important point: children learn in interrelated parallel tracks. It is not their way to "concentrate on one thing at a time." Not at all! The Hardy Boys and the trumpet shared center stage in Tan's life in the autumn of 1987.

As Christmas approached, "Let It Be" was clearly his favorite trumpet piece. We could see how proud he was to attack the high notes: he was deliberately playing "macho" in contrast to his sister's controlled, sparkling horn tone. Early in December I wrote in my diary:

> Tan crouches intently in the chair with the trumpet dangling carelessly between his knees. "What shall we play?" I ask him. "Let It Be," he says firmly. A brief piano introduction and we are under way. With eyes bulging and face flaming red he "squeezes" his way up to the D—and he is so proud! "I did it! Whoopee!" And we are both swaying to the rhythm of the music.

Progress on an instrument does not always occur without interruption, and Tan had his. My diary entry for January 25, 1988, tells the story.

> Tan had some very bad luck the last day of school before the teachers' strike began. First he got teased for wearing "girls' mittens." Then he got in a fight with a classmate and got kicked in the mouth, and as a result his two upper front teeth are now loose. Blood and tears. Grandma took him to the dentist, where he was thoroughly examined with X-rays, etc. He's not supposed to bite with those teeth for a long time. No trumpet-playing either. None. But as far as they can tell, the roots were not damaged. Can this possibly work out all right? He will have to have regular examinations for three years.
>
> Later in the day, the boy who had kicked Tan came to see him. He also brought his father and a model car—the world's reddest 1961 Jaguar, a JU 877E, made in Italy. "I'm sorry," he said. "I hope you'll be okay."

Two months later the dentist indicated that things were going well: "Just start playing again, Tan!" he said.

After such a long interruption, there was a lot of thawing in the trumpet playing that spring. We started with "Where Have All the Flowers Gone," and the trumpet playing blossomed like the flowers that sprang up through the last vestiges of winter's snow: coltsfoot in March, blue anemones in April, blankets of white anemones in May, pansies and violets in June, bluebells all summer and autumn. And Tan kept pace: "Down by the Riverside," "When the Saints Go Marchin' In," "Children of the Rainbow," "We Shall Overcome," "Waltzing Matilda," "Last Night I Had the Strangest Dream," "Pippi Longstocking," "He's Got the Whole World in His Hands," "Streets of Laredo," "My Own Land" (as a jazz waltz, with a modulation from F to A flat), and "Mary's Boychild," plus most of the well-known Christmas songs. By now it would have been unthinkable to Tan to leave his trumpet out of the Christmas festivities.

The trumpet sounds became steadily clearer, the lips steadily stronger, the high notes steadily surer: C-D-E-F. And then, finally, G, with an occasional lucky stab at A. Was Tan making music, or was he having fun? He was doing both! He was *playing* in two ways at once, and it would never have occurred to him to distinguish one from the other.

The first step in learning a new piece was always to sing it. We would sing the songs together—which often had the incidental benefit of giving him an English lesson. The result was that the rhythms and sounds of both text and music were well in hand before we began to work the piece out on the trumpet. This is important, for the feeling of the text must also come through in the textless sound of the trumpet. It must sing in the brass. We spent no time at all on exercises, nor did we concentrate on difficult passages or "getting the high notes." Our model was Tan's astonishing mastery of English the previous year, and we remembered that he hadn't spent five minutes drilling himself on "hard" words or formal grammar. So we relied on the Muse Within—his natural muse-ical learning competence—to carry him through, and went steadily on our way, not without learning some relevant music concepts in the process, and certainly not without considerable effort, but always in a spirit of play. We still did not use printed music.

How did we handle mistakes? Key signature problems? Sharps and flats? Modulations? *Such questions never arose* in the course of our playing together. They are adult, intellectual questions. Children don't think in those terms. The sense of the whole governs the mastery of the details—as when toddlers learn to synchronize the swinging of their arms with the movement of their legs as they pitch uncertainly across the floor. That, too, requires a lot of effort. If there are some wrong notes along the way—and there are plenty of them—perhaps the best thing an adult helper can do is to remember Norwegian poet Harald Sverdrup's paraphrase in "The Dandelion's Prayer": "Suffer the little children to come unto me, for they know not what weeds are." Then, perhaps, adults will be less inclined to intervene with a stern "No, that was wrong!" and children can continue on their merry way, carried along by the relentless beat of the music. Don't worry: children know when they make a mistake. But the freedom to continue demonstrates that something else is even more important than getting all the notes right: keeping the current flowing from body to horn. The *heart's* right to be a part of the process—indeed, to throw itself into the music-making without fear or reservation— is thereby established as an unconditional premise as the beginner strikes out into the unknown.

But are we losing good, swinging music in a cloud of sentimental mist? Not at all. Children are naturally discriminating, and they know without our telling them when they "get it right." They've had lots of experience with this sort of thing. They have endured sweat, fatigue, and more than a few scabs to master a variety of playground skills, and they have learned that the easiest way rarely leads to success. Indeed, they have often chosen the difficult way even when an easier way might have served just as well. As we noted earlier, for children the path to new knowledge and skills often involves *the triumph of inconvenience*. So they willingly play the same tune over and over again, until their lips ache and their fingers are stiff. But if they are to achieve mastery through all this effort, it must occur in the context of meaningful, muse-ical wholes that touch the heart and set the foot tapping. Give a young child dull exercises and printed music and you run a great risk that it will all die. Only moving feet cause hearts to beat: that is one of the secrets of the Muse Within.

The direct approach—through the child's own body and mind—allows the music to be governed by subjectivity and inner control. The child decides, the child shapes the result. Whether the note that is played is E-flat or E is strictly the child's own business. Experience is a hard taskmaster—quite literally. Mistakes along the way have motivated the child to try harder countless times before: that's how s/he learned to do a cartwheel, to jump from a swing, to ride a two-wheeler. But note: *the child is in charge,* and that is essential to the entire process. Freedom is the wellspring of learning.

If the child is presented with printed music from the outset, the whole experience changes. Now if you play E-flat instead of E, you are *wrong:* you have broken the requirement of the printed music that you play its way and no other. In the world of the beginner, the printed music too easily takes command of the entire process with its intimidating imperative: "Play exactly what is written!" Outer control is substituted for inner control. The subject is subordinated to the object. Internal desire is exchanged for external compulsion. Music is no longer the child's medium; instead, the child becomes the medium of the music notation. The entire process is devoid of human feeling. The direct contact of the body and heart with the instrument, which is decisive for the child's perception of music-making, is exchanged for indirect contact via the eye and the printed notes. The muse-ical temperature falls. Music is no longer experienced as something real, here and now; it is experienced only secondhand. But children must live in the present, the tangible, if their play and their learning are to have meaning for them.

By autumn Tan was playing his tunes with the same spontaneity he had exhibited the previous year when he "suddenly" started to speak English like a native-born American. He was no trumpet virtuoso, to be sure; there were no displays of lightning-fast fingering or triple tonguing, and his tone quality often left something to be desired. But rhythm was there, the beat was there. He did that part of the playing with natural fluency and feeling, as a musician—human-wise, one might say, not pupil-wise. Here, for example, is his version of "Where Have All the Flowers Gone." as transcribed by me in late November 1988.

The rhythmic pattern is quite sophisticated. Note the triplets, three against two, and the syncopation at many points throughout the piece. All this occurred easily and naturally in the manner of musicians who play by ear. For Tan such phrasing was part of a natural swinging beat. The piano was always there to support the sound of the trumpet with harmony and rhythm, thus providing the musical equivalent of moisture and sunshine to a growing plant. Clearly, the subtle phrasing would not have come about without the piano. That is not surprising, for children learn in *interaction* with wholes and interrelationships, through *spontaneous processes*.

The important point is that this rhythmically sophisticated ver-sion of the song was created not by a child prodigy but by a quite ordinary boy who was given the opportunity for an alternative type of musical training—an opportunity that is easy to provide. More than anything else, Tan's experience demonstrates the power of the learning processes of child culture, processes that are *natural to all children everywhere*. Their astonishing mastery of their

mother tongue is absolute proof of the effectiveness of these processes. *The skills involved in the direct learning of the language*— the
immediate grasp of the subtleties of intonation, rhythm, dynamics,
phrasing, and tempo—*can also be applied to the learning of music.*

How long would Tan have had to take lessons of the traditional
kind before he was able to play the above version of "Where Have
All the Flowers Gone?" Probably for several years. As a matter of
fact, many people have spent a long time learning all about syncopation and such without ever achieving Tan's spontaneity of execution. Another question is even more important: What is the
likelihood that a student taught by the traditional method will
preserve his/her contact with the essence of music as an immediate
and powerful energy field that unites heart with heart, music as
something organically developed from the spontaneous singing of
the child? I frankly doubt whether Tan would *ever* have reached
this point via the traditional route. There are indeed some
doughty people of great talent who manage it—not, I think,
because of but *despite* the endless drilling, reading of printed music,
and lonely practicing that are inseparable parts of the traditional
approach. But the majority of young music-reading students in
Western culture never get into the heart of music. The Muse
Within is reduced to silence.

Models and heroes are important to young people. Joe Montana, Michael Jordan, Bo Jackson—they are the embodiment of
both dream and reality. So why not old Satchmo, Louis Armstrong, regarded by many as greater than Montana, Jordan, and
Jackson put together? And after all, wasn't Tan's trumpet bought
in New Orleans, Armstrong's hometown?

It was time to do something new, so we went to a music store
and bought *Twenty Golden Hits: Satchmo at Symphony Hall 1947,* a
treasure trove of tunes known and loved all over the world:
"Muskrat Ramble," "Black and Blue," "St. James Infirmary,"
"Blueberry Hill," "Basin Street Blues." Just think of being able to
immerse yourself in music like that. All you have to do is put the
record on, and off you go!

Tan quickly became enamored of the jazz sound, and he could
see that his parents were also developing a sudden new fascination

with Louis Armstrong. Even his eighteen-year-old sister Tiril, a music lover with many heroes, discovered in Armstrong one she had hardly heard of before. That was important to a ten-year-old boy who desired a hero all his own.

"The world's best jazz trumpeter!"

"With bleeding iron lips."

"King Louis! Played circles around everyone else!"

Myths are re-created over and over again. And eyes shine anew over and over again—adults' as well as children's. Dreams and heroes beckon us toward better understanding, deeper insight, greater hunger for knowledge, for more playing, for more music.

Tan was clearly mesmerized by Louis Armstrong. He went straight to the library to look for a book about his hero and soon returned with a Norwegian translation of Jeanette Eaton's *The Story of Louis Armstrong*. It was not the best book about Armstrong, but Tan was especially pleased with it because he had taken the initiative to find it. He shut himself up in his room for a day or two and drank it in. He read about how Louis, at the age of thirteen, had formed a singing group that performed "Tiger Rag" in New Orleans's famous Storyville; about the countless spankings he received at the orphanage; that they called him Satchmo because when he smiled his mouth was as wide as a satchel, hence *satch*el-*mo*uth, later shortened; about the cruel teacher, Mr. Davis, who later relented and gave Louis a cornet and let him play in the orphanage band; about how he secretly listened to and learned from King Oliver. And how at last he became world-famous, played higher than anyone else had ever played, and was even honored by the Pope. King Louis!

Tan hungrily devoured the magic story of the life of his hero, and you could almost see him tightening his grip on his own New Orleans trumpet. He was ready to conquer new territory, and it was obvious to both of us that the new tunes had to be Louis Armstrong's. First listen, learn, catch the whirring of the wings— and then play. Come on, boy! Louis is waiting for you!

So we began. Tan quickly mastered "On the Sunny Side of the Street," playing it with a beat and feeling that faithfully mimicked Armstrong's recording. We both became giddy with excitement as the music took hold of us. Full speed! We even dared to improvise a little, introducing an extra triplet and ending with the trumpet clinging to high E before rising to a final G (concert F on a B-flat trumpet, of course).

My diary contains the following entry for January 28, 1989:

> Tan is exploding on the trumpet. One day we practiced "On the Sunny Side of the Street." In less than half an hour we were making music together like a couple of old pros. His tone was intense, full, daring. Think of it! Tan, who is usually so shy that he hardly speaks five words in an hour if anyone else is around.
>
> Yesterday we plowed through two new Armstrong tunes with the same kick: "That Lucky Old Sun" and "Blue Moon." This is what I call happiness.

We made another visit to the music store, this time for some collections of music that I had always wanted but until now had had no good reason to buy. Such a wealth! In a rapture I decided to buy them all: *Big Band Memories, The Best of the Swing Era, The Best Jazz Songs of All Time; 76 of the Greatest Standards,* including "God Bless the Child," "Boogie Woogie Bugle Boy," and "I'll Remember April." "Mood Indigo"—what about that tune! We plunged into it and felt the Muse Within leaping with joy. The young trumpet player really began to understand the idea of "blues." Here was music that expressed longing and pain, with unstable thirds and sixths. And the words were as blue as the music.

> You ain't be blue,
> No, no, no.
> You ain't be blue,
> Till you've had that mood indigo.

Tuva had not been participating in these jazz sessions. I was still accompanying her French horn playing, but the pieces her teacher gave her were from the classical repertoire, not jazz—and she was plainly jealous. And Tan was certainly not above quietly gloating over the fact that for once he—the baby of the family— was ahead of his sisters in something: they both clearly wished that they could play *his* music. He rubbed it in by playing his blues notes louder than ever, as if to say, "Hey, you guys, just listen to *me!*"

What to do? Trumpet and French horn are not a usual combination in the mainstream jazz tradition. Well, so what? We'll form a band anyway! Tan can play trumpet, Tuva French horn, Tiril tenor sax, and I the piano part. And that is what we did. My diary contains the following entry for January 29, 1989.

> Our little band started up Sunday with "Basin Street Blues." Tan played the lead, with a bright, daring tone. Tuva had a harmonizing part on the horn, and Tiril provided the "replies" on the tenor sax in the A section. In the B section, all three played together throughout. Tuva quickly picked up Tan's spontaneous syncopations. They all listen to each other and make subtle adjustments in response to the others' playing. Still a bit of wheezing here and there, but what a sound! It really swung! The Muse Within was there—in all of us. The combination of four instruments opened up a new world of music-making for us. There was no printed music: the children were all "playing by ear." I, of course, played the piano—and the result was a "full orchestra." Now all we are lacking is a suitable name for our little band. We got the A section

in pretty good shape before dinner. Now we have to get back to the
B section. Tuva smiled. This was it!

That afternoon when we started playing "Basin Street Blues"
together we all flew like birds, for the music gave us wings. We
could hear old Satchmo's gravel voice chuckling from above as we
added our voices to the chorus—imperfect amateurs, of course,
but perfectly happy nonetheless: "Basin Street is the street . . ."
Here was Camara's blue horse transformed into the magic of
music: *blues.*

Music has a way of penetrating deeper and deeper into the
body—into the movement of the muscles, as it were. That spring
Tan said to me, "Dad, when you play our songs while I'm upstairs
playing with my toys, my right hand starts fingering the trumpet
part all by itself." Children, it seems, can "hear with their fingers"
by means of a kind of analogical correspondence of ear and hand.

Our band is still playing, and we still feel some of the excitement
we felt the day we first discovered that we could make music
together. Our repertoire consists of standard tunes from the period between the wars: "Tenderly," played as a poetic jazz waltz;
"After You've Gone," also played lyrically and quietly, but with
an underlying syncopated twist. We also play some more rhythmical things: "Make Love to Me," with the lead alternating between
trumpet and French horn, and "Oh, Baby Mine," bouncy and
jovial. One of our "swingin'est" tunes is "Sentimental Journey,"
which sounds surprisingly good with simple parallel thirds between horn and trumpet and with the lead on the bottom. Very
slowly. Our "signature piece," of course, is "Basin Street Blues."

The children listen carefully to each other and respond sensi-
tively to each other's alterations of tempo and phrasing. This is the
spontaneous method in practice, carried along by the competence
natural to child culture. The band's lead trumpeter will continue
to play by ear for a few more years. He's doing fine without being
able to read music, and when he's ready he will learn it fast
enough. *There is no hurry.*

The musical progress we have traced above occurred in the
space of just one year in the life of a nine-year-old boy with a

trumpet—a boy who, like most children, also likes to play with cars, Legos, and balls. His resources for learning are those he shares with children the world over, for they are the common legacy of child culture. This boy also had the advantage, however, of a nearby adult who played the piano and provided an environment in which his inborn potential could find natural expression.

Not every child has a piano-playing parent, but there surely are many adults, music teachers, and older children in this world who can transpose and play well enough to accompany a beginning student—and more should be trained with precisely this role in mind. The important thing is to get on with it, to *try* an approach based on children's own ways of learning. Call it the "Red Rubber Ball" method if you like—the method rooted in the oral tradition of child culture. Many children are waiting for new and better ways to enter into the wonderful world of music, ways that are consistent with their inherent muse-ical natures. If we tap these resources, perhaps more children will go on making music because they experience it as incomparably enriching, and fewer instruments will be hidden away for good because they are so thoroughly detested.

Tan's story is important primarily as a concrete example of a deliberate attempt to harness children's spontaneous muse-ical competence. The same approach could of course be used with different instruments, different repertoire, and different patterns of practicing and playing together. The details can be infinitely varied in accordance with circumstances, including the temperaments of the individuals involved as well as the tastes and skills of the adult mentors. The unchanging point of reference, however, must be the unique life form and muse-ical learning competence that are the natural heritage of all children. Only as we keep this clearly in view and proceed accordingly will we introduce children to music in a way that holds promise of making it a vital and permanent part of their lives. In our own muse-ical version:

The band's there to meet us,
Children to greet us,

Where all *the kids* and *the adults* meet,
This is Basin Street!

Sounds and Notes:
Orality and Literacy in the World of Music

In *Orality and Literacy* (1982), Walter J. Ong discusses the relation
between literate culture and oral cultures, using the contrast between the spoken word and the alphabet as his basic frame of
reference. It is tempting to regard the notation system as the
"alphabet" of music and to think of the relation between sounds
and notes as identical to that between spoken and written words.
There are important differences, however. Notes are intended to
be sounded, whereas letters are intended for writing. The letters
that constitute a book have reached a final stage and live on in that
form in the context of literate culture. A novel or a scientific book
is not intended to be read aloud. A book stands on its own feet as
a final artistic or scientific product. Moreover, readers can easily
acquaint themselves with its content by reading it silently.

A musical score also represents something inherently artistic,
but to read it one must try to imagine what it would *sound* like. A
musical score does not realize its *telos* until it is sung or played for
its hearers. *The notes must take the form of sound in order to live.* With
language, there are just two stages in the process: first the oral,
then the written. Music, however, goes through three stages: oral,
written, then oral again. Music lives only in orality. Written music
is not music; it is simply a set of instructions for creating music.

A child who is asked to play a printed score must turn his
attention from the primary experience of making music (spontaneous singing within child culture, for example) to a kind of
secondary music-making in accordance with the notes on the
page. For many children, the result is that their ability to make
music in the primary sense withers and dies. Nothing comparable
occurs in the case of language: children's encounter with the
alphabet does not rob them of their oral competence (although it
can influence to some extent the way they speak the language).
Their oral musical competence, however, can be irretrievably lost
as a result of premature preoccupation with written music.

The two cases exhibit other differences as well. A much higher level of technical/motor skill is required to transform notes into music than to reduce language to writing. It is incomparably more difficult technically to play the piano than to write. The music notation system is also more complex than the system used for writing language. Whereas standard English is written with just twenty-six letters and a handful of punctuation marks, the music notation system employs literally hundreds of symbols of various kinds. Some are analogical (a crescendo sign, for example), others are abstract (e.g., the symbols denoting sharps and flats), and still others are words from a language other than the child's own (e.g., *adagio*). Thus, to paraphrase a famous text, narrow is the way to music via the printed page, and few are they who find it.

Notwithstanding these differences, there are enough similarities between the two cases to create similar problems for children trying to learn to read words and those trying to learn to read music. Ong has analyzed these problems in considerable detail with respect to written versus spoken language. Reformulating his analysis to fit the relation between experienced sound and printed notes, I find the following contrasts.

Experienced Sound	*Printed Notes*
Auditory	Visual
Inward experience	Determination from without
Subjectivity	Objectivity
Internalization	Externalization
Sensuality	Rationality
Warming up	Cooling down
Magic	Science
Spontaneity	Deliberation
Action	Observation
Transitoriness	Permanence
Dynamic	Static
Wholeness	Fragmentation
Socializing	Isolating
Sikia	Specialized sensation
Ngoma	Score

Obviously I do not mean to imply that the first column represents the unambiguously positive and the second column the unambiguously negative pole in each pair of contrasting characteristics. Written music constitutes a priceless part of our cultural tradition, a treasure trove of beauty and strength that none of us would willingly be without. Were it not for written music, the great creations of Bach and Mozart and Beethoven would have been lost forever, and all humankind would be inestimably poorer as a result. Notation is clearly indispensable as a means of preserving music. It is more than that, however: it has also channeled, organized, and released the creative powers of many composers in a way that would otherwise not have been possible. We are dealing here with psychodynamic processes that occur in the productive encounter of the human mind with the written word. The result of this encounter is the formation of what Ong calls "the literate mind." Orality and literacy are interdependent in a modern music society. As Ong says, "Both orality and the growth of literacy out of orality are necessary for the evolution of consciousness" (1982, p. 175).

The same holds for music, but because music is an audible form of expression it is even more important than in the case of language to maintain contact with living sound. This is especially so when the foundation is being laid, when one is trying to help children become spontaneously creative in relation to this medium.

PLAYING BY EAR IN FOLK CULTURE AND ART CULTURE

Folk cultures are oral cultures, and playing by ear is a part of folk culture. Norwegian folk music, Russian folk singing, American jazz, African *ngoma*—all are derived from folk cultures based on orality rather than literacy.

Though Western art music constitutes only a small part of the world's music, it has had an enormous impact on folk music in many parts of the world. It was apparently toward the end of the eighteenth century that European folk music began to come under the sway of art music's notation system. Swedish musicologist Jan Ling, in his book on European folk music (1989), says that folk fiddle-playing, especially, came under the influence of art music as individual fiddlers began to depend more and more on written music and to write down the folk dance music they played. Still, what they wrote down was never more than a bare outline, just enough to jog their memory. The essence of the music and the richness of its execution always lay far beyond the stylized transcription, for the very good reason that the notation system is incapable of capturing them in their entirety. Every professional musician knows, of course, that written music is only a series of clues to what the music itself—real live music that one can hear and enjoy—is supposed to sound like. But beginning music students typically perceive those written notes as holy writ before which they must bow in silent and intimidated reverence, whether the notes are those of a simple finger exercise or of *Für Elise* (in which the student all too often plays more and more slowly in the somewhat more difficult middle section—a common musical Waterloo for students with limited technical skill).

Although transcriptions have undoubtedly come to occupy a progressively greater role in Norwegian folk music in recent years, the origin of this music in an oral tradition is still evident to a careful observer. Consider a simple example, a dance tune for violin from the old mining town of Röros. We shall give it in two versions. The first is a copy of an early transcription of the basic melody with no embellishments. But note: nobody ever *played* it that way. The written notes were merely a framework within which each performer could improvise in countless ways, as is also the case in the modern jazz tradition. (*Lifligt* means "animated" and *vals* means "waltz.")

Here is the same dance tune transcribed in 1983 with additions and embellishments by Sven Nyhus, a contemporary fiddle player from Röros.

But note again: even this detailed transcription functions only as a framework, for many other subtle rhythmic details, as well as what one might call the "soul" of the dance tune, lie hidden deep within the oral tradition—as Sven Nyhus would be the first to admit. Indeed, he himself displays these "unwritten" elements of the oral tradition when he plays this piece that originated in the part of Norway where he lives.

Improvisation and playing by ear were still very much alive in the Western art music tradition in the eighteenth century. J. S. Bach, for example, was renowned for his extraordinary ability to improvise on the organ. All baroque organists had to master the thoroughbass (also called figured bass) system, learning to fill in the middle voices in accordance with directions in the form of Arabic numerals ("figures") above the bass notes. Indeed, this practice was once so common that the years from about 1600 to 1750 are sometimes called the thoroughbass period in Western music. Improvisation also served a practical purpose in the Lutheran worship service: chorales were to be sung by the congregation, and it was mandatory for the organist to invent a brief prelude to establish the pitch and the tempo before the singing began. The organ remains to this day the principal instrument for the exercise of the art of improvisation. Anton Bruckner (1824–1896) was nearly as renowned for his improvisational skill in his lifetime as Bach was a century earlier. Marcel Dupré (1886–1971) was an outstanding organ improviser in our own century. As a condition of entry to his classes at the Paris Conservatory, he required prospective students to demonstrate their ability to improvise a three-voice fugue on a theme given to them at the time of their entry exam. It is not surprising that many of his students are among the finest organists of our time.

Mozart, of course, was in a class by himself. Even as a child, his improvisational skills were legendary. It is said, for example, that the boy genius sometimes made a game of his performances by placing a coverlet over the keyboard and then creating astonishing improvisations for the enjoyment of his aristocratic audiences. It is well known that in all of his piano concertos Mozart designated a place in the first movement for a solo cadenza, i.e., an opportunity for the soloist (often Mozart himself in the first instance) to demonstrate his improvisational skill. It is less well known that other parts of his piano concertos are based on improvisation as well. Volkmar Braunbehrens, in his book on Mozart (1986), gives as an example the opening bars of the second movement of the famous "Coronation" Concerto in D, K. 537 (1788). In Mozart's handwritten manuscript, nothing is written for the left hand.

In performing the concerto, Mozart himself improvised a suitable part for the left hand but felt no need to write it down. In the orchestral score he wrote out parts only for the strings. For the winds he wrote *ad libitum,* thus giving the players an opportunity to display their inventiveness within the confines of the established key, tempo, style, mood, and thematic material of the piece. It is certain that the part indicated for the left hand in published editions of this concerto was written not by Mozart but by someone who decided it was advisable to give specific instructions here as well—contrary to the clear intention of the composer.

Jean Jacques Rousseau (1712–1778), a contemporary of Mozart and an avid composer himself, advocated playing by ear as the natural and correct way of learning music. In his great didactic novel *Émile* (1762), he wrote: "The reader has surely perceived that I, who am in no hurry to teach him to read words, also have no desire that he learn to read notes. . . . Instead of reading notes he can hear them, for a song is rendered much more authentically to the ear than to the eye."

During the nineteenth century, the practice of playing only

from written music became more and more dominant. One reason, perhaps, was the absence in southern Europe of the Lutheran tradition of improvising on chorales. There is a direct line from *Gradus ad Parnassum* (1725), the standard textbook in counterpoint by J. J. Fux, via J. G. Albrechtsberger (Beethoven's teacher), to the curriculum of the Leipzig Conservatory, the world's first such institution, established in 1843. This influential conservatory chose to follow the Fux tradition, giving great emphasis to written music. No doubt this was perceived as the practical and sensible thing to do at a time when music instruction was being transferred from the studios of private teachers to an institutional setting. Robert Schumann, however, who was a central figure at the Leipzig Conservatory when it was founded, was himself a brilliant improviser on the piano.

The influence of the Fux approach was further disseminated via the many études published during the nineteenth century. Muzio Clementi (1752–1832), a great keyboard virtuoso as well as a composer and teacher, published a large collection of them between 1817 and 1826, using the same title that Fux had used a century earlier. The type of instruction previously used for training composers was now applied to keyboard playing as the student was led through a long series of carefully designed exercises. The route to mastery was spelled out in detail: Clementi's études constituted what one might call a "Triptik to Parnassus." The student had but to follow instructions, progressing from easy to more difficult exercises, and at length he would reach the peak of Mt. Parnassus, home of the Muses. Clementi's études remain to this day standard fare for piano students at various levels of proficiency the world over, though the hope of reaching the top of the mountain remains an impossible dream for the vast majority of them.

The development of music publishing houses and music schools in Central Europe in the nineteenth century led to the creation and dissemination of a new type of music whose explicit purpose was pedagogical. Composers worked in close collaboration with their publishers. New institutions gave impetus to a rapid growth in music instruction, resulting in a flood of pedagogical publications that are still with us—a flood in which beginning students all too often sink before they learn to swim.

CHILDREN AND BIRDS: LEARNING BY EAR

It has often been observed that young children who move to a new locale are able to master a new language or a new regional accent so thoroughly that their speech is indistinguishable from that of the natives. The story of little Tan and the red rubber ball is one example. Swedish linguist Per Linell has summarized the prevailing view of this phenomenon as follows.

> Our capacity to learn foreign languages and dialects in a natural way seems to deteriorate at the onset of puberty. Under favorable circumstances, children can naturally become bilingual or multilingual, with perfect diction and grammar in both (all) languages. One who encounters and learns a new language after puberty, on the other hand, has a hard time mastering all the phonological, phonetic, and grammatical rules of the new language and avoiding the influence of the different rules of his/her mother tongue. The clearest and most common effects are evident in the pronunciation. Almost all people who learn a foreign language as grown-ups retain an accent, even if in other respects they have excellent command of that language. (1984, p. 112)

Some interesting parallels appear to exist between language acquisition in humans and song acquisition in birds. Research in this area has established that for many species of birds there are some especially sensitive phases for the acquisition of the song pattern (Clayton 1989), and that for some species—the song sparrow, for example—this sensitive phase is linked to the bird's development up to the time of sexual maturity. To put it simply: a young song sparrow, having learned the song pattern peculiar to its home territory, can change its dialect if it is moved to a region in which the pattern is somewhat different. It exhibits a learning plasticity during its "childhood" similar to that of human children. Once the bird reaches sexual maturity, with all the associated hormonal changes, its dialect is permanently fixed. (For a more thorough discussion of this topic, see Kroodsma and Miller 1982, Nottebohm 1984, Eales 1985, Nordeen and Nordeen 1988, and Clayton 1989.)

Humans, too, have what one could call an especially sensitive phase for language learning that ends with puberty. Linell (1984) suggests that this change in the capacity to learn language may be related to the fact that the brain begins to function differently at puberty. There is reason to believe that in human beings, as in birds, the especially sensitive learning phase is associated both with neurological development and with hormonal processes.

Whatever the underlying causes of the phenomenon, the unique learning ability of children is a well-documented and indisputable fact. Children learn their verbal mother tongue through the ear and the body, not via pencil and paper. They learn spontaneous singing, their muse-ical mother tongue, the same way in the context of child culture.

Ornithology as well as studies of language acquisition in humans further support the thesis that children's first music training should be communicated orally and based on hearing rather than on learning to read written music. Such an approach takes maximum advantage of the unique learning ability of children at a time when it is at its peak.

NOTATION AS A LIMITATION OF EXPRESSION

The *muse-ical imperative* lies deep in the heart of every professional musician and makes its presence known in those wonderful moments when they are at their best and the music flows as if from an inexhaustible well of indescribable beauty. In such moments the musician and the music are so intimately connected that they are virtually extensions—vital living parts—of each other.

The practice of following a printed score, however, often sets limits that are unknown in the aural tradition. The sight of a high C on a page of music represents an *external* imperative—bearing the authority of a revered composer—that can intimidate an internal imperative. Indeed, countless thousands of professional musicians have been intimidated in just this way. They see it looming before them, this magical high note, as if to say, "So high, and no higher, you shall play as proof of your professional adulthood—for that is the established limit for your instrument."

In the aural tradition there is no such authoritative barrier. For a musician in this tradition, the playing of others becomes a model, and at first a goal. But in this case internal desire, blissfully unaware of prevailing ideas about what is and is not possible, controls the entire process.

Lars Naess, a professional trumpeter in the classical tradition, has written to me as follows concerning the "established limits" for his instrument.

> Both reference works and textbooks on trumpet playing describe the trumpet's range as being from F-sharp below middle C to C two octaves above middle C and state quite definitely that these are the limits.
>
> . . . In the course of his professional studies or experience, an orchestral trumpeter is confronted with scores that exceed these limits. Except for Baroque music, which is not a part of ordinary symphonic literature, . . . one can easily pick out the composers who have violated the conventional limits. Wagner, in the Prelude to *Parsifal,* calls for a concert C two octaves above middle C *"sehr zart und ausdrucksvoll,"* Richard Strauss sends the trumpets up to high C-sharp and D in *Der Rosenkavalier, Salome, Electra,* etc. Not big changes, but big enough to create some notorious pitfalls for trumpeters.
>
> If we look at the jazz trumpeter, however, the situation is quite different. As early as the 1920s, Louis Armstrong began to play higher and higher with each successive record he cut. He often played high E, and routinely played on and around high C. By the 1930s and 1940s, high F was quite common among jazz trumpeters. In the 1950s Maynard Ferguson added a full octave, play-

ing F above high F—and Charlie Shavers, in a record released in 1948, played an octave above that (= the highest F on the piano). . . .

. . . The function of a jazz trumpeter is completely different from that of one who plays in an orchestra. He is more engaged in creating than in re-creating. The musical idea and the development of that idea come to the fore *while* he is playing. Ergo, the established limits disappear; the only remaining barriers are the performer's own physical and psychic resources. It was and is evident that the musical imagination quite easily led the creative jazz musicians beyond the acknowledged limits of the tonal range of their instrument. Therefore, playing very high notes has become a hallmark of jazz trumpeters in the same way that a "copper-red tone" is the ideal of orchestral trumpeters. . . .

Finally, a quotation from a record I once had of a jam session in which Dizzy Gillespie, Roy Eldridge, and others each played a solo passage in "Blue Lou." The writer of the program notes concluded his discussion of the titanic exegeses of "the leather-lunged men" with the words, "Take that—if you can. . . ."

It is said that some European trumpeters refused to believe their ears when they first heard Louis Armstrong's recordings in which he regularly played notes between high C and high E. They were sure he was playing an instrument especially constructed for this purpose and demanded to see it. Upon inspecting it, all they found was a well-worn trumpet from New Orleans with three ordinary valves—just like their own. It was the wail of pain and joy arising from his heart as well as his lungs that lifted Satchmo's trumpet sound "beyond infinity." Many children have also journeyed beyond infinity in imagination and song—just as boldly, just as existentially. Rusky found his way to Nangiyala, Per became a butterfly. That is the kind of experience young people are seeking when they first begin to play an instrument, whether or not they have any chance of reaching Satchmo's high E. If that desire is squelched they will cease to make music, no matter how long they may continue to take lessons out of loyalty to their doting parents.

THE ART OF TRANSPOSING MUSIC

Fun with transposition is a natural part of learning by ear. Because experiences within child culture familiarize children with rules and systems that must be mastered, it is easy for them to learn the logic of transposition once it is explained to them that the relationships among the scale degrees are the same and can be manipulated in the same ways in all keys. The tonic chord is built on the first step of the scale, the "home base" to which the music will eventually return, no matter where else it may go. The dominant chord is based on the fifth step of the scale and creates tension, "leaves you hanging." A chord built on the second step of the major scale creates yet other tonal colors, and when its third is raised it becomes the dominant of the dominant. A chord on the third step is called the mediant and leads easily into the minor modes.

Does that sound dry, complicated, and theoretical? Theoretical concepts are not difficult for children when they can be immediately converted into finger positions and music through songs they already know. They can learn theory effortlessly if it is presented to them in the right way—playfully, muse-ically. Unveiling the system gives them the joy of discovery and creates dexterity in fingers and sensitivity in ears.

I know that many music teachers who are also pianists feel inadequate at this point because they themselves never learned to transpose music. They didn't learn it as children, and now the train has left the station: to learn simple transposition at this late date, they feel, would be impossible. And so, time and again, they endure painful situations.

"Couldn't we take this song a little lower, Miss Petersen? We can't reach the high notes." (And they really can't. It's not easy to sing a high F when your voice is changing—especially in music class, where the girls titter every time your voice breaks.)

"I'm sorry," Miss Petersen says with obvious embarrassment. "I'm afraid I can't change keys on the spot, but maybe by next week I can prepare to play it in D. For now we'll have to do our best with what we've got." So they continue—in F major.

Happily, there are exceptions—teachers who have mastered the techniques of playing by ear and transposition in addition to conventional note-reading. Many, however—probably the vast majority—never acquired these skills. Nobody ever offered to teach them, and on the assumption that "teacher knows best," it never occurred to them to ask. Even as professional musicians and/or teachers of music, they are ill-prepared to respond to the needs of the moment in a natural and spontaneous way, for music is not a means of communication for them. The spontaneity of childhood has left them. They no longer believe that they can fly.

MUSIC AND NOTATION

Norwegian musicologist Dolores Grøndal has done some interesting research (1988) on the role of printed music in the playing process. The object of her study, undertaken at the Norwegian State Academy of Music, was to determine the influence of a score on the musical spontaneity of pianists in the process of learning a new piece. The study included both professional pianists and music students. Not surprisingly, Grøndal found that the professional pianists were much more adept than the students at maintaining their musical spontaneity while they were still dependent on the printed music. The professional pianists somehow grasped the music itself through the printed symbols; they didn't let the technicalities of the notation system prevent them from perceiving the music as something unified, whole, and personally engaging.

> It is very interesting to confirm that the teachers [the professional pianists] don't just "see" the printed score: they experience it in several ways. They "hear" sound, "perceive" movement and contact, "cognize" the printed notes . . . as if they were looking at a map, and simultaneously "see" the keys. In addition to all this, they also comprehend the score verbally in terms of chord structure, names of notes, etc. (1988, p. 29)

These experienced professional pianists exhibited something similar to the unitary sensation—the *ngoma*—of children. They did not merely perceive a part; they perceived the whole, both directly and bodily-auditively, in movement and sound. They spontaneously looked beyond the printed page as a pattern of visual symbols and directly perceived the music itself. The students, however, exhibited a much more fragmented relationship to the printed page and a correspondingly distant relationship to the music itself.

> This brings us to the central question: since there appears to be such a palpable difference between teachers and students, ought not the instruction to be especially directed toward training students to experience printed music with all their senses?
>
> . . . Will not the mastery of this skill give our students a quite different experience of music? And will it not help them to learn more quickly, and to enjoy it in a quite different way—and to continue playing? (p. 31)

Grøndal did not attempt to identify the possible causes of the rift between the music and the students' perception of the printed score. Thus she did not suggest the possibility of approaching music or a musical instrument directly, through the capacity for unitary sensation, rather than through the printed page. Nonetheless, her discussion can be construed as a contribution to *ngoma* pedagogy, for without discussing either children or child culture she has raised a question that once again calls to mind the original and unitary learning characteristic of children everywhere. Regrettably, most of us lose this capacity along the way in the labyrinths of intellectualization, specialization, and fragmentation that constitute the educational system. The professional pianists who perceived music whole represent the few who came through the system without losing this precious capacity. That is probably the underlying reason why they became professionals: they refused to let go of the music, and in the process saved themselves as well.

The Waning of the Muse Within

Teachers today remember with a condescending smile a time not so long ago when first-graders were introduced to reading in a highly mechanical way. "Dick. See Dick. See Dick run. Run, Dick, run." Dick and Jane and Sally. Father and Mother and Spot, the family dog. That was the world, the artificial world of words, in which children learned their ABC's.

Music instruction in many schools is still at the Dick and Jane stage. Here, for example, is a tune that Norwegian schoolchildren are often expected to play on the recorder.

The intent is obvious: to provide material for practicing fingering on the recorder for two notes, C and A. Melody and text are well suited to each other: both are banal. An introductory exercise such as this commits violence in three ways: against the instrument, against music, and—most important—against the poor child who must suffer through it.

Someone might object, "Isn't the melody similar to a song formula common to child culture everywhere? Isn't it in fact a good example of how to use material derived from child culture in the critical transition from spontaneous singing to mastering an instrument?" No. The song formulas of child culture are deliberately simple because they must be in order to serve their communicative function in the setting in which they are used. Such formulas are what they are because they are products of a living social context. The above ditty, with its "tu-tu-tu-tu-tu-tu-toot," is not. One does not approach child culture by mechanically appropriating its formulas and using them out of context. These formulas are at home only within child culture; without it they lose their magic and their meaning.

Similar exercises are produced by the music publishing industry in many countries, since books for beginners are a profitable commodity. The following example (Thompson 1936, p. 10), which first appeared over half a century ago, is from a graded series of instruction books that has gone through many editions and is still widely used by piano pupils the world over.

"Fun"?! What a letdown for eager young children—from spontaneous and joyous sensitivity to enforced wandering in a musical desert! The notes lie there demandingly, silent and heavy with authority. If you stray from the path marked out for you by the notes, be it ever so slightly, it's YOUR MISTAKE—and you have nobody to blame but yourself. If you succeed in getting all the notes right, there is still no guarantee that the result will be music. As the notes become more and more difficult to master, there is a constant struggle between the external demands of the printed score (perhaps augmented by those of the teacher) and the inner need for expression. The printed notes become a prison instead of a portal, confining expression instead of freeing it. Concentrating on the music as written usurps your energy, thus removing the physical dimension from the music-making. We have all witnessed the result: children who have tried for years to play the piano without ever getting physically involved in the process. The piano, for them, is an impediment to music rather than a glorious instrument with infinite possibilities for musical expression.

Is this an exaggerated account of the current state of affairs in the musical training of children? Perhaps, for here as elsewhere the world is not all black and white. Certainly there are cases— perhaps many cases—of pupils who thrive on the traditional score-based approach, making rapid progress toward a deeply fulfilling musical experience. The best of these pupils combine fine technique with a richly developed native muse-icality that is thrilling to observe. And it must also be said that there are plenty of pupils who have responded no better to the aural approach than have many of their peers to the exercise book. No matter what the approach, some children would rather go swimming.

Nonetheless, I think it cannot be denied that the tyranny of the printed score is a major factor in discouraging many beginning music pupils. In the docile acceptance of this tyranny lie the roots of the musical functional illiteracy that afflicts so many people who know something about the notation system but have lost the capacity to communicate music as a vital human reality. It is obvious that we are dealing here with a condition in many ways parallel to that of the secondary illiterates discussed earlier, who know the alphabet and can read words but who have never learned to read and write in the deeper sense, as a personally meaningful form of expression. The same dreary pedagogical story often repeats itself in the lives of children, whether the subject is reading and writing or music education. The effects, as we shall see, can be observed even in the professional adult music student.

The preface of the Thompson piano book from which we took the example above contains a statement defending the choice of material: "These melodies were written with careful thought and were kept as simple as possible in order that they would be within the grasp of a child's hand, which is, quite naturally, small." Yes indeed, the grasp of a child's hand *is* limited. The motor skills of a child's ten fingers are also limited. A human being's fine motor skills are usually not fully developed, from a neurological point of view, until about the age of ten. Why, then, should a child start playing the piano as a first instrument in any case? A child's need for play and meaning is enormous, as is the musical potential hidden in a piano. A premature encounter between child and piano runs the risk of doing violence to both. The child gets discouraged, the music ceases, and the piano—purchased in a moment of enthusiasm by ever-hopeful parents—gathers dust like the piece of abandoned furniture it has become.

Consistent with its commitment to mastery of the notation system as part of the learning process, Thompson has also published a companion volume to its introductory lesson book: *Note Speller*, "For the teachers who, for the sake of thoroughness, desire to have the pupil practice writing." The well-trained pupil, then, will advance simultaneously on two fronts, learning more and more about the notation system as s/he progressively masters the instrument. Whether or not we grant the legitimacy of the traditional approach, we must concede that the concern for integration is at least logical.

Some music teachers are so committed to the notation-system approach that they insist children be taught its elements *before* they start playing an instrument. In Norway, for example, it is by no means uncommon for children to be enrolled in a six- or twelve-month course in note-reading preceding their first lessons on an instrument. Knowing how to read music is the needle's eye through which children must pass before they can enter the kingdom—the right to make music on an instrument. The contract is clear and unambiguous: if you don't learn how to read music you can't experience the pleasure of playing an instrument. And that, to many children, is a penalty to be avoided at all cost, for in Norway it is regarded as an honor to play in the school band.

Look for a moment at the lesson on the next page, from a student workbook for a course of this kind taught in Oslo as recently as 1989 (the supposedly "correct" answers are given in each case). This exercise reminds me of the painful experience I once had trying to learn to swim. I was in the fourth grade, and all boys of that age who couldn't swim were required to take extra instruction. We knew that those who succeeded would get a silver patch, and that to get it you had to be able to swim twenty-five meters in deep, deep water. Unfortunately, our school didn't have a pool, so we had to practice on the gym floor. There we lay, on our bellies, practicing "swimming" hour after tedious hour. "Arms forward! Stroke! Arms forward! Stroke!" the teacher wheezed rhythmically, over and over again. The predictable re-

---

<u>Lesson 3</u>

Here is a row of notes. Can you clap, beat time, and say "boom"
and "bah" at the right places? Try!

♪ ♫ ♪ ♫ ♪ ♫

Sometimes the rows of notes get very long. Think of how many
notes there are in <u>Twinkle, Twinkle Little Star</u>. You can also
think about how confused you would get if we didn't use commas
and periods in writing our language.

   Example: "Now you must get up Billy it's late school starts
            in five minutes you must not get late again today
            do you hear me"

We would get confused in the same way if the notes were just
strung out without being divided into small groups.

To divide up the row of notes we use a vertical line.
It is called a <u>BAR LINE</u>.
The small groups of notes <u>before</u>, <u>between</u>, and <u>after</u> the bar
lines we call <u>measures</u>.

                 measure   measure   measure

              ♫ ♫ ♪ ♪ ♫ ♪ ♫ ♪

                    bar line bar line

How many bar lines are there in this row of notes? <u>2</u>
And how many measures did you find? <u>3</u>

If you replace each quarter note with two eighth notes you will
see that each of the three measures has the same number of notes.
DO THIS:

          ♫ ♫ | ♫ ♫ | ♫ ♫

How many eighth notes were there in each <u>measure</u>: <u>4</u>

We could call this a <u>four eighth-note measure</u> (4/8).

It is most common to call this <u>TYPE OF MEASURE</u> a 2/4

        (two quarter-note measure) | It is because ♪ = ♫ |
                                     |
                                     | Thus   4/8 = 2/4

---

sult was that we got slivers in our hands and scabs on our elbows,
but we never learned to swim. No silver patches were given out
when the training finally came to an end. Not one. The water was
in another world, miles away from our dingy little gym.

   Music instruction without music in your ears is like swimming
instruction without water. You get slivers in your soul.

AUNT LIL AND "RUSTLE OF SPRING"

He was thirteen years old and just beginning to show signs of a voice change. Tall as a telephone pole, a bit stooped, and as ungainly as only a pubescent boy can be. "Nothing but arms and legs," his father said.

Aunt Lil was sixty-five, on the threshold of old age. Her fingernails were meticulously polished, always in a color that matched her lipstick, and her fingers sparkled with a multitude of gold rings. The scent of pungent perfume perpetually surrounded her.

He was a piano student, she was his teacher. Aunt Lil. Everybody's Aunt Lil.

Like many others, he was nauseated by her perfume and had recently hit on the idea of stuffing little wads of cotton in his nostrils before going to his lesson. Fear of everything female can run pretty deep in a thirteen-year-old boy.

"Just a little nosebleed," he mumbled when Aunt Lil asked with alarm whether he had hurt himself.

"Every week?" she asked sweetly when he came to his lesson with cotton in his nose for the fifth week in a row. He nodded silently and sat down sullenly on the piano stool with Aunt Lil in her chair close beside him. They had been sitting like that, once a week, for almost five years now, every Thursday right after school, from two-thirty to three-fifteen. Today, however, was no ordinary Thursday. The week before, Aunt Lil had given him a new piece that demonstrated a high level of confidence in him: Sinding's "Rustle of Spring," Op. 32, No. 3. No beginner's piece, this! It was something for really advanced students.

"Well, young man," Aunt Lil warbled happily, moving her chair closer to him, "I can hardly wait to see what you have accomplished during the past week. How did it go?"

It is hard to speak clearly with cotton in your nose, so instead of answering he started playing. He was there to play, not to engage in chit-chat. The composer had written *agitato*. That makes sense, the boy thought to himself as his heart knotted up in apprehension: D-flat major, endless mounds of thirty-second notes, and an increasingly frantic race in the left hand—the one that always gave him the most trouble in fast passages.

The first few measures went fine, with the melody in the left hand and the spring breeze rustling above.

RUSTLE OF SPRING

Christian Sinding. Opus 32 Nr. 3

But soon it was to get much worse.

He played away as beads of sweat began to form on his brow. The cotton wads made it hard to breathe. His left hand began to stiffen as if to protest the wild ride on which it was being taken. In desperation he stepped on the pedal, held it down firmly, and changed the left-hand arpeggios into a diffuse cascade of sound. Didn't his version, different though it was from what Sinding had written, sound at least a *little* like a rustle of spring? He stole a quick glance at Aunt Lil sitting there in her prewar padded chair. Wasn't she smiling? Yes! She was entranced!

"Lovely!" she said excitedly. "What a 'Rustle of Spring'! My, how you must have practiced during the past week!"

Aunt Lil, sensitive as she was, must have let herself be totally carried away by her pupil's pedal version of Sinding's masterpiece. Impressed with what she was hearing, she clearly did not notice all the sloppy left-hand improvisations he had substituted for the "impossible" arpeggios.

From that day forward, playing the piano was a totally different experience for that young man. Aunt Lil's unintended tolerance for inventiveness opened up a new world of exciting possibilities at the keyboard. The printed music lost its absolute power over him. He was free—free to express himself, free to make music— and he threw himself into it with a vengeance. Who could stop him? Not Christian Sinding, who was long since dead. Not Aunt Lil, who was apparently beginning to lose her hearing. He himself was now in charge: whatever *his* ear approved was permitted.

He began to rush through the popular hits of his day, songs like "Love Letters in the Sand" and "Only You." At first he bought the expensive sheet music, but little by little he began to play by ear, which was both cheaper and better. He quickly picked up the harmonic clichés that are the stock in trade of pop music, found ways to improve on them, and before long was able to stand on his own defiant feet in the world of music. He continued to take lessons from Aunt Lil for another six months, a pedal player on Thursdays and a happy improviser the rest of the week. But the oscillation between the two musical worlds—the others' and his own—became increasingly difficult.

The day he took his last lesson from Aunt Lil he went without cotton wads in his nose. He also got a haircut, the kind Aunt Lil's generation liked in those days. The barber had clipped him close all the way around and well above the ears. He felt like he had been scalped.

"How cute you look with that new haircut!" Aunt Lil said smilingly as she opened the door.

"I have a new song I want to play for you," he said seriously.

"Really?" she said. "For me?" Her heavily rouged cheeks seemed to grow just a shade redder.

The song had been carefully chosen. After all, wasn't it Aunt Lil who had first taught him notes and a certain amount of technique? And wasn't it she who had also given him the opportunity to go his own way on the piano, whether or not she intended to?

So he began, in C major, with a generous sprinkling of velvety minor and diminished seventh chords along the way: "You are my special angel, sent from up above. . . ." Aunt Lil smiled even more broadly than she had during that first lesson with "Rustle of Spring." In fact, she blushed. She looked almost angelic.

As he was leaving, he handed her a piece of sheet music he had bought out of his meager allowance. It was his going-away present to her. On it he had written "To Aunt Lil from one who plays by ear. New Born." He closed his eyes, plunged into the cloud of perfumed air that engulfed her, and gave her a hug. It wasn't nearly as bad as he had feared. Then he was gone.

He didn't say it in so many words, but Aunt Lil understood. He wouldn't be coming for lessons anymore. He brushed his hair forward Elvis-style as he bounded down the stairs from the fifth floor, inwardly exulting at his newfound freedom. With his left hand sliding happily on the handrail he took the last eight steps in a single jubilant leap: ". . . I feel your touch, your warm embrace, and I'm in heaven again!" The echo of the song was still reverberating in the stairwell as he stepped out into the sunshine and closed the door behind him.

THE INSTRUMENT AND THE BODY

French philosopher Maurice Merleau-Ponty is one of many who have disputed Descartes's dualistic view of man, arguing instead that the body is both the origin and the center of the process of perception. Merleau-Ponty writes about the communicative relation of the human body to the world and about the body as the basis for instrument/human relations. Norwegian philosopher Carl Erik Grennes has applied Merleau-Ponty's views specifically to the musician's relation to his instrument.

> Merleau-Ponty gives several examples of this mode of existence. It is typical of human beings to relate to their environment by means of instruments. The typewriter constitutes an extension of my body

in that it makes possible my work as a writer. We can see this point even more clearly in the relation of a blind person to his/her cane. The cane is not, for the blind person, a physical object apart from the body: it is an extension and an amplification of the body's sensing apparatus. . . . In the same way, one cannot correctly describe a musician's relation to his/her instrument in terms of a body manipulating a physical object. The musician has "tuned" his/her body to the instrument just as s/he has "tuned" the instrument to the body. . . . In modern terminology one could say that body and instrument constitute a "system" that collectively exhibits the property of "mind." (1984, p. 18)

Here we are dealing once again with a type of *ngoma* and *sikia* whose roots lie in childhood's ecology of perception. Musicians live in creative symbiosis with their instruments. A horn player's lips *hear* as they make contact with the mouthpiece in the act of playing. Fingertips in position on the black and white keys of the piano call forth creative powers that are otherwise merely latent possibilities. The instrument does not reduce possibilities; it enhances them, realizes them. The musician and the instrument, in the act of making music together, become one entity. Each without the other is artistically mute. United they become more than the sum of two disparate entities, and in moments of authentic creativity they collaborate to create music with wings.

Earlier we discussed Winnicott's view that creative play serves a key function as a bridge-builder between inner and outer worlds. In the encounter with a musical instrument, it is important for the child to build a bridge—via instrument as extension of body—from the inner muse-ical need for expression to the audible realization of this need in the outer world, i.e., the music. Moreover, the sound produced in the outer world must *satisfy* the child's inner need if the playing is to "ring true" and thereby give meaning to the child's own life. This is what makes the choice of an instrument suitable to the child's specific physical, emotional, and cultural circumstances so critically important. It is also why children should be encouraged to develop the direct channel between ear and body, without the distraction of printed music. The principle is as easy to understand as it is difficult to put into practice: the closer the contact between child and instrument, the closer the child's contact with music.

Emphasis on the physical dimension of musical performance led Roland Barthes to distinguish two types of music:

> . . . the music one listens to, the music one plays. These two musics are two totally different arts, each with its own history, its own sociology, its own aesthetics, its own erotic; the same composer can be minor if you listen to him, tremendous if you play him (even badly). . . . The music one plays comes from an activity that is very little auditory, being above all manual (and thus in a way much more sensual). It is . . . a muscular music in which the part taken by the sense of hearing is one only of ratification, as though the body were hearing—and not "the soul." (1982, p. 149)

In the discussion of Merleau-Ponty, Grennes cites the blind person and his/her cane as an example of organic sensing, with body and hand extended by means of an indispensable instrument. Many musicians will recognize this type of sensing from their own experience of playing an instrument. Look, for example, at pictures of Louis Armstrong playing his trumpet: he closes his eyes during his improvisations. The performer gets even closer to the instrument and the music, the feeling of oneness becomes even more intimate, when the eyes are closed. Introspection into one's own soul also becomes deeper—as if the metal of the trumpet turned into gold when Armstrong touched it.

WHEN AND WHAT?

Two questions are often asked regarding the music training of children: When should they begin to play an instrument, and what kind of instrument should they learn to play first? There are no easy answers to these questions, but we can derive some guidelines from what we now know about children's muse-ical development and the forms of learning characteristic of child culture.

My first suggestion is: *Don't start them on an instrument too soon.* The transition from spontaneous singing to the mastery of an instrument is a critical one, and children are often subjected to the demands of instrumental instruction before they are physically, neurogically, or psychologically ready for it. It takes time to develop as a human being. Many things must be in place before a child is ready to find pleasure in playing an instrument. The fine motor skills of the fingers must be adequately developed. The lateralization of the left and right hemispheres of the brain must be well along. The child must have had sufficient time to be a child, frolicking with friends and playing children's games, without undue pressure from adults to do other things. There are already enough burnouts and dropouts among music students without adding to the number by pushing children into something for which they are not yet ready.

Someone might say, "But what about Mozart, the child prodigy *par excellence?* He certainly started playing an instrument at a very early age and was a true virtuoso by age six. And do we not read from time to time about other young prodigies—Mozart's offspring, so to speak—who are masters on an instrument while they are still in grade school? What about them?"

The example of Mozart—or of the occasional child prodigy who gives a brilliant performance of Beethoven's Fifth Piano Concerto before the age of ten—is hardly relevant to our topic. Most children master *the normal tasks of childhood* in their own way and in their own good time. They acquire an astonishing fund of knowledge, language, and social codes as part of their natural development, without the help of adult specialists or academic pedagogy. It is when the learning resources of children are pressed too soon into the service of tasks set by others that problems may arise, both in education generally and with respect to music instruction in particular. Starting a child on an instrument at a very young age is rarely a shortcut to musical virtuosity, but it is often a prelude to disaster. For every child prodigy there are tens of thousands of other children who have suffered defeat in their first encounter with an instrument and have given up the idea of ever playing an instrument for the rest of their lives.

Of course we should share with our children from infancy forward the values we believe in. Starving the natural hunger for learning is also a serious problem in the upbringing of children. During the preschool years, however, we should be in no hurry to impose on children our carefully formulated ideas of what they should be doing. All too often we give children suggestions and shortly thereafter expect them to comply, in a kind of immediate "pedagogical harvest." A young child may indeed take delight in hearing a Mozart sonata. Far too many children are given an altogether too limited musical diet during their upbringing, with unfortunate results for their aesthetic development. Hearing a Mozart sonata can strike a chord in children at many different levels, enriching their emotions and their imagination, their play and their thinking. Mozart's music can enter organically into their everyday lives as a vital part of their minds and activities—but on *their* terms. That is quite different from expecting the child to sit at the piano and learn to *play* that same Mozart sonata. Here, through an instructional system motivated not by the child's own needs but by parental ambition, Mozart is made to stifle the Muse Within in a way that he himself surely would not have condoned.

The child's first and most important instrument is *singing*, with the body itself as the resonance chamber, string, and bow. We have had occasion to observe how important spontaneous singing is for children everywhere. All children need singing as an integral part of their development as human beings. It is part of the natural mechanism whereby children, from infancy onward, master the complex skills of language and interpersonal communication. No external demands based on *bel canto* aesthetics must be allowed to hinder this important development.

It is only fair to note that some representatives of the art music tradition have also challenged the one-sided cultivation of the *bel canto* ideal and have defended the legitimacy of other types of singing and vocal expression. Luciano Berio, for example, has composed a piece for solo female voice ("Sequenza III," 1966) that not only breaks new ground but also seems to me to be rooted in many ways in the muse-ical mother tongue of childhood. It exhibits much of the expressive richness and vocal experimentation on the boundary between speech and song that are characteristic of spontaneous singing. It is similar in some ways to Per's song about the butterfly. Berio's performance instructions, which he lists alphabetically in the "preface" to the song, reflect a universe of vocal expressive nuances that all children are familiar with in their spontaneous play, in smooth transitions between song and speech, which for them are but two shimmering sides of the same coin.

> anxious, apprehensive, bewildered, calm, coy, distant, distant and dreamy, dreamy and tense, echoing, ecstatic, extremely intense, extremely tense, fading, faintly, frantic, frantic with laughter, gasping, giddy, impassive, increasingly desperate, intense, joyful, languorous, muttering, nervous, nervous with laughter, noble, open with laughter, relieved, serene, subsiding, tender, tense, tense with laughter, tense muttering, urgent, very excited and frantic, very tense, whimpering, whining, wistful, witty

Berio is well aware that this attempt to suggest some of the vocal subtleties he desired in the performance of his song represents nothing more than a composite stylization of infinite possibilities. If the song is to come to life in a muse-ical way, it clearly must be performed by an artist who is so mature as a human being that she dares to incorporate an unabashed childishness as an important element among her vocal resources.

After some experience with spontaneous singing, the most natural next step for many children will be drums and other rhythm instruments, in genuine *ngoma* combination with singing and play. Here, too, there is nothing wrong with permitting children to start early provided they are allowed to use these instruments in their own way, as part of their spontaneous play and muse-ical communication. Speaking, singing, dancing, and beating the drum should be intertwined as closely as possible, with the natural rhythm of the children's language and songs as the controlling framework. For a long time it will seem more natural for the children to beat the drum with their hands and fingers rather than with drumsticks, for in this way their bodies are in immediate contact with the drum. Some children will start drumming directly on their bodies in time to their singing, a common practice in the African tradition. Adults can create a framework for children's drumming by playing, dancing, and singing with them. I think children also find it exciting and meaningful to beat time to recorded music, in the process learning to match their rhythm to that of professional performers. The important common element here is that the youngsters are learning by participating functionally and directly in a musical context that carries them along. Adults must make sure that children are given such opportunities, for that is how they learn. Self-motivated learning in companionship with others always works better for children than formal instruction. It is child culture's own recipe.

With genuine *ngoma* sensing, it is impossible to think of drums without dancing and singing. The pounding of the feet on the ground and the pounding of the hands on the drum are experienced as different manifestations of one and the same inner movement. If one vibrates, so does the other. If one stops, both stop. Such is the ecology of the muse-ical mind.

> Danish music educator Bernhard Christensen reports that at a folk festival in Yugoslavia . . . he was very impressed with a drummer whom he was unable to see during the performance because the performers were sitting in an orchestra pit.
>
> After the performance, therefore, he went backstage to interview the drummer, who turned out to be a boy about five or six years old! Christensen asked him through an interpreter to demonstrate some of the dance rhythms he had played earlier, but all the boy could produce now were some clumsy, vague rhythmic patterns. He seemed to grow more and more subdued and confused until one of the dancers went out on the stage and started to dance.
>
> Then, when he was able to connect the music to some meaningful background, i.e., the dancer's movements, the boy regained his former confidence and again produced all the complex patterns that earlier had made such a strong impression on the audience. But simply as patterns, apart from the dancing and the movements of the dancers, they evidently didn't exist for the boy. (Sundin and Sääf 1971, pp. 6–7)

So long as we are dealing only with singing and drums, it is relatively easy to think of music-making as an organic extension of children's play. The world still hangs together, and neither the child nor the music nor the instrument is driven out of Eden. Then comes the critical phase, music education's rite of passage: the transition from spontaneous music-making as a form of play to a melody-producing instrument that requires technical proficiency to play.

In the Western world, the piano has long been the instrument of choice for children's first experience of this kind. If we look at the matter from the child's point of view, however, there are many reasons not to start with this instrument—not, at least, in the traditional way. Consider the following polarities between the characteristics of a small child and the daunting requirements of a piano.

The Child	*The Piano*
•Short finger span	•Requires larger hands
•Limited lateralization	•Requires independence between left and right hand
•Limited development of fine motor skills	•Requires fine-motor-skill use of all ten fingers
•Music and physical movement are one	•Requires sitting still on a bench for extended periods
•Body, singing, and breathing are one	•Breathing is not directly related to music-making
•Needs companionship	•Requires practicing and playing alone

A five-year-old can play with a piano—pick out melodies, discover chords, and so on—and there is certainly nothing wrong with letting a seven-year-old learn to play by chord symbols, adding things by ear, if s/he really wants to. Children have different interests and skills, and they develop at their own pace. Again, we should not be in too great a hurry. *Classical* piano playing—the kind adapted to the requirements of the instrument rather than those of the child—is generally best delayed a couple of years for most children. I think the piano-playing of most children would definitely benefit rather than suffer from such a delay.

Dmitri Shostakovich's mother, herself a professional piano teacher educated at the St. Petersburg Conservatory, understood this point. As a small boy, Dmitri showed no great interest in playing the piano. He preferred to play with his playmates, and his mother gladly approved. Not until he was nine years old did she start giving him formal piano lessons. In waiting so long she demonstrated, in my opinion, that she was both a wise teacher and a good mother.

Wind instruments, on the other hand, are suitable for children in a number of ways.

1. Many of them make fewer fine-motor-skill demands than the piano and require less independence between the left and right hand.
2. They preserve the direct contact between breathing, mouth, body, lungs, and abdominal muscles that is so important for children's forms of cognition.
3. They allow the child to move while s/he is playing. S/he can literally walk around, creating the music bodily as well as instrumentally. "I move—and I learn!"

Child culture itself seems to exhibit a natural propensity for wind instruments. When children play, they make blowing sounds of many kinds. Every observer of children has seen this, and it revives memories of childhood: whistling, blowing on a blade of grass, producing real musical sounds on a willow flute, creating a "jug and bottle" band. Such experiences are part of the foundation on which a child's future musical development can be built. Learning is meaningful to the extent that it is related to past experience, modifying and expanding what is already known.

There are many wind instruments from which to choose. Among the relevant considerations are the child's temperament and identification with musical "heroes." Some may like the mellow, pastoral sound of the French horn, others the more aggressive sound of the trumpet. Such instruments as the tuba and the trombone obviously should wait a few years, until the body is strong enough and the arms long enough to handle them.

There is of course no advance guarantee that a wind instrument will give a child a good experience with music, such that the child, after the first few lessons, will clutch the instrument to his/her bosom and promise to be faithful till death. The child's relation to the instrument and to music must be built on the interests, skills, and resources developed through past experience. Learning must be child-centered, not instrument-centered, for *the child is the main instrument. Sikia* ecology of feeling, mind, and body is the crucial starting point for playing any instrument. If the child is not getting in tune with the Muse Within, there will be no real music-making, no matter how beautiful and costly the mechanical instrument at hand. So long as this basic concept is understood and observed, a variety of methods may be used to move forward—methods that allow child and music to become united as closely and naturally as child and pail and shovel in a sandbox.

The wind instrument that has been used most frequently in classroom instruction is the recorder. Indeed, the recorder is the only instrument many children have an opportunity to play. The memory of the sour, squeaking sounds produced by thirty beginning recorder players has cured plenty of children of whatever interest they may have had in learning to play an instrument of any kind. They have no way of knowing that what they experienced is a regrettable misuse of a fine solo instrument that has a rich tradition in music history.

My recommendation for an alternative to the recorder for use by beginners in a classroom setting is the melodica, a type of mouth organ on which the pitch is varied by depressing the keys on a small keyboard. The melodica has several advantages.

1. It requires little in the way of fine motor skills (much less than the recorder). It is possible to play melodies holding the instrument in just one hand; thus there is no need for subtle coordination between the left and right hands.
2. No special blowing technique is required.
3. No special lip or tongue skills are required.

4. The keyboard, with its black and white keys, gives the child a clear visual impression of the chromatic scale (much clearer than the recorder).
5. It provides for the possibility of simple chords (which the recorder does not).
6. The sound of a roomful of beginners trying unsuccessfully to play in unison is not as unpleasant as that of an equal number of beginners playing recorders out of tune.
7. Fingering skills acquired in playing the melodica can be transferred to both the accordion and the piano.

Is the melodica capable of producing "ordinary music"? Of course it is. Indeed, a skillful player can produce music that really swings! Jazz musician Joseph Zawinul, for example, played the melodica on one piece in the album *Mysterious Traveller*.

It is also very important here, as with all instrumental instruction, that teachers make it clear that they regard the instrument with respect. They must also be able to play the instrument and show enthusiasm for it. The sharing of enthusiasm is fundamental in learning processes. Children are used to learning by example, along a line that goes from imitation and accommodation to assimilation, to use Piaget's terms. The teacher's own playful music-making on the instrument often means more to the children than anything s/he might say during the music lesson.

When the music instruction of children is being discussed, the question of the Suzuki method inevitably arises. All informed music educators know about the astonishing results achieved by this method in Japan, where very young children learn to play the violin under the powerful influence of a symbiotic relationship with their mothers. Clearly, the success of the method underscores the importance of musical listening and hearing-based rote playing rather than printed music. The combination of emotional fellowship between mother and child and the approximation to playing by ear has made the Suzuki method very effective.

On the other hand, the Japanese, with their traditional sense of thoroughness and system, have pressed the musical socialization process forward in a manner that clearly reflects adult ambition and standards and can hardly be said to be grounded in the inherent values of child culture. Without a doubt, the Suzuki method has produced a large number of competent violinists. Strikingly few of the world's top violinists are Suzuki products, however. Might this not be related to the fact that these children—even the gifted violinists among them—do not experience an optimal development from playing children to musicians, and that many of them, too, end up as burnouts? They showed so much promise as children, but they never fully realized it—not, in any case, to the extent hoped for by their teachers. How many of them continue to play as amateurs, and how many have quit playing altogether? And why? It would be most interesting to see the results of some research on these questions.

Attempts to transplant the Suzuki method to countries with totally different cultural and social structures have also proven somewhat problematic. Just as the Kodály method had its origin in Hungarian culture and folk music, so the Suzuki method was based on some unique features of Japanese culture, not least the unusually tight family structure, with the mother playing a very special care-giving role (Suzuki 1977). Suzuki saw this in his own country and adapted his method accordingly. But the same situation does not exist in Western countries, where different values prevail and the mother plays quite different familial and social roles. Nonetheless, attempts are constantly being made to transplant the Suzuki method *in toto* to the United States and other countries. If Suzuki's goals are to be realized outside Japan, however, it is his *ideas* that must be employed, not by mechanically copying his methods but by creatively adapting his pedagogical principles to other cultural settings. The child and the music must be firmly rooted in the cultural reality of the child's own country. Only then can the Suzuki method open exciting new perspectives for children. Unfortunately, it is an international Suzuki—Suzuki *sans* the specifically Japanese qualities, and strongly influenced by Western aesthetics—that largely dominates the contemporary music market today. The beginners' volumes in the piano instruction books published in Princeton by Suzuki Method International, for example, are quite similar to the corresponding volumes of the Thompson series in their lack of muse-icality. Little remains here of old Suzuki's burning vision of a learning process involving mother and child in symbiotic playing by ear.

Children are generalists. They have to develop a variety of skills in order to participate in the teeming comradeship of child culture. Specialization occurs more often than not as a result of the encouragement of adults, who are constantly looking for signs of a promising talent that may someday become great and famous. Thus talented little dancers are carted off to ballet lessons, talented young ballplayers to Little League, and talented young voices to choir practice. That is not all bad, of course, but children also need freedom—time and space to maintain their versatility, their well-roundedness. Why should a child play just one instrument, by the way? There are so many instruments, with so many different sounds and timbres. If children really learn to play one instrument, it will not take them long to master another. They will already know what it is to make music with their whole being. Thus one can well imagine a child who first plays drums and then trumpet, going on as a teenager to master the piano or the violin, the synthesizer or the electric guitar—and reveling in a muse-ical manifold that provides ever new and alluring opportunities for the singing of the Muse Within.

LEARNING TO READ MUSIC

We have seen in the foregoing that there are many reasons—historical, developmental, physiological, neurological, and biochemical—why children's first experience with an instrument should be by ear, without the distraction of printed music. This is the natural gateway to instrument playing for children. The ability to play by ear will add a vital dimension to the bearer of the Muse Within for the rest of his/her life, enriching the experience of music-making in countless ways.

Eventually, however, the child should learn to read music. When? And on what basis? For many children the encounter with printed music is a disappointment, a "downer." For others it proves to be an enrichment and a welcome aid in music-making. Which it is depends on the pedagogy employed in introducing it to the child.

There are many different forms of notation, from simple chord symbols for a guitar accompaniment to the complete score of a piano sonata. It is important, therefore, to adapt different kinds of notation to the differing needs of students. Notation should be introduced progressively, and with due attention to the different age groups.

If we assume that children start playing an instrument at age eight or nine, it is probably best to let them spend at least a couple of years playing by ear before introducing notation. By then they should have come to feel the instrument as a part of themselves—like the blind person with a cane—and the time will be ripe for the introduction of notation. It goes without saying that this phase, too, must occur on an organic foundation, not simply as something that is done because it has always been done in the past. Children themselves should feel a need for notation and understand what they are going to do and why.

Printed music can be presented as an aid to memory when a child has learned so many pieces that it is difficult to remember them all. Thus learning to read music is perceived to have a practical purpose and is not a meaningless task pursued for no apparent reason. Or the need for printed music can arise when a group of children play together: it helps them keep track of who is to play what and when, thus organizing their cooperative effort in a way that makes sense to them. Since they have already developed a close and muse-ical relationship to their instruments, there is now no danger that they will end up as mere mechanical note-players. Everything they have learned about genuine music-making can be carried over into their playing by note—which, of course, is what true musicians have always done.

Musical notation can enable a child to play music so complex that it would otherwise be almost impossible to learn. In this case, printed music becomes a completely natural ticket to the playing of a kind of music that many children want to be able to play. The teacher should introduce the child to the score the first time through, demonstrating how the notes on the printed page can be transformed into resounding music. The child listens and perhaps plays along as s/he begins to grasp the outlines of the new piece. Once the piece has been learned, the score should be put aside as the child resumes playing in the accustomed manner—from a *sikia* kind of memory, in direct contact with his/her own listening ear, and instrument, and fingers, and body. Be careful, however, not to underestimate what a child can learn *without* the help of written music. Children can easily learn a two-part Bach invention directly, without a printed score, if the teacher demonstrates it for them in meaningful phrases and gives them an opportunity to repeat what they have heard.

Allowing for individual differences, it appears that puberty is for many children the ideal time to introduce printed music. At puberty, under the heavy influence of today's school system, children make the transition to systematic understanding and thinking in abstract and symbolic categories. Research also indicates that a change occurs in the division of functions between the left and right hemispheres of the brain at this stage, partly as a result of the maturation of the corpus callosum, the band of white fibers forming the neurological link between the two hemispheres. At the same time, the emergence of the sex hormone appears to weaken the ability to learn "by ear" and reproduce both verbal sounds and music.

The onset of puberty, then, is a time when children are more prepared than previously to understand the symbolism of musical notation and use it to their own advantage. Of course, they can learn the theory of notation earlier as a purely intellectual exercise, but such learning is likely to be confined to a rather superficial understanding of the literal significance of the various symbols. For most children, the understanding of musical notation never gets beyond this purely descriptive, *iconographic* level (see Panofsky 1980). They remain on the outside, able only to look in through the window at the music represented by the printed notes. But the understanding of a printed score should reach a deeper, *iconological* level, where the notes on the printed page are perceived as signs pointing toward real music—music that is sensed with subjective immediacy in mind, body, and instrument, and in the very act of producing the sound. That is the level achieved by the professional pianists studied by Dolores Grøndal. For them, the notes were music, directly perceived as bodily movement and audible sound. To achieve such an intimate relationship between the notation and the music, however, a similarly intimate relationship must already have been established among the child, the instrument, and the music. Printed music, i.e., notation, at best can only enrich a muse-ical intimacy that is already there.

Typical beginning students have no such basis for dealing with the printed music. They are normally expected to accomplish all of the following tasks simultaneously.

1. Learn the mechanics of the instrument.
2. Develop the physical skills required to play the instrument (mouth, fingers, etc.).
3. Learn the rudiments of music theory relevant to the playing of the instrument.
4. Correlate all of the above with a deeper approach to iconological note-reading and authentic music-making.

It is absurd to think that this formula—conflicting, as it does, with so much of what we know about children and how they learn—could have any hope of success except in a few rare cases. The high dropout rate in schools of music and the frequency of psychological problems among advanced music students are both related, in my opinion, to this mindless violation of the Muse Within. The expectations prove to be unreachable for most. Even among those who continue to the more advanced levels of music training, there are many who still suffer the effects of the manner in which they were introduced in childhood to the serious study of music.

For students who play an instrument capable of producing chords, a natural first step toward note-reading is often playing by chord symbols, a common practice in popular music and jazz. Chord symbols can be found in music of many different genres and at various levels of difficulty, so there is plenty of opportunity for variation and progression. They constitute in many ways an ideal halfway house between the complete freedom of playing by ear and the constraints of a conventional musical score. In a piece consisting of a simple melody line with chord symbols added, the notation does not function as an authoritative multitude of demands that the intimidated young student is sternly admonished to obey. Its role is one the student can readily understand and appreciate: to be a helping hand, to point the way toward the music s/he is to create. The notational framework is open, not closed. Certain chords are written in only as suggestions and support, not as unalterable commands. New chords can be introduced, old ones eliminated, as often as one pleases. And not least: with chord-symbol notation, the demands of the music can be adapted to the student's stage of development with respect to fine motor skills. A prepubescent child, for example, can begin to play the guitar as soon as his/her hand is big enough to grasp the neck of the instrument.

The relative openness of the chord-symbol system is an invitation to students to try their wings, give their imaginations free rein, find new sounds, do a bit of improvising on the piano. It also creates a natural and functional basis for transposition, both on the piano and on the guitar (the use of capotasto is mandatory!). Songs must, of course, be played in a key that is comfortable for the singers. Ideally, students who are about to learn note-reading have already had a good deal of experience with transposition as an integral part of their experience of playing by ear.

For many, the next step will be a natural and organic transition to the mastery of conventional music notation, the gateway to the inexhaustible riches of the world of music. Now the student can explore at will the musical treasures created by the great masters. Note well: *playing by ear is not the opposite of classical note-reading but its natural presupposition.* It is the experience that ensures that the child's playing will be the singing of the Muse Within, not merely the mechanical depressing of valves or keys. Teachers and parents must learn to be patient. Children need time to mature, musically as in other respects.

It may appear that what I have described is an upward progression from the primitive and simple (playing by ear) through the somewhat more sophisticated (chord-symbol playing) to the culturally approved and truly valuable stage (note-reading). That is not my intention. Playing by ear, chord-symbol playing, and note-reading are simply three different playing traditions, each valuable in its own way. Some people will always prefer to play by ear and will find much enjoyment in so doing. Others will be especially attracted to chord-symbol playing and will have no desire to learn another method. And still others will find their musical home in the note-reading tradition.

What I am urging is not a relaxation of artistic standards but greater breadth in our concept of what is musically legitimate. If we compare the different music traditions, we should not look only at the degree of originality and complexity exhibited by each. By such criteria, the singing of a simple child's song will always be judged inferior to, say, a performance of Mozart's *Magic Flute*. But other qualities are also important—for example, genuine musicianship, authentic presence, touching the heart of the listener. Judged by these criteria, a simple ballad or a rock hit may well exhibit more true quality than a traditional performance of an operatic aria. It is, among other things, a question of the meaningfulness of what is created at the moment of the performance. Conservatories and other institutions of advanced music study could do much to enlarge our vision in this area, for the world looks to them to lead the way with respect to musical standards.

THE TEN COMMANDMENTS OF TRADITIONAL MUSIC TRAINING
The introduction to note-reading in the traditional manner may strike many students as a kind of parody of the Ten Commandments.

1. Thou shalt have no music gods other than mine.
2. Thou shalt not misuse the key signatures.
3. Thou shalt regard printed music as holy.
4. Thou shalt honor corrections and exercises, for then it will go well with thee and thou shalt live long in the music school.
5. Thou shalt not play wrong notes.
6. Thou shalt not transgress the tempo markings.
7. Thou shalt not create fermatas where none are indicated in the printed music.
8. Thou shalt not forget the accidentals.
9. Thou shalt not covet thy neighbor's ability to play by ear.
10. Thou shalt not covet other music forms or techniques or anything else that is thy neighbor's.

The setting within which the commandments are delivered is typically the well-ordered weekly lesson, where both teacher and student know in advance most of what is going to happen. The students have practiced the assignment enough to know exactly where their weak points are. The teacher, having assigned the same piece to innumerable other children through the years, also knows where problems are going to arise—for this student, and for others yet unborn. The instrumental repertoire is in many ways a legacy that is passed on from generation to generation through private lessons and as part of the permanent core curriculum of the music schools. After half an hour the ordeal is over, and though the relative amounts of praise and criticism may vary from time to time, by and large it has proceeded as both teacher and student knew it would. Having been through it together many times before, either of them could have written the script.

Striking the wrong key on a piano is not fatal. You can't be jailed for it. Neither is it morally reprehensible, as many piano students tend to feel. It does not warrant the bad conscience it often creates. It only seems to be such a serious offense if the teacher frowns, makes the student stop, and—however mildly— corrects him or her on the spot. It is the *fear* of making a mistake that is fatal.

Teachers should not criticize children for making mistakes. Rather, they should show the children how to play the passage in question—and praise them when they succeed. That this advice is so old as to sound almost banal does not detract from its continuing validity. If playing wrong notes takes on too negative a character, the result can be so stultifying for the child that the Muse Within is silenced forever.

Music teachers who tend to be overly critical of student mistakes might have something to learn from current theories about how best to teach children to write. It is now widely accepted among elementary educators that it is unwise to call attention to all the mistakes in the writing of young children (Smith 1982, Graves 1983, Dysthe 1987, Holm 1988). There has been agreement on this point for half a century as far as first-graders are concerned, and the tendency today is to observe the same principle for older children as well. It is to be hoped that it will gain wide acceptance throughout the world. Critical and mechanical correction of every little error diminishes the importance of the content of the writing and places it at a distance from the child and his/her need for expression. Formal training in writing, necessary though it is at the proper time, must not be carried on in such a way as to impede the child's grasp of the language or his/her powers of expression. A mechanically correct text that has every "i" dotted, every "t" crossed, every word correctly spelled—but is stiff and devoid of all human feeling—is not the goal we should be seeking. If the superficial relationship of secondary illiterates to written language is ever to be overcome, it can only be through an authentic identification of the *writer*—his/her deepest human interests and concerns—with the content of what s/he writes.

Conventional taboos must also be overturned with respect to early music training. No great harm is done, for example, if a child "mistakenly" substitutes an E-flat for an E-natural in the opening phrase of "Baa, Baa, Black Sheep" (as sung by Norwegian children).

The expected and the unexpected can be joined together: that is one of the basic principles of creativity. In the above example, major and minor exist side by side in a way that adds a dash of humor to this delightful little piece. A quick-witted teacher might remark to an "erring" piano student, "Well, there *are* both black and white ones in a flock of sheep, aren't there?" The child would learn the important lesson that even mistakes can be turned to good advantage.

Remember that children have been taking similar liberties with their songs, both musically and textually, throughout childhood. Why shouldn't they do the same when they begin to play an instrument? Is it the teachers who are paralyzed at the thought of such freedom and unwittingly communicate their fear to the student? Do they feel that they somehow lose authority and control if the child departs from the printed score and goes off on a flight of fancy? Is this what gets in the way? If a child comes to note-reading with a background in playing by ear and improvisation, a "mistake" can well become an opportunity to create something new and interesting. Perhaps it will be something playful, something idiosyncratic, something that picks up and develops the humor implicit in the inadvertent juxtaposition of major and minor. For with a bit of imagination, the E-flat can become the basis for a brand new version of "Baa, Baa, Black Sheep." We must never forget: children *can* fly. Music teachers especially must never forget, for the magic moment when a child, if encouraged, might take flight often occurs during what in other respects may seem to be an ordinary music lesson.

The teacher must dare to show the way, to be an example for the child. "Baa, Baa, Black Sheep" as a hilarious mixture of major and minor? What fun! And off they go, teacher and student—together. The teacher's degree of openness to such adventures will set the standard, for children generally are game for any amount of play, amusement, audacity, and wonder. If, for the sake of simplicity, the teacher retains the prescribed harmonization, the introduction of an E-flat here and there—and perhaps a few other notes foreign to the harmony—will constitute nothing more than a little extra color within a familiar framework. It is an old technique often used in music traditions less restrictive than ours. Blues playing, for example, makes ample use of this technique: the key is established, and the melody is then spiced with "deviant" notes expressing the mood and emotion of the moment. Children quickly understand such things and make them their own. Humor and serendipity stimulate the hunger for knowledge. They can also decrease fear, with lasting effect. In the hands of a competent and daring teacher there is no danger of chaos and formless nonsense. On the contrary, teacher and student will create priceless opportunities to make music together spontaneously—which is quite the opposite of what actually occurs in all too many music lessons.

What I am proposing is not a mere possibility, a fancy: I have observed it in practice on many occasions. It is the kind of moment that keeps music alive as a channel of experience renewed from day to day in the life of the child.

Let us not make children grow up feeling pangs of guilt every time they play a note that isn't in the score. Let us rather give them permission, when they play a "wrong" note, to incorporate it into a new version of the piece, seemingly stumbling along, like Charlie Chaplin falling down the stairs in one of the old silent films. This, too, calls for form, work, practice, because improvisation requires well-developed listening skills as well as dexterity and confidence in the fingers. These just happen to be somewhat different skills— ones more deeply anchored in the heart and soul—than those required to follow a printed score meticulously.

It is important not to leave children entirely to their own resources in making such attempts, for without help and direction they can quickly become discouraged. They tend to be extremely self-critical and are likely to be very hard on themselves unless they are taught otherwise. Immerse them and their music in an environment that gives constant encouragement and support. Draw them into the fellowship of a muse-ical communion of saints that is profoundly human precisely because it is authentically muse-ical. Let them, in this context, experience the unique power of music as the voice of the Muse Within. Some children, under such circumstances, will achieve results so far beyond the ordinary that even the most skeptical teacher will be forced to abandon conventional ideas about what can reasonably be expected of young musicians.

Trust and inner confidence during the early years are in most cases the best guarantee against later performance phobias. One would think this point would be obvious, but in view of the amount of anxiety and stress created by the existing system of music instruction one feels compelled to emphasize it. None of us, admittedly, knows the complete answer to the problems of note panic, mistake phobia, or stage fright. I think the suggestions given here point in the right direction. Let each reader, each parent, each teacher go on from here—with both careful planning *and* improvisation.

Music Without Fear

Anxiety, stage fright, and the like often stand between individuals and the music they are attempting to play. The technical and interpretive skill required to perform the music seem so formidable to many people that the connection between them and the music is broken; making music becomes a matter of playing with as few mistakes as possible rather than playing as well as possible. For them, the glass is always half empty rather than half full.

This anxiety follows many students of music in varying degrees even into the conservatory and beyond. We are all familiar with the symptoms: fear of blundering, disinclination to play for others, sweating, knotted stomach, heightened adrenaline production, trembling, dry mouth, wet palms. These symptoms are well known to adults as well as children, professionals as well as amateurs. Anthony Kemp (1981) has made a systematic study of the problem. At the Norwegian State Academy of Music a study of stage fright and performance anxiety is currently under way, among other things to determine whether the pedagogical approach in the academy may itself contribute to the problem. Psychologist Knut Olseng reports, for example:

- several instances each year of students fainting at their recitals;
- widespread use of medications (e.g., beta blockers and mild sedatives) to get rid of stage fright;
- sporadic use of marijuana by students to help them get through especially demanding periods of practicing.

Of approximately one thousand musicians studied, Olseng found that nearly half the female students were excused for some period of time during the year because of psychosomatic symptoms related to their studies. Olseng writes:

What struck me was the fact that those who had such symptoms experienced a great deal of stress in their work. They were subject to stage fright, they felt that their job or their academic progress threatened their self-respect, they had to avoid many situations involving solo playing, and so on. . . . In my work as a psychologist at the Norwegian State Academy of Music I encounter a number of students who have failed—fine people who simply have not been able to withstand the psychological pressure and the demands placed on them by their teachers, their fellow students, their families, themselves. . . .

How in the world can we get living and thinking music students to truly live on the stage? Do we kill the most promising musical performers before they ever get off the ground because we lack the knowledge and techniques about the learning process itself? (1989)

A recent study of classical musicians in the United States revealed that almost half of them experience psychosomatic problems associated with playing and public performances. More than a quarter of them were regular users of beta blockers such as propranolol, which is a prohibited substance for Olympic athletes (Lockwood 1989). We know, of course, that some musicians also use narcotics for the same reason.

The causes of stage fright and performance anxiety among music students and professional musicians obviously do not lie entirely in the instructional system used in the schools of music. These schools merely reinforce the problems inherent in the kind of instruction that the students received as children. For that and other reasons it is important to discuss as openly and objectively as possible—and perhaps with a clearer idea of what we are doing—what might be done differently in the music instruction of children. Tendencies to anxiety may of course show up in many other areas of life as well. Again, the form of music instruction simply reinforces a preexisting disposition. For music's sake, as well as the child's, let us do everything possible to rid music instruction of needless anxiety.

"Music has charms to soothe a savage breast, / To soften rocks, or bend a knotted oak," wrote William Congreve in *The Mourning Bride*. Music is capable of *reducing* tension and anxiety. That is why there is such a specialty as music therapy, and why we sometimes leave a concert feeling renewed and uplifted in the depths of our souls. Music is not merely part of life's decoration: it is a unique life force. Thus it is vital to understand as much as we can about the Muse Within, and to discuss music and children, music and music education, music and human communication.

Some institutions of advanced music education are in the pro-

cess of critically examining their present practices. The Guildhall
School of Music and Drama in London, for example, has recently
instituted a type of music training quite different from that of other
professional music schools in England and on the Continent.
Dance and awareness of one's body are important here, as are
improvisation, meditation, and communication. Musicians are
encouraged to get in touch with themselves again as pulsating,
muse-ical human beings. The need for this is very great, according
to Peter Renshaw and Peter Wiegold, creators of the Guildhall
program. Many professional musicians feel a need for a new
artistic vitality and immediacy. Some of the ideas implemented at
Guildhall have recently been espoused in Sweden—for example,
at the Music Academy in Gothenburg. In Norway, work is under
way at the University of Oslo to develop theories and techniques
in support of new and more effective forms of music instruction,
not least for children and young people. This book is one result of
that effort.

Music Experience and the Importance of a Rich Repertoire

When I heard Per sing his butterfly song, I learned something
about child culture that I will never forget. Filled with admiration,
I was forced to revise all my former beliefs about what kinds of
songs small children are capable of singing—indeed, what kinds
of music they are capable of *liking*. This matter turns on something
much more important than what children are able to assimilate
and perhaps reproduce in a recognizable form: it is at root a
question of what they are capable of *experiencing*. It is we adults who
set limits at this point, because we—practical, sensible people that
we are—think there *are* limits to the kinds of music children can
enjoy, and that these limits must be respected. But the imagination
and emotional receptivity of children know no such limits, either
for songs or for other music. The butterfly song is quite complex
rhythmically, melodically, and with respect to tonality. Most musically trained adults would have to go through it several times to
commit it to memory. Per, however, was just five years old, and
he had a speech defect of such severity that he was barely able to

say his own name clearly enough to make himself understood. Nonetheless, something "clicked" for Per when he heard this song. He instantly and effortlessly made it his own—singing it, to be sure, in his own unique way. As a matter of fact, it soon became the favorite song of Per's entire class. Whoever first advanced the theory that "simple little children require simple little songs" must never have been a child, for it patently contradicts the facts.

Research on the spontaneous singing of Norwegian preschool children (Bjørkvold 1985) shows that children are generally attracted to challenging and complex songs—the kind that rarely find their way into songbooks for children—if they are given an opportunity to get acquainted with them. Like anything else we seriously expect children to respond to, such songs must be presented to them by adults who believe in the value of what they are offering without worrying about what is "suitable" for children. In children's natural, almost voracious quest for new challenges, this seems to be one side of their bold creativity. It is an integral part of the triumph of inconvenience in childhood, the urge to seek challenge as an expression of the will to life. Children would rather climb a real tree, dangerous though it may be, than content themselves with the jungle gym solicitous adults have provided for them. Those same children would rather sing "The Many-Color'd Butterfly" than most of the clapping and hopping songs found in typical songbooks for young children. And they are at least as fascinated by the poems of Longfellow and Whittier and Frost as by the simpler fare they are often given. Let us not give them stones when they are asking for bread.

A large body of research has established a close link between what children receive in the way of literary and language impressions during the first years of life and their language competence later on. The relationship is simple enough: the richer the language environment, the greater the verbal competence of the person growing up in that environment. The lesson is clear: Read frequently to your children; they need stimuli from all kinds of good literature. Spend time talking to your children; they need to be enriched by the many varied nuances of human language. It is encouraging to note that in both Norway and the United States there is growing interest on the part of authors as well as parents in the quality and diversity of children's literature.

The same lesson applies, *mutatis mutandis,* to the sphere of children and music. Children, as we have seen, weave music into their play as an integral part of their communication with one another. It is deeply embedded in their spontaneous, muse-ical mother tongue. The richer this material in the early stages of life, the better prepared the child to comprehend and express his/her own experience of reality. Children have a natural disposition to receive, to "take in" what is presented to them. A broad musical experience in childhood will obviously enrich and invigorate the later stages of life. We who care about children and music need to make it clear to voters and school boards that music education is not a "frill" that can be dispensed with when budgets are tight. On the contrary, it is a vital part of children's development as human beings, and its neglect will cause irreparable harm.

It must also be said, however, that the selection of songs offered to children in the schools I have observed leaves much to be desired. There is all too often a deadening sameness about them, a decided lack of musical and textual daring. Virtually all of them, for example, are in a major key. In my study of the spontaneous singing of Norwegian preschool children (Bjørkvold 1985) I found that approximate ninety percent of the songs introduced by teachers were extremely simple and in major keys—and Norwegian music is known for its preference for minor and modal keys! Can it be mere coincidence, then, that the children's clear-cut favorite of all these songs was "The Many-Color'd Butterfly"—the only *modal* song they were given an opportunity to hear? Why do we assume that children are capable of enjoying only songs that we ourselves consider textually simple and musically uninteresting? Why do we continue to inflict upon children what someone has called "major poisoning" a century or more after Grieg, Debussy, and others permanently changed the Western world's concept of tonality?

As a first step toward abolishing the "monopoly of the major," children should at least be given much more exposure to the rich repertoire of songs in minor keys that abound in the song literature of many nations. This would also provide a dimension of cultural diversity as the children learn songs from other countries—perhaps, in some cases, in the original languages. Make use of the resources in your community. Find someone from Latin America to teach the children some Spanish songs, someone from France or Germany to teach them French or German songs. You will be amazed at the authentic sound of their accent after only brief instruction by a native speaker. And it goes without saying that American children should be exposed to a variety of songs within the American repertoire as well—folk songs, ballads, show tunes, spirituals, blues, and so on. Teach them the songs that *you* think are interesting and fun to sing, and don't worry about whether or not they are generally regarded as "suitable" for children. It doesn't take children long to figure out whether the adult who is leading them believes in and likes a song. Present songs that you can sing with heartfelt enjoyment, and children will listen with their hearts. The result will be a human alliance between adult and child based on physical nearness and shared experience of a kind that television cannot duplicate.

CHILDREN AND CONTEMPORARY MUSIC

Because it represents a break with convention, modern music— music not securely anchored in some kind of tonality—has a unique capacity to liberate the imagination. Children are virtuosos with respect to imagination and should by all means be introduced to such music. Moreover, the introduction should occur early enough that they are still able to approach it with an open mind. Much of this music, including electronic music, has been recorded and could easily be incorporated as a dynamic element in connection with such activities as role playing, puppet shows, and improvised dancing. "But surely," someone will object, "modern music is too difficult for children to comprehend." Not at all. It is only *we adults* who consider modern music "too difficult" for children. If we think back to the spontaneous singing of children we know that such music is *not* foreign to them, for their *fluid/amorphous* songs typically contain elements of free-tonal invention that sound very "modernistic."

The leap from fluid/amorphous songs in the sandbox to art

music in the concert hall is shorter than we might think. Many
instances could be given of modern compositions best understood
as mature artistic expressions of the same musical urge that creates
the spontaneous singing of children. For example, Norwegian
composer Knut Nystedt, who is well-known in the United States
as a composer of sacred choral music, employs graphic notation
in the opening bars of *Exultate*, op. 74.

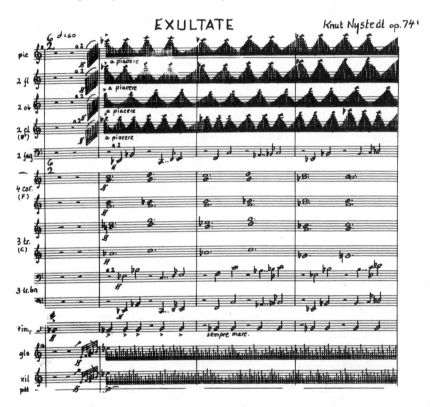

The precise meaning of this notation is that the performer is to
improvise *glissandi* within the prescribed limits—a clear case of
stylized fluid/amorphous song in an advanced artistic setting. Another example of the same phenomenon appears in a concerto for
viola and chamber orchestra by the modern Russian composer V.
Barkauskas.

American composer John Cage has gone beyond merely employing the fluid/amorphous song form in an original composition. With a genuinely childish touch, he has also created his own version of juvenile art.

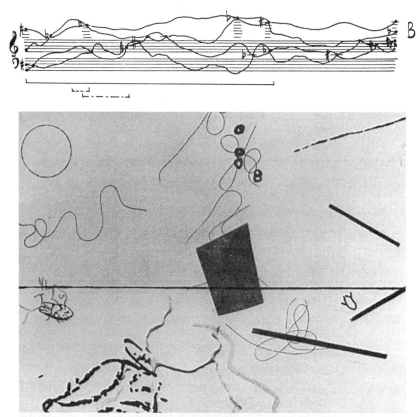

Déreau, number 3

Norwegian music history furnishes a striking example of a composer who was profoundly influenced by the atonal spontaneous
singing of a child. Fartein Valen (1887–1952) was the foremost
representative of atonal music in Norway. His style was extremely
unpopular among his own countrymen during the period between
the two world wars, when nationalism in the spirit of Grieg—
albeit without his genius—held sway in Norwegian music. Music
historian Olav Gurvin gives this account of how Valen was emboldened by the singing of a young boy to continue on the path
he had chosen.

> Arne, a son of the composer's nephew, . . . was also very musical.
> At the age of five or six he could sit and improvise vocally—i.e.,
> he did not sing a definite melody, but sat and picked out notes here
> and there on one or two vowels. One day Valen noticed that the
> boy did not use the usual diatonic major or minor scales, but
> selected notes here and there from the chromatic twelve-tone scale.
> He was, in a way, singing "atonally." This occurred at the time
> when Valen was on the verge of . . . totally abandoning tonal music,
> but was sometimes in doubt about whether this really was the right
> thing to do. Perhaps there was something in the objection he had
> often heard—that "atonal music" was not natural, that it was
> nothing but intellectual constructs and fabrications. But when a
> child could sing in this way, then it had to be natural. Nor could
> there be any obstacle to using the chromatic scale directly, outside
> the major/minor system. Arne's song strengthened his confidence
> that he was on the right path despite the objections of his critics.
> (1962, pp. 130–31)

Exposing children to modern music, then, does more than
create an important opportunity for broader musical competence
as the basis for a subtle and enriching investigation of their own
reality. Acquainting them with the musical vocabulary of such
modern masters as Stravinsky, Shostakovich, Schoenberg, Valen,
Cage, Ligeti, and Nordheim can also be viewed as a consolidation
of their identity. In many instances, upon hearing this music,
children will have an experience of *déjà entendu,* for it will strike

them as a kind of external recognition and confirmation of their inherent identity.

There is every reason to protect this modernistic haven in the hearts of children, especially as they approach school age. So much that is dear to them is threatened by the many dualisms that will suddenly be imposed upon them: beautiful/ugly, right/wrong, successful/unsuccessful, nice/naughty, happy/sad. When the neat systems of adults threaten to make the whole world look as flat as a North Dakota prairie, it might be a good thing for children to be able to call to mind some impressions from topsy-turvy musical modernism that spurn all such systems, thus preserving a necessary element of irrational tension and disorder in their lives. There has to be something to challenge all the rules, introduce the joker, and make the game worthwhile. It is common knowledge that the concert programs of most of the major orchestras in the Western world strongly favor the music of the past. The music of the twentieth century is performed far less frequently than that of the eighteenth and nineteenth centuries. Music education, too, favors the music of the past. The performers of tomorrow concentrate on the music of yesterday, thereby preparing themselves to give the public what it allegedly wants and what keeps the turnstiles turning: the secure successes of yesteryear. It is a vicious circle: the public gets what it wants, and as familiarity grows, it increasingly wants what it gets.

It goes without saying that we must continue to hear the music of the great masters. The world would be infinitely poorer without this priceless legacy. But if we become too myopic in our reverence for the past—too narrow, too smug—we run the great risk of reducing our homage to an empty cultural and pedagogical ritual. Music then loses its power to break through the boundaries of our lives and becomes instead a servant of convention and a defender of the very limits it once sought to transcend.

"There are two kinds of composers: living and dead. The dead ones are the best," wrote a high school student in an essay on composers. The repertoire used in most music instruction reflects a similar opinion, for the works of contemporary composers are rarely included. I think it is especially important, however, that students hear much more of this music than they do at present. With their unique sense—indeed, their deep inner need—for overstepping the boundaries, children must have an opportunity to experience the exhilaration of their own time, whose music aims not only to confirm and gladden but also to disturb, to say something new. Christopher Small, in a discussion of the repertoire used in music instruction, has written, "Once a work has made the transition to classic it can never, however we may try, revive its power to disturb our sensibilities. It may continue to delight us, to move us, to astonish us even, but it can never provoke us" (1977, p. 161).

It is true that much contemporary music written for pedagogical use is technically demanding and thus too difficult for children (though music that "sounds strange" to the teacher is often excluded under the *guise* of being too difficult). Contemporary composers should address the challenge of writing more music that is within the competence of young players. So much more "old" music is accessible to children that it is perhaps not surprising that they rarely encounter music written since World War II. No doubt it is unrealistic to think that anything like "equal time" can ever be achieved for contemporary music. Nonetheless, through a combination of playing *and* listening—vast numbers of recordings are available—it should not be difficult to give children a much more adequate introduction to contemporary music than most of them are currently receiving.

In addition to contemporary art music there is a large repertoire of ballads and popular songs accessible by means of chord-symbol playing. These, too, often reflect the contemporary scene both textually and musically, in a way that the "serious" music tradition cannot. Teachers should not be intimidated by the fact that children and young people are usually much more up-to-date on the latest hit tunes. Rather, they should use their students' prior interest in this music to motivate them in the mastery of their instruments. As always, however, teachers should select pieces they think have musical interest.

My studies of children's spontaneous singing show that their repertoire of standard songs typically covers a surprisingly wide range. I heard Norwegian children singing songs that had been handed down in the living tradition of child culture for at least three or four generations—a cultural legacy from perhaps as long as 150 years ago. This continuity is extremely important not only for the cultural identity of the children but for that of the whole nation. And each generation makes its own contribution to this legacy. The songs of the current generation are important if the chain of cultural continuity is to remain unbroken. The songs of today's children will soon become the "golden oldies" of tomorrow's parents.

THE KODÁLY SYSTEM

One of the most widely used systems of music education for children is the Kodály system, which relies heavily on *solfeggio*, Hungarian folk music, and five-tone scales (pentatonicism). From a purely historical point of view, the Kodály system must be seen as an outgrowth of the patriotic currents that swept through Hungary after the breakup of the Austro-Hungarian Empire. World War I had just ended, and Hungary sought to free itself from its powerful neighbor politically, economically, and culturally. Austria had always been the dominant partner in the Austro-Hungarian union; now it was time for Hungary to find its own national and cultural identity. That was no easy task, for mighty Austria had produced some of the brightest luminaries in the pantheon of European music: Haydn, Mozart, Schubert, Mahler, Schoenberg. How could Hungary compete with such giants?

Kodály's idea was strikingly simple: Hungarian folk music, which was deeply rooted in the hearts of his countrymen and in the history of old Hungary, could serve as a rallying force for the Hungarian people. Kodály was especially interested in folk songs because of their close relationship to the Hungarian language. This, he saw, was music that moved and united people. Kodály's vision, then, was of a country that achieved cultural freedom and national independence through folk music. He sought to realize his dream by working in several interrelated arenas simultaneously: as a composer, as a musicologist, and later as a music educator.

As a music educator, Kodály knew exactly what he was doing, and he was extremely effective. And Hungary's political authorities understood and endorsed his cultural-political vision. Because of his proven ability as a composer, his knowledge of Hungarian folk music based on original research, and the evident power of his pedagogical theories, Kodály was able to secure the government's cooperation in carrying out the most comprehensive nationwide musical-political action plan the world has ever seen. Hungarian children of all ages, preschool through puberty, were given a steady diet of Hungarian folk music. They learned its singular rhythms, intervals, motives, and songs—and of course they learned about pentatonicism, which looms so large in Hungarian folk music. The entire program was carried out systematically according to a comprehensive design, with a carefully planned progression from beginning to end. Kodály's and Bartók's compositions, which were built on the same Hungarian tradition, further strengthened the project and lent it a measure of international artistic prestige.

The results were impressive. Hungarian folk music really did play a role in creating a new sense of national consciousness and dignity. Singing and music instruction became important elements in the new wave of independence that swept over Hungary. In due course, people began streaming in from all over the world to visit this new mecca of music education, to admire the vigor, the vision, the system, the results. And rightly so.

Unfortunately, the international music community drew a false conclusion from what the visitors had seen and heard. So great was the admiration for Kodály's pedagogy and his five-tone scales that music educators fell at his feet like new converts before a revered guru. His system was imported into country after country, apparently with no serious misgivings about the fact that it had its origin in Kodály's fierce nationalism. The system had proven its effectiveness; all that was needed was to translate these Hungarian materials into other languages, and soon the whole world would be singing. The five-tone scale was construed as a kind of primordial scale, without a corresponding foundation in the musical legacy of the various national cultures. It is true, of course, that examples of indigenous pentatonic tunes can be found in other countries as well. It is also true that Kodály himself had entertained ideas about the possible universality of pentatonicism. But to flood five continents with unmodified Kodály materials on so slim a basis was to take a very big step.

The international Kodály devotées ignored one of Kodály's main points: that the music used in the education of children must have a *national mooring* in the folk culture of the children's own country if it is to have national value and importance. Kodály's vision can be applied elsewhere, but only (as with the Suzuki method) by *adapting* it to the unique circumstances of other national cultures. In Hungarian folk music, five-tone scales are an important element. The same is true of traditional Hungarian children's songs. That is why pentatonicism was such a prominent feature of Kodály's system.

Why should Norwegian, American, Russian children—indeed, children all over the world—be fed a steady diet of pentatonic songs? What is the scientific or historical justification for exalting pentatonicism as the universal key to music literacy? It cannot be the kind of musicological research Kodály conducted on Hungarian folk music, which offers little evidence to support the claim of universality. And this is the case whether one studies traditional "adult" folk music or the singing of children.

As a matter of fact, my research in three highly disparate child cultures suggests that pentatonicism is *not* an especially typical feature of the singing of preschool children. It is not characteristic of fluid/amorphous songs or song formulas or standard songs in the national cultures of Norway, Russia, or the United States. One does occasionally find standard songs with pentatonic elements— in Russian folk music, for example—but pentatonicism is not typical of the indigenous music of any of these countries.

The Kodály enthusiasts' crowning proof of the universality of pentatonicism has always been the alleged universality of the teasing formula (which is in fact relatively unknown in Russia, as we have seen). This formula, it is claimed, is clearly based on the five-tone scale and thus confirms the universal validity of the Kodály system.

But wait: the teasing formula contains only *three* different notes. Where are the other two notes to support the pentatonic origin of the formula? A pentatonic scale consists of five different notes, usually with the fundamental tone repeated at the top as confirmation that the scale is complete. For example:

That the teasing formula can *fit into* a pentatonic scale does not at all imply that it is *based on* that scale. This simple formula can "fit into" a number of scales, including several different five-tone scales as well as the diatonic major scale.

Speculation that the formula might nonetheless be based on a five-tone scale is further weakened when children themselves expand it in one way or another, for they leave little doubt about which scale they have in mind. This version, for example, which emphasizes the teasing element, is well-known among children throughout Scandinavia.

The ending of this formula actually contains the half step E-F, which completely destroys any reference to a pentatonic scale.

The enthusiastic adoption of the Kodály system without adequate critical thought is yet another example of how an adult interpretation of child culture forces concepts and phenomena into settings where they really do not belong. It is our own concept of the world that determines our understanding and interpretation of the world, thus rendering our perception more or less selective. Just as our adult concept of "music" is not directly applicable to children's culture (it obstructs our view if we try to make the facts fit into it), so the scales constructed by well-meaning adults may not always be adequate to encompass children's own tunes and feeling of tonality. Perhaps we should even allow for the possibility that at least some of the spontaneous singing of children—their fluid/amorphous songs and their song formulas—is not tied to *any* specific scale. Perhaps we should say instead that it is characteristic of these songs that they exhibit *scale independence*. Such a view becomes quite plausible if we abandon preconceived ideas about scales and simply allow our hearing to be guided by what children are actually singing.

In Norway, where a large body of folk-music material has been preserved thanks to the efforts of collectors since the 1840s, researchers have investigated the possible occurrence of a pentatonic scale in Norwegian folk music. Only a handful of melodies in this vast body of material can be persuasively shown to have undeniably pentatonic elements. Realistically, these few melodies constitute a rather slim foundation for the future development of pentatonic music in Norway. Nonetheless, Kodály's five-tone scales are still alive in Norway, as in so many other countries, thanks to the efforts of an active circle of disciples who will never forget the overwhelming impressions received during their numerous pilgrimages to Budapest.

These remarks about Kodály and pentatonic music should not be construed as a dismissal of pentatonic children's songs in and of themselves, either in Norway or elsewhere. Pentatonic scales and songs have a legitimate place as elements of a larger whole as we seek to introduce children to the wonderful diversity of the world of music. My objections to the Kodály system have to do with its one-sided emphasis on pentatonic music and its domination of elementary music education in so many parts of the world. Kodályism, if I may use the term, is especially worrisome when the detailed teachings of the Hungarian master become the alpha and omega of training programs for elementary music teachers—the future teachers of young children—and when the alleged natural affinity of the children themselves for pentatonic music is used as the crowning argument for the excellence of the system. Such programs are launched without adequate study of either the children or the music of the national culture of which they are a part. Thus they proceed without the kind of basic research normally required as a minimal condition of any such venture in Western society.

This book presents—for the first time anywhere, so far as I am aware—a systematic transcultural body of material that might serve as the basis for a discussion of the distinctive characteristics of the singing of preschool children. Similar research should, of course, be undertaken in many other parts of the world, but it is not too early to initiate a discussion of a music pedagogy for children based on studies of child culture.

Teachers trained in the Kodály method, too, should participate in an objective exchange of ideas concerning a music pedagogy for children constructed on this basis. Much needs to be done in many areas. Pentatonic music can be a valuable—but not a dominating—element en route to the goal that the followers of Kodály desire as much as the rest of us: a music pedagogy for children based on children and child culture.

FROM THE MOZART SHADOW TO GRADUS AD PARNASSUM

In the middle of the eighteenth century, public attention was focused on children by two impressive figures: Jean-Jacques Rousseau and Wolfgang Amadeus Mozart. Both had a great deal to do with the subsequent music training of children, though in very different ways.

In Rousseau's *Émile,* the child, the original human being, was placed in the center in the training and upbringing of people for a better and more enlightened society. It was Rousseau who, in this connection, coined the slogan "Respect childhood!" Children themselves and their natural, spontaneous willingness to learn were the means and the end, in contrast to an artificial, stilted adult culture that Rousseau scorned.

Mozart was six years old when *Émile* was published, and it is one of those rare coincidences of history that the two complemented each other: *Émile* strengthened Wolfgang and Wolfgang strengthened *Émile.* To many, the two appeared to represent the theory and the actuality of one and the same phenomenon. For was not young Wolfgang the embodiment of the very ideal about which Rousseau had written? Was he not the divinely gifted child who could do everything and outshone everyone in learning and other achievments? Was not Wolfgang in a way *Émile* himself, Rousseau's ideal child, who appeared in the fullness of time at the precise moment when history was ripe for him, at the height of the period of the Enlightenment, and by his very being presented incontrovertible evidence of the astonishing natural ability of all children? That was the perception of many.

The reality was quite different. Far from being a personification of *Émile*, young Mozart was obliged to represent much that was quite the opposite of the ideal advocated by Rousseau. Within a year after the publication of *Émile*, the seven-year-old boy set out on his first great European tour accompanied by his eleven-year-old sister, Nannerl, a prodigy in her own right, and his very ambitious father, Leopold. The tour lasted for three years and included numerous appearances before royalty and nobility in several of the major capitals of Europe. Where was the freedom and naturalness that Rousseau advocated in this ostentatious display of a child prodigy in an adult world? What Leopold Mozart presented in little Wolfgang was by no means a child of nature in Rousseau's sense. He was a little boy whose father dressed him up like a little man, and the music he was expected to play was that which suited the tastes of his adult mentors.

It was, of course, astonishing: this dazzlingly gifted little boy was able to perform the most difficult music more brilliantly than even the most accomplished adult performers of his day. It is important to note, however, that it was by this adult standard that Mozart was judged to be so brilliant. The demonstrations of his genius in the courts of Europe had nothing to do with respect for the distinctiveness of childhood in relation to that of adulthood. This was adult culture implanted in a child. It was a musical apotheosis, the endorsement of art culture by an innocent child. The counterfeit culture of the courts thereby secured, while it lasted, the cloak of innocence in the form of a little boy, a cloak that it sorely needed to cover its ill-concealed decadence.

Ever since that time, Mozart has been the ultimate yardstick by which proposals regarding music education are measured. His example established a pattern: start early, and progress steadily and as rapidly as possible toward the heights, *Gradus ad Parnassum*. The pattern continued with Beethoven, whose father reportedly scolded and beat young Ludwig and reminded him of what Mozart had accomplished. Beethoven, as we know, survived it rather well. Some children are strong—but many are not. The idea of pushing children to achieve in the manner of Mozart took firm root in the Western mind. Children played and labored, stumbled and clambered, step by tedious step. *Poco a poco morendo.*

The dream of producing another Mozart became, in a way, part of the mythology of music training, albeit reduced to somewhat more realistic dimensions. The dream remained, and remains, in one form or another in the hearts of many parents: "Let us start early and see what happens! Maybe you, my little daughter, or you, my little son, have at least a trace of Mozart in your blood?" Those are the thoughts that tempt us as we enroll our children with a music teacher at the earliest possible time. And why not? Have we not read of children who played at Carnegie Hall at the age of eight, studied with one of the world's greatest pianists at ten, and at age twelve were giving concerts all over the world? Why, then, should my son, my daughter, not do the same?

Innumerable children in generation after generation have had to live and toil beneath the long shadow of Mozart. This Mozart shadow, the symbol of the adult world's dream of outstanding musical accomplishment, is not always recognizable as such. For most parents it exists more as an unspoken but nonetheless constant undercurrent in our subconscious world of hopes and dreams, where it gently motivates us as a good father or mother to take our children to their weekly music lessons—as we secretly harbor the thrilling thought that we are doing our part to bring to fruition the fragments of genius that have been entrusted to our care. The thought is similar to that of winning the lottery: we read each week of others who have done so, and the idea that *we* might win some day hovers in our consciousness as something that is neither an idle dream nor a concrete expectation. The music teacher, who has seen so many children give up altogether after a year or two of lessons, is typically more realistic about each child's prospects. Once in a while, however, even a music teacher feels the Mozart shadow and the towering peak of Parnassus looming overhead. Parental expectations sometimes become almost palpable, and who can deny that the teacher of a prodigy, or even of an ordinary mortal who makes a successful performance debut, acquires thereby some reflected glory and status among his/her peers?

We all know that many children, the vast majority, fall by the wayside someplace along the way to the pinnacle of Parnassus. Some people regard this as a kind of music-pedagogical version of Darwin's theory of the survival of the fittest. In Sweden, for example, there was, as a result of a national policy, a significant increase in the number of children enrolled in music schools in the 1960s and 1970s. This increase, however, did not produce a corresponding increase in the music activity of the adult population during the years 1965–1987 (Nylöf and Nordberg 1988). According to official statistics the percentage of adults in Sweden who currently play a music instrument is apparently no higher than it was a quarter of a century ago.

In music schools in Sweden today, approximately 180,000 children are taking instrument lessons. The corresponding number in Norway is about 60,000. In Norway, as in Sweden, the vast majority give up before they reach puberty. The situation in Russia, as we noted earlier, is also reported to be disturbing.

It is, of course, unrealistic to expect that all of these children should continue to play an instrument for the rest of their lives. People have a right to turn away from music, too, if other things in life seem more important to them. Nonetheless, one cannot help but wish that a greater proportion of the tens of thousands of children who toddle off to music lessons at the age of six or seven would, as adults, continue to enjoy music as participants as well as listeners. To be sure, one can be authentically muse-ical without playing an instrument, but music-making is one of the important ways in which the Muse Within enriches the lives of Muse-bearers. What happened to all those other children who started out on the road to Parnassus?

The path from child culture's spontaneous singing, via class singing in school, choral singing, and intensive vocal training to the singing of art songs and arias in the concert hall, is the story of an increasingly more discriminating selection process. Not everyone is capable of playing Mozart sonatas or singing Verdi arias. Moreover, learning to perform the sonatas of Viennese Classicism or the arias of grand opera *does* require long and intensive training. We need to understand, however, that other types of singing and music performance can also be important, worthwhile, and meaningful—not necessarily for the concert hall or the opera stage, but for the hundreds of thousands of people who will never sing or play in the glow of the footlights but who nonetheless experience the restless longing of the Muse Within. It can mean so much: a way of staying in touch with one's inner self, a special and intimate kind of sharing with one's children, a muse-ical hearth around which one can gather with one's friends. For the Muse Within, who finds a voice in the spontaneous singing of children, is, as we have seen, the continuing power of creativity in every human life.

Gradus ad Parnassum has no place for people like Per. He and tens of thousands of monotones are written off as "unmusical" long before anyone would think of signing them up for music lessons. They are thrown onto music's scrap heap, permanently deprived of a life-giving means of expression in the name of aesthetics. I am reminded of the touching observation of a Swedish songwriter: "The forest would be terribly quiet if only the birds with the best voices were allowed to sing."

It is understandable that music teachers become excited when they discover a child with a beautiful voice, one that appears to have potential for use in a chorus or even as a solo voice. The focus of their interest, after all, is the transmission of the song repertoire and the *bel canto* tradition to the next generation of singers. The favored children, the chosen few, will then be taught to sing in the manner of adults—in the spirit, one might say, of *Gradus ad Parnassum*. They are perceived as the links—the important links, in any case—between the mass of preschool children and the polished choruses and the music schools. It is unfortunate, however, that in this preoccupation with the favored few the needs of the many are neglected. Muse-icality is renounced in the name of musicality, and the forest that should resound to the mighty voice of all humanity singing *ad libitum* grows eerily silent.

It is when adult standards derived from the world of art music are used to judge the musical progress of children that the selection process becomes so heartless and the dropout rate so great. That society generally and music teachers in particular continue to impose such standards on children to whom they ought not to be applied is a result not of cultural intolerance but of inadequate knowledge. Much of the responsibility lies with the academic community, for not enough research has been done to generate a critical, systematic body of knowledge about children's distinctive muse-icality as the basis for a more adequate pedagogy. We researchers have been much more interested in such issues as when children are capable of hearing the difference between major and minor, or between ¾ and ⁴⁄₄ time—experimental psychology—than in trying to understand muse-ical communication among children. It is obvious that huge problems must arise between children and music instruction based on adult concepts when, for example, it is at least questionable whether the very concept of music that prevails in the adult community may not be misleading when applied to the early music training of children. As we have seen, child culture's *ngoma* denotes a much wider sociomusical phenomenon than the term "music." A broadly contextual perspective must be adopted in order to understand children's point of departure and distinctive way of expressing themselves—in a word, their muse-icality. It requires us to adopt an anthropological/psychological understanding of music in place of the prevailing elitist/idealistic one.

A pedagogical approach based on a broader and more inclusive view of music and muse-icality would undoubtedly benefit that vast majority of children who will learn to play an instrument or sing in a choir *con amore* with no thought of professional specialization. It is my opinion, however, that this approach would also benefit the small minority of children and young people who will choose to become professional musicians. Why? Because human development *through* music is an important precondition for formal training *in* music (see Ruud 1983). Regardless of the goal being pursued, it is of fundamental importance to take care of and nourish and encourage the expression of the Muse Within each child, each young person, each human being. If our system of music education fails to do this, it loses its legitimacy.

American composer Charles Ives, who for many years was reviled for his avant-gardism, tells a poignant story about the off-key singing of his friend John Bell.

> Once when Father was asked: "How can you stand it to hear old John Bell (who was the best stoneman in town) bellow off-key the way he does at camp meetings?" his answer was: "Old John Bell is a supreme musician. Look into his face and hear the music of the ages. Don't pay too much attention to the sounds. If you do, you may miss the music. You won't get a heroic ride to heaven on pretty little sounds." (Cowell 1955, pp. 23–24)

The kind of beauty that Ives's father discerned in the singing of old John Bell is present also in the singing of children if we will but listen for it. It lies at the heart of their muse-icality, like an irresistible power in voices that must sing in order to live. If through a misguided preoccupation with what is "pretty" and "right" we lose this muse-ical foundation, we lose our ability to make authentic music of any kind.

Musicality, then, is but a part, a specific dimension, of muse-icality. Insofar as musicality is humanly rooted in muse-icality, it will thrive and blossom, whatever its expression, style, and tradition.

The German city of Leipzig is one of the great music centers of the world. It was here that Johann Sebastian Bach spent half of his adult life. Here, too, the world's first music conservatory was established, under the leadership of such luminaries as Felix Mendelssohn and Robert Schumann. Above the organ in the Gewandhaus concert hall in Leipzig hangs an old motto attributed to Seneca of Rome: *Res severa est verum gaudium* (A serious thing is a true joy). The spontaneous singing of children is one of these true joys, no less than the music of Bach, Schumann, Mendelssohn, and Ives. The route to a muse-ical Parnassus goes not through technique and upward but through children's own culture and inward.

A collage in three languages: "Music," "Freedom," and "I Love You" in Norwegian, English, and Russian.

7

"If You Love Somebody, Set Them Free!"

Of course it hurts when buds begin to waken.
Why else would spring delay its coming so?
Why else would all this store of fervent longing
    lie bound within a sheath of ice and snow?
The tender bud lay sleeping through the winter.
What now begets this gnawing sense of lack?
Of course it hurts when buds begin to waken:
    it hurts the bud that grows—
    and that which holds it back.
                    —KARIN BOYE
                    (Trans. W. H. Halverson)

KILL THE REFEREE!

Deep within the heart of every teenager lie the remnants of spontaneous singing as a legacy from early childhood. Now and then, at critical moments, the primal forces come to the fore once again.

I was watching a soccer match. The team that had been my favorite since childhood was playing, and it was a big game. If they won, they would remain in the first division. If they lost, they would fall into the second division and be written off as also-rans. It was no laughing matter, for in Norway we take soccer as seriously as Americans take baseball and football.

The stadium was filled with several thousand fans like me, damp with nervous sweat. Around me were mostly fans of the opposing team, laughing and cheering and having a good time. A bunch of young people in their late teens with caps and scarves in black and gold completely dominated the bleachers.

They had every reason to celebrate. Their team was ahead 3–0, and only five minutes of playing time remained. It looked pretty hopeless, and I was on the verge of tears. My heroes were about to go down to dishonor and defeat! I began to imagine the gloating headlines in the Monday newspapers and felt that I had been personally subjected to ridicule. The fans of the opposing team had some pneumatic noisemakers, and now, in the closing minutes of the match, they wailed a deafening howl of victory. My adrenaline was flowing. I was so angry I thought I was going to explode.

Then it happened. The referee blew his whistle and pointed authoritatively: penalty in our favor. An eerie stillness came over the crowd. I felt a twinge of hope as I awaited the inevitable. Finally a hint of justice in this cruel world!

The opposing fans were dumbfounded. What was going on? They shook their heads in beery disbelief and stared dumbly at the playing field. Then, as if someone had given a signal, they threw away their noisemakers and their black-and-gold caps and began to yell with murder in their eyes.

Kill   the   ref!   The   ref   is   cra- zy!

Their teenage voices bristled with aggression. The sound of artificial noisemakers was no longer enough for them. The situation called for an expression of naked anger, and nothing would do but a derisive song dredged up from the marrow of their bones, where it had been indelibly inscribed in childhood. The chant continued right up to the final whistle. As far as the fans were concerned, their song had annihilated the referee once and for all.

The goalie was faked out and the penalty kick hit the mark. We scored! But the other team won 3–1. We languished in the second division from then on.

THE PRIMAL CRY AND PUBERTY

In the autumn of 1986, a comprehensive survey was conducted among American teenagers to determine what they regarded as the most important things in their lives. Choosing from a list of fifty-four items, they collectively ranked "music" number one, "teachers and school" number fifty-four. "Mother" came in at thirty-one, "father" at forty-eight.

Primal cries and puberty. Life and love. The Muse-bearer awakens to a stormy new chapter during the teenage years. All the creative potential of child culture surges inexorably forward in powerful new forms.

- new eroticism and sensuality
- new need for nearness
- new curiosity
- new clownishness
- new need for independence
- new testing of limits
- new need for identity
- new intransigence
- new upheaval
- new *why*'s
- new fantasies and dreams
- new emotionality
- new irrationality
- new improvisations
- new existentiality
- new life ecology
- new sense of group comradeship

Winnicott, who attempted to apply his psychodynamic theory of play to the upheaval of adolescence, had some laconic words of wisdom for the weary parents of teenagers, particularly those who made a sincere effort to be creative in their parenting. Later, with pain and rejoicing, they reaped their tumultuous reward, with the candor they had encouraged as living proof of the authenticity and crushing strength of the onset of adolescence.

> If your children find themselves at all they will not be contented to find anything but the whole of themselves, and that will include the aggression and destructive elements in themselves as well as the elements that can be labeled loving. There will be this long tussle which you will need to survive. . . .
>
> If the child is to become adult, then this move is achieved over the dead body of an adult. (I must take it for granted that the reader knows that I am referring to unconscious fantasy, the material that underlies playing). . . . But it is wise to remember that rebellion belongs to the freedom you have given your child by bringing him or her up in such a way that he or she exists in his or her own right. In some instances it could be said: "You sowed a baby and you reaped a bomb." (1971, pp. 143, 145)

The upheaval is naturally directed at least as strongly against school and society as against parents. As we all know, the tensions between and among the adolescent, school, and society are a common theme in rock culture. We can trace this theme in a long list of films from *Blackboard Jungle*, with Bill Haley's "Rock Around the Clock," to such later and far more implacable variations as Pink Floyd's *The Wall*.

As noted earlier, the school traditionally has not contributed to the further development of the type of existentially conditioned creativity that children bring with them from child culture. School culture reflects adult culture in that it tends to split up rather than to unify. In the United States as in Norway, music is treated as little more than a footnote in the curriculum, despite the fact that it ranks high among teenagers' personal interests. So many American high school students are so disengaged from English instruction, I am told, that as many as one out of three who enter university study are obliged to take remedial work in their own language before they are ready to begin baccalaureate-level work. At the other end of the spectrum, the number of students whose writing creativity is truly nurtured by the school curriculum is distressingly small. Indeed, some teachers are frankly intimidated by students whose inherent creativity leads to writing that contradicts the teacher's idea of what constitutes a "proper" school essay.

But young people find ways to pursue their musical needs outside the school curriculum. Music is one of their principal means of expressing their dreams and their turmoil, their rage and their identity.

Adolescent music culture is a clear extension of childhood's music culture, its *ngoma*. It is powerful, spontaneous, articulated, and existential. Many rock artists are perfectly aware of this relationship. A spokesman for the Eurhythmics (Annie Lennox and David Stewart), for example, said in an interview with the news daily *Dagens Nyheter* preceding a concert in Stockholm in October 1986: "One must be like a child the whole time, seeing and experiencing everything as if for the first time. Then creativity is seething. This is not a way of looking at things that comes easily, but it is our damned duty to take care of it."

An important debate is under way in the United States at the present time regarding the relationship between the stilted language instruction in school and the development of the language of rock culture as an alternative form of expression. Robert Pattison, one of the major participants in the debate, has suggested that the popular immediacy and energy of rock has created a new type of literacy in American society. His ideas are similar in some ways to both Freire's views on the pedagogy of the oppressed and Enzensberger's admiration for the vitality of the culture of the illiterate. They also relate closely to Ong's discussion of literacy and orality and the emergence of a new *secondary orality* (1982). Pattison, himself a specialist in English literature, claims that rock is the teenagers' and the new society's idiomatic form of expression.

Correct English, and the mechanical literacy of the middle classes that spawned it, have alienated the writing population. . . . Today a universal system of mechanical language use according to inflexible rules has helped create two literacies. One is the established literacy taught in schools. The other is a popular literacy keyed to the spoken language of the people. . . .

The new literacy is not a by-product of cultural delinquency but a felt need among its users. It has evolution on its side, and its claims will be heard. Heard is the right word, for . . . the new popular literacy is one of the ear more than the eye. The development of electronic media has facilitated its growth, and it finds its readiest means of ideological expression in music. . . .

Electronic media are a powerful stimulant to the development of a literacy centered on the spoken word. They threaten established literacy by offering a continuous stream of vernacular raised to the level of popular art—an art without the restraints of correct English. . . .

Rock demands respect as the first art form of the new literacy. Its lyricism is full of vigor and wit. . . . The opponents of rock condemn it by the aesthetic canons of the old literacy which it is the point of rock to reject. Implicit in rock is a new set of standards of beauty and language. . . . Those who venerate the principles of the old print literacy will likely abominate rock, and indeed rock invites their abomination. . . .

The new literacy, operating through the electronic media, will compel the established literacy of middle-class authority to become looser and more idiomatic. . . . If we are lucky, the resulting mongrel product will be a literacy effective enough to serve the needs of social organization and technological development but sensible enough to maintain rapport with the vitality of spoken language and the need of the population for a sublime sense of language. If we are unlucky, . . . we will have two literacies, one of authority operating through print and known only to an elect handful of scribes trained at elite universities, the other propagated through electronic media and embodying the people's aspirations for an incarnation of the Word in the daily affairs of life. This second result would represent a severing of the body from the soul of our culture. It would pit class against class as well as literacy against literacy. It would be the end of the American experiment. (1982, pp. 201–207)

Rock as a cultural phenomenon is connected to upheaval and resistance, both of which loom large in the lives of most teenagers. Pattison writes of this in a later book, with specific reference to American culture.

Frank Sinatra singing "My Way" is old-fashioned pop in a regressive jazz tradition, but Sid Vicious singing the same song is rock, pure and simple. The Sinatra version is an old man's song whose mature theme is the acceptance of life as it is. The Vicious version is a young rebel's denunciation of everything old, smug, and wistful. (1987, p. x)

ROCK MUSIC IN THREE CULTURAL SETTINGS

Rock as a form of protest manifests itself differently in different countries despite its position as international mass-media culture. The conflicts prompting the protest are in many ways dissimilar, for example, in the United States, Norway, and Russia.

In the United States, much of the underlying friction at first consisted in an ambivalent relationship between white and black culture. American rock developed with explosive rapidity and attracted vast numbers of white middle-class youth. What they wanted, however, was not black culture *per se,* but only its element of sensuous rebellion against what they perceived as white culture's bland banality as expressed in school and society. And Elvis Presley, "The King," was an undeniably white artist with an undeniably black soul—"imitation black rhythm on genuine white hips," as Pattison put it (1987, p. 33). The combination had enormous appeal. Not only was it a powerful expression of rebellion, but it was at the same time culturally legitimate, a professionally planned marketing program by the rock king's agent, Sam Phillips, and Sun Records. The commercial market could safely accommodate such a product at a time when racism and racial segregation were widely tolerated in many areas of American society.

Today, rock has become a mass-cultural refuge that cuts across generational and racial boundaries. It has become a vehicle through which personal needs find expression in fantasies, dreams, and drugs, not least as a counterbalance to the increasing inflexibility and emotional monotony of the information society. Such sentiments are shared by teenagers and forty-year-olds alike, and are forcefully expressed by both groups.

According to Pattison, American rock never became truly political because American society, despite its many social and political differences, is not in the last analysis an aggregation of social classes. The United States, he says, is still inspired by the immigrants' utopian ideal of a society with freedom and justice for all, far removed from all thought of nobility, royalty, and inherited privileges. Such a society will necessarily have little room for political rock, in sharp contrast, for example, to Great Britain, where the rock music of the larger cities took on the character of political and social protest.

To understand the role of rock music in Norway, we must remember that this onetime home of the Vikings is a relatively small country with no superpower aspirations. Moreover, its language, which exists in two official versions and hundreds of dialects, is spoken by very few people elsewhere in the world. In this setting, then, much of rock's vitality consists in a linguistic-cultural rebellion that has both a national vs. international dimension and a local vs. national one. English (including American English), the international *lingua franca* of rock, has been important in and of itself as a means of expression for Norwegian teenagers who have felt confined by their own language. Many of them are tired of the constant concern over details of spelling and grammar as they write a seemingly endless series of themes in their Norwegian classes at school. They need something more powerful: rock music, foreign-sounding words supported by electric guitars and hypnotic rhythms! Rock is communication and emancipation through music, as in earliest childhood.

Imported rock music has had another advantage for Norwegian

youth: they could sing the language "their way," free from school control. The English emanating from old 45-rpm records was musical magic, pure and simple. It constituted what one might call "meaningful gibberish" to young people seeking a meaning deeper than that of words. Norwegian teenagers donned Elvis clothing and hairstyles and sang with genuine passion: "Yoo-waintnawtinbøddahowndogg!" This was American English from Memphis, Tennessee; it was the mother tongue of rock. It was "rock" English, and as such it bore little resemblance to the "proper" English they were supposed to learn in school. It was verbal protest with rock music as medium.

Rock in Norway has also taken another turn that is quite distinctively Norwegian. The country has been embroiled for over a century in a language controversy (New Norwegian vs. Dano-Norwegian) that has pitted rural people against city people, blue-collar workers against business and professional people, the political left against the political right. The official policy is to treat both forms of the language more or less equally; Norwegian radio and television, for example, are required by law to use each of them for a specified number of hours a week. Many Norwegians, however, speak a local or regional dialect that is neither pure Dano-Norwegian nor pure New Norwegian, and they tend to be quite contemptuous of the whole matter. This contempt has found expression in an indigenous form of rock music that draws much of its power from the defiant use of a local dialect. It is a peculiarly Norwegian way of saying, "A plague o' both your houses."

In Russia, rock found its home primarily in the clash between East-European/Russian and Western culture. For Russian youth in the former USSR, rock provided a little breathing space in a society characterized by censorship, cultural and political dogma-tism, and numbing conservatism. Alla Pugatsyova, heavily made up and at times a platinum blonde in the style of Marilyn Monroe, was one of the most popular artists in the Soviet Union in the 1980s. She thrilled millions of fans as she challenged established limits and political-cultural taboos with her remarkable combina-tion of sentimental mellifluence, idiomatic Russian lyrics, and occasionally pounding American rhythms. The result was a musical-cultural mutation with enormous power.

The late Vladimir Vysotsky used the rock idiom in many of his songs as a vehicle for his own provocative texts. This was authentically Russian rock, with music functioning as a means of passionate protest during the cultural freeze of the Brezhnev era. The lyrics, often political in nature, were such that his music could be performed only in private gatherings, out of view of the ever watchful secret police. It was underground music. Vysotsky's death in 1980 was never officially announced in the newspapers or on radio or television. Nonetheless, hundreds of thousands of devoted fans filed through the streets of Moscow toward Vysotsky's own Taganka theater on the day of his burial. His sneering voice and pounding guitar had become the voice of millions of his oppressed countrymen, despite the efforts of officialdom to make him invisible.

The explosive growth in the number of rock bands in Russia at the present time is one of the most telling signs of the reality of the policy of *glasnost.* It is said that over one hundred thousand new rock bands were formed in that vast country during a recent two-year period, many with an unmistakably Western stamp in both their music and their image. Many of the country's leading lyricists are writing texts for this new music movement that is sweeping the land, thereby injecting a vital new element into Russian literature and Russian society.

THE POWER OF THE TRANSITORY

Whatever its cultural setting, the inner meaning of rock is always the same: rebellion and existence. Rock culture derives most of its energy from the music, for it is the music that heats up the fans and fills the stadium or the amphitheater with electricity. The music is what rock culture is finally all about. It is the essence of its language, the clenched fist of its stance.

From the very beginning, starting with Bill Haley's "Rock Around the Clock," the music itself has carried the message of dissent. Much of the harmony used in rock was borrowed from the blues, much of the melodic idiom from country-western. Rock music, however, was always more antisentimental than either of these, often to the point of being brutally primitive. It had no time for subtlety or circumlocution: its lyrics dealt directly with feelings and with sex. It was leather jackets, motorcycles, and pounding rhythms as energy raised to a higher power. That is how it began, in the 1950s version of youth culture. Here stood the rock musician himself as a representative of folk culture's oral tradition—spontaneous, physical, visible, audible—in clear contrast to the white tie and tails of the classical concert hall.

Rock lyrics are, of course, unthinkable apart from the reckless sound and erotic beat of the music. The words and the music dynamically interact, like light and shadow under a hot sun. Rock's primal cry and hammering texts get their desired vulgar power from the emotional subcellar of the music. Sound amplified far beyond the pain threshold hits you in the chest like a horse's kick—and paradoxically, in so doing creates possibilities for a new type of deeply craved sensibility. Each listener becomes, as it were, an oasis of calm in the eye of the storm. Rock concerts become suggestive purification rituals that could never occur in either home or school. All the trappings of the theater—makeup, lighting, scenery—create the setting for an intense sharing of sensuality and experience. The performer is the medium, the painted clown, the high priest, if only he is good enough and has a message that can work the magic his listeners are seeking. Then he will sing—Ronia-like—with an inner urge that will not be silenced.

The incessant energy of rock culture is a product of the turbulence of puberty. It is erotic and dreamy, emotional and unstable, wild and rebellious, vehement and vulnerable, naïve and visionary. It is play pursued in deadly earnest, a muse-ical rainbow bridge between the inner and outer worlds in the often chaotic daily life of the teenager.

Discussions of the quality of rock music frequently degenerate into a confrontation between the "high" culture of the adult world and the "low" culture of teenagers. Rock is compared to Beethoven and inevitably fares poorly. "The big difference," an internationally known symphony conductor declared recently, "is that in five years nobody will know who Bruce Springsteen is. Rock has a brief, social function. Beethoven's music is still living after 150 years."

Such a comparison is beside the point. Rock and Beethoven are not two manifestations of the same phenomenon; they are different phenomena. It makes no more sense to compare them than to compare Beethoven and Cubism, or Beethoven and environmentalism. *Of course* a Beethoven symphony exhibits qualities of form, counterpoint, instrumentation, thematic development, and harmony that go far beyond anything in the very best examples of rock music. But those qualities, admirable as they are in art music, would not enhance the quality of rock. The two phenomena are incommensurable. Rock is a type of music, to be sure, but its function and meaning are fundamentally different from those of art music.

As a musical experience associated with youth, rock has to do above all with processes of psychological and cultural identity. Fads in music, fashion, and idols are important symbols through which the individual and collective quest for identity is made evident. Without a moment's hesitation, the rocking adolescent chooses the vulgarities of the day over the music of the ages in order to establish a position from which to withstand the enormous pressure of adult society. It is a matter of entering adulthood on one's own terms. From this perspective, indifference toward the undisputed beauty of the works of the masters is part of the psychology and dynamics of adolescent rebellion, which is as elementary as it is necessary. Rock is music as friction, music as a wild declaration of independence. Beethoven's Ninth Symphony could never serve this purpose for millions of young people, however exquisite, however honored by music lovers throughout the world. The symphony conductor's smug dismissal of Bruce Springsteen was in fact a confirmation of rock's necessity and value for a purpose Beethoven's symphonies were never intended to serve.

The nature of rock is such that teenagers need not limit themselves to the role of mere spectator. It is relatively easy to learn a few simple guitar chords and rhythms, rig up the necessary equipment, and become a rock musician—in your own band. This is the source of much of rock culture's existential strength and power of identification: it looks for all the world as if there is a straight and easy road from fandom and its surfeit of dreams to superstardom and its abundance of wealth and fame.

That the life expectancy of most rock music is so brief in no way contradicts the assertion that such music plays a uniquely important role in the lives of countless teenagers. On the contrary, rapid turnover is a corollary of rock culture's function and dynamics so long as it continues to serve its original purpose. It is precisely its transience that gives it its strength. If this music were to become durable, it would lose the raw effectiveness of the moment. It can be possessed only in the pulsating present, only in the flash of exploding revolt. *Carpe diem.* Seize the day. Each new group of fifteen-year-olds has *its* urgent need to find *its* way into the future—*now.* And each new group of fifteen-year-olds makes *its* selections, in a complicated balance between individual rebellion and commercial manipulation. Rock as provocation and revelation is always today's rock, never yesterday's, over and over again. Meanwhile, the older teenagers are inexorably pushed closer and closer to the adult world, where rock evokes pleasant feelings of nostalgia and Beethoven's Ninth Symphony waits patiently in the wings.

THE ETERNAL TEENAGER

Many generations of teenagers have experienced a wonderful surge of happiness in a band, on a dance floor, at a rock concert, or in front of a stereo. Beatniks, teddy boys, mods, glitterrock, punks, heavy metal, and New Wave—the preferences change from generation to generation. There are different idols, clothing styles, and haircuts; different music, texts, and dances; different sounds, rhythms, and superstars; different cultural and racial backgrounds; different modes of politicization and social awareness; different degrees of flight, aggressiveness, and apathy.

These fluctuations have provided vitally important outlets for the convulsions of adolescence, with music as the medium. Rage, for example, can be expressed in a guitar solo rather than in violence and blind destruction. The need to cry out, to express oneself, can find an accepted outlet in a rock song, divorced from society's traditional sex-role stereotypes (Fornäs, Lindberg, and Sernhede 1988). Boys, too, can weep under the ritual protection of song. The numbers speak for themselves: about ninety percent of the rock musicians in Scandinavia are males. When the school put up barriers, when language got in the way, when parents appeared as threatening oppressors—music *welcomed* them with open arms. It became a key to understanding the confusion in the recesses of their own minds as well as the confusions in the larger world. The rock songs they love with such reckless passion are thundering manifestations of teenagers' need to survive on their own terms. A Norwegian rock musician spoke for teenagers everywhere when he was asked, "What is it about rock that is so phenomenal?"

> Freedom. Absolute freedom. For me, rock has been the locus of freedom ever since I was thirteen or fourteen years old. A retreat where I could go to be myself. Where I had something that didn't belong to anybody else. This was mine! That's how I've felt about it ever since I first heard the Doors, Hendrix, and Eric Burdon. (*Arbeiderbladet,* April 25, 1987)

This statement reveals one of rock's many paradoxes: it evokes genuine feelings of individual freedom in the midst of a global mass culture. The Doors belong to millions at the same time that they are yours and yours alone.

Today, however, rock's "locus of freedom" is no longer restricted to teenagers. The sociocultural situation has changed dramatically since the early days of rock. For one thing, rock itself has evolved through the years; today's rock is different because of what has gone before. Moreover, the explosive development of the music industry has created a drive for ever larger markets. Most important of all, perhaps, is the fact that the place of rock today is different than in the 1950s and 1960s. Early rock, for better or worse, was exclusively an affair of the adolescent world.

That is no longer the case. The market has long since conquered vast numbers of people in their twenties, thirties, and forties who relish the opportunity to fan the embers of endless puberty. Elvis's life as a rock star began when he was a teenager and ended when he was a middle-aged man. He couldn't read music, but he could sing—always with raw soul in his voice, always with the pelvic gyrations that were his trademark, always with the phallic potency and pounding rhythms of his electric guitar. His fans adored him and wouldn't let him go. They all aged together—rock, Elvis, and the fans. The music was so much a part of them that they couldn't abandon it without losing themselves. As Pattison says, "Rock devises strategies to avoid the inevitability of age and the necessity of transcendence. Rock defines youth not in years but in thrills. . . . Rock's generation is comprised of spiritual, not chronological cohorts" (1987, pp. 100, 101).

That many of rock culture's top international artists are now middle-aged is something the mass media take for granted. Neither the market nor the listening public will willingly let go of a rock artist like Tina Turner. Today's teenagers must share a Mick Jagger or a Stevie Wonder with a large audience of ex-teenagers in a way that would have been unthinkable when rock was in its infancy. That rock is so widely appreciated and enjoyed enables it to serve as a direct, emotional means of expression—a matter of great importance for large numbers of people in a society that is steadily becoming more bureaucratic, more technocratic, more specialized. It is, one might say, a healthy alternative to Valium. It is a product of teenage culture that has come to serve purposes that cut across generational lines.

Is the emergence of "family rock" an indication of the stupefying effects of media culture? Hardly. That older generations choose to cling to a musical form that helped them cope with life and its manifold challenges at a critical time in their development shows, rather, that human beings have the capacity to retain some of the sensitivity and immediacy characteristic of adolescence. But family rock cannot serve as the voice of adolescent rebellion. Not everything can be shared. Teenagers need a violent voice that is uniquely theirs, one that expresses their strident demand for independence. They must have their own music and artists and idols—music that is shockingly different from that of their parents, and indeed, everyone except their own peers. If the rock everybody enjoys starts to feel too stifling, the inner upheaval at the heart of adolescence must and will find other forms.

Commercialism, too, constantly threatens to transform the harsher elements of adolescent culture into something totally harmless. The commercial half-life of each new phenomenon of adolescent protest grows steadily shorter. Each new musical manifestation of such protest has but a brief moment in the sun before it is declawed and its roar transformed into a gentle purr. Today's scandal will be tomorrow's convention. The punk teenager thinks to shock her elders with the wildest hairdo imaginable—and one fine day she encounters a refined, middle-aged dowager who has just been given the same hairstyle at her local beauty shop.

There's More to It Than Rock Music

Not all teenagers, of course, satisfy their insatiable appetite for music with a steady diet of rock and other forms of popular music. It is commercially useful to the music industry to keep rock culture continually in the public eye, even though it gives a distorted and one-sided picture of the musical interests of young people. Away from the footlights and the pounding world of rock, many teenagers express their individuality through other types of music: jazz, classical music, choral music, ballads, and band music (which plays an important role in the musical lives of teenagers in both Norway and the United States). Many of them find genuine pleasure and meaning in several different types of music. It is not unusual, for example, for a fifteen-year-old to enjoy playing John Philip Sousa in the school band and to listen with equal enjoyment to rock, jazz, Vivaldi, and Mozart at home.

Perhaps we should say with Plato that each human being, each adolescent, is tuned in his or her own unique way, with his or her own built-in modulations and mood changes. Different personalities and temperaments resonate to different types of instruments, both as listeners and as performers. It is a wonderfully rich mélange:

- the mellow tone of the French horn
- the crass eroticism of the tenor saxophone
- the introspective lyricism of the Spanish guitar
- the piercing assertiveness of the trumpet
- the swinging waltz of the accordion
- the exquisite Chopin of the grand piano
- the infinite longing of black gospel songs
- the mighty fugues of the pipe organ
- the steady beat of the Dixieland tuba
- the satiny smoothness of a choir
- the seductive sensuality of the cello
- the sparkling aural cornucopia of the symphony orchestra
- the screaming distortions of the electric guitar
- the husky breathing of the harmonica
- the crisp sound of a double-stopped violin
- the brazen glissando of the trombone

The Muse Within sings in an infinite variety of voices—voices that differ from instrument to instrument, from genre to genre, from performer to performer, from listener to listener, from mood to mood.

Teenagers drink eagerly from the fountain, taking into their hearts the music they have chosen as their own. This is their refuge, their oasis when everything else becomes a desert. Hour after hour, day after day, week after week, year after year, they are engaged in a tireless quest for those rare, magical moments when the music on the outside—the music that everyone can hear—corresponds exactly to the singing of the Muse Within. Such elusive moments are their Holy Grail, the goal of their deepest longings, the impossible dream they are still innocent enough to dream—and sensitive enough to find, especially in eroticism and music. The muse-ical life force has acquired a new dimension in the transition from childhood to adolescence: *"Canto et amo, ergo sum!"* "I sing and I love, therefore I am!"

THE SLUMBERING STORM

Night has fallen, and sixteen-year-old Anne is in her room—her own private space, the place where she is free. Books, tabloids, clothing, guitar, cosmetics, records, cassettes, hair dryer, and pictures of her boyfriend lie strewn about in wild disorder. All the pictures and posters on the walls are hanging upside down. Protest. The jogging shoes under the chair are of different colors, one blue and one red. The fool's hallmark. That, too, is protest. Over the bed hangs a hand-lettered slogan, scrawled out defiantly in thick red India ink: "As long as you continue to vandalize our future we will refuse to have anything to do with your present."

Anne lies curled up under the blankets, sound asleep, half child and half adult. Vulnerable, yet incredibly strong. The storm is slumbering, preparing for another passionate day. The pillow, as always, is stained with hair coloring. Smudgy remnants of black mascara ring her eyes.

Cozy bedtime singing with the rest of the family is ancient history now. At sixteen, she has long since replaced the songs of childhood with her own Walkman. She sleeps with the earphones clasped tightly over her ears, and the music—her music—infuses and colors her nightly dreams. For even at night she is tirelessly searching for happiness. An unexpected chord can give relief from pain and hate. A happy turn of melody can be like a kiss of joy in a moment of musical ecstasy. The Muse Within is never at rest in a seething teenager.

The cassette player on the dresser is playing, too, giving her insatiable heart a double dose of music. It sits and booms away, there among piles of schoolbooks and tabloids and cheap paperbacks. It is playing so loudly that the whole house reverberates with its sound. The words of Pink Floyd's "The Postwar Dream" penetrate the darkness.

Should we shout,
Should we scream,
"What happened to the postwar dream?"
Oh, Maggie, Maggie, what did we do?

Outside the sixteen-year-old's door a father pauses for a moment, desolate and bewildered. Helplessly, he realizes that the music from the cassette player excludes him as if he were a total stranger. This girl—Daddy's little girl, who had always been so close to him—is now so unbelievably far away.

"That's how it has to be," say those who stand on the periphery of the struggle for independence.

"We are bleeding," say those who stand in the center of the struggle.

He understands, and he *wants* to do the right thing. But what good are rational formulas when both the chaos and the concern are bound to runaway blue horses?

On the door to Anne's room hangs a Sting poster marking the entryway to her world. The words—absolute and imperative—strike him like an arrow in the heart and make him shudder: *"If you love somebody—set them free!"*

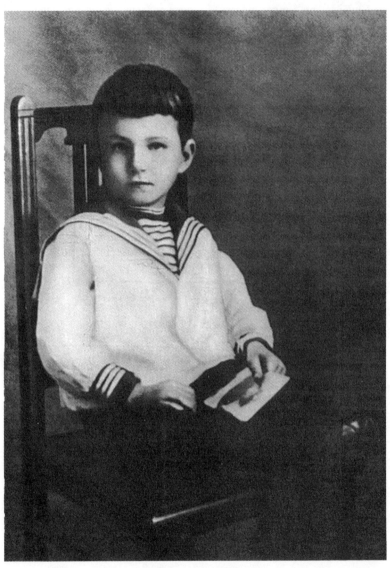

Dmitri Shostakovich

8

The Muse Under Siege

> The childhood shows the man,
> As morning shows the day.
> —JOHN MILTON, *Paradise Regained*

THE CHILD AND THE ARTIST

A child's eye and a child's ear live on in the mature artist, in whom the playful temperament of *homo ludens* is manifest in artistic form. Wonder begets originality, childlikeness begets power. Thus armed, the artist is able to combat the tyranny of convention and foster the growth of new vitality.

One can observe this phenomenon in the paintings of many of the great artists. What would a giant like Picasso have been without the childlikeness that gives energy and depth to so many of his mature works? He once said, "It has taken me a whole lifetime to learn to draw like a six-year-old." His famous *Bathers with Beach Ball*, for example—a profoundly childlike painting—was created when he was forty-six.

History affords numerous examples of the adult world's con-

Bathers with Beach Ball

tempt for adult manifestations of qualities associated with child-hood. Western society has always held reason in higher regard than play. The word "childish" (and its counterparts in other languages) has an undeniably negative ring to it. At the same time, however, there is in our society an undercurrent of admiration and respect for children and the qualities of childhood as vital sources of enrichment for the whole of life. That undoubtedly is why the English language has another word—"childlike"—that means essentially the same thing as "childish" but with positive instead of negative connotations. To be like a child in ways regarded as undesirable is to be child*ish;* to be like a child in ways regarded as desirable is to be child*like.*

What does it mean, then, to be childlike? Astrid Lindgren, the renowned Swedish writer of children's stories, said in her eighties, "It's a kind of playfulness in one's approach to life that is quite good to have, in my opinion" (Bøhle 1988a). The *playfulness* of childhood contains a measure of authentic sensitivity that restores

the immediacy of reality to the adult human being, thereby reinforcing his or her vitality. Ashley Montagu calls this the process of
"growing young" (1981). Childlikeness is by no means a sign of
infantile regression. On the contrary, it is both a source and a
proof of continuing vitality and strength—in Pablo Picasso, in
Astrid Lindgren, in every adult bearer of the Muse Within.

Psychoanalysis sheds further light on this matter with its emphasis on the dynamic interaction of different dimensions of the
psyche as a key to the understanding of human creativity. We are
the sum of everything we have been in the past. The experience
of each day, each year, each developmental stage, is recorded
within each of us, as if on a built-in flight recorder. This is not how
most of us have been taught to think about ourselves. We have
been taught to think in linear terms, with each new moment fully
supplanting those that preceded it. One unfortunate result is that
our other—latent—ages are removed from the sphere of active
consciousness, and our concepts of "age" and of the self are
rendered unnecessarily shallow. This is a more serious matter than
it might appear, for as we confront the flickering play of light and
shadow that we call reality, we desperately need all the resources
nature has placed at our disposal—our capacities for feeling and
understanding in their full height and depth and breadth. The
various age strata that live on within us equip each of us with a
remarkable instrument having many different registers and timbres, and we must use various combinations of stops, as it were,
if we are to realize the fullness of our humanity. Music, poetry,
dance, painting, sculpture—and not least, contact with playing
children—can give renewed life to these age strata in adults who
may have been unaware that they were even there. For the Muse-
bearer, age is not linear but helical.

The experience of "cumulative aging" is perhaps most apparent in the life of the creative artist. Astrid Lindgren once spoke of
it quite explicitly in an interview.

There is a subsoil in one which, I assume, is full of experiences that
one had as a child. For in childhood one experienced with such

enormous intensity everything that one experienced. And it is clear
that when I am going to write a book, all I can do is reach into my
inner self and pull out something from that time or from what I was
at that time. . . . We have all of our years within us, from earliest
infancy right up to the present. . . . Human beings are by nature
more or less childlike, but I suppose I am perhaps a little more
childlike than most. (Bøhle 1988a)

Infantile regression is stagnating and confining, the very opposite
of creative. Creative processes, on the other hand, have the artistic
goal of satisfying the present moment's need for expression in a
way consistent with contemporary reality. In such processes,
childlikeness becomes a dynamic element in development and
human growth, i.e., in *life progression*. Edith Cobb touches on this
in *The Ecology of Imagination in Childhood* (1977).

The point is that it is not the moments of regression that empower
actual creativity—an idea often proposed in psychoanalytic studies
of creativity. It is the capacity for returning reductively to the use
of universals, to the "materials" that furnish human beings with the
power to create imagery, that inspires adult creativity. . . .

To "become as a child" is a far more subtle idea than is generally
assumed. The drive and ability of the poet (and in a far simpler
form, of the child) to become what he wishes to know or understand derives from a combination of wonder and a sense of "something far more deeply interfus'd," an acceptance of not knowing,
which brings with it a special type of humility infused with joy. (pp.
94–95, 107)

What we are speaking of here is the mature artist's pulsating
vitality and creative potential, of which the child's intrepid playfulness and insatiable curiosity—without a rational safety net—are
integral parts. The power of discovery inherent in childlike wonder is among the things that appear in a refined and seasoned
form in mature artists—in their striving, their talent, their inspiration, the products of their creative work. The child and the artist

are blood relatives, bearers of the Muse Within. Both feel the inner drive of a compelling muse-ical imperative, naturally operative in the child, artistically cultivated in the poet, the painter, the sculptor, the composer. Childlikeness as a wondering and inventive quest for understanding is an essential presupposition for creativity for both: *Canto — ergo sum!*

"MUSE-ICAL," "CREATIVE," "AESTHETIC," AND "ARTISTIC": A CONCEPTUAL CLARIFICATION

According to the ancients, as we have seen, the Muses were created so that the world might have a voice, a concrete mode of expression. Their frame of reference was an Olympian world inhabited by a plethora of divine beings, the "immortals." The Muses were conceived as goddesses who through word, dance, and song could change the world. Beauty and truth were regarded as one. Needless to say, our discussion of the Muse Within is not an exercise in reified mythology. Our subject is the human being, the *muse-ical* human being, through the various stages of life. Our focus is on the internal source of authentic expression as a key to what is humanly true and thus meaningful.

From the muse-ical dimension springs the power to create: muse-icality is the ground of creativity. Without a power of muse-ical expressivity uniquely our own, none of us would be able to shape the raw stuff of existence into a human life. *All* normal, healthy children have this power as well. Every day they must exercise their creativity in order to go beyond yesterday's achievements, to widen their horizons, in their determined conquest of an ever larger and deeper life arena.

Creativity can express itself *either* aesthetically or nonaesthetically. If the former, the result is an embodiment of beauty in one or more of its myriad forms. Drawing and coloring pictures, or shaping objects out of sand or clay, are classic examples of children's creativity expressed in an aesthetic mode. But the boy who fashions a go-cart out of a few scraps of wood and some cast-off wheels is also being creative, albeit not primarily in an aesthetic way. The primary goal of his creativity is function, not beauty.

Both modes of creativity emerge, however, from the same source. They are, we might say, twin gifts of the Muse Within.

If creativity in its aesthetic mode is carefully nourished in a person who has shown special talent for such expression—if it is trained and perfected through years of study and hard work—it may at length achieve an *artistic* form. This achievement is possible only for the few. But note well: the fact that artistic creativity is reserved for the few does *not* mean that other aesthetic expressions—the nonartistic ones—are less important. They are simply creative expressions of another type, valuable in their own way and in their own right. That is why it is wrong—*conceptually* wrong—to compare, say, Mozart's "Exultate Jubilate" with the spontaneous singing of kindergarten children.

Nonetheless, the artist and the child have much in common. They drink from the same muse-ical fountain. Both have the capacity, each in their own way, to *inspire*—to breathe life into— our muse-ical self.

The muse-ical bond between the child and the artist, traversing the entire distance from ordinary people to the genius, binds *all* of us together in something universally human. The artist, even the greatest of artists, does not belong to another world, unapproachably removed from the rest of us. Even the art of a genius belongs inherently to you and me as well, for *muse-ically* we are all kin. The artist who creates a thing of beauty must ultimately draw his inspiration from a source that is the birthright of every human being.

Thus far I have tried to show forth the vital role of the Muse Within in the lives of ordinary people. Indeed, the inherent muse-icality of all human beings is our principal theme, and we shall return to it in our concluding chapter. Now, however, we are going to look more closely at the role of the Muse Within in the life and work of a great artist. Deeper insight into the artistic perspective will further enrich our understanding of the astonishing breadth and depth and creative power of the Muse Within. To understand the creative artist is also to understand an important dimension of ourselves.

Our focus in this chapter will be on the music of Dmitri Shostakovich. This is art music, the product of a genius, to be sure—but it is also music that emerged from the muse-ical depths of a fellow human being, music that can only be understood against the background of the cultural and political forces convulsing the society in which this man, this artist, lived his life. Dmitri Dmitrievich Shostakovich: as the twentieth century draws to a close, we can trace a line from this name and this man's music directly to the revolution that changed the political landscape of Europe and turned the whole world on its head. Powerful forces are unleashed when the voice of the Muse Within resounds among us!

DMITRI SHOSTAKOVICH: GENIUS AND FELLOW MUSE-BEARER

Dmitri Shostakovich is an example of a mature artist whose life and work demonstrate in an especially poignant way the resourcefulness as well as the urgency of the muse-ical imperative. The Muse Within, as Pindar said, is the voice of creation. It *must* sing or it will die. Just as life itself takes a variety of forms adapted to differing conditions, so also the Muse Within appears in various manifestations appropriate to the Muse-bearer's stage of development and circumstances of life. The Muse sings in the primal cry of the newborn infant, in the spontaneous singing of the young child, in the authentic musical experience of the adolescent, in the inspired creativity of a Mozart, a Beethoven, a Shostakovich. The mature composer's link with childhood as a continuing source of muse-ical inspiration is particularly evident in the case of Shostakovich, for whom calculated playfulness—a deadly serious game of "let's pretend"—became the means whereby the Muse Within was able to sing even, as it were, in prison.

A YOUTHFUL UPHEAVAL BASED ON GOGOL

Shostakovich was born in St. Petersburg in 1906. The city, Peter the Great's vaunted "window to the West," exhibits in its history as well as its literature and music a fascinating blend of beauty and ugliness, laughter and angst, convention and scandal. It was in the glittering salons of St. Petersburg's wealthy aristocrats that Push-

kin's *Eugene Onegin* once wandered spleenfully about. It was in
the deserted back alleys of St. Petersburg that Nikolai Gogol's
pathetic Akaky Akakyevich stumbled through the winter fog looking for the tattered overcoat that had been stolen from him. Here
was social criticism with a vengeance, unmistakably reflecting
harsh reality but spiced with bizarre satire and allegorical fantasy.
It has been said that all subsequent Russian literature is derived
in one way or another from Gogol's "The Overcoat." Indeed, this
is in some ways an understatement, for many key figures in Russian and Soviet *music* also have Gogolian roots. Shostakovich, as
we shall see shortly, linked his first musical revolt to Gogol.

Shostakovich grew up at a time of seething ferment in Russian
cultural life. Cubism began to have a strong impact on Russian
painting as early as 1908. Shortly thereafter, abstract art came to
the fore. Russian lyric poetry exhibited a similar defiance of established conventions. Symptomatic of the prevailing attitude was the
title of the 1912 manifesto of the Futurists: "A cuff on the ears of
the public taste."

Russian music was slower to respond to the currents of the
times. In Russia, too, with its rich music tradition, the conservatory lived up to its name: a place where things are *conserved*. Like
Stravinsky a generation before him, Shostakovich felt that the
conservatory was *too* conservative. A fundamental revolt against
the reigning authorities was only to be expected in the course of
his maturation as a human being and artist. Stravinsky had defied
the authorities by going to France, where he composed the revolutionary *Rite of Spring*. Shostakovich stayed in his homeland and
composed *The Nose*—as pronounced a break with established
opera convention as *Rite of Spring*, written some fourteen years
earlier, had been with the ballet-music tradition.

The break was important on many different levels. Among
other things, it was an adolescent revolt: it cleared the air and
created a certain distance between the young composer and the
teachers whom on another level he both respected and loved. But
of course it was also more than an expression of adolescent independence. It represented a decisive departure from established
aesthetic norms.

That Shostakovich's break with the past occurred precisely in this genre gave it unusual shock value, for opera was the *sanctum sanctorum* of Russian art music. Among the operatic jewels of which Russians were inordinately proud were Glinka's national operas, Mussorgsky's *Boris Godunov*, Tchaikovsky's Pushkin operas, and Rimsky-Korsakov's operatic settings of Russian fairy tales. A Soviet composer did not challenge this lofty tradition unless he felt himself ready to beard the lion in the lion's own den. Shostakovich was ready—but he could not have foreseen how many lions he would have to fight.

In some respects, Shostakovich's iconoclasm was in line with the cultural-political ideology of Russia in the 1920s. The political and aesthetic revolutions were seen as interrelated. The new society needed new and preferably revolutionary aesthetic ideals adequate to the vision of the new regime. This line of thinking was advanced at the highest levels of government, where Anatoly Lunacharsky, himself a lover of the arts, held the post of minister of culture. In 1927, when Shostakovich began working on *The Nose*, the aesthetic environment in the Soviet Union was still permissive as a heated debate raged over aesthetic standards suitable for a socialist society. Shostakovich himself became a member of the Association for Contemporary Music, whose aesthetic ideals were diametrically opposed to those of the more orthodox Russian Association for Proletarian Music. An early and outspoken opponent of the crass proletarianization of both folk and art music, Shostakovich was able, at first, to express his views openly.

But political repression of nonconformists was on the upswing during the later 1920s, a development unsettling to many artists, including Shostakovich. His desire to make a purely political statement was a further reason for composing *The Nose*. The dynamics here are similar to those observed in an earlier chapter: the child's compelling inner need to exceed established boundaries. The composer, like the child, must daily mobilize every cognitive, emotional, and physical resource to make new conquests of *terra incognita*.

THE NOSE: FROM LAUGHTER TO ANGST

Shostakovich's youthful opera is based on one of the stories in Gogol's celebrated collection of Petersburg tales. Written in 1836, its central idea is even more absurd than that of "The Overcoat," the lead story in the cycle. *The Nose* was, in the first instance, a powerful allegorical attack on the frightful human oppression and pervasive control that prevailed under Czar Nicholas I, but Shostakovich saw that it applied with equal acuity to the circumstances of his own day. The opening of the story (as translated by Constance Garnett) gives it an air of realism, but the reality quickly becomes intertwined with the most remarkable details and events.

An extraordinarily strange incident took place in Petersburg on the twenty-fifth of March. The barber, Ivan Yakovlevich, who lives on Voznesensky Avenue (his surname is lost, and nothing more appears even on his signboard, where a gentleman is depicted with his cheeks covered with soap suds, together with an inscription "also lets blood")—the barber Ivan Yakovlevich woke up rather early and was aware of a smell of hot bread. Raising himself in bed he saw his wife, a rather portly lady who was very fond of drinking coffee, engaged in taking out of the oven some freshly baked loaves.

"I won't have coffee today, Praskovya Osipovna," said Ivan Yakovlevich. "Instead I should like some hot bread with onions." (The fact is that Ivan Yakovlevich would have liked both, but he knew that it was utterly impossible to ask for two things at once, for Praskovya Osipovna greatly disliked such caprices.)

"Let the fool have bread: so much the better for me," thought his wife to herself. "There will be an extra cup of coffee left," and she flung one loaf on the table.

For the sake of propriety Ivan Yakovlevich put a jacket over his shirt, and, sitting down at the table, sprinkled some salt, peeled two onions, took a knife in his hand and, assuming an air of importance, began to cut the bread. After dividing the loaf into two halves he looked into the middle of it—and to his amazement saw something there that looked white. Ivan Yakovlevich probed at it carefully with his knife and felt it with his finger. "It's solid," he said to himself. "What in the world is it?"

He thrust in his fingers and pulled it out—it was a nose! . . . Ivan Yakovlevich's hand dropped with astonishment, he rubbed his eyes and felt it: it actually was a nose, and, what's more, it looked to him somehow familiar. A look of horror came into Ivan Yakovlevich's face. But that horror was nothing compared to the indignation with which his wife was overcome.

"Where have you cut that nose off, you monster?" she cried wrathfully. "You scoundrel, you drunkard, I'll go to the police myself to report you! You villain! I have heard from three men that when you are shaving them you pull at their noses till you almost tug them off."

But Ivan Yakovlevich was more dead than alive: he recognized that the nose belonged to none other than Kovalyov, the collegiate assessor whom he shaved every Wednesday and every Sunday.

After this beginning we are given a glimpse of the victim himself as he unsuspectingly awakens and discovers the catastrophe.

Kovalyov the collegiate assessor woke up early next morning and made the sound "brrrr . . ." with his lips as he always did when he woke up, though he could not himself have explained the reason for his doing so. Kovalyov stretched and asked for a little mirror that was standing on the table. He wanted to look at a pimple which had appeared on his nose the previous evening, but to his great astonishment there was a completely flat space where his nose should have been. Frightened, Kovalyov asked for some water and a towel to rub his eyes; there really was no nose. He began feeling with his hand, and pinched himself to see whether he was still asleep: it appeared that he was not. The collegiate assessor jumped out of bed, he shook himself—there was still no nose. . . .

After a wild chase through the streets of St. Petersburg, Kovalyov sees his nose alighting from a carriage outside the Kazan cathedral (which still stands on Nevsky Prospect, St. Petersburg's main street).

> [The nose] was in a gold-braided uniform with a high collar; he had on buckskin trousers and at his side was a sword. From his plumed hat it might be inferred that he was of the rank of a civil councilor. Everything showed that he was going somewhere to pay a visit. He looked to both sides, called to the coachman to open the carriage door, got in, and drove off.
>
> Poor Kovalyov almost went out of his mind; he did not know what to think of such a strange occurrence. How was it possible for a nose—which had only yesterday been on his face and could neither drive nor walk—to be in uniform!

Kovalyov finally gets his nose back after enduring a series of experiences that derisively expose the corrupt authorities and scoundrels in the Russian bureaucracy.

Seemingly innocuous, but for that very reason doubly caustic, Gogol's conclusion mimics the matter-of-fact tone of the opening paragraphs. In so doing, he makes fun of the crushing oppression of the government of Nicholas I.

> So this is the strange event that occurred in the northern capital of our spacious empire! Only now, on thinking it all over, we perceive that there is a great deal that is improbable in it. Apart from the fact that it certainly is strange for a nose supernaturally to leave its place and to appear in various places in the guise of a civil councilor, . . . how did the nose get into the loaf, and how about Ivan Yakovlevich himself? . . . no, that I cannot understand, I am absolutely unable to understand it! But what is stranger, what is more incomprehensible than anything is that authors can choose such subjects. I confess that is quite beyond my grasp, it really is. . . . No, no! I cannot understand it at all. In the first place, it is absolutely without profit to our country; in the second place . . . but in the second place, too, there is no profit. I really do not know what to say of it. . . .

Brilliantly playful? Yes, indeed! And what should the Czar's poor censors and hangmen say about this absurd confusion? At first they flatly banned the novel. Gogol persisted, however, and eventually got permission to publish it. The crafty and pointedly disarming concluding paragraphs evidently had their intended effect. And besides, a silly story about a lost nose surely couldn't be *so* dangerous! That the loss of a nose might, for example, also have to do with the loss of human identity in a profoundly inhuman society was not easy to prove. Through the clever use of allegory, Gogol slipped beyond the limits of censorship and political control. His very existence as a visionary writer demanded that he break through these limits. Thus he employed a variety of literary devices that exploded existing literary conventions. The muse-ical imperative triumphed once again.

Mikhail Bachtin (1979) has shown that genuinely carnivalistic features abound in Russian literature. Bachtin focused especially on the writings of Dostoyevsky, but the same characteristics are clearly present in Gogol's works. Dostoyevsky's writings were in fact directly inspired by Gogol's Petersburg stories with respect to both subject and style. Moreover, one can trace a direct line from the style of Gogol and Dostoyevsky in the nineteenth century to that of Shostakovich in the twentieth. It will be illuminating for our purposes, therefore, to note some of the features identified by Bachtin in the works of these three giants of Russian cultural life.

1. The eccentric, as a counterweight to logical reason.
2. The grotesque-paradoxical, the warped mirror that shatters and distorts the prevailing dogmatic hierarchy of values, norms, and rules.
3. The scandalous, which turns the ritual laughter of the carnival into a symbolic polemic against the social and political conditions of the time.
4. Unusual psychic states, with nightmarish dreams, psychological breakdowns, and wild ravings.
5. Unacceptable associations and connections, irrespective of social rank and personal feelings. The high become low and the

low become high. In the old carnival tradition, the fool becomes
king. In Dostoyevsky's great novel *Crime and Punishment,* a whore
becomes the Madonna. And in "The Nose," a tiny human nose
becomes a powerful government official.

It is evident, then, that "The Nose," transcending the established limits of literary convention, stands firmly in an indigenous
tradition of literary carnivalism—and with powerful effect. What
Shostakovich did was to clothe Gogol's nineteenth-century allegorical farce in the garb of avant-garde twentieth-century music.
Shostakovich was breaking new ground in European music history. With its mixture of styles, grotesque fancies, and clownish
lunacy, his music was fully on a par with Gogol's text. As events
unfolded, Shostakovich never again had an opportunity to compose anything as modernistically vital as this opera. At twenty-
one, he was still innocent and at heart as invincible as a child in
his artistic temerity.

The opera employs a variety of musical styles. Praskovya Osipovna, the barber's screeching wife, yells out her profanities in a
manner that is much closer to a primal cry than to Italian opera.
This is not the *bel canto* of art music but the *mal canto* of revolt.
Alban Berg, who visited Leningrad and sampled its music in the
1920s, used this style of singing in *Wozzeck.* Kovalyov's singing
approaches the style of the art song, but on his lips it sounds
distorted, ironic, a parody of the real thing. Kovalyov is so super-
cilious as the government official, so pompous in his imagined
superiority to the masses, that he can only express himself in
grandiose clichés. Shostakovich cunningly gives him vocal lines
reminiscent of the Baroque *opera seria,* the most dignified type of
old-fashioned opera song. But the combination is ridiculous, like
a bride in a flowing white wedding gown, boxing gloves, and army
boots. Kovalyov wakes up and tries to clear the phlegm from his
throat by singing. He coughs, yawns, stretches, and unaware of
what has happened begins to sing a hopelessly stilted and pompous recitative—*without a nose!*—producing some ludicrous musical
effects of the highest order.

Shostakovich used a musical style appropriate to the personality of each of the central characters in the opera. He gave them melodic characterizations that were in fact of sociolinguistic origin. As he himself formulated the underlying idea in his preface to the opera, "The vocal parts are built on the intonation of the spoken language. . . . I wanted to create a synthesis of the art inherent in the words and music." Each person was assigned a specific style paradoxically tied to his/her social rank, all the way from the frightened poor people to the nose itself as the civil councilor. The pecking order of the social code, as evident in Russian society in Shostakovich's day as in Gogol's, was here set forth in sharp and truly innovative musical categories. Shostakovich also broke new ground in his psychological characterizations.

Let us look briefly at one scene. The barber, having been thoroughly upbraided by his shrewish wife, leaves the breakfast table with the nose wrapped in a towel. Laden with a heavy sense of guilt, he sets out through the streets of St. Petersburg. He must get rid of the nose as quickly as possible. The fatal proof of his guilt must be disposed of, every trace must be removed. He hurries toward the Neva River, where he intends to throw the nose away, feeling as he goes that everyone is watching him. It is a classic case of the paranoia of the malefactor. Shostakovich first expresses the barber's erratic course through the city with a simple, hectic little theme that then becomes the subject of a canon. The barber's pulse quickens: surely everyone can see that he has done something terribly bad! The music quickens as well. The canon motive is passed from one instrument to another, steadily growing more and more chaotic, with less and less regard for the established rules of imitation. The barber walks faster and faster. Disquiet turns into anxiety and anxiety into terror. The theme gets lost in a confused jumble of instrumental sounds and shouting voices that seems to have no structure or direction. The barber's pounding pulse is indicated with heavy orchestral strokes that can be heard through the cacophony.

The inevitable occurs: the barber's wild dash through the

streets attracts attention. A policeman challenges him in a bellowing, authoritarian voice, and in a register that breaks all the rules
of operatic propriety: "Stop! Come here!" The barber goes into
shock and his mind snaps. The theater goes totally dark, intentionally shocking the audience as well. The anxiety explodes as an
experience that the viewers share with the wretched barber. The
audience is inexorably drawn further into the black hole of lunacy
as Shostakovich unleashes an orgy of percussion effects unlike
anything ever heard previously in a European concert hall. For
almost four minutes the theater reverberates to the bewitching
whisper and thundering sound of a percussion orchestra. The
percussionists, according to Shostakovich's original score, were to
be placed at various locations around the perimeter of the theater.
This was opera as it had never been staged before, far in the
forefront of the music theater of that day.

Another noteworthy innovation in Shostakovich's opera was his
occasional use of the instruments as coactors in the play. A typical
example is the famous scene in which Kovalyov wakes up and
discovers that his nose is missing. The instruments have a rollick-
ing good time here as they engage in an almost organic interaction
with Kovalyov's physical movements. An eerie glissando duet for
violin and trombone mirrors in sound Kovalyov's sleepy motions
as he sits on the edge of the bed stretching, coughing, and clearing
his throat. The music is an *analogical imitation* of the physical movements, just as the spontaneous singing of children often is. The
Icelandic word for "composer"—*tonleikar,* one who plays with
sounds—preserves an important concept that many languages,
including English, have lost. In composing the music for *The Nose,*
Shostakovich showed himself to be a *tonleikar,* playing like a child
and like a mature illusionist at one and the same time.

Shostakovich does not maintain his modernistic musical language throughout the entire opera. Avant-garde sections, in the
very forefront of the music of his time, appear alongside naïvely
simple sections written in an almost folk style. But it is precisely
such juxtapositions, intermixing what appear to be totally incom-
patible types of music in an almost postmodernist manner, that
give the opera much of its carnivalistic flavor.

In 1836, when Gogol published "The Nose," Russian society was tightly controlled by artistic and political censors. One could say that Gogol, with his marvelous sense of the allegorical and the fantastic, hid behind the symbolic mask that he himself created. The mask is an integral part of the carnival. The use of a mask, where you represent yourself as someone other than the person you really are, can be said to be a carnivalistic element in Gogol's Petersburg stories.

In old Russia, as a matter of fact, the mask of the carnival was not the only kind available to provide a façade for criticism of reigning authority. Russian tradition provided another kind of mask—the *yurodstvo*—that served a similar purpose. Moreover, the wearer of a *yurodstvo* mask was perceived to be imbued with a special—indeed, sacred—protection and inviolability. A *yurodivy* was originally a religious figure, an eccentric vagrant completely outside normal society. In the popular mind, the *yurodivy*'s strangeness was perceived as a sign of his holiness. Under the cover of this presumed holiness, a *yurodivy*, allegedly possessing supernatural wisdom and spiritual gifts, could speak out independently, even prophetically, about the society and the people beside and among whom he lived. Leo Tolstoy, in *Childhood, Boyhood, Youth,* writes that the *yurodivy* Grisha "spoke enigmatic words that many regarded as prophecies." The *yurodivy* was free to say anything he pleased. It meant bad luck for anyone who bothered or interfered with him. Not even the czar dared to touch him.

Gogol, of course, was no *yurodivy* in the traditional sense of the word. It seems clear, however, that as a prophetic speaker of the truth and a critic of society he played a kind of *yurodivy* role in his writing.

While Gogol needed a mask in order to write "The Nose," Shostakovich composed his opera in the full light of day. The music to *The Nose* is the real Shostakovich, immediate, direct, unfeigned.

BEHIND THE MASK

Shostakovich soon bitterly regretted his boldness in *The Nose.* A portent of what was to come occurred in 1928, when he presented in Moscow a seven-movement suite for tenor, baritone, and orchestra from the opera, which had not yet been performed. The reactions among his traditional adversaries were more violent than before. The tone was more vitriolic, and the criticism showered down upon him like a hailstorm.

In 1929, a major turning point occurred in Soviet cultural life when Lunacharsky was dismissed as minister of culture. Stalin had initiated his first five-year plan the preceding year, and as part of his strategy for fulfilling that plan he needed someone who could be counted on to bring cultural life to heel. Andrei Zhdanov, who would soon become infamous as the feared hangman of culture, was Stalin's choice for the job. It was under the watchful eyes of Zhdanov and his lieutenants, then, that Shostakovich's opera had its premiere in 1930. Fourteen sold-out performances followed, and the audience response was enthusiastic. Judged by normal criteria, the opera was an enormous success. Unfortunately for Shostakovich, normal criteria did not apply to cultural life in the Soviet Union. The conservative clique, emboldened by the repressive new leadership at the Ministry of Culture, viewed these performances as pure provocation. The opera was characterized as "a hand grenade from an anarchist," and violent accusations were hurled at the hapless young composer. Boris Asafyev, the foremost musicologist in the Soviet Union and Shostakovich's ally in the Association for Contemporary Music, came to his defense, characterizing the opera as a brilliant musical embodiment of Gogol's fantasy world—but to no avail; Soviet officialdom had already made up its collective mind. After two performances in 1931, the opera was stopped for good. Thirty years were to pass before *The Nose* was again performed in the Soviet Union.

Shostakovich had obviously underestimated the reaction his opera would arouse. In that decisive year of 1931, when his music was condemned for the first time by the censors in the Kremlin, Shostakovich was already well along on his next opera, *Lady Macbeth of the Mtsensk District*. He realized immediately, of course, that he was in a difficult situation. There was great danger that his freedom to compose would be taken from him, danger that his next opera would suffer the same fate as his first. His solution was to play the role of a *yurodivy*. Thus, in 1931, Shostakovich publicly criticized his earlier work, even going so far as to borrow the rhetoric the bureaucracy had used against him: "I think an artist should serve the greatest possible number of people. I always try to make myself as widely understood as possible, and if I don't succeed, I consider it my own fault" (1980, p. 31).

The following year, when Zhdanov pushed through a reorganization of the Soviet composers' associations, Shostakovich felt he had to publicly criticize *The Nose* more directly. He wanted his next opera to be performed, and he tried to assure the authorities that he was now using a more moderate musical language than he had employed in *The Nose:* "The music of *Lady Macbeth* differs greatly from that of my last opera, *The Nose.* An opera, when it comes down to it, is meant to be sung, and all the vocal parts in *Lady Macbeth* are melodious and cantilena-like" (1980, p. 34).

The ploy succeeded. In January 1934 *Lady Macbeth* was staged in both Leningrad and Moscow, and again the reception was enthusiastic. The oppressed woman as revolutionary and heroine was obviously a theme to which many of Shostakovich's compatriots could relate. It is evident from Shostakovich's notes from this period, however, that he himself remained uneasy. The invective that had been hurled at him and his music after the premiere of *The Nose* had hurt him deeply. Since then, music censors had been appointed to ensure conformity with the standards of socialist realism. Shostakovich tried to put some distance between himself and what had transpired earlier in order to lessen the possible impact of official disapproval of *The Nose* on his new opera. He was especially aware that the new authorities were enamored of lyrical old melodies—cantilenas—and he attempted to steal their thunder in the public debate.

> I tried to achieve maximum simplicity and expressiveness in the musical language of the opera. I cannot accept the theory—at one time commonly held here—that there should be no vocal line in modern opera, or that the vocal line is merely a spoken part, in which intonation should be stressed. An opera is above all a vocal work, and the singers should attend to their immediate duty—of

singing, not speaking, declaiming, or intoning. All the vocal parts are based loosely on the cantilena style, exploiting the full potential of that rich instrument, the human voice. (1980, p. 46)

Who is it who is expressing himself in this way? Is it, as one might think, a sly and unprincipled opportunist who knows which way the wind is blowing and trims his sails accordingly? Or is it a *yurodivy* who is playing out a charade in order to preserve the opportunity to compose music at all? A correct understanding of Shostakovich's life and work turns on this issue. Who was the real Dmitri Shostakovich? What did he really think? Why did he write the way he did? Was he for Stalin or against him? Western Europe struggled with these questions, with growing confusion and increasing political indignation, but with no awareness of the *yurodivy* tradition as a possible explanation of what Shostakovich was doing. According to a widely discussed book by Solomon Volkov (1980), editor of *Sovietskaya Muzyka,* this tradition is crucial to a proper understanding of Shostakovich's life after 1934.

Stepping on the road of *yurodstvo,* Shostakovich relinquished all responsibility for anything he said: nothing meant what it seemed to, not the most exalted and beautiful words. The pronouncement of familiar truths turned out to be mockery; conversely, mockery often contained tragic truth. This also held for his musical works. . . .

His decision was not made suddenly, of course; it was the result of much vacillation and inconsistency. Shostakovich's everyday behavior was determined to a great degree, as was the behavior of many authentic old Russian *yurodivye* "for Christ's sake," by the reaction of the authorities, which were sometimes more intolerant, sometimes less. Self-defense dictated a large portion of the position of Shostakovich and his friends, who wanted to survive, but not at any cost. The *yurodivy* mask helped them. It is important to note that Shostakovich not only considered himself a *yurodivy,* but he was perceived as such by the people close to him. The word *yurodivy* was often applied to him in Russian musical circles. (1979, pp. xxvi–xxvii)

For some time it appeared that Shostakovich's *yurodivy* strategy was going to work. From 1934 to 1936, *Lady Macbeth* was performed more than eighty times in Leningrad and more than a hundred times in Moscow; it was successful to a degree unparalleled in Communist Russia. In the icy cultural climate of the time, this was truly sensational. The writers were prevented from writing, but music was still relatively free. And what music it was! Galina Vishnyevskaya, leading soprano star at the Bolshoi Theater after World War II and a close friend of Shostakovich (she later sang Lady Macbeth in the opera), characterizes this music thus.

> *Lady Macbeth* seems to me the most lifelike and vivid portrait of the composer during the happiest time of his life. Here we see him as God made him: the young genius, who embodies an amazing combination of intellect, well-honed talent, and unbridled temperament. Here he wrote heedlessly and from the heart. Everything in the opera is open—the tremendous scale of passions and the brilliant humor. (1984, p. 351)

But the very success of the opera became the source of its, and its composer's, undoing. In December 1935, throwing caution to the winds, Shostakovich allowed *Lady Macbeth* to be moved to Moscow's famous Bolshoi Theater, the most important opera house in the Soviet Union. Then the bubble burst. It mattered no longer that the opera employed a somewhat more moderate musical language than that used in *The Nose*. Nor was it of any help to Shostakovich that he had publicly voiced a certain amount of self-criticism. The performance of *Lady Macbeth* at, of all places, the Bolshoi Theater was an unacceptable provocation, an impudent challenge to the norms of socialist realism, and it could not be tolerated. Shostakovich was becoming dangerous, and it was time to cut him down to size. *Pravda*, the voice of the Kremlin, took up the issue. There should no longer be any doubt about what was proper and permissible in the Soviet fatherland. The country needed positive heroes and good old folk tunes, not defiant murderesses as opera heroines and not musical modernism. The article, enti-

tled "Chaos Instead of Music," castigated both the composer
and his opera.

> From the very first moment the listener is unnerved by a stream
> of deliberately inharmonious sounds. . . . While our . . . music
> critics swear oaths of fidelity to socialist realism, [the Bolshoi
> Theater], in staging Shostakovich's opera, is preparing to pre-
> sent a manifestation of the rawest type of naturalism. . . . Every-
> thing in it is raw, primitive, and vulgar. . . . It is clear enough
> that the composer has never asked himself what the Soviet re-
> public expects from its music. He has made music into a code
> and distorted it to such a degree that it can be appreciated only
> by aesthetic formalists who have lost all sound taste. (January 28,
> 1936)

The Nose was the principal reason for the attack, *Lady Macbeth*
the immediate occasion. The Bolshoi's production of the latter
was summarily stopped. Shostakovich's Fourth Symphony, which
was in rehearsal with the Leningrad Philharmonic, was removed
from the program just before its planned premiere. Shostakovich
felt officially executed. He had been branded an enemy of the
people—a *vrag naroda* in Russian. Thus stigmatized, he would
spend the rest of his days in chronic fear of what might happen to
him—perhaps imprisonment, or even more likely, liquidation.
Such things actually happened to many of his friends during the
reign of terror that now raged unchecked in Russia. Vsevolod
Meyerhold, for example—the stage director with whom Shostakovich had worked on the Leningrad production of *The Nose*—
was executed in 1939.

A full century before Shostakovich's *The Nose*, the great Alexander Pushkin had identified laughter, compassion, and angst as the
principal traits of the Russian poet (Meyerhold 1934). Pushkin's
characterization of the Russian poet is a remarkably apt description of Shostakovich's music as well. In *The Nose*, these elements
are portrayed in the precise order in which Pushkin listed them:
it opens with laughter, which quickly yields to compassion and

angst. After the banning of *The Nose*, when Shostakovich began literally to fear for his life, what occurs in his music is more than a mere change of style. One could say that the reigning emotions exchanged places, the emotional chemistry became different. After the *Pravda* attack, angst became the dominant element, though compassion and laughter were not forgotten. After all, Shostakovich *was* a Russian. Once he became a marked man, however, the sequence in his music was always from angst to laughter, never the reverse. The change is evident in his Fifth Symphony, the first work he composed after the *Pravda* attack. It remains evident fully twenty-four years later in Symphony No. 13, the "Babi Yar" symphony. We shall, therefore, look in some detail at these two important works.

THE FIFTH SYMPHONY: IN THE CLAWS OF FEAR

We all remember from childhood how to play a role, to pretend. Children have a natural ability to throw themselves into role-playing with such abandon that they really experience the emotions appropriate to the role at any given time. At such moments, play becomes, in a sense, reality. Children know, of course, the difference between then and now, ourselves and others, reality and fantasia. They use language with remarkable sensitivity to indicate nearness and distance, role assignments, and role limits. Changes in accent, inflection, or vocabulary function in child culture as lightning-swift muse-ical costume changes that distinguish role from role and play from reality. With one tone of voice a child is obviously playing the role of teacher; with another, a split second later, that same child is a timid little boy or girl. It is as if playing children have an innate capacity for metacommunication (Bateson 1972).

Children also play other kinds of roles—social, psychological—to protect themselves, adapt to new situations, find breathing room, survive. This is how they maintain a healthy relationship to reality as they undergo the process of socialization. Thus role-playing is a well-developed skill in all of us, a legacy from both the real and the make-believe worlds of childhood.

For Shostakovich, the whole of life soon became a matter of role-playing—and he felt, with considerable justification, that his life depended on his playing it well. The *Pravda* assault in January 1936 was the fateful turning point. For a time, Shostakovich wrote nothing at all. The shock simply left him stunned. For a long while he considered suicide. As the will to live slowly returned, however, it was clear to him that continued silence was no solution. The creative urge was too strong for that. When at length he resolved to resume his work as a composer, he adopted the role of a *yurodivy* in his professional life as a survival strategy. It was his version of the triumph of inconvenience. He donned the *yurodivy*'s mask and mounted the high wire in a desperate attempt to balance the conflicting demands of words and actions, personal integrity and public identity, the muse and the commissar. This was bound to take its toll—psychologically, physically, and in terms of his creative powers. "I was in the claws of fear," he once said of his life at that time (Volkov 1979, p. 140). He needed, as Volkov suggests, to claim as his own the words of an oft-quoted prayer that is as well-known in Russia as it is in the United States: "Lord, grant me the strength to change what can be changed, the strength to bear what can't be changed, and the wisdom to know the difference."

With music, the prayer could be uttered without words, purely instrumentally. The Russian writer Ilya Ehrenburg, who had also been a victim of Stalin's censors, is reported to have said once after a Shostakovich concert, "Music has a great advantage: Without mentioning anything it can say absolutely everything." Apparently this music escaped the comprehension of the authorities who had hearts that beat but did not understand, eyes that looked but did not see, ears that listened but did not hear. At the same time, this music was filled with meaning for untold millions of Russians who heard and understood each theme in Shostakovich's music. They understood because they shared his fate, because they, too, were oppressed and persecuted. His music became their medium of protest as they endured a regime of terror and censorship, a regime that had to be challenged—by the masses, too. The music spoke to them and on their behalf in their own code, in their own muse-ical mother tongue as Russians.

We have several eyewitness accounts of the premiere of Shostakovich's Fifth Symphony, when the now legendary Yevgeny Mravinsky made his debut as principal conductor of the Leningrad Philharmonic. The Leningrad concert hall was elegantly austere, with its white marble, classic lines, soaring columns, heavy silk drapery, and ornate chandeliers. Volkov gives us a glimpse of what transpired there on November 21, 1937.

> [This date] can be considered a watershed day in the musical fate of Shostakovich. The hall of the Leningrad Philharmonic was overflowing: the cream of Soviet society—musicians, writers, actors, artists, celebrities of every kind—had gathered for the premiere of the disgraced composer's Fifth Symphony. They were waiting for a sensation, a scandal, trying to guess what would happen to the composer, exchanging gossip and jokes. After all, social life went on despite the terror.
>
> And when the last notes were sounded, there was pandemonium, as there would be at almost all later Soviet premieres of Shostakovich's major works. Many wept. Shostakovich's work represented the effort of an honest and thoughtful artist confronted by a decisive choice under conditions of great moral stress. The symphony is riddled with neurotic pulsations; the composer is feverishly seeking the exit from the labyrinth, only to find himself, in the finale, as one Soviet composer put it, in "the gas chamber of ideas."
>
> "This is not music; this is high-voltage, nervous electricity," noted a moved listener of the Fifth, which to this day remains Shostakovich's most admired work. The symphony made it clear that he spoke for his generation, and Shostakovich became a symbol for decades. In the West his name took on an emblematic quality for both the right and the left. Probably, no other composer in the history of music had been placed in so political a role. (1979, pp. xxxi–xxxii)

Once again we see the power of the Muse Within as a fundamental theme. A feeling, an understanding, an experience that transcends established boundaries is formulated by the composer, then shared by those who hear his music. The concert hall in Leningrad must have been filled with Muse-bearers on that November evening when the Fifth Symphony was played publicly for the first time. They experienced the music not as an isolated aesthetic phenomenon or routine entertainment but as something vitally important for their lives under the bloody yoke of terror. It was not only Shostakovich's muse who sang in that packed concert hall in Leningrad. The Muse sang in the baton of the conductor, in the instruments of the orchestra, and in the aching hearts of those who listened with rapt wonder to the uncanny beauty and power of the music. For the Muse can sing her reassuring song even in the midst of human suffering, even under siege. The Muse, to paraphrase Hemingway, can be besieged, but she can never be defeated.

This is how Galina Vishnyevskaya describes the Fifth Symphony: "Listening to it, we become aware of the agonies he lived through. Shostakovich speaks on the events of those years with more passion and courage than any writer or painter who bore witness to those times. The Fifth Symphony was a turning point not only in his creative life but in his outlook as a Russian. He became the chronicler of our country; the history of Soviet Russia is nowhere better described than in his compositions" (1984, p. 212).

It seems clear, then, that Shostakovich's Fifth Symphony was a pivotal work in the political as well as the cultural history of the Soviet Union. Let us look at it more closely as we try to understand how it managed to speak so muse-ically and so forcefully to the composer's compatriots at a particularly difficult period in their country's history.

Each question we ask leads to yet other questions. How did the composer of this mighty symphony survive as a human being and as a musician? Millions of his contemporaries were liquidated. How did he avoid Stalin's execution lists without annihilating his own creativity? How did he—only thirty-one, still a young man with so much of his creative work yet undone—deal with his enemies and his friends as a *yurodivy* composer "in the claws of fear"?

Shostakovich knew perfectly well what Stalin's music censors demanded of him as they sat there in the front row of the concert hall listening to the premiere of the Fifth Symphony. They wanted traditional tonality, clear melodies and themes, and transparent orchestration, without noise and confusion. And Shostakovich gave them all that, as if he were throwing bones to starving hounds. The contrast between the modernism of *The Nose* and the opening of the Fifth Symphony is striking. Everything seems to be back in place again, as in the good old days when major was major and minor was minor. The principal theme settles down on a sturdy and clear tonic of D. Theme after theme is presented with crystal clarity by various solo instruments. All are melodic and singable, just as socialist realism required. Moreover, they are developed in conventional ways, with extensive use of canon imitation. The Stalinists no doubt nodded approvingly and smiled like Cheshire cats as the exposition continued with its singular simplicity. Shostakovich, they must have thought, had changed his ways. He had become their man. This was music as music ought to be in a workers' paradise, music with a positive tone and form, music appropriate for the celebration of the twentieth anniversary of the Revolution. But they heard only what was on the surface. They were like the members of the king's court in Edward Rowland Sill's "The Fool's Prayer."

> The jester doffed his cap and bells,
> And stood the mocking court before;
> They could not see the bitter smile
> Behind the painted grin he wore.

But Shostakovich's friends and fellow sufferers strained their ears to hear something else, something more, *beneath* the new simplicity. They sat on pins and needles and listened for hidden signals in the music, for the "bitter smile" of the *yurodivy* behind the mask. Where was the *real* Dmitri Shostakovich? Was he still alive and well? Was the rebellion still there, the integrity, the critique, the honesty? A crucial question, for it was their *common* rebellion and integrity that they longed to hear reaffirmed. And they were not disappointed. As the symphony progressed, they found everything they were looking for set forth with enormous power. The triumph was all the more gratifying because they knew that Stalin's henchmen were sitting there congratulating themselves, without the slightest inkling that what they were hearing was a powerful expression of contempt for everything they represented.

Every game has its rules and conventions. One needs to understand them in order to appreciate fully the artistry and originality of any given example. In Shostakovich's Fifth Symphony, the first movement is in standard sonata form. The structure of a traditional first movement is as follows.

— Slow introduction.
— Exposition: a principal theme and a secondary theme, contrasting in character and temperament, are placed in opposition to each other, thus creating tension according to a classical dialectical mode of thought.
— Development: both themes are developed in such a way as to further increase the tension.
— Recapitulation: the opening themes are restated, clarified in light of the development. Opposition and contrast are smoothed out in such a way that the two together constitute a new whole (synthesis).
— Coda: short summing up of the entire movement.

A sophisticated concert-going Soviet audience would of course have been thoroughly familiar with this outward structure. They would also have been acquainted with Shostakovich's earlier music and his distinctive style. Thus the audience was in a good position to judge his progress as a composer, his increasing mastery of his craft, from one work to the next. For this audience, however, music was more than merely playing with musical tones, a sound game enclosed in its own autonomous universe. Unlike Westerners, Russians—deeply formed by nineteenth-century czarist totalitarianism—were accustomed to interpreting music as political and social commentary. For them it was entirely natural to listen to Shostakovich's symphony as a musical delineation of the place of the human individual and of humanity in Soviet society in the 1930s. As Galina Vishnyevskaya said, "he became the writer of [Russia's] history."

One can analyze this symphony in traditional musicological terms—its formal structure, its themes, its harmony, its orchestration, and so on. Such analysis has its value and leaves little doubt that by traditional standards alone, Shostakovich was one of the great symphonists of our time. To many Russians, however, his music holds a deeper meaning. Their view might almost be expressed as a paraphrase of Martin Luther's formula regarding the Eucharist: in, with, and under the musical qualities—the tonality, the themes, the development, the instrumentation—there is a supra-musical reality that can be perceived by those who look for it. For Russians, art has often had what might be called prophetic overtones. It has been regarded—at times, and by some—as a type of *yurodivy* pronouncement possessing visionary power. Speaking to this point, Russian film maker Andrei Tarkovsky made a statement shortly before his death that applies with equal force to his own films and to Shostakovich's symphonies.

> For Russians, . . . it is still the case—as it always has been—that culture and cultural works have a kind of spiritual, mystical, or, if you will, prophetic significance. . . . Here in the West, on the other hand, culture has long since become a commodity, the consumer's property. (1988, p. 71)

Adopting the terminology used throughout this book, we may say that Shostakovich's music can be understood as a particularly poignant manifestation of the kind of existential seriousness observed in the spontaneous singing of children and the musical revolt of adolescence.

In what follows, then, I propose to try to look at this great symphony through Russian eyes—to understand, so far as a non-Russian can understand, what it meant to Shostakovich's compatriots in the 1930s, and perhaps what it means to Russians today. This, I may say, is how I was first introduced to the Fifth Symphony by my fellow students at the Leningrad Conservatory in

1968. This approach to Shostakovich's music is employed in several works by Russian musicologists (e.g., Orlov 1961).

The nonmusical background against which the Fifth Symphony should be understood is the momentous tension between Shostakovich and Stalin, and between further artistic activity and totalitarian control. The sharply hewn theme hurled out in the opening measures lets us know immediately that this symphony is the creation of a composer who has *not* resigned but on the contrary is ready to continue the struggle. It is, as someone has said, "a clenched fist."

Many have identified the principal theme that follows with Shostakovich himself, the symphony's human subject. The theme's character is such as to express a clear break with established conventions. According to standard practice, the principal theme within sonata form is supposed to be virile and precisely delineated. The contours of this one, however, are more or less vague, as if it were a musical portrayal of a stunned composer who is now stumbling about in search of a solid place to stand. And while Stalin's censors noted only that the theme ended on a good solid D, the rest of the audience followed the theme's original movements in a scale that was neither D minor nor D-Phrygian but purely and simply D-Shostakovich.

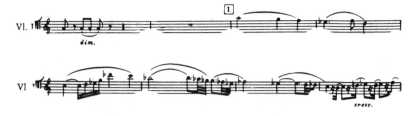

The essence of Shostakovich's originality and identity was still intact, despite the *Pravda* attack and the ban on atonality.

The secondary theme, too, has a story to tell. It is beautiful and poetic, with dense, undulating chords. The composer has even allowed himself the luxury of a shimmering harp in the accompaniment. The associations were immediately evident: innocence, imperturbability, childhood. The theme, however, is harmonized in E-flat minor, traditionally regarded as the most somber of all the minor keys and quite outside the normal harmonic pattern of sonata form. It is "a ray of hope, like a little strip of azure-blue sky between dark clouds," as one Russian commentator described it.

The development is announced with an abrupt change of mood. The piano suddenly enters as a foreign element in the orchestral sound, with a brutal, chopping motive in a low register.

Rattling trumpet sounds are then heard, giving the music a more aggressive flavor. Soon the snare drums take the lead, creating a military air that leads to an insistent fortissimo with whirling march rhythms. The dam breaks, the avalanche roars with unrestrained fury. The themes are distorted and brutalized. The orchestra grows into a colossus. Low-voiced brass instruments increasingly dominate the sound. Clearly, it is Stalin's Soviet Union that is being depicted here, with the venomous duality of meaning characteristic of the *yurodivy* tradition. "A thundering tribute!" shouted Stalin's men triumphantly. "The march of the evil powers!" observed Shostakovich's friends knowingly, in silent dialogue with the composer.

Only in the recapitulation is the tension fully released. Contrary to normal practice, the secondary theme is stated first. The effect is startling. Gone, now, is the melancholy of the opening section. The theme is transferred from E-flat minor to D major, where it sounds bright and life-affirming. It is like the calm after a fierce storm. It is, one might say, a Russian version of Beethoven's classic pattern of "from struggle to victory."

But where is the principal theme? Normally it is the *first* theme to be played in the recapitulation. It represents, we remember, Shostakovich himself. What, then, has become of the composer? The solution to this puzzle is obviously critical to an understanding of the underlying message of the symphony. We are left wondering for some time, but the answer comes just before the end of the movement: he is there, but in disguise! As the movement ends, the principal theme is heard once again, so altered as to be hardly recognizable: abbreviated, inverted, a lovely little flute solo that slowly fades into silence.

It is as if one momentarily glimpsed a face behind a darkened window, the face of a *yurodivy*, Dmitri Shostakovich.

The second movement contradicts convention in yet another way. Usually, though even Beethoven sometimes diverged from tradition here, second movements in symphonies are in a slow tempo, as if to give listeners an opportunity to catch their breath after the typically dramatic pace of the first movement. But Shostakovich has other ideas. Instead of offering his listeners a moment of rest, he immediately thrusts them into one of his derisive scherzo movements. After exposing so much evil in the first movement, perhaps it seemed to Shostakovich that *humor,* not relaxation, was the psychologically appropriate form of contrast. In the two outer sections the humor ranges from imitations of laughter in the lower wind instruments (listen especially to the bassoon) to swirling dance tunes (waltz, ländler, mazurka) with real oompah-oompah accompaniments, ironic rhythmic irregularities, absurdly pompous horn fanfares, and bombastic drums. It is a true *danse macabre,* both savage and poetic.

In the midst of this boisterous humor, the little clown suddenly appears—a real human being, helpless, vulnerable, stumbling about as if confused. This is Dmitri Shostakovich as a Charlie Chaplin figure—but remember the bitter smile. Cautiously he lifts his violin to his chin and somewhat hesitantly plays a simple little solo. It doesn't go too badly, though of course he misses a note or two as real clowns always do. He plays a brief encore, this

time on the flute. He concludes his little solo with an ungainly
clown scale, half in minor, half in major. The clown's life is, after
all, a mixture of tears and laughter.

Shortly thereafter the clown turns up again. He wants so much
to please his audience, over and over. He starts to play his now
familiar solo one more time, but he is drowned out by the orchestra. Comical? Perhaps. He tries again, and again he is clubbed
into submission by the superior power. That's how it always
happens at the circus, and Shostakovich, as a true Russian, loved
the circus. The clown is there to be shoved aside and forgotten. He
is insignificant. The orchestra takes over completely. The thematic material introduced at the beginning of the movement is
taken up again, this time with a concentrated pizzicato section in
the strings, a lavishly clownish adornment conceived by a composer thrust into the abyss of angst. It is obvious that Shostakovich
is here employing humor to keep the angst under control. When
he was a child, perhaps, like children everywhere, he learned to
whistle in the dark. Now, in the darkness of Stalin's Russia, his
whistling took another form.

As this robust orchestral repast continues, the audience is doing what every circus audience does: waiting impatiently for the reappearance of their favorite character, the clown. He *must* show his face again before the show is over. And sure enough, he gives his fans one last little glimpse of himself. The clown knows now that he is going to be clubbed as soon as he appears. Everybody in the audience knows it too, and true to the psychology of circus audiences everywhere they vacillate between laughter and compassion as they await his fate. The little clown does not disappoint them. He tries one last time, ever so cautiously, to sing his song, this time in the sad, fragile voice of the oboe (see score, pp. 312–13). The impish lightness of the melody has disappeared; all that remains of the original theme is its rhythm. But that is enough. As the clown is chased out of the circus ring in the concluding measures of the movement, we, the audience, know perfectly well who has really won. For we know that the clown is indestructible; he will always come back, as long as there are circuses, and people to enjoy them.This scherzo, then, which has an ABA structure, is a simple little Charlie Chaplin comedy in musical form. At one level, it is pure music; at another, it is about Dmitri Shostakovich and his desperate life situation. Non-Russians, too, can follow the story if we know what to listen for.

The third and fourth movements have several common features. Both start out in a minor key and end in major. The symbolism is easy to understand and has been used ever since Bach's day: the major ending stands for light, catharsis, release, and hope. This turn in the last section of the symphony gave it a therapeutic function, a kind of mental boost for countless terrified and suppressed people in Russia of the 1930s. That the official censors explicitly interpreted the major mode in this same section as a demonstration of confidence in the bright future of Stalin's Russia is another matter. Shostakovich, we may say, was able to have it both ways: his enemies thought he had capitulated, but his friends knew better. Thus he was able to continue his work as a composer without losing his integrity.

Both movements make use of elements drawn from the preceding two movements. The principal theme from the first movement

reappears in the third, altered, to be sure, but easily recognizable, as if it were the composer's alter ego.

A variant of the lovely secondary theme from the first movement also reappears in the fourth. This time it is assigned to the horn, which now, logically enough, has lost much of its lyricism. Opposition exacts a price.

Soon the snare drums also return, like an echo from "the march of the evil powers" in the first movement. In this movement, however, the snare drums are not permitted to grow in significance. Symbolically, they are soon required to make way for the concluding coda, which with almost astonishing abruptness shifts the mood to one of festivity, with elements of light and hope. Is the composer perhaps throwing another bone to a panting censor?

Despite these similarities, the third and fourth movements are very different in character. The opening of the third movement is almost hymnodic, in sharp contrast to the almost raucous laughter with which the preceding movement concludes. High emotional tension prevails throughout the movement. I am reminded of the words of August Strindberg in "Stadsresan" upon hearing Beethoven's *Appassionata*.

All that is scornful in life, the cynical, scoffing demeanor
That jests at the things we hold sacred,
    and sneers at our higher emotions,

That calls for devotion and honor,
    and laughs at the ones who possess them;
Life as a hostage, fast bound
    by poor humankind's varying fortunes,
Threatens to strike what we love
    most of all, to wound and disfigure—
This is the soul of the music, the wordless, powerful poem,
Shouting and weeping in impotent
    rage over life's cruel misery.
(Trans. W. H. Halverson)

Recent Russian musicologists have characterized the third movement as introverted, with an almost raw display of the composer's own angst. Typical of the movement is the following oboe solo, whose phrasing and intonation are suggestive of the human voice. The loneliness, the feeling of forsakenness, are perhaps even more prominent here than in the principal theme of the first movement and the clown melody of the second.

After the premiere of the Fifth Symphony, it was the third movement that Stalin's musicologists, led by the infamous I. Nestyev, found it most difficult to swallow. Where was the optimism required by socialist realism? It was nowhere to be found in this movement, which was criticized as an "expressionistic etching of petrified fright." The music, they said, contained the "color of resignation and pallor of death" and had "a hysterical, demented tinge." One quickly recognizes *Pravda*'s abusive terminology.

The transition to the fourth movement is intended to shock the listeners: from the quiet pianissimo on which the third movement ends we are suddenly thrust into an explosion of sound, forte fortissimo, with thundering timpani. Some critics reacted with contempt: "[The portrayal of] suffering's pathos in several places gets perilously close to naturalistic screeching and yelling," said one of them (see Meyer 1980). Again we detect the terminology of *Pravda*, where "naturalism" was a dreaded pejorative that could have far-reaching consequences for an artist's future. And despite the fact that the symphony clearly ended in a major key, with both timpani and trumpet fanfares, the critics did not think the last movement was optimistic and positive enough to outweigh the basically tragic tone set in the preceding movements. It was what one Russian critic aptly called "an *optimistic* tragedy in four movements," but a tragedy nonetheless. This paradoxical ambiguity must have seemed strange to the authorities in the midst of their celebration of the twentieth anniversary of the Revolution.

Be that as it may, Shostakovich survived the presentation of his Fifth Symphony. He had cleverly soothed his opponents by giving it a clear tonal foundation, melodious themes, military-sounding marches, pounding timpani, and a resounding conclusion in a major key. Most important, he had been publicly critical of his own past and had given the symphony an ironic subtitle: "An artist's practical reply to deserved criticism." Were these the words of a *yurodivy?* Of course. But who could prove it?

In 1938, nearly a year after its premiere, Shostakovich made his first public statement regarding the symphony.

> My latest work may be called a lyrical-heroic symphony. Its basic ideas are the sufferings of man, and optimism. I wanted to convey optimism asserting itself as a world outlook through a series of tragic conflicts in a great inner, mental struggle.
>
> During a discussion at the Leningrad section of the Composers' Union, some of my colleagues called my Fifth Symphony an autobiographical work. On the whole, I consider this a fair appraisal. In my opinion, there are biographical elements in any work of art. Every work should bear the stamp of a living person, its author, and it is a poor and tedious work whose creator is invisible. (Volkov 1979, p. 72)

We who read Shostakovich's words and listen to his music can only try to interpret such a statement as best we can, knowing that it is a *yurodivy*'s mixture of official platitudes and genuine candor.

After Shostakovich's death, Volkov published a highly revealing statement the composer once made about the relationship
between Stalin and an artist who was also a *yurodivy:*

> Yes, I'll say it again: Stalin was a morbidly superstitious man. All
> the unforgiven fathers of their countries and saviors of humanity
> suffer from it, it's an inevitable trait, and that's why they have a
> certain respect for and fear of *yurodivye*. Some people think that the
> *yurodivye* who dared to tell the whole truth to czars are a thing of the
> past. . . . But the *yurodivye* aren't gone, and tyrants fear them as
> before. There are examples of it in our day. (1979, p. 192)

THE THIRTEENTH SYMPHONY

Stalin died on March 5, 1953, and it soon became apparent that
his successors in the Kremlin would be somewhat more tolerant
of protest than he had been. The greater freedom of the post-
Stalin era is reflected in a poem by the poet and protest singer
Bulat Okudzjava written circa 1960.

THE BLACK CAT

In a drab, unlighted hallway
Stands the stairwell to our flat;
There, at home within the darkness,
Dwells a big black alley-cat.

Evil lurks behind his mustache
As he leers in fiendish glee.
Other cats meow and wail;
This one taunts us silently.

Mice and rats are not his targets
As he lays his cunning plans;
This cat terrorizes tenants
Who resist his harsh demands.

Sallow eyes dart hither, thither
As he crouches in his lair.
Everyone must do his bidding:
Prying eyes are everywhere.

Craftily he rules his kingdom,
Licks his fangs and has his way,
Hones his claws and preens his whiskers,
Ever ready for the fray.

That's why life is not so pleasant
In our gloomy Russian house:
We've become the helpless victims
In a game of cat and mouse.
(Trans. J.-R. Bjørkvold and W. H. Halverson)

This thinly veiled allegory about the reign of terror and the longing for a more open society was widely sung by Okudzjava. By 1960, Stalin's body had been removed from the mausoleum on Red Square, and the political and cultural restraints effected during his rule had been significantly relaxed. It was now possible to be openly critical of the once-feared ruler, so the poet felt free to entertain his fellow citizens with a sarcastic allegory about the dictator-cat who made life so miserable for so many.

For Shostakovich, the exhilaration of having outlived his worst enemy was tempered by the sad irony that Sergei Prokofiev, his great companion in suffering, died on the same day as Stalin. Shostakovich was now the only Soviet composer of international standing who had survived the Stalin era. His would be the only music to be heard on both sides of the Iron Curtain as a cultural-political statement about the situation in the Soviet Union after the death of Stalin. People would be asking: Were there now opportunities for a new standard, for a new sense of freedom, for a clearing of the air, for muse-ical criticism?

Shortly after Stalin's death Shostakovich began work on his Tenth Symphony (the "thaw" symphony). His own initials (D–E-flat [= Ess]–C–B [= H]) constitute one of the important musical motives in this symphony. In the climax of the last movement, this motive is shouted out by the full orchestra as if to affirm as forcefully as possible, "I, Dmitri Shostakovich, have survived Stalin!"

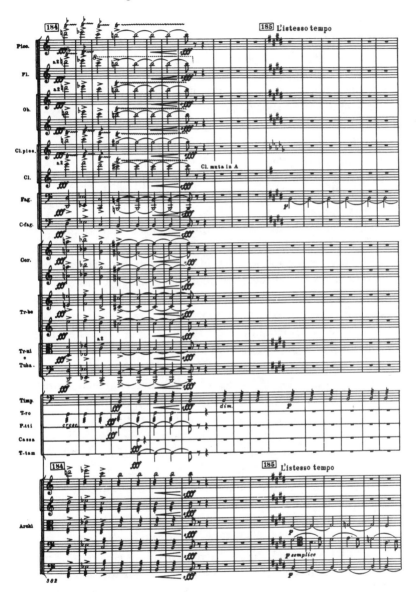

Many years later Shostakovich referred to the second movement of this symphony as a portrait of Stalin—*post mortem et festum,* so to speak. Thus both the composer and the tyrant were made integral parts of Shostakovich's first major work after Stalin's death.

After a long and tortuous discussion in the Soviet Composers' Union, where the symphony was first condemned as "formalistic," Shostakovich was finally rehabilitated in the winter of 1954. The Tenth Symphony was officially declared to be a masterwork. The thaw continued, culminating in Nikita Khrushchev's famous "de-Stalinization" speech at the Twentieth Party Congress in 1956. Later that year Shostakovich was given an opportunity to publish an article in *Pravda*. Twenty years had passed since the *Pravda* article that had so profoundly changed Shostakovich's life as a composer. Now, with the implicit support of Khrushchev himself, Shostakovich was able at last to criticize his persecutors in the Composers' Union openly.

The year 1958 saw some further important developments toward greater artistic freedom in the Soviet Union. Khrushchev needed the support of the artists in his continuing struggle with the conservative wing of the political leadership, for it was no secret that some prominent hawks were beginning to call for his ouster, especially after the revolt in Hungary. In May 1958 the Central Committee published a decree criticizing the notorious Zhdanov conference of 1948, where both Prokofiev and Shostakovich had once again been stripped of all honors and condemned as enemies of the people. The 1958 decree explicitly rehabilitated them, declaring them "gifted composers," though it reaffirmed the cultural-political validity of the 1948 conference. It was obvious that Khrushchev needed the borrowed luster of Shostakovich's international reputation to enhance his own credibility, not least in relation to the West, where signs of liberalization in the official attitude toward artistic expression were closely watched. With much public fanfare, Shostakovich was now awarded the Soviet Union's highest honor, the Lenin Prize.

But the same year also witnessed an unexpected chill in the midst of Khrushchev's thaw. The push in this direction came from the West, for in November 1958 Boris Pasternak was awarded the Nobel Prize in Literature. His selection was widely viewed in the Soviet Union as a deliberate provocation, and it had immediate consequences for Soviet cultural life. Once again the West looked on as a Soviet man of letters was persecuted and isolated. Pasternak's last novel, *Doctor Zhivago,* was banned in the Soviet Union. In 1960 Pasternak died, obviously deeply troubled by the harassment to which he had been subjected.

Shostakovich, meanwhile, was in a stronger position than he had ever been before in his life: officially rehabilitated, recipient of the Lenin Prize, perhaps the best-known representative of Soviet culture in the world. He could no longer be publicly denounced. The politicians had played their Shostakovich card, making him invulnerable. Confident of his strength, Shostakovich chose to make his own artistic statement, to unleash a veritable battering ram in the midst of the tense cultural-political situation that prevailed in the Soviet Union at the time. The battering ram was Symphony No. 13, the "Babi Yar" symphony.

It was 1962, the year John F. Kennedy and Nikita Khrushchev looked each other in the eye over the Cuban missile crisis and— as Americans love to recall—Khrushchev blinked. For Khrushchev, it was a humiliating and damaging defeat that subjected him and his policies to severe criticism by his opponents among the top leaders of the Communist Party. A number of cultural figures, including Shostakovich, sent a letter directly to Khrushchev and the Central Committee defending the policy of cultural liberalization and attacking the neo-Stalinists. Yevgeny Yevtushenko, perhaps the foremost poet and rebel of the "thaw" generation, published his famous poem "Stalin's Heirs."

We carried him from the mausoleum.
But how remove Stalin's heirs from Stalin!
. . . .
While Stalin's heirs walk this earth,
Stalin, I fancy, still lurks in the mausoleum.

It was this defiant Yevtushenko whom Shostakovich chose as his artistic partner in the creation of the Thirteenth Symphony, which should be understood as one of many manifestations of a broad musical protest movement that emerged in the Soviet Union during the 1960s. The previous year, Yevtushenko had published "Babi Yar," the poem regarded by many as the quintes-

sential representative of the spirit of the thaw. It is based in the first
instance on the true account of a pogrom that occurred near Kiev
during World War II in which some 34,000 Jews were massacred
by the Nazis. Yevtushenko makes this tragic episode the starting
point for a poetic treatment of humankind's suffering and humankind's shared responsibility for that suffering.

What was it about Yevtushenko and his poem that impressed
Shostakovich so deeply? Partly, of course, it was the sheer power
of the poetry. Beyond that, however, he seems to have been
fascinated by the idea of the Jew as the incarnation of suffering
throughout history. He himself had written songs to Jewish texts
during the late 1940s, though it was not possible to publish them
at the time: the Babi Yar massacre was perpetrated by the Nazis,
not the Russians, but anti-Semitism was rampant in Soviet society
as well. Shostakovich understood the persecuted Jew because he
himself had been persecuted for most of his adult life. He was not
a Jew, but as the representative of a whole generation of suffering,
persecuted, and massacred Russians he felt almost as if he were.
Yevtushenko's poem must have sounded to the composer like an
authentic expression of his generation's and his own life crisis.

I am each old man here shot dead.
I am every child here shot dead.
Nothing in me shall ever forget! . . .

No doubt Shostakovich was also impressed with Yevtushenko's
boldness. Here was a voice from a new generation of Russian
artists who dared to speak with complete openness and with a
combative power that must surely have been thrilling to an aging
yurodivy artist. Yevtushenko's exceptional skill as a reader of his
own poetry, which gradually won him a large and enthusiastic
audience, further underscored this boldness. Yevtushenko could
fill an entire sports stadium with listeners who were deeply moved
by his words, for he wrote of things they had experienced in their
lives and in their souls. Here there was no mask: Yevtushenko met
his audience directly, face to face.

Shostakovich was now fifty-five, Yevtushenko twenty-nine.

Shostakovich realized that together they could create shock waves throughout Soviet society. As a poem, "Babi Yar" had already spread through the country like wildfire. The time was ripe for the composer to remove the mask. He would include "Babi Yar" in his next symphony, using a bass soloist and male chorus to convey Yevtushenko's powerful text.

The Thirteenth Symphony was written during a period of hectic creativity in Shostakovich's life. There was something almost Mozartian about the feverish pace at which he worked. He was busy revising *Lady Macbeth*—banned ever since the fateful *Pravda* attack in 1936—which in its new form was retitled *Katerina Izmailova*. At the same time he was paying homage to his favorite composer, Modest Moussorgsky, by orchestrating "Songs and Dances of Death"—a labor of love in more ways than one, for throughout most of his adult life, Shostakovich had looked death in the eye as a creative composer. The presentation of Moussorgsky's song cycle in new garb was so important to him that he himself conducted the premiere performance (his debut as a conductor). In sharp contrast to the Moussorgsky songs, filled as they are with somber funereal motives, stands Shostakovich's String Quartet No. 9, also completed in 1962. His goal in the quartet, according to his own statement, was to give expression to the childlike side of his nature, and it is, indeed, a musical manifestation of play and lightheartedness. Is this simultaneous preoccupation with death and playfulness evidence of a split personality? Not at all, but it *is* typically Russian.

The Thirteenth Symphony runs the gamut of human emotions from pathos and horror to humor and innocence, but with the power of Yevtushenko's "Babi Yar" as the mental and emotional center. It was begun in the summer of 1962 as Shostakovich lay in the hospital with a partial paralysis of his right hand. Physical pain and the memory of several decades of psychological torment somehow combined to unleash a mighty torrent of creative energy. The Muse Within demanded to be heard more importunately than ever, and he began to compose like a man possessed. Once again he would write music that scoffed at the established limits—limits Shostakovich had felt compelled to observe for most of his creative life. By December the symphony was ready. Both the symphony and *Katerina Izmailova* were in fact premiered just two days apart as 1962 ebbed to a close. The unmasked Shostakovich was heard from once again, and once again the music censors had their work cut out for them.

Shostakovich had first conceived the symphony as a single-movement work based entirely on "Babi Yar." As he composed, however, it grew in concert with his increasing temerity and became a five-movement work for bass solo, male chorus, and orchestra, with a playing time of over an hour. The movements have the following subtitles, all taken from Yevtushenko's poems.

First: Babi Yar (Adagio)
Second: Humor (Allegretto)
Third: In the Store (Adagio)
Fourth: Fears (Largo)
Fifth: A Career (Allegretto)

The theme of *persecution,* present throughout the symphony, is treated with an openness previously unheard of in Soviet society.

The first movement, as we have indicated, deals with the persecution and mass execution of the Jews at Babi Yar. The key is B-flat minor, and a funereal mood is created by the somber tolling of bells. The chorus represents "the voice of the people," as in countless dramatic works from the Greek tragedies to *Boris Godunov.*

The second movement shows how persecution also leads to suppression of what is perhaps the victim's most important survival weapon: *humor.* But though an individual human being may be hounded to death, humor can never be destroyed.

Czars, kings, emperors,
sovereigns of all the earth,
have commanded many a parade,
but they could not command humor. . . .

The merging of humor and the *yurodivy* theme in a cunning survival strategy is obvious. The contrast in mood between the first and second movements—from the horror of Babi Yar to the jocularity of this portrayal of humor—is almost grotesque, but altogether typical of Shostakovich. At the same time, the placement of this movement immediately following the musical treatment of the Babi Yar tragedy gives it a greater feeling of depth and seriousness than any of Shostakovich's earlier treatments of the same theme. The music races along with tremendous displays of power, brutal time changes, and piping flutes ("clown's pipes," as they are called in Yevtushenko's poem). At the point where humor has been executed and has returned, Shostakovich begins a purely instrumental section laced with gallows humor as he quotes the melody of one of the songs in his early work, "Six Songs to English Texts." The original text, which is of Scottish origin, depicts the dance of the condemned man beneath the tree where he was to be hanged.

> Sae rantingly, sae wantonly,
> sae dauntingly gaed he;
> he played a spring and danced it round,
> below the gallows tree.

Remember the clown in the second movement of the Fifth Symphony? Here he is again, eternally human, eternally the same, always having his head chopped off but permanently indestructible.

The third movement ("In the Store") deals with another survival resource in Soviet society: women. In a country where food as well as freedom is in perpetually short supply, it is the women, "their families' guardian angels," who somehow manage to secure enough food to survive. "It is shameful to short-change them!" sing the bass soloist and the men in a rather somber adagio movement that reflects the grayness of the housewife's daily life and also contrasts with the jocularity of the preceding movement.

The fourth movement ("Fears") depicts the paralyzing angst that is the natural consequence of persecution. Musically, this movement is slow and somber, with an introductory tuba solo against a quiet background of deep strings, but the percussion quietly warns of evil lurking nearby. This is deepest, darkest night, and a black Stalin-cat prowls ominously in the darkness.

In the text the poet looks back at the fear that once gripped the land, and that might still be paralyzing the souls of men even as he writes.

Fears are dying out in Russia.
And while I am writing these lines,
at times unintentionally hurrying,
I write haunted by the single fear
of not writing with all my strength.
(Trans. Andrew Huth)

Yevtushenko's text is astonishingly descriptive of Shostakovich's own experience as a creative artist. It is as if someone had finally found the words to describe what it was like to spend a quarter of a century "in the claws of fear."

The concluding movement, too, is highly autobiographical in character. Here the famous Renaissance astronomer Galileo serves as the composer's alter ego. Galileo, as we know, was persecuted for endorsing the Copernican theory that the earth revolves around the sun, not the sun around the earth. Confronted by the superior force of the inquisitors, he was forced to recant his heretical views publicly. It is said that when it was all over he whispered to himself, *"Eppur si muove!"*—"And yet it moves!" Galileo spent the rest of his life playing a kind of *yurodivy* role, much as Shostakovich was to do some three centuries later.

Musically, the scherzo-like final movement is similar in character to the second. The clown will enter the ring one more time. The bassoon is given the honor of representing him.

Zigzagging along with no identifiable climax, this theme might be described as anticareerist. Its meaning is clear: such, outwardly observed, were the careers of both Galileo and Shostakovich, apparently without direction, lost in a labyrinth of persecution, inquisition, censorship, and terror. The point is stated directly in the concluding lines of the poem on which the movement is based.

I believe in their sacred belief,
and their belief gives me courage.
I'll follow my career in such a way
that I'm not following it!

It would soon become apparent that a symphony based on "Babi Yar" was not going to see the light of day without serious opposition. Rumors that Shostakovich was composing such a work were rampant throughout the summer of 1962. Many tongues had wagged when Yevtushenko's poem was published the previous autumn, but the thought that these seditious verses might now be linked with the music of the great Shostakovich—which would be heard by millions of people in the Soviet Union and throughout the world—was more than Stalin's heirs could tolerate. Such a symphony would almost certainly defy most of the taboos upon which the fragile armistice between the political leaders and the cultural community was based. Since nobody had yet heard the music, however, only one course of action was open to them: to attack Yevtushenko and the poem "Babi Yar." Yevtushenko was younger than Shostakovich and less well-known internationally, so a move against him would not arouse as much opposition. Thus an attack on Yevtushenko seemed to the Stalinists the best way to abort the Thirteenth Symphony before it reached full term.

Galina Vishnyevskaya, whose friendship with Shostakovich placed her very close to the events that were intended to prevent the public performance if not the creation of the "Babi Yar" symphony, has written a detailed account of what happened.

In the Central Committee's Department of Agitation and Propaganda, the riffraff were already poking around. The papers published a review of "Babi Yar" in which Yevtushenko was charged with ignoring the role that the Russian people played in the destruction of Nazi Germany, distorting the truth about the victims of fascism, and so on.

Vedernikov [the bass soloist] called me at home. "Listen, Galka. I got the music from Shostakovich and agreed to sing, but, you know . . . I can't." . . .

When . . . I told [Shostakovich] that Vedernikov had refused to sing, he wasn't all that astonished: it was as if he'd been expecting it. The Party had already demanded that the text be revised or they would ban the performance. [Shostakovich] responded by saying he would not change a single line, and would make no cuts. Either it was produced as written, or they could cancel the premiere.

Yevtushenko hurried around Moscow, pulling out all the government stops at his disposal, while I looked for another soloist. (1984, pp. 276–77)

As an obvious countermove in the ongoing power struggle, Yevtushenko published both "Stalin's Heirs" and "Fears" in late October 1962. Both probably came into being, at least in their present form, as a consequence of the struggle with the authorities over the symphony. "Fears" was in fact written specifically for the symphony and provided yet another reason for the authorities to try to prevent its premiere. The alarm sounded. Nobody had yet seen the full score except the composer himself.

On December 17, 1962, the day before the scheduled premiere, a meeting was held in Moscow between the political leadership and a large number of artists. Loud voices were raised demanding that the premiere be canceled. After the meeting, Khrushchev had a conversation with Yevtushenko about "Babi Yar" and evidently demanded that at least some lines of the text be changed. On the day of the scheduled performance, an attempt was made to get the chorus to withdraw. Yevtushenko persuaded them to continue, however, saying that he was responsible for the texts, not they.

At the last minute, the bass soloist who had been chosen to replace Vedernikov was ordered to substitute in an opera performance at the Bolshoi that same evening. Without a bass soloist there could be no performance of the Thirteenth Symphony. This time it was world-renowned orchestral conductor Kyril Kondrashin who saved the day: he arranged for another substitute to handle the role at the Bolshoi and rescued the scheduled soloist for the symphony. Just a few hours before the premiere was scheduled to begin, official permission was given for the performance to proceed. Shostakovich had won, and without compromise.

Why did the authorities finally relent? Had Shostakovich, after all, become too eminent for them to attack? Would a public silencing of Shostakovich have become too big a burden in the propaganda war between the United States and the Soviet Union, especially in the aftermath of the Cuban missile crisis? Or was there a secret agreement with Yevtushenko, who had obviously been pushed very hard?

Vishnyevskaya reports that they were not sure the symphony was really going to be played until they heard the opening bars from the orchestra. The seats normally occupied by government officials were conspicuously empty during the concert. The area just outside the concert hall was heavily patrolled by the police. The planned television broadcast of the concert was not permitted. And in the printed program there appeared not one word of Yevtushenko's text. The thaw was over. This was a blast of arctic air such as the Soviet Union was soon to experience again with distressing frequency under the harsh rule of Leonid Brezhnev.

A few days later the symphony was scathingly criticized in the press, whereupon Yevtushenko published a new version of "Babi Yar." The changes were substantial. Russia's heroism during World War II was emphasized; the poet's identification with the Jews was greatly softened; the identification with the crucifixion of Christ was removed altogether; the Russians' own sufferings were placed on an equal footing with those of the Jews. Most important of all, perhaps, for official Soviet politics, Russia's victory over fascism was introduced as a theme in the poem. Khrushchev's pressure on Yevtushenko had obviously had an effect: the young poet had been brought to heel. That he later insisted to Western reporters that he had not been pressured to make these changes only shows that he, too, had now learned how to play the role of a *yurodivy*. The revolutionary poet of the thaw had merely been stripped of many of his illusions, and like Shostakovich in his young manhood, he had been forced to don a mask.

In February 1963 the Thirteenth Symphony was performed using the revised version of Yevtushenko's poem. Shostakovich's powerful symphony of protest survived in disguise pending the day when "Babi Yar" could once again show its true face. One single work, a symphony, had created permanent changes in the official cultural policies of a powerful government, despite countless efforts by officialdom to tone it down. It is the oft-told but ever true story of the remarkable power of the violin over the rifle. The Muse-bearer is strong, even when bound by the chains of evil men.

WHEN A WHOLE SOCIETY WAKES UP—WITHOUT A NOSE!

How has Shostakovich's Thirteenth Symphony fared more recently in Russia, where swiftly moving events have at last destroyed the Stalinist engines of suppression? As far as I am aware, as of this writing the original version has not yet been played in St. Petersburg's main concert hall—which, ironically, now bears the name of the composer. To mark the fortieth anniversary of the infamous 1948 purge, however, *Sovietskaya Muzyka* published a scathing critique of the government's treatment of Shostakovich and his music. The government's handling of the matter, according to the article, had "done irreparable damage to the national culture . . . and such actions must henceforth be unthinkable" (Golovinski 1988). One must, therefore, assume that in due course the original version of Shostakovich's great symphony will also be heard in his native land.

The very word *glasnost* implies such a hope, if one takes the etymology of the word at face value. Usually translated incorrectly as "openness," it is associated with the old Russian word for "voice" (*glas*). *Glasnost*, in other words, is an inherently *muse-ical* concept, related to the basic idea underlying the ancient myth of the birth of the Muses: to give the world a voice in order thereby to change it.

In the meantime, the politics of *glasnost* is steadily making the visionary description of Russian society contained in Shostakovich's opera *The Nose* a current reality. The remnants of Stalinism are being stamped out everywhere. People executed for "crimes against the state" or declared traitors under the former regime are being rehabilitated. Many powerful leaders are being accused of corruption and thrown out of power. Leningrad has once again become St. Petersburg.

Cultural life in Russia today is a seething cauldron of change. Yevtushenko's "Babi Yar" has finally been republished in its original version (Yevtushenko 1987). Pasternak's *Doctor Zhivago* is now being acclaimed as a masterpiece and was presented serially in the prestigious journal *Novy Mir* (Egeberg 1989). The exiled Alexander Solzhenitsyn has also been rehabilitated. His most important work, *The Gulag Archipelago,* a powerful attack on the Soviet government's systematic persecution and imprisonment of millions of its own citizens, is being published in the same journal. Shortly before his death, Andrei Sakharov was honored for his courageous life and work and permitted once again to take his seat in the Soviet Academy of Science. And Russian high school students were excused from taking their final exam in history because the contents of the school's textbooks were openly acknowledged to be false. The old Communist regime is being attacked in a constant flow of new films, books, and music. *Dies irae:* it is as if the Muses are intoning a final requiem over the ruins of the Soviet empire.

Thus it was not just Gogol's Kovalyov who, a century and a half ago, woke up one morning without a nose. The political identity of a whole society has suddenly disappeared. Hundreds of thousands of Stalin's heirs stand unclothed—and un-nosed—before the mirror of history as a whole political culture has been rendered noseless. The demand for freedom toppled the Communist governments of Europe in the autumn of 1989. One politician after another lost his nose, in land after land: Poland, Hungary, Czechoslovakia, Romania, Bulgaria. Overnight, as it were, two Germanies resolved to become one, and in less than a year it was a *fait accompli.* And Mstislav Rostropovich, himself a refugee from his Stalinist homeland, sat in the open air beside the Berlin Wall and played the most important solo of his life. Bach. A solitary cello tone with a deep, rich vibrato rose victoriously through the rusty, blood-stained barbed wire, penetrated the Iron Curtain, and reached the heavens. The Muse sang, and the wall came tumbling down.

THE POWER OF MUSE-ICAL WONDER

Thus it is that the Muse-bearer can, with astonishing acuity, see into the future. Muse-bearers of all ages possess what Edith Cobb has called "the vulgar wisdom of child and poet." The little blue horse gallops along. The fictional story of *The Nose* becomes, in its own way, truer than true. For the Muse-bearer, one plus one is never exactly two: an element of restlessness always remains. It is the restlessness and innovative power of this muse-ical wonder that shatters the confining limits of the Euclidian square. This is what makes music swing in the human soul and gives poetry the overwhelming power that causes even the mighty to tremble. They all knew this—Gogol, Shostakovich, Meyerhold, Yevtushenko. It is the secret of the untamable logic of the muse-ical mentality and of the clown's apparent clumsiness as he stumbles about the circus ring. It is the power of childlikeness in the creative adult human being—even under siege.

"RIGHT NOW THE ACCORDION
IS THE ONLY THING THAT HELPS"

It was the afternoon of August 20, 1991. A whole world trembled in fright. Mikhail Gorbachev had been deposed as president and was under virtual house arrest at his dacha in the Crimea. Yanayev had assumed control of the Soviet Union.

We all followed the unfolding drama on our television screens: on this afternoon a column of tanks rolled threateningly into Red Square in the heart of Moscow. Loaded machine guns atop the tanks were all aimed in the same direction: toward the walls of the Kremlin, toward the parliament building of the Russian Federation. Tonight the Kremlin was to be stormed. Tonight Yeltsin was to suffer the same fate as Gorbachev. He, too, was to be silenced by the power of the evil empire.

Red Square was filled with a mighty throng of people. Barricades of cars and busses were put up in front of the brick walls of the Kremlin. In a bittersweet twist of fate, the people now found themselves defending the Kremlin as the last bastion of freedom. The seething crowd was shouting and crying. Enraged mothers scolded soldiers who sat stonefaced in the turrets of their tanks.

A song, a simple Russian waltz, was heard in the midst of the confusion. The TV camera panned Red Square, searching out the source of the song: a young Russian and his accordion. One leg braced defiantly on the tank tread, his accordion pressed tightly to his breast, he raised his gravelly voice toward the afternoon sky.

A TV reporter fought his way through the multitude and up to the singing young man. Clearly moved by the apocalyptic seriousness of the moment, he stretched his microphone forward and asked, "Does it help to play the accordion at a time like this?" The young Russian stopped singing, loosed himself from the spellbound magic of the music, and smiled. "Right now the accordion is the only thing that helps!"

Clutching his instrument, he started the song once more—an innocent melody as a shield against tanks and guns. And people sang and sang, as night slowly descended over the onion domes of Vasily Cathedral. The soldiers prepared for the final assault.

We all know how it ended. The tanks never breached the Kremlin walls. By the next day they were gone. Yanayev and his cohorts fled. Humanity had won—and the Muse rejoiced within.

9

Old Age

Age does not make us childish, as they say.
It only finds us true children still.
—GOETHE, *Faust*

In the fullness of time, human beings reach that stage of life known as "old age." Physical strength diminishes, and often mental acuity as well. Life is nearing its end. But as long as we live, the Muse Within lives too. Indeed, it is often she who preserves vitality, maintains priceless identity, and gives life dignity. Though much is forgotten and much passes away, though bodies and minds grow weary with age, still the undying echo of childhood's song and childhood's play continues to vibrate deep within. Here, in the depths of the soul, is the inexhaustible spring from which we drank as children, and to which we return again and again throughout our lives. As life nears its close, the Muse Within can bring color to wrinkled cheeks and a remarkable youthfulness to arthritic legs.

GRANDMA'S CIRCLES

Grandma had always loved singing. As a young girl she had sung in the church choir in her hometown. She was proud of that. Her pastor had called her "Hymn-Josepha" because she knew more hymns by heart than anyone else in the choir. "But he wasn't too happy to see me winking at the boys in the pews when I stood up by the pulpit to sing a solo!" she once told her wide-eyed grandchildren with a chuckle.

When Josepha was old enough to have a little money of her own, she bought an inexpensive guitar and even attended an evening school to take a few lessons. She never got beyond three chords in G major and two in D major, but that was enough to accompany most of the songs she wanted to sing. Especially "The Alpine Rose," one of her all-time favorites.

Sometimes in the evening, after Grandma had had time to enjoy a hot red-wine toddy, the children would ask her to sing "The Alpine Rose."

"All the verses or none at all!" she always said.

"All!" the children shouted. And so, warmed by the hot toddy as well as the shining eyes of the children, she sang the melodramatic old ballad from beginning to end, all fourteen verses.

High up in the Alps' eternal whiteness,
Where the foot of man has never trod,
Grows the Alpine rose in radiant brightness,
Clinging to a frozen clump of sod.

In the valley lived a comely maiden,
Beautiful as any Alpine flower!
Many were the suitors who came calling
Hoping to win both her hand and dower. . . .

Needless to say, the ballad ends tragically.

"Farewell father, mother, sisters, brothers,
Farewell all whom happiness awaits!"

Like one possessed, she climbed the icy mountain,
And leaped to share her lover's grisly fate.

And of course Grandma loved all the immigrant songs that had found their way back to Norway. These were songs about Norway and America, about parting and danger and longing for home. Seven of her brothers and sisters had gone to America to escape the poverty of their homeland, and most of them she never saw again. On her sofa was a decorative pillow with a big Norwegian flag embroidered on it. It had been a gift from her older sister Hilda, who lived in Brooklyn. Beneath the flag, Hilda had stitched the opening words of perhaps the best-known Norwegian-American immigrant song of all: *Kan du glæmme gamle Norge?* ("Can You E'er Forget Old Norway?"). We children could never quite understand why Hilda should have given Grandma that pillow, for it was obvious that she, who had lived there all her life, could never "forget old Norway." She had never even been to Sweden, whose border was less than a hundred miles from her home. But that pillow—her "America pillow," as she called it—was her favorite, no doubt about it. Logic and familial affection don't always go hand in hand.

Grandma wrote long letters to her relatives in America. She was especially diligent about writing to her cousin Gudrun, who had been her closest childhood friend. She had a huge collection of letters received from Gudrun through the years, for she never could bring herself to throw any of them away. And she would sing out her deep longing for the loved ones she had not seen for so many years in a plaintive, quavering voice, trying to wring the last drop of pathos from each word.

Wherever we may roam,
Our thoughts return to home,
To mother, father, loved ones by the score.
And many times each day,
The mem'ries steal away,
To my old, beloved home on Norway's shore.

But now Grandma was old and tired. Not even the guitar and a hot red-wine toddy worked the magic they once did. We grandchildren had begun to say among ourselves that she was in "Twilightland." We hadn't just made up that name either. It came from a children's story that Grandma herself had read to us when we were younger, and we remembered that Twilightland was a place where "it didn't matter if your legs hurt, because in Twilightland everyone can fly."

Everyone can fly! That was something we children understood, for we did it all the time when we played together. So, we thought, everything is surely fine for Grandma in Twilightland.

One day I had what I thought was a brilliant idea. I was looking over a new book by a colleague of mine—a collection of children's songs as they were sung in Trondheim, an old city in central Norway. The thought suddenly occurred to me: "Grandma would enjoy listening to these songs! She loves singing so much, and it would give her a chance to hear some children's songs and spend an evening with one of her grandchildren at the same time. Surely a combination like that will bring back some sparkle to those tired old eyes!"

We laid our plans carefully, inviting her over for an evening of song, fun, and fellowship. After an opening round of hugs and words of welcome I fixed her the strongest hot toddy I knew how to make, and the children showered her with loving attention. Cake and coffee were scheduled to follow later in the evening.

Then I sat down at the piano. I started with "Crazy Canute," which I knew had been one of her favorite songs ever since her youth. It was a sentimental old street ballad that I knew by heart because Grandma and others in the family had sung it so often through the years.

> He lives in a hut near the mountain wall,
> That pitiful, strange old man,
> And roundabout it the birch trees grow,
> His only friends in the land.
>
> . . . .

He, too, was once a carefree young lad,
With a family, and good looks to boot,
But tragedy struck, he withdrew from the world,
And his name became "Crazy Canute." . . .

We all enjoyed singing that song when Grandma was with us. She sighed contentedly, took a big swallow of toddy, and looked expectantly at me. She wanted more. How about some of those children's songs I had been talking about?

"Tom Brown's Baby" seemed like a good choice. I knew that Grandma liked this one too, so brimming with confidence I began.

Tom Brown's baby had a cold upon its chest, . . .
And they rubbed it with camphorated oil.

It is amazing how quickly an old woman's mood can change from contentment to irritation. I couldn't even see her as I sat there at the piano, but an uneasy feeling in the back of my neck told me that something was wrong. I turned around, and sure enough she was looking a little bewildered, almost as if I had somehow offended her. "Humph!" I heard her mutter to herself. "It's *John,* not *Tom.*"

Somewhat uncertainly, I quickly switched to another song known to all Norwegian children, "Take the Ring and Pass It 'Round." Surely, I thought, I can't get into trouble with this one.

Take the ring and pass it 'round,
On and on until it's found.
Now the ring is hidden well.
Who has got it: can you tell?

I stole a quick look over my shoulder to see how I had done, and what I saw was not reassuring. The look on Grandma's face this time was nothing so benign as bewilderment. Her cheeks flamed with anger, and her raven eyes glared at me like burning coals.

I felt like a little boy who had just been caught trying to steal a cookie.

"Jon-*Ro*-ar!" she fairly shouted at me. Her voice was as firm as it had been when I was a little boy, and it bristled with indignation. "Where did you get that nonsense? The last line is supposed to be 'Hey, who's got it: can you tell?' "

"I'll show you," she said defiantly as she struggled to her feet. And she did. She began to sing, clapping her hands and swaying rhythmically from side to side. She forgot that her balance wasn't very good, forgot that she needed a cane to stand. She had emerged from Twilightland, and for one glorious moment she was a child again as she sang the words the *right* way—the way they were sung when she was young.

> Take the ring and pass it 'round,
> On and on until it's found.
> Now the ring is hidden well.
> Hey, who's got it: can you tell?

"*That's* how it's supposed to be, young man!" she said triumphantly. "If you're going to sing a song, you should sing it right!"

"But Grandma," I protested, "in *this* book it says, 'Who has got it: can you tell?' I was just . . ."

She cut me off. "Don't try to teach *me* how to sing this song. I played the ring game to that song as a little girl twenty years before your mother was born. The book is wrong!"

I know now that I should have stopped right there, but I didn't. The plan for the evening was to share some of the songs from this book with Grandma, and I wasn't ready to give up on it. My next choice was "London Bridge Is Falling Down."

> London bridge is falling down,
> Falling down, falling down.
> London bridge is falling down,
> My fair lady.
>
> Build it up with iron bars,
> Iron bars, iron bars.

Build it up with iron bars,
My fair lady.

That was too much for Grandma. "Iron bars, my eye!" she shrieked. "It's 'Build it up with sticks and stones!' I want to go home—*now!* Get me a taxi! Humph! Iron bars!"

Nothing could placate her. Another toddy, Grandma? Cake? Coffee? A little time with the children? No! The evening was over, and she was going home. She wouldn't accept a ride from her wayward grandson, nor would she let me pay the cab fare. She was angry, she was offended, and she would go home on her own terms—in a taxi, paid for out of her own meager funds. Period.

Not until she had stormed out the door did I begin to understand what the problem was. The book I was using was a collection of children's songs *as they were sung in central Norway*. That was the whole idea of the collection. But Grandma was from southern Norway, and where she came from these songs were sung with numerous subtle differences. It was deeply offensive to her museical self to hear her grandson implicitly endorsing a song tradition that was not hers. To her that seemed like disloyalty, treachery, a kind of sacrilege. These songs, in the exact form in which she had learned them, were part of her identity, part of her very self. The unauthorized version promulgated by her normally dutiful grandson simply could not be tolerated. She felt compelled to say in her own Archimedean way, "Don't disturb my circles!"

The evening Grandma stomped out of our apartment—lips pursed, eyes flashing—she looked younger than she had for many years. But that was the last time I saw her emerge from Twilightland. It was her last hurrah, but it was a performance her grandson will always remember.

UNCLE OLAF AND
THE GOLDEN WEDDING WALTZ

Uncle Olaf and Aunt Jenny had been married for fifty years, and the occasion was to be celebrated with a big Golden Anniversary party. A large number of relatives, friends, neighbors, and former coworkers were invited to a nearby banquet hall to share in the festivities.

The bridegroom had aged considerably in recent years. He didn't go outdoors much anymore, even though he had spent most of his life in the construction industry. He tottered when he walked, and had trouble going up and down stairs. His hearing had also begun to fail.

"What!" barked Uncle Olaf whenever we asked him a question.

We children thought he barked because he was angry, and were just a little afraid of him.

"Uncle Olaf isn't really angry," Aunt Jenny explained gently. "He talks loud because he can't hear very well anymore."

But Aunt Jenny knew that Uncle Olaf also barked because he *was* angry. He was angry about growing old, angry about his increasing infirmity. He had certainly never read Dylan Thomas, but he knew in his bones the truth of that poet's famous lines.

> Do not go gentle into that good night,
> Old age should burn and rave at close of day;
> Rage, rage against the dying of the light.

Aunt Jenny was still as light on her feet as a girl skipping rope. She invited the young people to come and visit anytime, and to bring their friends. And every autumn the tree in her yard yielded the world's best yellow plums—which Uncle Olaf steadfastly refused to pick.

"Dammit, Jenny, you can't just let the kids sit there and eat green plums!" Uncle Olaf used to grumble. But Aunt Jenny, ignoring him, would set a huge bowl of overripe yellow plums on the table and let us eat to our hearts' content.

Uncle Olaf had once had several hobbies, but one by one he had abandoned them. Now he did nothing but watch television, although Norwegian television at the time carried programming only a few hours each day. He didn't mind: he was perfectly content to watch the test pattern, which continued to fill the screen when no program was on the air. He could sit and stare at it for hours. No matter what was on television, he watched it. Not until the weather report was finished and the station signed off for the night was he ready to go to bed.

"But Olaf," Aunt Jenny would sometimes say, trying her best to be diplomatic, "must you sit and look at that awful program?"

"How the hell am I supposed to know it's an awful program until I've watched it?" he would reply with irrefutable logic — whereupon he would remain glued to the "tube" until the beautiful female announcer smilingly wished the viewers a pleasant good-night. Uncle Olaf always smiled back at her.

Actually, Uncle Olaf still had one hobby to supplement his addiction to television. He played the harmonica. On the rare occasions when the television was turned off, more often than not he would get out the harmonica he used to play "in the workmen's shed at the construction site" and strike up a tune. It was a C-major instrument, the simplest kind of harmonica you could buy.

The relation between the harmonica and chewing tobacco has probably never been discussed in music literature, but for Uncle Olaf the two belonged together like beer and pretzels. "It takes a little chewin' to get the music swingin' right," he would say through his stained dentures with a wink at us children, knowing full well that Aunt Jenny, the world's most meticulous housekeeper, hated this habit with a passion. He had been blowing chewing tobacco into his harmonica for over sixty years, and we knew that Aunt Jenny loved to hear him play in spite of the tobacco juice and filth associated with it. She often said, "If it hadn't been for the harmonica, I would never have married him." Then she would add, "Well, he was also a heck of a dancer when he was young, but" — and you could hear the pride in her voice — "it was the harmonica that gave him the rhythm!"

Gave him the rhythm? We had a hard time picturing Uncle Olaf as "a heck of a dancer" as we watched him hobbling around among the guests at the Golden Wedding celebration. He was wearing his best suit, and in the breast pocket he had tucked his precious harmonica. No pretty little handkerchief for him. No-siree. Uncle Olaf thought decorative handkerchiefs were "nothin' but foolishness." "All us guys in the construction business used the *natural* method," he always insisted when Aunt Jenny tried to refine his habits. We understood that the issue really had to do with his identity as a workingman, a carpenter. A certain uncouthness went with the territory, and he wasn't about to give it up just because he had grown old.

"Hey, Dad!" one of his sons suddenly announced, "The 'Golden Wedding Waltz' is next. Aren't you going to ask your bride for this dance?"

All the guests formed a circle and began to clap rhythmically. We children looked apprehensively at each other: did they really have to embarrass him in this cruel way? Couldn't they see that Uncle Olaf's tottery old legs had all they could do to bear the weight of his body when he was standing still? He certainly had not tried to use them for dancing for at least twenty years.

The committee that had planned the party had located an old Victrola and a 78-rpm recording of the "Golden Wedding Waltz." This part of the celebration was going to be carried out in style, with authentic sounds from Olaf and Jenny's youth. "What a neat idea," we thought to ourselves, though we still had our misgivings about the wisdom of subjecting the honorees to the humiliation from which there was evidently no avenue of escape.

The record was placed on the turntable and the phonograph wound up till we thought the spring was going to break. The last thing anybody wanted was for the old Victrola to run down before the dance was finished! There we stood in a large circle surrounding the bridal pair, looking on with affectionate admiration, slightly nervous about how they would handle the situation. And there they stood in our midst, seemingly unperturbed, like two innocent children. Aunt Jenny was beaming, and Uncle Olaf— well, Uncle Olaf was still himself, grumbling under his breath and seemingly bored by "all this fuss." But he would do what he had to do.

The rusty old spring set the record spinning and a very *low*-fi sound filled the hall, but it was a sound from Uncle Olaf and Aunt Jenny's youth. And a miracle happens — a *muse-ical* miracle: Uncle Olaf becomes a different person. He is like the dog in the old Victrola ads who hears "his master's voice": the familiar strains of the music of yesteryear strike a responsive note in the depths of his soul, and he is suddenly transformed. The Muse waves her magic wand, and the frog becomes a prince, the lamb becomes a lion. The old man forgets his infirmities and for one glorious moment is young again. And Aunt Jenny was right: he *is* one heck of a dancer!

The hormones of youth begin to course powerfully through his body under the intoxicating influence of the music he remembers so well. Beaming through eyebrows that suddenly seem less gray, he grasps his Jenny and draws her close. There is strength in those loving hands. He places them on her hips, then slowly moves them downward until they are resting gently on her buttocks. This is how he had held her, how all young men held their partners at the country dances, when they were young. It has an immediate effect on both of them. Jenny blushes demurely and lovingly tightens her grip on Uncle Olaf's stooped neck. Hands and bodies communicate wordlessly as the old dancers move with astonishing grace across the floor.

Uncle Olaf crouches down, leans far back, and plants his heels firmly on the floor. He and Jenny are in perfect balance. Their bodies begin to whirl around and around, in perfect coordination with the beat of the waltz. They lean lower and lower with each revolution, as if to scorn the law of gravity as well as the ravages of time. They swing to the left and to the right. They whirl across the dance floor, gliding along in a constant accelerando, helped by the centrifugal force generated by their whirling bodies. Uncle Olaf's thighs are as supple as those of a speed-skater. His feet never leave the floor: he just glides and glides, rotating on his heels, around and around. Jenny blushes more and more, lets herself be led, seduced. She knows her role and plays it well. She leans her upper body farther and farther back, forcing her lower body ever more tightly against his. Her old breasts are extended toward him in a way they probably have not been for thirty or forty years. And she is so proud! "Look! He can dance! My guy can still dance! *We* can still dance!"

And Uncle Olaf, bridegroom of fifty years, tobacco-chewing harmonica player, TV nut, and one heck of a dancer, suddenly becomes aware that he has won his bride all over again. Proudly, he extends his body, then bends his knees and sinks down almost to the floor. "Ho-ho!" he bellows triumphantly as the sweat runs down his cheeks. "Ho-ho!"

Everyone understands that this is just how he did it at the neighborhood dance hall in years gone by, when he and Jenny were young. And everyone knows beyond a shadow of a doubt that he has rarely done it since they were married and got bogged down in the daily routine of making a living and raising a family. His eyes glisten as if to say, "By God, I haven't forgotten how to dance, have I!"

And he hadn't. Dancing bodies have their own memory, their own intelligence. Dance movements implanted in the body in one's youth create patterns that can never be removed, patterns that are preserved by the Muse Within. Muse-bearers remember with dancing bodies.

Olaf and Jenny dance their "Golden Wedding Waltz" to the end, whirling about like the young lovers they once were. Their bodies are pressed together in a sensuous V as they cling to each other more tightly than ever. Their wedding rings glisten as if they, too, understand the magic spell of this special moment. His hands are still on her buttocks, hers still wrapped tightly around his neck. He even manages to sweep his bride off her feet and lift her up into the air. He grasps her around the waist and lifts her, synchronously and rhythmically, just as the waltz comes to an end. He is the king of the dance floor once again.

And there we spectators stood, bewildered and shy, encircling them. Family, neighbors, coworkers, friends. Not a soul among us considered venturing out on the dance floor while Olaf and Jenny were dancing their "Golden Wedding Waltz." Their entrancement held us spellbound, and we could only watch in mute wonder.

Soon the "Golden Wedding Waltz" gave way to the Beatles, who were all the rage at the time, and the spell was broken. Now the rest of us could dance. The old Victrola had done its job and was moved out to the cloakroom. The Beatles required another sound: twin speakers and electric amplification.

Olaf and Jenny sat down to catch their breath. They had played their part. For them, the whole evening began and ended with the

"Golden Wedding Waltz." A scant three minutes of indescribable joy dancing together on a big dance floor: that was all. It was like a fireworks display: magnificent while it lasted, but oh, so brief!

They lived together—happily, in their own way—for many years thereafter, but they never stepped on a dance floor again. Uncle Olaf resumed his life as a role model for couch potatoes, watching the test pattern on the TV screen, swearing angrily at the slightest provocation, chewing tobacco, and occasionally playing his harmonica. And Aunt Jenny continued to offer the children who came to her house the world's juiciest yellow plums, autumn after autumn.

TAPPING FEET CAUSE HEARTS TO BEAT

She isn't so terribly old, really. Seventy-five, that's all. But her body is much older. In just a couple of years she has turned into a fragile, emaciated little wisp of a thing. She weighs only about eighty pounds, and even so, her back is scarcely able to bear the weight. Two broken hips have made it so hard for her to walk that even a trip from the sofa to the bathroom is long and painful for her. It is only with great effort that she is still able to struggle up from the sofa into a standing position in front of her walker. She depends on willpower and Darvon.

Her eyes, though, are young; they still shine as brightly as ever. It is as if they have taken over her whole face as they peer out from under her tousled gray hair.

"Hey! Nothing is more important than singing and music. That's what I've always said."

She has stuck to that, always. It's not that she has spent much time making music during her life. She has never played an instrument. But she can *listen.* If the music touches her heart, she gets totally absorbed in it.

Her son, making his regular Friday visit, knows this. His most appreciative fan is crouching there on the sofa once again, waiting for him to start playing.

The old Zimmermann piano is badly out of tune. The C-sharp just above middle C makes an awful sound, so he quickly resolves to avoid anything requiring him to play that note. E-flat major should be safe. He begins, "moderato, with feeling": "I'm in the mood for love, simply because you're near me . . ." It surely was not the shining eyes of a wizened old woman that Jimmy McHugh and Dorothy Fields were thinking of when they wrote this song. But so what? The music works its magic instantaneously. Her eyes grow misty, and the son knows that his mother is lost in happy memories of a time long ago when the world was full of beautiful women and dashing young men. *Heaven is in her eyes.*

The son senses her mood. This is no time for nostalgic tears! He starts playing a cheery boogie-woogie bass pattern in C major, gets mixed up, then switches to another Jimmy McHugh and Dorothy Fields hit from a golden past: "Just direct your feet to the sunny side of the street!" Above the feeble sound of the piano, mother and son are both, as it were, hearing the bright, clear sound of Louis Armstrong's trumpet joining in: Satchmo at Symphony Hall, 1947. The son, hamming it up, does his best to imitate Satchmo's gravel voice as he hunches over the keys, bellowing to high heaven. And the dear soul is laughing for the first time in many weeks. Hasn't she got sunshine in her hair?

"He's a bit off his rocker, that fellow," she chortles contentedly.

"Cuckoo," he replies.

"The crazy boy," she sighs.

And the son starts laughing, too. He turns up the tempo several notches, molto, molto. "Give me five minutes more, only five minutes more, of your charms . . ." Their eyes meet as he continues playing. They are in a magic circle of muse-ical communication that goes back to a time long ago when they played "peek-a-boo" together. Mother and son. Then and now. He looks down at her right foot, old and crippled. It is all rhythm! It is beating time. *Tapping feet cause hearts to beat.*

When does death come?

"When the brain stops working," say some.

"When the heart stops beating," say others.

"When the foot stops tapping," says the bearer of the Muse Within.

Postludium

As long as the human race continues to exist, the Muse will be among us, for the Muse Within is part of the pulsating soul of every human being.

Every second of every day, babies are born into the world. Each of them, like each of us when we were young, continues the muse-ical discovery of the universe. Their experience of discovery is part of the human heritage we all share. These children of today and tomorrow do what the Muses once did at the foot of Mount Olympus under the proud, watchful eyes of Zeus and Mnemosyne. "They sing and play / Their childlike way," infusing life with meaning. Here lies nothing less than a continuous hope for the survival of the human race, whose history is the never-ending song of the Muse Within.

Bibliography

Akerø, Marit (1987). "Fantasi som skapende transcendens." *Kontur* 2, February. Oslo.

Alkersig, Mette, and Mette Riemer (1989). *Spontansangen—en del av børnenes egen kultur*. Egtved.

Åm, Eli (1989). *På jakt etter barneperspektivet*. Oslo.

Anyanwu, K. (1987). "The Idea of Art in African Thought," in Guttorm Fløistad, ed., *Contemporary Philosophy: A New Survey*. Vol. 5, *African Philosophy*. Dordrecht, Boston, and Lancaster.

Applebee, Arthur N., Judith Langer, and Ina V. S. Mullis (1987). *The Nation's Report Card: Learning to Be Literate in America*. Report no. 15-RW-01, NAEP, Princeton.

Ayres, Jean A. (1979). *Sensory Integration and the Child*. Los Angeles.

Bachtin, Michail (1979). *Problemy poetiki Dostoevskogo*. Moscow.

Barthes, Roland (1975). *Roland Barthes*. New York.

Barthes, Roland (1982). *Image—Music—Text*. London.

Barthes, Roland (1988). *Barthes*. New York.

Bastian, Peter (1988). *Inn i musikken—En bok om musikk og bevissthet*. Oslo.

Bateson, Gregory (1972). "A Theory of Play and Fantasy," in *Steps to an Ecology of Mind*. New York.

Berefelt, Gunnar (1981). "Barns kreativitet, en försummad resurs." *Abrakadabra*, April. Stockholm.

Berefelt, Gunnar (1987). "Leka bör man annars dör man," in *Barns skapande lek*. Center for the Study of Child Culture, University of Stockholm.

Bergström, Gunilla (1977). *Hvem kan redde Albert Aberg?* Oslo.

Bergström, Matti (1988). "Music and the Living Brain." *Acta Philosophica Fennica* 43. Helsinki.

Bjerke, André (1977). *Samlede dikt*, vol. 1. Oslo.

Bjørkvold, Jon-Roar (1979). *Barnas egen sangbok*. Oslo.

Bjørkvold, Jon-Roar (1984). *Komponist og samfunn—Hanns Eislers musikk i lys av liv og skrifter. Schönberg og Brecht*. Oslo.

Bjørkvold, Jon-Roar (1985). *Den spontane barnesangen—vårt musikalske morsmål*. Oslo.

Bjørkvold, Jon-Roar (1987). "Sangens betydning i barnas kultur," in *Barns skapande lek*. Center for the Study of Child Culture, University of Stockholm.

Bjørkvold, Jon-Roar (1988a). *Fra Akropolis til Hollywood—Filmmusikk i retorikkens lys*. Oslo.

Bjørkvold, Jon-Roar (1988b). "Our Musical Mother Tongue—World Wide," in Ragnhild Söderbergh, ed., *Children's Creative Communication*. Lund and Kent.

Bjørlykke, Bjørn (1989). *Språkutvikling og språklæring—Språksystem og kommunikasjon hos barn i førskulealder*. Oslo.

Blacking, John (1973). *How Musical Is Man?* Seattle.

Blekastad, Milada (1974). "Comenius og den pedagogiske eros," in Tore Frost and Egil A. Wyller, eds., *Den platonske kjærlighetstanke gjennom tidene*. Oslo.

Bøhle, Solveig, ed. (1988a). "Astrid Lindgren, en bondedatter fra Småland." Radio program, NRK, November 1. Oslo.

Bøhle, Solveig, ed. (1988b). "Man skal leva sitt liv så at man blir vän med döden." Radio program, NRK, November 2. Oslo.

Bouij, Christer (1984). *Dmitrij Sjostakovitsj och den sovjetiska kulturpolitiken*. Dissertation, University of Uppsala.

Boye, Karin (1953). *Samlade skrifter*, vol. 10. Stockholm.

Bråten, Stein (1988). "Dialogic Mind: The Infant and the Adult in

Protoconversation," in M. E. Covallo, ed., *Nature, Cognition and System I.* Dordrecht.

Braunbehrens, Volkmar (1986). *Mozart in Wien.* Munich and Zürich.

Bronfenbrenner, Urie (1963). *The Making of the New Soviet Man: A Report on Institutional Upbringing in the USSR.* Cornell University, Ithaca.

Bronfenbrenner, Urie (1970). *Two Worlds of Childhood: U.S. and USSR.* New York.

Bronfenbrenner, Urie (1979). *The Ecology of Human Development.* Cambridge, Mass.

Bronowski, Jacob (1978). *The Origins of Knowledge and Imagination.* New Haven and London.

Bull, Tove (1984). "Talemålsbasert lese- og skriveopplæring," in Marit Anmarkrud, ed., *Grunnleggende lese- og skriveopplæring,* Oslo.

Cage, John (1982). *Etchings 1978–1982.* Crown Point Gallery, Oakland, Calif.

Camara, Dom Helder (1985). *Tusen grunner til å leve.* Oslo.

Campbell, Carol A., and Carol M. Eastman. "Ngoma: Swahili Adult Song Performance in Context." *Ethnomusicology* 28 (no. 3). Michigan.

Campbell, Sammie M. (1984). *Kindergarten Entry as a Factor in Academic Failure.* Dissertation, University of Virginia.

Carling, Finn (1988). *Dagbladet,* May 5. Oslo.

Carlsen, Kari, and Arne Marius Samuelsen (1988). *Inntrykk og uttrykk— Estetiske fagområder i barnehagen.* Oslo.

Chimondo, Steve (1987). "The Aesthetics of Indigenous Arts." *Review of Ethnology.*

Clayton, N. S. (1989). "Song, Sex and Sensitive Phases in the Behavioral Development of Birds." *Tree* 4 (no. 3). U.K.

Cobb, Edith (1977). *The Ecology of Imagination in Childhood.* New York.

Condon, William S., and Louis W. Sander (1983). "Neonate Movement Is Synchronized with Adult Speech: Interactional Participation and Language Acquisition." *Science.*

Cowell, Henry (1955). *Charles Ives and His Music.* New York.

Dale, Erling Lars (1986). *Oppdragelse fri fra "mor" og "far"—Pedagogikkens grunnlag i det moderne samfunn.* Oslo.

Dalin, Per (1988). "På tide å se elevene som en ressurs." *Aftenposten,* January 27. Oslo.

Dalin, Per (1990). "Utdannelsesrevolusjonen i Sovjet-Unionen." *Aften-posten*, June 20. Oslo.

Dam, Hanne (1989). "Skolen på hovedet." *Information*, June 3–4. Copenhagen.

Dantlgraber, J. (1970). *Kreativität und Erziehung—Uber den Einfluss der elementaren Musik- und Bewegungserziehung des Orff-Schulwerkes auf die Kreativität*. Dissertation, University of Salzburg.

DeCasper, Anthony J. (1980). "Of Human Bonding: Newborns Prefer Their Mothers' Voices." *Science* 208.

DeCasper, Anthony J., and M. J. Spence (1982). "Human Fetuses Perceive Maternal Speech," Paper for the International Conference on Infant Studies, Austin, Texas.

DeCasper, Anthony, and M. J. Spence (1986). "Prenatal Maternal Speech Influences: Newborns' Perception of Speech Sounds." *Infant Behavior and Development* 9. Norwood, N.J.

DeCasper, Anthony, et al. (1986). "Familiar and Unfamiliar Speech Elicit Different Cardiac Responses in Human Fetuses." Paper for the International Society for Developmental Psychobiology, Annapolis, Maryland.

DeWoskin, Kenneth J. (1982). *A Song for One or Two: Music and the Concept of Art in Early China*. Michigan.

Diderichsen, A., V. Rabøl Hansen, and S. Thyssen (1989). 6 *år—og på vej i skole*. Copenhagen.

Dneprov, E., V. S. Lazareva, and V. S. Sobkina, eds. (1991). *Vserossiiskoe obrazovanie v perechodnyj period: Programma stabilizatsia i razvitija*. Moscow.

Donaldson, Margaret (1979). *Children's Minds*. London.

Duve, Anne-Marit (1975). "Analfabeter i velferds-Norge." *Sinnets Helse* 5. Oslo.

Dysthe, Olga (1987). *Ord på nye spor*. Oslo.

Eales, Lucy A. (1985). "Song Learning in Zebra Finches: Some Effects of Song Model Availability on What Is Learnt and When." *Animal Behaviour* 33 (no. 4).

Eaton, Jeanette (1971). *Historien om Louis Armstrong*. Oslo.

Egeberg, Erik (1989). "Glasnost og perestrojka—er det *egentlig* noe i det?" *Ergo* 1. Oslo.

Egorova, V., ed. (1967). *Dmitrij Sjostakovitsj*. Moscow.

This collection presents a wealth of interesting information about Shostakovich—autobiographical material, recollections and comments by contemporaries and friends of the composer, and a number of stylistic analyses of his works.

Eisenberg, R. B. (1976). *Auditory Competence in Early Life: The Roots of Communicative Behavior.* Baltimore and London.

Elkind, David (1981). *The Hurried Child: Growing Up Too Fast Too Soon.* Reading, Mass.

Elkind, David (1988). *Miseducation: Preschoolers at Risk.* New York.

Elkind, David, and Samuel Sava (1986). "Some Educators Concerned over 'Superbaby' Burnout." *Los Angeles Times,* Betty Cuniberti, November 20.

Elsness, Turid Fosby (1989). *Sesam sesam,* ABC med lærerveiledning for 1. klasse, NTB-pressemelding. *Arbeiderbladet,* March 2. Oslo.

Ende, Michael (1983). *The Neverending Story.* Trans. Ralph Manheim. New York.

Enerstvedt, Ase (1976). "Om barnekulturen—Et forsøk på å se dens særtrekk som kulturform." *Forskningsnytt* 5. Oslo.

Engdahl, Horace (1983). "Tecknets utopi—Roland Barthes och paralitteraturen." *Bonniers Litterära Magasin.* Stockholm.

Enzensberger, H. M. (1986). "Til analfabetens pris." *Samtiden* 2. Oslo.

Ericson, Gertrud, Ingrid Lagerlöf, and Alf Gabrielsson (1990). "Barn, dans och musik," in *Barn och musik.* Center for the Study of Child Culture, University of Stockholm.

Eriksen, Trond Berg (1989). *Nietzsche og det moderne.* Oslo.

Evans, Tordis Dalan (1984). "En oversikt over Colwyn Trevarthens teori om spedbarnets sosiale utvikling." *Barn—Nytt fra forskning om barn i Norge* 1. Trondheim.

Falbel, Aaron (1989). *Friskolen 70: An Ethnographically Informed Inquiry into the Social Context of Learning.* Dissertation, MIT, Cambridge.

Fernald, A. (1976). "The Mother's Speech to the Newborn." Paper for the Max Planck Institute for Psychiatry, Munich.

Flesch, Rudolf (1956). *Why Johnny Can't Read—and What You Can Do About It.* New York.

Fløgstad, Kjartan (1986). *Det 7. klima.* Oslo.

Fornäs, Johan, Ulf Lindberg, and Ove Sernhede (1988). *Under rocken.* Stockholm and Lund.

Freire, Paulo (1970). *Pedagogy of the Oppressed.* New York.

Freire, Paulo (1985). *The Politics of Education: Culture, Power and Liberation.* Granby, Mass.

Friss, G. (1966). "Die Musikgrundschule," in S. Frigyes, ed., *Musiker-ziehung in Ungarn.* Stuttgart.

Fux, Johann Joseph. *Gradus ad Parnassum* (1725), in Alfred Mann, ed., (1967), *Sämtliche Werke, Serie VII: Theoretische und pädagogische Werke,* vol. 1, Graz.

Gardner, Howard (1982). *Art, Mind and Brain: A Cognitive Approach to Creativity.* New York.

Gardner, Howard (1983). *Frames of Mind: The Theory of Multiple Intelligences.* New York.

Gardner, Howard (1991). *The Unschooled Mind: How Children Think and How Schools Should Teach.* New York.

Gerhardt, Rolf, and Ivar Hansen (1982). "Hva kan Forsvarets sesjons-tester fortelle om nivået i skolen." *Skoleforum* 22.

Goethe, Johann Wolfgang von: *Wilhelm Meisters Wanderjahre.* Vol. 17, *Goethe Gesamtausgabe* (1969). Munich.

Gogol, Nikolai. "The Nose," in *The Complete Tales of Nikolai Gogol* (1985). Trans. Constance Garnett, revised by Leonard J. Kent. Chicago and London.

Golovinskij, Grigorij (1988). "Tak cto proizoslo v 1948 godu." *Sovjetskaja Muzyka* 8. Moscow.

Gourlay, Kenneth A. (1984). "The Non-Universality of Music and the Universality of Non-Music." *The World of Music* 28 (no. 2). West Berlin.

Graff, Ola (1985). *Joik som musikalsk språk.* Master's thesis, University of Oslo.

Graves, Donald H. (1983). *Writing: Teachers and Children at Work.* Ports-mouth, N.H.

Grennes, Carl Erik (1984). "Kroppen som filosofiens *sted*—M. Merleau-Pontys filosofi." *Samtiden* 6. Oslo.

Grimm, J. and W. (1885). *Deutsches Wörterbuch.* Leipzig.

Grøndal, Dolores (1988). "Notebildet—synsinntrykk eller sanseopp-plevelse." *Musikk og Skole* 1. Oslo.

Gruska, G. (1978). Modellversuch "Künstler und Schüler" Berlin II. I:

Bundesminister für Bildung und Wissenschaft: Modellversuch "Künstler und Schülern" Zwischenbilanz in zehn Berichten. Bonn.

Gurney, N. and E. (1965). *The King, the Mice and the Cheese.* New York.

Gurvin, Olav (1962). *Fartein Valen—En banebryter i nyere norsk musikk.* Oslo.

Gustafsson, Björn, and Sol-Britt Hugoh (1987). *Full fart i livet—en väg til kunskap.* Mjölby.

Handerer, H. (1974). *Musik—Bildungsbedeutsamkeit des Faches Musik in der Primarstufe.* Regensburg.

Hanshumaker, James (1980). "The Effects of Arts Education on Intellectual and Social Development: A Review of Selected Research." *Arts Education.* Urbana, Ill.

Hansson, Hasse, and Birgitta Qvarsell (1983). *En skola för barn.* Stockholm.

Hoffmann, C., and Würsten, R. (1976). *Der Einfluss eines vermehrten Singunterrichts auf Hauptfächerleistungen.* Dissertation, Psychologisches Institut der Universität Bern.

Holen, Astrid (1983). "Barns sangaktivitet i 1 1/2–3-årsgrupper i barnehagen." *Dansk årbok for musikforskning,* vol. 14. Copenhagen.

Holm, Signy (1988). *Leselyst og skriveglede.* Oslo.

Hood, Burrel Samuel III (1973). *The Effect of Daily Instruction in Public School Music and Related Experiences upon Non-Musical Personnel and School Attitudes of Average Achieving Third Grade Students.* Ed.D. dissertation, Mississippi State University. *Dissertation Abstracts International* 34.

Hovdhaugen, Even (1976). *Språkvitenskap—en elementær innføring.* Oslo.

Hsüan, Chang (1968). *The Etymology of 3000 Chinese Characters in Common Usage.* Hong Kong.

Huizinga, Johan (1955). *Homo Ludens.* London.

Hurwitz, Irving, et al. (1975). "Non Musical Effects of the Kodály Music Curriculum in Primary Grade Children." *Journal of Learning Disabilities.* (March).

Ibsen, Henrik. *Catilina, in Ungdomsskuespill og historiske dramaer 1850–64, dikt* (1962).

Ibsen, Henrik. *Peer Gynt,* in *Fra Brand til Keiser og Galilæer 1866–73* (1972). Oslo.

Jacobsen, Rolf (1985). *Nattåpent.* Oslo.

Jensen, Odd Harald, and G. Flottorp (1985). *The Effect of Controlled Sound Stimuli on the Heart Rate of Human Fetuses.* Oslo.

Johnsen, Lillemor (1981). *Integrated Respiration Theory/Therapy.* Oslo.

Johnson, Frederick, ed. (1971). *A Standard Swahili-English Dictionary.* Oxford.

Kalsnes, Signe (1984). *Hvorfor slutter elevene i musikkskolen? En beskrivelse av ulike forhold i og utenfor musikkskolen.* Master's thesis, State Academy of Music, Oslo.

Kantrowitz, Barbara, and Pat Wingert (1989). "How Kids Learn." *Newsweek,* April 17.

Kemp, Anthony (1981). "The Personality Structure of the Musician." *Psychology of Music* 9 (no. 2).

Kjerschow, Peder Christian (1988). *Schopenhauer om musikken.* Oslo.

Kleiva, Turid, and Bodil Røyset, eds. (1981). *Paa børnenes eget talemaal— Dialekt i barnehage og skule.* Oslo.

Klem, Lone (1985). "Med mot til å møte kaos." *Dagbladet,* December 17. Oslo.

Klosovskij, B. N. (1963). *The Development of the Brain and Its Disturbance by Harmful Factors.* New York.

Kodály, Zoltán (1974). *The Selected Writings of Zoltán Kodály.* Budapest.

Koestler, Arthur (1965). *The Act of Creation: A Study of the Conscious and Unconscious Processes in Humor, Scientific Discovery and Art.* New York.

Kolata, Gina (1984). "Studying Learning in the Womb." *Science* 225.

Kormann, A. (1972). *Der Zusammenhang zwischen Intelligenz und Musikalität unter entwicklungs- und kreativitätpsychologischem Aspekt.* Dissertation, University of Salzburg.

Kroodsma, Donald E., and Edward H. Miller, eds. (1982). *Acoustic Communication in Birds.* Vol. 2, *Song Learning and Its Consequences.* New York.

Larsen, Steen (1984). *Børnenes nye verden.* Copenhagen.

Ledang, Ola Kai (1988). "Musikkbegrepet i Afrika og Europa," in *Det Kgl. Norske Videnskabers Selskabs Forhandlinger 1988.* Trondheim.

Leontjev, A. A. (1976). *Udviklingsproblemer i psyken 1–2.* Copenhagen.

Levin, Henry M., Gene V. Glass, and Gail R. Meister (1984). *Cost Effectiveness of Four Educational Inventions.* Center for Educational Research at Stanford, project report 84 A 11.

Lewis, C. S. (1985). *The Magician's Nephew.* New York.

Lilliestam, Lars (1988). *Musikalisk ackulturation från blues til rock—En studie kring låten Hound Dog.* Göteborg.

Lind, John (1980). "Music and the Small Human Being." *Acta Paediatrica Scandinavica.* Stockholm.

Lindgren, Astrid (1975). *The Brothers Lionheart.* Trans. Joan Tate. New York.

Lindgren, Astrid (1985). *Ronia, the Robber's Daughter.* Trans. Patricia Crompton. New York.

Linell, Per (1984). *Människans språk.* Lund.

Ling, Jan (1989). *Europas musikhistoria—Folkmusiken.* Göteborg.

Lockwood, Alan H. (1989). "Medical Problems of Musicians." *New England Journal of Medicine* 320 (no. 4).

Madsen, Clifford K., and Jere L. Forsythe (1973). "Effect of Contingent Music Listening on Increases of Mathematical Responses." *Journal of Research in Music Education* 21 (Summer).

Mehren, Stein (1971). *Veier til et bilde.* Oslo.

Merriam, Alan P. (1964). *The Anthropology of Music.* Illinois.

Meyer, Krzysztof (1980). *Dmitri Schostakowitsch.* Leipzig.

Meyerhold, Vsevolod (1934). *Chaplin og Chaplinismen.* Oslo.

Milne, A. A. (1970). *Now We Are Six.* New York.

Montagu, Ashley (1981). *Growing Young.* New York.

Montague, Mary E. (1961). *The Effects of Dance Experiences upon Observable Behaviors of Women Prisoners.* Ed.D. dissertation, New York University. *Dissertation Abstracts* 23.

Montessori, Maria (1981). *The Secret of Childhood.* New York.

Morsing, Ole (1987). "Børn og skabende arbejde—et stykke Danmarkshistorie og et aktuelt bud på nye livsformer." *Norsk pedagogisk tidsskrift* 1. Oslo.

Muckle, J. Y. (1988). *A Guide to the Soviet Curriculum: What the Russian Child Is Taught in School.* New York.

Nielsen, Carl (1927). *Min fynske barndom.* Copenhagen.

Nielsen, Steen (1985). *Mennesker og musik i Afrika.* Gjellerup.

Nietzsche, Friedrich (1899). *Also sprach Zarathustra,* in *Nietzsches Werke,* vol. 6. Leipzig.

Nobel, Agnes (1984). *Hur får kunskap liv? Om konst och eget skapande i undervisningen.* Stockholm.

Nordeen Kathy W., and Ernest J. Nordeen (1988). "Projection Neurons Within Vocal Motor Pathway Are Born During Song Learning in Zebra Finches." *Nature* 334 (July 14).

Norton, Natalie J. (1973). *Symbolic Arts: The Effect of Movement and Drama upon the Oral Communication of Children in Grade Two.* Ed.D. dissertation, Boston University School of Education. *Dissertation Abstracts International* 34.

Nottebohm, Fernando (1984). "Birdsong as a Model in Which to Study Brain Processes Related to Learning." *The Condor* 86 (no. 3, August).

Nyhus, Sven (1983). *Fel'klang på rørosmål—Fra slåtter og danser i egen familie-tradisjon til nyere samspillformer.* Oslo.

Nylöf, Göran, and Jan Nordberg (1988). *Kulturbarometern i detalj—Tema musik.* Statens Kulturråd, publik- och programforskning, Stockholm.

Oberborbeck, K. (1970). *Phantasie und Musikerziehung im Kindesalter—Der Einfluss der elementaren Musik- und Bewegungserziehung (Orff-Schulwerk) auf die Phantasieentwicklung von Kindern.* Dissertation, University of Salzburg.

Oksaar, Els (1988). "Aspects of Creativity—International Strategies of Mono- and Multilingual Children," in Ragnhild Söderbergh, ed., *Children's Creative Communication.* Lund and Kent.

Okudzjava, Bulat (1988). *Romanze vom Arbat—Lieder, Gedichte.* Berlin.

A rich collection of original texts and German translations, with explanatory notes.

Olofsson, Brigitta Knutsdotter (1987). *Lek för livet.* Stockholm.

Olseng, Knut (1989). "Job-Reality for Musicians and Teachers of Music in Norway." Paper, Bolkesjø-seminar, April 7.

Ong, Walter J. (1982). *Orality and Literacy: The Technologizing of the Word.* Bristol.

Opdal, Paul Martin (1987). "Barn som filosofer." *Norsk pedagogisk tidsskrift* 4. Oslo.

Ordzjonikidze, G. (1967). "XIII simfonija D. Sjostakovitsja," in V. Egorova, ed., *Dmitrij Sjostakovtisj.* Moscow.

Orlov, G. (1961). *Simfonii Sjostakovitsja.* Leningrad.

Osterberg, Dag (1984). "Kropp og omverden." *Samtiden* 6. Oslo.

Panofsky, Erwin (1980). "Ikonografi og ikonologi," in Bent Fausing and Peter Larsen, eds., *Visuell kommunikation.* Copenhagen.

Papousek, M., and H. Papousek (1981). "Musical Elements in the Infant's Vocalization: Their Significance for Communication, Cognition, and Creativity." *Advances in Infancy Research* 1. New Jersey.

Pattison, Robert (1982). *On Literacy: The Politics of the Word from Homer to the Age of Rock.* New York.

Pattison, Robert (1987). *The Triumph of Vulgarity: Rock Music in the Mirror of Romanticism.* New York.

Paynter, John (1970). *Sound and Silence: Classroom Projects in Creative Music.* London.

Pearce, Joseph Chilton (1985). *Magical Child Matures.* New York.

Pettersen, Veslemøy (1985). "Musikk som kommunikasjon sett i et utviklingsperspektiv." Master's thesis, University of Oslo.

Plato. *Laws* (1920). Trans. Benjamin Jowett. London.

Porzionato, Giuseppe (1989). "Atteveta motorea e competenza musicale," in *Pedagogia e didattica del movimento corporeo nell' educazione musicale di base,* 20th European Conference, Corale Goriziana "C. A. Seghizzi," Gorizia.

Postman, Neil (1982). *The Disappearance of Childhood.* New York.

Postman, Neil, and Charles Weingartner (1971). *Teaching as a Subversive Activity.* New York.

Poulsen, Sten Clod (1980). *Udviklingsbetingelser for den alsidige personlighed— En problematisering of musiske fag og musisk virksomhed i skole og uddannelsesforløb.* Copenhagen.

Puretz, Susan L. (1973). *A Comparison of the Effects of Dance and Physical Education on the Self-Concept of Selected Disadvantaged Girls.* Ed.D. dissertation, New York University. *Dissertation Abstracts International* 34.

Qvarsell, Birgitta (1987). *Barn, kultur och inlärning.* Stockholm.

Read, Herbert (1958). *Education Through Art.* New York.

Revers, W. J., and H. Rauhe (1978). *Musik—Intelligenz—Phantasie.* Salzburg.

Rico, Gabrielle Lusser (1983). *Writing the Natural Way.* Los Angeles.

Rishaug, Harry (1980). *Messingblåseren—Melodibok 1.* Oslo.

Rommetveit, Ragnar (1972). *Språk, tanke og kommunikasjon—En innføring i språkpsykologi og psykolingvistikk,* 2d ed. Oslo.

Rousseau, Jean-Jacques. *Emile ou de l'éducation* (1966). Paris.

Ruud, Even (1983). *Musikken, vårt nye rusmiddel—Om oppdragelse til og gjennom musikk i dagens samfunn.* Oslo.

Sachs, Curt (1977). *The Wellsprings of Music.* New York.

Sacks, Oliver (1986). *A Leg to Stand On.* London.

Sarfi, M., D. Smørvik, and H. Martinsen, (1984). "Why Does My Baby

362

Cry? Maternal Beliefs About Causes of Crying in 2–16 Weeks Old Infants." Paper, University of Oslo.

Schenk, Robert (1989). "Musiker dopad vid slutredovisning!" *Månadsbladet*, no. 5, 1988–89, Göteborg University.

Selmer-Olsen, Ivar (1987). "Ugh, ugh, pølse med lugg," in NAVFs Norwegian Center for Child Research, report no. 13, *Barn og humor*. University of Trondheim.

Selmer-Olsen, Ivar (1988). "Hvorfor henge seg opp i bagateller, når det fins trær?" *Norsklæreren* 5. Oslo.

Selmer-Olsen, Ivar (1990). *Barn imellom— og de voksne*. Oslo.

Seuss, Dr. (1957). *The Cat in the Hat*. Boston.

Shaw, Barbara A. (1974): *A Language-Art Acquisition Approach to Teaching Art and Its Effect on Oral Language Development and Reading of Preschool Children*. Ed.D. dissertation, University of Georgia. *Dissertation Abstracts International* 36, 178a.

Shelter, Donald J. (1987). "The Inquiry into Prenatal Musical Experience: A Report of the Eastman Project 1980–1987." Paper for the International Music and Child Development Conference, Denver, Colorado.

Shostakovich, Dmitry. *Shostakovich: About Himself and His Times* (1980).

This book, published in English in the USSR for distribution abroad, should be viewed as a complement to Solomon Volkov's *Testimony* (see below). A collection of "counter-memoirs," it is documentary and factual, in contrast to Volkov's anecdotal and literary approach. It presents excerpts from Shostakovich's writings and public statements from 1926 to the end of his life. Here we find several sides of Shostakovich, from *yurodivy* statements full of official platitudes to candid openness (during the war, for example). Stylistic analysis is important for a proper understanding of this material: Shostakovich's language varies from period to period, depending on the prevailing political-cultural climate. The original text, of course, is a better source for such analysis than the English translation.

Shugar, Grace Wales (1988). "The Nature of Peer Discourse: Participant Structures for and by Children," in Ragnhild Söderbergh, ed., *Children's Creative Communication*. Lund and Kent.

Simpson, Donald J. (1969). *The Effect of Selected Musical Studies on Growth in General Creative Potential.* Ed.D. dissertation, University of Southern California. *Dissertation Abstracts International* 30, 502a.

Sjölund, Arne (1978). *Sovjetisk förskolepedagogik.* Lund.

Skoglund, Christer (1987). "Några föreställningar om kreativitet och skapande genom tiderna," in *Barns skapande lek.* Center for the Study of Child Culture, University of Stockholm.

Small, Christopher (1977). *Music — Society — Education.* London.

Smith, Frank (1982). *Writing and the Writer.* London.

Snow, C. E. (1977). "The Development of Conversation Between Mothers and Babies." *Journal of Child Language* 4. Cambridge.

Søbstad, Frode (1988). *Førskolebarn og humor.* Dissertation, University of Trondheim.

Söderbergh, Ragnhild (1979–80). "Sprakanvändning vid dockskapslek." *Nysvenska studier,* 59–60. Lund and Kent.

Söderbergh, Ragnhild (1988). *Barnets tidiga språkutveckling.* Stockholm.

Söderbergh, Ragnhild, ed. (1988). *Children's Creative Communication.* Lund.

Steinfeld, Torill (1986). *På skriftens vilkår — Et bidrag til morsmålsfagets historie.* Oslo.

Stender-Petersen, Ad. (1952). *Den russiske litteraturs historie,* vol. 3. Copenhagen.

Stern, Daniel (1977). *The First Relationship.* Cambridge, Mass.

Strindberg, August (1918). "Stadsresan," in *Samlade skrifter,* vols. 37–38. Stockholm.

Sundberg, Ove Kristian (1979). "Musiske perspektiver i Platons dialog *Lovene." Studia Musicologica Norvegica,* no. 5. Oslo.

Sundberg, Ove Kristian (1980). *Pythagoras og de tonende tall. Oslo.*

Sundin, Bertil (1963). *Barns musikaliska skapande.* Stockholm.

Sundin, Bertil (1977). *Barnets musikaliska värld.* Lund.

Sundin, Bertil (1982). *Barnen och de sköna konsterna.* Stockholm.

Sundin, Bertil (1986). "Mera glädje, mindre nit." *Musikkultur* 4. Stockholm.

Sundin, Bertil (1988). *Musiken i människan.* Stockholm.

Sundin, Bertil, and Annika Sääf (1971). "Förskolebarn och rytm — Perception och återgivande av auditiva rytmiska mönster." Nordisk Sommeruniversitet, Stockholm.

Suppan, Wolfgang (1984). *Der Musizierende Mensch — Eine Anthropologie der Musik.* Mainz.

Suzuki, Shinichi (1977). *Kunnskap med kärlek—Ett sätt att utbilda och fostra.* Gislaved.

Suzuki Piano School, vol. 1 (1978). Suzuki Method International. Princeton, N.J.

Sverdrup, Harald (1983). *Samlede dikt 1948–82.* Oslo.

Swanwick, Keith (1988). *Music, Mind and Education.* London.

Tarkovskij, Andrej (1988). "Kunst, frihet, ensomhet—Samtale med Andrej Tarkovskij." *Arken* 3–4. Oslo.

Taube, Evert (1977). *75 viser/dikt.* Oslo.

Thompson, John (1936). *Teaching Little Fingers to Play.* Ohio.

Thurman, Leon, Margaret Chase, and Anna Peter Langness (1987). "Reaching the Young Child Through Music: Is Pre-Natal and Infant Music Education Possible?" in Jack Dobbs, ed., *International Music Education, ISME Yearbook,* vol. 14. Austria.

Trageton, Arne, and Vivian H. Gullberg (1986). *Barns skapande leik.* Oslo.

Trevarthen, Colwyn (1978). "Intersubjective Exchange and Transfer of Understanding in Infancy." *British Journal of Educational Psychology* 48 (February). Edinburgh.

Trevarthen, Colwyn (1983). "Interpersonal Abilities of Infants as Generators for Transmission of Language and Culture," in Alberto Calvino and Michele Zapella, eds., *The Behavior of Human Infants.* London and New York.

Trevarthen, Colwyn (1987). "Sharing Makes Sense: Intersubjectivity and the Making of an Infant's Meaning," in R. Steele and T. Threadgold, eds., *Acquiring Culture: Cross Cultural Studies in Child Development.* Kent.

Trevarthen, Colwyn (1988). "Infants Trying to Talk: How a Child Invites Communication from the Human World," in Ragnhild Söderbergh, ed., *Children's Creative Communication.* Lund and Kent.

Uphoff, James K., and June Gilmore (1985). "Pupil Age at School Entrance: How Many Are Ready for Success?" *Educational Leadership,* September. Alexandria, Virginia.

Uphoff, James K., June E. Gilmore, and Rosemarie Huber (1986). *Summer Children: Ready or Not for School?* Middletown, Ohio.

Usova, A. P. (1974). *Unterricht im Kindergarten.* Berlin.

Varkøy, Øivind (1984). *Legitimering av musikk i oppdragelse og undervisning—*

En idéhistorisk skisse og ideenes nedslag i norsk skole. Master's thesis, University of Oslo.

Verny, Thomas (1982). *The Secret Life of the Unborn Child.* London.

Vetlugina, N. A., ed. (1980). *Samostojatel'naja chudozestvennaja dejatel'nost' doskol'nikov.* Moscow.

Vishnevskaya, Galina (1984). *Galina: A Russian Story.* Trans. Guy Daniels. San Diego, New York, and London.

Volkov, Solomon (1979). *Testimony: The Memoirs of Dmitri Shostakovich.* Trans. Antonina W. Bouis. New York and London.

As editor of *Sovietskaya Muzyka,* the journal of the Soviet composers' union, Volkov was for many years at the center of Russian musical life. His book has been justly criticized on many counts. In 1983 I had a long conversation with Maxim Shostakovich, the composer's son, after he had fled to the West. Maxim vouched for the book's genuineness in the sense that it undoubtedly is the product of a collaboration between Volkov and Shostakovich. Maxim identified formulations in the book and an anecdotal style that were clearly derived from his father's customary way of expressing himself. But though the book is genuine enough as far as it goes, Maxim nonetheless maintained that it is not wholly representative of his father and what he stood for. Maxim thought the book was quite complete in its coverage of his father's relationship with Stalin and his regime. He was more critical of the book's characterizations of other musicians, especially Prokofiev. If Shostakovich himself had written the book—and Maxim emphasized that it was Volkov's book, not his father's—the discussion of Prokofiev would have been considerably more subtle.

Vygotskij, Lev S. (1987). *Psichologija iskusstva.* Moscow.

Vygotsky, Lev S. (1975). *Thought and Language.* Cambridge, Mass.

Weavers, Kitty D. (1971). *Lenin's Grandchildren: Preschool Education in the Soviet Union.* New York.

Weber, Ernst (1981). *Bessere Bildung mit mehr Musik? Bericht über Versuche mit erweitertem Musikunterricht in der Schule.* Amt für Unterrichtsforschung und -planung der Erziehungsdirektion. Bern.

Welhaven, Johan Sebastian (1943). *Samlede digterverker,* vol. 10. Oslo.

Wergeland, Henrik (1954). *Mennesket. Samlede skrifter,* vol. 5. Christiania.

Wiggen, Geirr (1979). "Dialektbruk i morsmålsopplæringa, særlig den første lese- og skriveopplæringa," in Jo Kleiven, ed., *Språk og samfunn*. Oslo.

Wilson, Frank R. (1986). *Tone Deaf and All Thumbs? An Invitation to Music-Making for Late Bloomers and Non-Prodigies*. New York.

Winnicott, D. W. (1971). *Playing and Reality*. London.

Wolfe, P. H. (1969). "The Natural History of Crying and Other Vocalizations in Infancy," in B. M. Foss, ed., *Determinants of Infant Behaviour*. London.

Wootton, Mary L. (1968). *The Effect of Planned Experiences Followed by Art Expression and Discussion on Language Achievement of First-Grade Pupils*. Dissertation, Arizona State University. *Dissertation Abstracts* 29, 2617a.

Yevtushenko, Yevgeny (1966). *The Poetry of Yevgeny Yevtushenko, 1953–1966*. Trans. George Reavey. London.

This edition presents Russian and English versions of the poems in parallel columns, thus giving non-Russian readers a good introduction to Yevtushenko's work. "Stalin's Heirs," "Babi Yar," "Humor," and "Career" are among the poems included here.

Yevtushenko, Yevgeny (1987). *Stichotvorenija i poemy*, vol. 1. Moscow.

Ziehe, Thomas, and Herbert Stubenrauch (1982). *Ny ungdom og usædvanlige læreprocesser*. Copenhagen.

Acknowledgments

Grateful acknowledgment is made to the following for permission to reprint copyrighted material: From "The Nose," in *The Complete Tales of Nikolai Gogol* (London: Chatto & Windus, 1923). English translation copyright © 1923, renewed 1950, by the Estate of Constance Garnett. Reprinted by permission of Random Century Group, London. From *The Magician's Nephew* by C. S. Lewis. Copyright © 1955 by C. S. Lewis. Reprinted by permission of HarperCollins Publishers Limited, London. From *The Brothers Lionheart* by Astrid Lindgren. Copyright © 1973 by Astrid Lindgren. English translation copyright © 1975 by Brock Hampton Press Ltd. Reprinted by permission of Viking Penguin, a division of Penguin Books, USA, Inc. "Realities," from *Day By Day* by Robert Lowell. Copyright © 1977 by Robert Lowell. Reprinted by permission of Farrar, Straus & Giroux, Inc. *Baigneuses au Ballon* by Pablo Picasso, 1928. Private collection. Reproduced by permission of Acquavella Galleries, New York. Photograph facing chapter 3 by Arnaud de Wildenberg/Sygma. Reproduced by permission of Sygma, New York. From *Early Poems* by Yevgeny Yevtushenko, translated by George Reavey. Copyright © 1966 by Marion Boyars Publishers, Ltd. Reprinted by permission of Marion Boyars Publishers, Ltd., New York, London.

INDEX

Akerø, Marit, 45
Albrechtsberger, J. G., 194
Alkersig, Mette, 80
Anyanwu, K., 49–50, 84, 113–14
Applebee, Arthur N., 140–41,
    142–43, 144
Armstrong, Louis, 172, 182–84,
    186, 197, 198, 212, 348
Arnold, Matthew, 168
Asafyev, Boris, 294
Asbjørnsen, P. C., 34

Bach, Johann Sebastian, 190,
    192, 224, 254, 255, 311,
    331
Bachtin, Mikhail, 289–90
Balakirev, M. A., 86–87

Barkauskas, V., 238
Barthes, Roland, 39, 212
Bartók, Béla, 244
Bastian, Peter, 51
Bateson, Gregory, 25, 34, 299
Beatles, The, 175–76, 346
Beethoven, Ludwig van, 190,
    194, 213, 250, 268, 269,
    283, 308, 309, 314–15
Bell, John, 254
Berg, Alban, 290
Berio, Luciano, 214–15
Blacking, John, 83–84
Bøhle, Solveig, 36, 278, 279–80
Borodin, Aleksander, 86–87
Boye, Karin, 257
Bråten, Stein, 11
Braunbehrens, Volkmar, 193
Brezhnev, Leonid, 266, 329

Brock, William E., 140
Bronfenbrenner, Urie, 19, 58–59
Bronowski, Jacob, 163–64
Bruckner, Anton, 192
Burdon, Eric, 270
Bush, George, 59, 142

Cage, John, 239, 240
Camara, Helder, 119, 186
Campbell, Kenneth A., 145
Chaplin, Charlie, 231, 309, 311
Chase, Margaret, 5
Chekhov, Anton, 39
Chomsky, Noam, 16
Chopin, Frédéric, 273
Christensen, Bernhard, 216
Clayton, N. S., 195, 196
Clementi, Muzio, 194
Cobb, Edith, 25–27, 51, 77, 128,
      161–62, 280, 332
Comenius, John Amos, 25
Condon, William, 15–16
Congreve, William, 233
Cui, Cesar, 86–87

Dalin, Per, 148–49, 154
Dam, Hanne, 155
Darwin, Charles, 251
Debussy, Claude, 236
DeCasper, Anthony, 3–5, 6, 7,
      13–14, 15, 16
Descartes, René, 43, 50, 210
DeWoskin, Kenneth J., 52–53

Donaldson, Margaret, 16
Doors, The, 270
Dostoevsky, Feodor, 77,
      289–90
Dupré, Marcel, 192
Duve, Anne-Marit, 143
Dysthe, Olga, 228

Eales, Lucy A., 196
Eaton, Jeanette, 183
Egeberg, Erik, 331
Ehrenburg, Ilya, 300
Eisenberg, R. B., 3
Eldridge, Roy, 198
Elkind, David, 144–45
Ellington, Duke, 13
Engdahl, Horace, 39
Enzensberger, Hans Magnus,
      139–40, 144, 261
Ericson, Gertrud, 159

Falbel, Aaron, 155
Ferguson, Maynard, 197–98
Fernald, A., 14
Fields, Dorothy, 348
Flesch, Rudolf, 145–46
Flottorp, G., 5
Fornäs, Johan, 270
Forsythe, Jere L., 158
Freire, Paulo, 133–34, 138, 144,
      172, 261
Frost, Robert, 235
Fux, Johann Joseph, 194

Gabrielsson, Alf, 159
Galileo, 326–27
Gardner, Howard, 133, 159
Garnett, Constance, 286
Gerhardt, Rolf, 144
Gillespie, Dizzy, 198
Gilmore, June, 145
Glass, Gene V., 154–55
Glinka, Mikhail, 86, 93–94,
    285
Goethe, Johann Wolfgang von,
    156, 335
Gogol, Nikolai, 284, 286, 288,
    289–90, 291, 293, 294, 331,
    332
Golovinskij, Grigorij, 330
Gorbachev, Mikhail, 97, 149,
    166, 167, 332
Gotsdiner, Arnold, 98
Gourlay, Kenneth, 51–52
Graves, Donald H., 228
Grennes, Carl Erik, 210–11,
    212
Grieg, Edvard, 86, 236, 240
Grimm Brothers, 46
Grøndal, Dolores, 200, 201, 224
Groven, Eivind, 75–76
Grundtvig, N. F. S., 165
Gurney, Eric, 4
Gurney, Nancy, 4
Gurvin, Olav, 240
Gustafsson, Björn, 159

Hanshumaker, James, 156, 157,
    158–59
Haydn, Joseph, 243
Hemingway, Ernest, 302
Hendrix, Jimi, 270
Hershiser, Orel, 103
Hitler, Adolf, 58, 167
Holiday, Billie, 112
Holm, Signy, 228
Hood, Burrel Samuel, III, 158
Hope, Laura Lee, 137
Hsüan, Chang, 53
Huber, Rosemarie, 145
Hugoh, Sol-Britt, 159
Huizinga, Johan, 24
Huth, Andrew, 326

Ibsen, Henrik, 43, 126
Ives, Charles, 254, 255

Jackson, Bo, 182
Jackson, Mahalia, 112
Jacobsen, Rolf, 163
Jagger, Mick, 271
Jensen, Odd Harald, 3, 5
Johnsen, Lillemor, 129
Johnson, Frederik, 49
Jordan, Michael, 103, 182

Haley, Bill, 260, 266
Hansen, Ivar, 144

Kabalevsky, Dmitri, 93–94
Kantrowitz, Barbara, 155

Kemp, Anthony, 232
Kennedy, John F., 60, 321
Khrushchev, Nikita, 320, 321,
    328, 329
King, Martin Luther, Jr.,
    112
King, Ronnie, 172
Klem, Lone, 169
Klosovsky, B. N., 7
Kodály, Zoltán, 156, 157, 221,
    243–48
Koestler, Arthur, 39
Kondrashin, Kyril, 328–29
Kroodsma, Donald E., 196

Lagerlöf, Ingrid, 159
Langer, Judith, 140–41, 142–43,
    144
Langness, Anna Peter, 5
Ledang, Ola Kai, 52
Lenin, Vladimir I., 58
Lennox, Annie, 261
Leontiev, A. A., 59, 88
Levin, Henry M., 154–55
Lewis, C. S., 55
Ligeti, György, 240
Lindberg, Ulf, 270
Lindgren, Astrid, 35, 36, 42–43,
    137, 278, 279–80
Linell, Per, 195, 196
Ling, Jan, 190
Lipman, Matthew, 164
Lockwood, Alan H., 233
Longfellow, Henry Wadsworth,
    235

Lowell, Robert, 123
Lunacharsky, Anatoly, 285, 294
Luria, Alexander, 88
Luther, Martin, 305

McHugh, Jimmy, 348
Madsen, Clifford K., 158
Mahler, Gustav, 243
Marcus Aurelius, 130
Martinsen, Harald, 15
Meister, Gail R., 154–55
Mendelssohn, Felix, 254, 255
Merleau-Ponty, Maurice,
    210–11, 212
Merriam, Alan P., 80
Meyer, Krzysztof, 315–16
Meyerhold, Vsevolod, 298, 332
Mill, Irving, 13
Miller, Edward H., 196
Milne, A. A., 73
Milton, John, 277
Moe, Jørgen, 34
Monroe, Marilyn, 265
Montagu, Ashley, 279
Montague, Mary E., 158
Montana, Joe, 182
Morante, Elsa, 169
Moussorgsky, Modest, 86–87,
    91–93, 285, 323
Mozart, Leopold, 249
Mozart, Nannerl, 249
Mozart, Wolfgang Amadeus,
    190, 192–93, 213, 214, 227,
    243, 248–50, 251, 252, 272,
    282, 283, 323

Mravinsky, Yevgeny, 301
Mullis, Ina V. S., 140–41,
    142–43, 144

Naess, Lars, 197–98
Nestyev, I., 315
Nicholas I (Czar of Russia), 286,
    288
Nielsen, Carl, 171–72
Nielsen, Steen, 52
Nietzsche, Friedrich, 44
Nixon, Richard M., 60
Nordberg, Jan, 251
Nordeen, Ernest J., 196
Nordeen, Kathy W., 196
Nordheim, Arne, 240
Norton, Natalie J., 158
Nottebohm, Fernando, 196
Nyhus, Sven, 191–92
Nylöf, Göran, 251
Nystedt, Knut, 238

Oksaar, Els, 66
Okudzjava, Bulat, 317–18
Oliver, Joe "King," 183
Olsen, Vivian Zahl, 78
Olseng, Knut, 232–33
Ong, Walter J., 48, 54, 131, 139,
    188, 190, 261
Opdal, Paul Martin, 164–65
Orff, Carl, 156
Orlov, G., 306
Owens, Jesse, 28–30, 34, 103

Panofsky, Erwin, 224
Papousek, H. and M., 14
Pasternak, Boris, 320–21, 331
Pattison, Robert, 141–42,
    261–63, 264, 271
Pestalozzi, Heinrich, 156
Phillips, Sam, 263
Piaget, Jean, 6, 16, 34, 132,
    135–36, 220
Picasso, Pablo, 38, 277, 278,
    279
Pindar, 54, 283
Pink Floyd, 260, 274
Plato, 1–2, 7, 54–55, 86, 156,
    161–62, 272
Porzionato, Giuseppe, 27
Postman, Neil, 100–102, 137
Poulsen, Sten Clod, 160
Presley, Elvis, 263, 265, 271
Prokofiev, Sergei, 87, 93–94,
    318, 320
Pugatsyova, Alla, 265–66
Puretz, Susan C., 158
Pushkin, Alexander, 283–84,
    285, 298–99

Reagan, Ronald, 60
Renshaw, Peter, 234
Riemer, Mette, 80
Rimsky-Korsakov, Nikolai,
    86–87, 285
Rostropovich, Mstislav, 331
Rousseau, Jean-Jacques, 135,
    193, 248–49
Ruud, Even, 253–54

Sääf, Annika, 216
Sachs, Curt, 114
Sakharov, Andrei, 331
Sander, Louis W., 15–16
Sarfi, M., 15
Sava, Samuel, 145
Schiller, Friedrich, 25
Schoenberg, Arnold, 240,
    243
Schopenhauer, Arthur, 38–39
Schubert, Franz, 54, 243
Schumann, Robert, 194, 254,
    255
Selmer-Olsen, Ivar, 41
Sernhede, Ove, 270
Seuss, Dr., 3–4
Shavers, Charlie, 197–98
Shaw, Barbara A., 158
Shaw, George Bernard, 162
Shelter, Donald J., 5
Shostakovich, Dmitri, 41, 87,
    218, 240
Shugar, Grace Wales, 17,
    18
Sill, Edward Rowland, 303
Simpson, Donald J., 158
Simpson, O. J., 34
Sinatra, Frank, 263
Sinding, Christian, 207–9
Skoglund, Christer, 39
Small, Christopher, 84–85,
    242
Smith, Frank, 228
Smørvik, D., 15
Snow, C. E., 14
Socrates, 2, 161–62
Söderbergh, Ragnhild, 80

Solzhenitsyn, Alexander, 331
Sousa, John Philip, 272
Spence, M. J., 4
Springsteen, Bruce, 72, 267–68
Stalin, Josef, 167, 294, 296, 300,
    302–3, 304, 306, 308, 310,
    311, 315, 317, 318, 319,
    321, 327, 328, 330–31
Stern, Daniel, 15
Stewart, David, 261
Sting, 275
Strauss, Richard, 197
Stravinsky, Igor, 87, 240,
    284
Strindberg, August, 314–15
Stubenrauch, Herbert, 128
Sundberg, Ove Kristian, 1
Sundin, Bertil, 216
Suzuki, Shinichi, 220–22,
    245
Sverdrup, Harald, 179

Tarkovsky, Andrei, 305
Tchaikovsky, Peter I., 54, 93–94,
    285
Thomas, Dylan, 342
Thompson, Francis, 150
Thompson, John, 203, 204, 205,
    221
Thurman, Leon, 5
Tolstoy, Leo, 293
Trevarthen, Colwyn, 12–14, 15,
    16, 17–18, 19
Turner, Tina, 271
Twain, Mark, 162

Uphoff, James K., 145
Usova, A. P., 59, 88

Valen, Fartein, 240
Vedernikov, 328–29
Verdi, Giuseppe, 252
Verny, Thomas, 3, 5
Vetlugina, N. A., 87–88
Vicious, Sid, 263
Vishnyevskaya, Galina, 297, 302,
      305, 327–28, 329
Vivaldi, Antonio, 272
Volkov, Solomon, 296, 300, 301,
      316, 317
Vygotsky, Lev, 6, 16, 87–88,
      96
Vysotsky, Vladimir, 266

Wagner, Richard, 197
Warner, Gertrude Chandler,
      137
Washington, George, 59

Wayne, John, 32, 99
Weber, Ernst, 157–58
Wergeland, Henrik, 75–76
Whittier, John Greenleaf, 235
Wiegold, Peter, 234
Wingert, Pat, 155
Winnicott, D. W., 44, 128, 211,
      260
Wolfe, P. H., 15
Wonder, Stevie, 271
Wootton, Mary L., 158
Wordsworth, William, 136

Yeltsin, Boris, 332
Yevtushenko, Yevgeny, 321–23,
      326, 327, 328, 329, 330,
      331, 332

Zawinul, Joseph, 220
Zhdanov, Andrei, 294, 295,
      320
Ziehe, Thomas, 128